Ontology and the Lexicon

T0382146

The relation between ontologies and language is at the forefront of both natural language processing (NLP) and knowledge engineering. Ontologies, as widely used models in semantic technologies, have much in common with the lexicon. A lexicon organizes words as a conventional inventory of concepts, while an ontology formalizes concepts and their logical relations. A shared lexicon is the prerequisite for knowledge-sharing through language, and a shared ontology is the prerequisite for knowledge-sharing through information technology. In building models of language, computational linguists must be able to map accurately the relations between words and the concepts that they can be linked to. This book focuses on the integration of lexical resources and semantic technologies. It will be of interest to researchers and graduate students in NLP, computational linguistics and knowledge engineering, as well as in semantics, psycholinguistics, lexicology and morphology/syntax.

CHU-REN HUANG is Chair Professor in the Department of Chinese and Bilingual Studies at the Hong Kong Polytechnic University, and Research Fellow at the Institute of Linguistics, Academia Sinica in Taiwan.

NICOLETTA CALZOLARI is Director of Research in Istituto di Linguistica Computazionale at the CNR in Italy.

ALDO GANGEMI is senior researcher at the Institute of Cognitive Science and Technology of CNR (Italy), and coordinator of the Semantic Technology Lab.

ALESSANDRO LENCI is a researcher in the Department of Linguistics at the University of Pisa.

ALESSANDRO OLTRAMARI is a Research Fellow in the Laboratory for Applied Ontology, Institute of Cognitive Science and Technology at the Italian National Research Council.

LAURENT PRÉVOT is an Associate Professor at the Université de Provence.

Studies in Natural Language Processing

Series Editor:
Steven Bird, University of Melbourne

Editorial Board Members:
Chu-Ren Huang, The Hong Kong Polytechnic University and
  Academia Sinica
Christopher Manning, Stanford University
Yuji Matsumoto, Nara Institute of Science and Technology
Maarten de Rijke, University of Amsterdam
Harold Somers, Dublin City University
Suzanne Stevenson, University of Toronto

This series offers widely accessible accounts of the state-of-the-art in natural language processing (NLP). Established on the foundations of formal language theory and statistical learning, NLP is burgeoning with the widespread use of large annotated corpora, rich models of linguistic structure, and rigorous evaluation methods. New multilingual and multimodal language technologies have been stimulated by the growth of the web and pervasive computing devices. The series strikes a balance between statistical versus symbolic methods; deep versus shallow processing; rationalism versus empiricism; and fundamental science versus engineering. Each volume sheds light on these pervasive themes, delving into theoretical foundations and current applications. The series is aimed at a broad audience who are directly or indirectly involved in natural language processing, from fields including corpus linguistics, psycholinguistics, information retrieval, machine learning, spoken language, human-computer interaction, robotics, language learning, ontologies, and databases.

Also in the series
Douglas E. Appelt, *Planning English Sentences*
Madeleine Bates and Ralph M. Weischedel (eds.), *Challenges in Natural Language Processing*
Steven Bird, *Computational Phonology*
Peter Bosch and Rob van der Sandt, *Focus*
Pierette Bouillon and Federica Busa (eds.), *Inheritance, Defaults and the Lexicon*

Ontology and the Lexicon

A Natural Language Processing Perspective

Edited by

Chu-Ren Huang

Department of Chinese and Bilingual Studies
The Hong Kong Polytechnic University
Institute of Linguistics, Academia Sinica

Nicoletta Calzolari

Istituto di Linguistica Computazionale del CNR, Italy

Aldo Gangemi

Institute of Cognitive Science and Technology
Italian National Research Council

Alessandro Lenci

Department of Linguistics
Universitá degli Studi, Pisa

Alessandro Oltramari

Institute of Cognitive Science and Technology
Italian National Research Council

Laurent Prévot

Laboratoire Parole et Langage
Université de Provence, France

CAMBRIDGE
UNIVERSITY PRESS

Shaftesbury Road, Cambridge CB2 8EA, United Kingdom

One Liberty Plaza, 20th Floor, New York, NY 10006, USA

477 Williamstown Road, Port Melbourne, VIC 3207, Australia

314–321, 3rd Floor, Plot 3, Splendor Forum, Jasola District Centre, New Delhi – 110025, India

103 Penang Road, #05–06/07, Visioncrest Commercial, Singapore 238467

Cambridge University Press is part of Cambridge University Press & Assessment,
a department of the University of Cambridge.

We share the University's mission to contribute to society through the pursuit of
education, learning and research at the highest international levels of excellence.

www.cambridge.org
Information on this title: www.cambridge.org/9781009342476

First published 2010
First paperback edition 2022

A catalogue record for this publication is available from the British Library

ISBN   978-0-521-88659-8   Hardback
ISBN   978-1-009-34247-6   Paperback

Contents

Contributors

The editors

CHU-REN HUANG, CHIEF EDITOR' is a research fellow at the Institute of Linguistics, Academia Sinica and a chair professor at the Department of Chinese and Bilingual Studies at the Hong Kong Polytechnic University. He is a member of ICCL, and past president of ROCLING and LST. He has played an important role in the development of Chinese corpus and computational linguistics since he received his PhD in linguistics from Cornell University in 1987. He currently serves on the editorial boards of Cambridge Studies in Natural Language Processing, *Journal of Chinese Linguistics*, *Computational Linguistics and Chinese Language Processing*, *Journal of Chinese Information Processing*, and *Language Resources and Evaluation*. He directed or co-directed the construction of Sinica Corpus, CKIP Lexicon, Sinica BOW, and Chinese WordNet. He was an organizer of OntoLex 2005, 2006, as well as a special session on upper ontology and NLP for NLP-KE 2003. His recent research foci include discovery of conventionalized ontology in written language and ontology-driven comparative studies of cross-lingual lexica.

NICOLETTA CALZOLARI graduated in Philosophy from the University of Bologna and is Director of Research at Istituto di Linguistica Computazionale of the CNR in Pisa, Italy. She received an honorary doctorate in philosophy from the University of Copenhagen in 2007. She has promoted internationally the fields of Language Resources and Standardization, and her research fields include human language technology, corpus linguistics, lexical semantics, knowledge acquisition, integration and representation. She has coordinated a large number of international and national projects, currently coordinating the FLaReNet EC project. She is a member of ICCL, of the ACL Exec, vice-president of ELRA, chair of the Scientific Board of CLARIN, and member of many International Committees and Advisory Boards. She has been invited speaker, member of program committees, organizer for numerous international conferences and workshops, and general chair of the last three LRECs and of COLING-ACL-2006. She is co-editor-in-chief, with Nancy Ide, of the journal *Language Resources and Evaluation*, Springer.

ALDO GANGEMI graduated in philosophy from the University of Rome 'La Sapienza' in 1989 and then studied medical informatics, knowledge representation, and knowledge engineering with grants from the Italian National Research Council (CNR). He is currently senior researcher at the CNR Institute of Cognitive Sciences and Technology in Rome, and head of the Semantic Technology Lab. He also co-founded the Laboratory for Applied Ontology. His interests include ontology engineering, knowledge management, the Semantic Web, semiotics, and cognitive linguistics. His work on ontology engineering and conceptual modelling dates back to 1992, when he pioneered the application of ontologies to knowledge organization systems. His current research focuses on pattern-based ontology design, collaborative modelling, hybridation of NLP, lexical and semantic resources, and meta-models for heterogeneous knowledge integration. He has published more than 100 refereed articles in proceedings of international conferences, journals, and books, and has been involved in several projects funded by both the European Union and industrial companies (either as research partner or consultant). He is responsible at CNR for the EU projects IKS, NeOn and BONy, and has worked in the seminal ontology-related EU projects Galen, WonderWeb, OntoWeb, Metokis, and the Eureka project IKF. He has co-organized the first Formal Ontology and Information Systems Conference FOIS 1998, and the Linguistic Resources and Evaluation Conference, LREC 2006, and he is chairing the next European Knowledge Engineering and Knowledge Management Conference, EKAW 2008, as well as several workshops such as WORM at ODBASE2004 (focusing on regulatory ontologies), LEGONT at ICAIL2003 (focusing on legal ontologies), CORONT at EKAW2004 (focusing on core ontologies), and OPSW at ISWC2005 (focusing on ontology design patterns for the Semantic Web), the EON06: Ontology Evaluation for the Web Workshop at WWW2006, OntoLex: the ontology/lexicon interface at ISWC2007, and SWAP2008. He serves in the Programme Committees of main conferences in his field (KR, ISWC, WWW, FOIS, LREC) and gives invited academic and industrial talks, courses, and tutorials. He has acted as a reviewer for the EU-IST framework programmes and the Italian Ministries of Research and Industry.

ALESSANDRO LENCI is a researcher at the linguistic department of Pisa University and a member of the Institute of Computational Linguistics (ILC-CNR) also in Pisa. He is the author of numerous publications and has taught various courses concerning ontologies and the lexicon. His research interests concern computational linguistics, natural language processing, and cognitive sciences. More particularly he has actively contributed to the following topics: cognitive and computational models of the lexicon, verb aspect, acquisition and representation of lexical knowledge, computational models of syntax, natural language learning, term extraction, and ontology learning.

ALESSANDRO OLTRAMARI received the Master degree in philosophy at the University of Padua in 2000 and PhD in Cognitive Science at the University of Trento in 2006. He has been a Research Fellow at LOA since 2000, where he mainly studies the methodological and applicative aspects of the integration between ontologies and computational lexicons. In this context, he used to be co-organizer of the main event in the field, the workshop 'OntoLex', in 2004 (Lisbon), 2005 (Jeju Island, Korea), and 2006 (Genoa). He has been visiting research associate at Princeton University (USA), guest of the Laboratory of Cognitive Science (WordNet group). He is author of about thirty scientific papers in the field of formal and applied ontology, computational linguistics, philosophy of mind, and cognitive semantics. His scientific interests include the foundational aspects of artificial intelligence, analysis of metaphor, affective computing, and human-machine interaction. Since January 2007 he has also collaborated with Cogito S.r.l. in the development of linguistic technologies.

LAURENT PRÉVOT obtained his PhD in computer science and formal linguistics at Toulouse Research Institute of Computer Science (IRIT). He has been a post-doctoral research fellow for several years, first at the Laboratory for Applied Ontology (ISTC-CNR), where he has sharpened his competence in knowledge representation and ontological analysis; then at the Institute of Linguistics of the Academia Sinica (Taipei) where he has contributed to research on the interface between ontologies and lexical resources; and finally at the CNRS within the Syntax and Semantics Research Unit (CLLE-ERSS) of Toulouse University. He is now an associate professor in linguistics at Provence University and a member of the laboratory 'Parole et Langage'. His research interests also include discourse semantics as well as semantics and ontology of interaction and communication.

Other contributors

COLLIN F. BAKER, Project Manager, International Computer Science Institute, San Fransisco, USA

STEPHEN BEALE, Research Assistant Professor, Department of Computer Science and Electrical Engineering University of Maryland Baltimore County, USA

STEFANO BORGO, Researcher, Laboratory for Applied Ontology, Institute for Cognitive Sciences and Technology, Trento, Italy

GOSSE BOUMA, Associate Professor, Department of Information Science, University of Groningen, The Netherlands

PAUL BUITELAAR, Senior Research Fellow and Head, Unit for Natural Language Processing, Digital Enterprise Research Institute, National University of Ireland, Galway, Ireland

RU-YNG CHANG, PhD student, Multimedia Human-Machine Communication Lab, Department of Computer Science and Information Engineering, National Cheng Kung University, Tainan, Taiwan

YA-MIN CHOU, Assistant Professor, National Taipei University, Taipei, Taiwan

CHRISTIANE FELLBAUM, Senior Research Scientist, Department of Computer Science, Princeton University, USA

NICOLA GUARINO, Head, Laboratory for Applied Ontology, Institute of Cognitive Science and Technology, Trento, Italy

EDUARD HOVY, Director, Natural Language Group, Information Sciences Institute, University of Southern California, Los Angeles, USA

AURAWAN IMSOMBUT, Researcher, Department of Knowledge Management Dhurakij Pundit University, Bangkok, Thailand

ASANEE KAWTRAKUL, Associate Professor, Department of Computer Engineering, Kasetsart University, Bangkok, Thailand and Deputy Director, National Electronics and Computer Technology Center, Bangkok, Thailand

HSIANG-BIN LI, Research Assistant, Institute of Information Science, Academia Sinica, Taipei, Taiwan

SUJIAN LI, Associate Professor, Institute of Computational Linguistics, Peking University, Beijing, China

WENJIE LI, Assistant Professor, Department of Computing, The Hong Kong Polytechnic University, Hong Kong

QIN LU, Professor, Department of Computing, The Hong Kong Polytechnic University, Hong Kong

BERNARDO MAGNINI, Senior Researcher, HLT Research Unit, Trento, Italy

CLAUDIO MASOLO, Research Scientist, Laboratory for Applied Ontology, Institute for Cognitive Sciences and Technology, Trento, Italy

MARJORIE MCSHANE, Research Associate Professor, Department of Computer Science and Electrical Engineering, University of Maryland, Baltimore county, USA

JORI MUR, PhD Student, Department of Information Science, University of Groningen, The Netherlands

SRINI NARAYANAN, Group Leader, Artificial Intelligence, International Computer Science Institute, University of California, Berkeley, USA

SERGEI NIRENBURG, Professor, Department of Computer Science and Electrical Engineering, University of Maryland Baltimore County, USA

ADAM PEASE, Principal Consultant and CEO, Articulate Software, San Francisco, USA

PATRICK PANTEL, Senior Scientist, Yahoo! Labs, Santa Clara, USA and Research Assistant Professor, Information Sciences Institute, University of Southern California, Los Angeles, USA

ANDREW PHILPOT, Research Scientist, Information Sciences Institute, University of Southern California, Los Angeles, USA

JAN SCHEFFCZYK, Solution Architect, E.ON IS GmbH, Hannover, Germany

MANUELA SPERANZA, Researcher HLT Research Unit, Trento, Italy

LONNEKE VAN DER PLAS, Post-Doctoral Researcher, Language Technology Laboratory, Department of Linguistics, University of Geneva, Switzerland

Preface

Why should I read this book?

The mapping between knowledge representation and natural language is fast becoming a focal point of both knowledge engineering (KE) and computational linguistics (CL). Ontologies have a special role to play in this interface. They are essential stepping stones (a) from natural language to knowledge representation and manipulation and (b) from formal theories of knowledge to their application in (natural language) processing. Moreover, the emergence of the Semantic Web initiative presents a unique opportunity to bring research results in this area to real-world applications, at the leading edge of human-language technology. An essential and perhaps foundational aspect of the mapping between knowledge representation and natural language is the interface between ontologies and lexical resources. On the one hand, their integration includes, but is not restricted to, the use of ontologies (a) as language-independent structures of multilingual computational lexicons and (b) as powerful tools for improving the performance of existing lexical resources on various natural language processing (NLP) tasks such as word-sense disambiguation. On the other hand, lexical resources constitute a formidable source of information for generating ontological knowledge both at foundational and domain levels.

This current volume aims to be an essential general reference book on the interface between ontology and lexical resources. Given the fast developments in this new research direction, we introduce a general framework with a terminology to accommodate both ontological and lexical perspectives. However, to show its relevance and its direction of development, the focus of the book is on the current applications of such a framework. The chapters present an up-to-date overview of contributions to the field, from both CL and KE communities. Hence it constitutes a self-contained reference from introduction to the domain to the latest applications and tools developed.

Intended audience

We hope this book presents a productive dialogue among the following communities: those from the CL research community who are interested in ontology and ontologies, those from Semantic Web and KE communities who pay special attention to natural language, and those from the linguistic community who want to know how lexical knowledge can be formalized and computed. As suggested by the title, this book not only aims to reduce the gaps among these research communities, but does so on a solid ground provided by a precise framework and definitions on all sides. The book should be accessible to Master and PhD students and has been used as material for such a course.

Issues and scope

The scope of the book can be summarized by the issues it covers. The value and relevance of this book will be determined by how many of these issues remain valid or central to the research areas in the future:

- What are ontologies and lexical resources?
- What are the benefits of considering them simultaneously?
- What kind of integration can be made between these knowledge systems?
- What are the benefits of such an integration (for their respective research domains)?
- What are the applications benefiting from this integration?

Some more precise questions are addressed:

- How can NLP treatments help build knowledge resources?
- How are lexical resources used in NLP applications?
- Can we improve current knowledge resources and how?
- What is the role of formal ontology in this context?

In addition to a general framework to address the above issues, specialists already familiar with the domain will find state-of-the-art exploratory application of recent theoretical development as well as complete development of known techniques on new domains and languages. The book introduces a new perspective with a focus on Asian languages, bringing new challenges to this new area.

How the book came about

The majority of papers in this book were from the emergent OntoLex workshop series, initiated in 2000 and held in 2002, 2004, 2005, 2006, 2007, and 2008. A selection of contributors from the 2002, 2004, 2005, and 2006 workshops were invited to submit their papers, complementing other invited submissions. The papers were rigorously reviewed by reviewers invited by the Studies in Natural Language Processing editorial board, as well as by the editors of this volume. They are also cross-commented on by other authors. The editors worked in parallel on the introductory and the roadmap chapters.

Notation

In this book, the following conventions have been adopted for referring to the various WordNet-related objects:

- WordNet is a registered proper name referring to the Princeton WordNet.
- The term 'wordnet' is a common noun that refers to all lexical knowledge bases built following to some extent the original Princeton WordNet design.
- Many language wordnets, however, do use the template of 'Language WordNet', such as Italian WordNet and Chinese WordNet. This is not to be confused with the original WordNet.

As for notational issues:

- *Words* or *terms* are in italics
- CONCEPTS are in small capitals
- Synsets, { *synonymous set, synset, ...* }, are in bracketed italics. Note that the set provided does not have to be complete. For example, the synset { *dog, domestic dog, Canis familiaris* } can be simply referred to by { *dog* }. Also, sometimes the synset is given by a word indexed by a number, e.g. { *dog_2* }. In this later case, the synset corresponds to the second sense of the word *dog*.
- **Relations** are in boldface.

Acknowledgements

We would like to thank first and foremost the three editorial assistants, Li-wu Chen, Helen Kai-yun Chen, and Sophia Y. M. Lee, who spent numerous hours correcting and typesetting more than four versions of all the papers. This book could not have been completed without them. Steven Bird, the editor in chief of the Cambridge Studies in Natural Language Processing (SNLP) series, as well as several anonymous reviewers, also painstakingly read through and made comments on different versions of this book. This book improved greatly because of their contributions. We would also like to thank all of the contributors, who persevered through the long process. In particular, we would like to thank the few authors whose papers we were not able to include in the end because of other editorial considerations. Their contribution to research on the ontolex interface is by no way diminished by this omission. Colleagues at the Chinese WordNet group of Academia Sinica who helped us set up a website as well as process different versions of the chapters are Javan Ming-wei Hsu and I-Li Su. Editors who helped us check grammatical and stylistic errors are Professor Kathleen Ahrens, Maureen Kealy, and Colleen Lippert. Lastly, we thank the Cambridge University Press team in charge of the SNLP series, in particular Helen Barton, for their firm support and guidance in seeing this book through the publication process. Any remaining errors are, of course, ours.

Part I

Fundamental aspects

1   Ontology and the lexicon: a multidisciplinary perspective

Laurent Prévot, Chu-Ren Huang, Nicoletta Calzolari,
Aldo Gangemi, Alessandro Lenci, and
Alessandro Oltramari

1.1   Situating ontologies and lexical resources

The topics covered by this volume have been approached from several angles and used in various applicative frameworks. It is therefore not surprising that terminological issues arise when the various contributions to the domain are brought together. This volume aims to create synergy among the different approaches and applicative frameworks presented.

Ontologies[1] are commonly defined as specifications of shared conceptualizations (adapted from Gruber, 1995 and Guarino, 1998b). Intuitively, the *conceptualization* is the relevant informal knowledge one can extract and generalize from experience, observation, or introspection. The specification is the encoding of this knowledge in a representation language (See Figure 1.1, adapted from Guarino, 1998b).

At a coarse-grained level, this definition holds for both traditional ontologies and lexicons if one is willing to accept that a lexicon is something like the linguistic knowledge one can extract from linguistic experience. However, a crucial characteristic of a lexicon is that it is linguistically encoded into words. In order to understand more subtle differences one has to look closer at the central elements of ontology creation: *conceptualization* and *specification*. What distinguishes lexicons and ontologies lies in a sharper interpretation of these notions.

Ontologies and semantic lexical resources are apparently similar enough to be used sometimes interchangeably or combined into merged resources. However, lexicons are not really ontologies (Hirst, 2004 and Chapters 12, 13). For example, synonymy and near-synonymy are very important relations for semantic lexicons, while there is no room for them in formal ontologies where concepts should be unambiguous and where synonymic terms are

---

[1] We follow here the accepted differentiation between Ontology (the philosophical field) and ontologies (the knowledge representation artefacts).

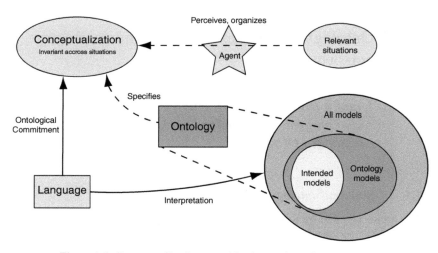

Figure 1.1 Conceptualization, specification and ontology

grouped under the same concept. From the ontological viewpoint the issue of synonymy is external and transparent to the ontological representation. Ontological discussions take place once synonymy issues have been resolved. Another example is the information about word usage (e.g., register) offered by lexicons but not relevant for traditional ontologies. Overall, linguistic resources, such as lexicons, are made of the linguistic expressions and not of their underlying concepts, while linguistic ontologies contain such underlying concepts.

The knowledge these resources attempt to capture has a very different nature, and in order to improve the management of the so-called *ontolex interface* it is useful to consider in some detail their differences, as we will see in the following subsections.

More practically, the important distinction we make in this volume is the supposed difference between formal and linguistic ontologies. According to the traditional view, formal ontologies are logically captured and formally well-formed conceptual structures, while linguistic ontologies are grounded on human language and are therefore 'linguistically conventionalized', hence often not formally precise, conceptual structures. The formal/linguistic opposition hides a much richer and layered classification that can be unveiled by sharpening the analysis of the resources in terms of conceptualization and specification.

At a terminological level, computational lexicons, lexical resources or relational lexicons differ from each other in a non-trivial way. However, since this book deals specially with natural language processing (NLP) and Semantic Web issues, the lexical resources we consider are machine-readable and are therefore synonymous with *computational lexicons*. Finally, since relations are essential components of computational lexicons, we also take *relational lexicon* as a synonym in the context of this book.

The interface between ontology and lexicon (the ontolex interface hereafter) is born out of their distinct yet related characteristics. A lexicon is about words, an ontology about concepts, yet they both represent shared conceptualization, from the perspective of conventionalization. For applications in human-language technology, a lexicon establishes the interface between human agents and knowledge. For applications in the Semantic Web (Berners-Lee *et al.*, 2001), an ontology enables the machine to process knowledge directly. It is in this context that the ontolex interface becomes a crucial research topic connecting human knowledge to web knowledge.

1.1.1 Conceptualization

The nature of a conceptualization greatly depends on how it emerged or how it was created. Conceptualization is the process that leads to the extraction and generalization of relevant information from one's experience. A conceptualization is the relevant information itself. A conceptualization is independent from specific situations or representation languages, since it is not about representation yet. In the context of this book, we consider that conceptualization is accessible after a specification step; more cognitive-oriented studies, however, attempt at characterizing directly the conceptualizations (Schalley and Zaefferer, 2006). Every conceptualization is bound to a single agent, namely it is a mental product which stands for the view of the world adopted by that agent; it is by means of ontologies, which are language-specifications[2] of those mental products, that heterogeneous agents (humans, artificial or hybrid) can assess whether a given conceptualization is shared or not and choose whether it is worthwhile to negotiate meaning or not. The exclusive entryway to concepts is by language; if the layperson normally uses natural language, societies of hybrid agents composed by computers, robots, and humans, need a formal machine-understandable language.

To be useful, a conceptualization has to be shared among agents, such as humans, even if their agreement is only implicit. In other words, the conceptualization that natural language represents is a collective process, not

---

[2] Language here is no more than a representational formalism and vocabulary, and therefore is not necessary a natural language, but could be, for example, a predicate logic and a set of predicates and relations constituting the vocabulary of the theory.

an individual one. The information content is defined by the collectivity of speakers.

Philosophers of language consider primarily linguistic data and introspection for drawing generalizations to be used as conceptualizations for building natural language ontology. Traditional lexical semanticists will use mainly lexical resources as a ground for the conceptualization. Cognitive scientists might broaden the range of information sources, possibly including other perceptual modes such as visual or tactile information (see Section 1.3.1).

In our understanding, this is how a *linguistic ontology* is distinguished from a *conceptual ontology* that does not restrict its information sources to language resources. These kinds of ontology that acknowledge the importance of the agent conceptualization are called *descriptive* ontologies and they are opposed to *revisionary* ones (Strawson, 1959). A *descriptive ontology* recognizes natural language and common sense as important sources for ontological knowledge and analysis, while *revisionary ontology* refutes this position and is committed to capture the intrinsic nature of a domain, independently from the conceptualizing agents (see Masolo *et al.*, 2003; Guarino, 1998b, and Section 1.3.2).

In *lexical ontologies*, conceptualization is based on linguistic criteria, more precisely information found in lexical resources such as dictionaries or thesauruses. In many cases they are slightly hybrid since they feature mainly linguistic knowledge but include in many places world knowledge (also called encyclopedic or common-sense knowledge). Lexical ontologies are interesting because of the special status of the lexicon in human cognition. Indeed there are two notions of lexicon. A lexicon can be defined as a collection of linguistically conventionalized concepts, but in a more cognitive framework it is a store of personal knowledge which can be easily retrieved with lexical cues. In the context of this volume, we focus on the former definition of *lexicon*.

Engineering and application ontologies that have conceptualization grounded in shared experiences among experts are also relevant in the NLP context. How such ontologies can be integrated with more generic ontologies is of great interest in this volume (see Chapters 13 and 17, which explicitly deal with this issue).

Finally, a further refinement is introduced between linguistic conceptualizations derived from one unique language (monolingual linguistic ontology) or from several languages (multilingual linguistic ontology). Although language-based, the further generalization obtained through crosslinguistic consideration renders the conceptualization less dependent on surface idiosyncrasies. The issue is then to determine whether the conceptualizations based on different languages are compatible and, if not, how to handle them. Multilingual issues are extremely important for obvious applicative purposes, but their development might also help to investigate the complex relationship between language, culture, and thought. A recurrent question for both cognitive science/NLP is the existence/need of a distinction between the so-called conceptual level (supposedly language independent) and the semantic level that would be deeply influenced by the language. These issues will be developed further both in the sections devoted to cognitive approaches (Section 1.3.1) and to NLP applications (Section 1.4.3).

The conceptualization process is a crucial preliminary for ontology construction. However, it is not the focus of this book and we encourage the reader to consult the more cognitive oriented contribution made in Schalley and Zaefferer, 2006.

1.1.2 Specification

The second operation is specification, as an ontology specifies conceptualization in a representation language. Apart from the level of complexity and explicitness, what is crucial is that ontologies, as language-dependent[3] specifications of conceptualizations, are the basis of communication, the bridge across which common understanding is established.

The nature of this language leads to the second main source of differentiation for ontologies. *Formal ontologies* are expressed in a formal language, 'informal ontologies' are, for example, expressed in natural language, and *semi-formal ontologies* combine both.[4] An important aspect of this distinction is the exclusion of ambiguity from formal ontologies while it is ubiquitous in semi-formal ones. However, this cannot be a blind generalization. Ontologies may be extremely rigorous and precise although formulated in natural language, and formality alone does not ensure rigour and precision.

Linguistic ontologies use the word senses defined in lexical resources (either informally or semi-formally as in WordNet) to create the concepts that will constitute the linguistic ontology. This move is a difficult one and if not performed carefully can lead to poor resources from an ontological viewpoint (see Chapter 3 for details on this problem). Still, in principle, nothing prevents a linguistic ontology from being formal.[5] It is the difficulty of such a project that makes linguistic ontologies only 'semi-formal'. More precisely

---

[3] Language-dependent does not mean here dependent to any given natural language but to the language used to formulate the ontology.

[4] Etymologically the 'formal' of 'formal ontology' also comes from the idea of not focusing on one area of knowledge but on principles equally applicable to all areas of knowledge. As such they operate at the level of the form rather than of the content. However, the more straightforward aspect of formality versus informality is emphasized here.

[5] Moreover, it is important to make the distinction between a linguistic ontology and an ontology of linguistics. The latter is an ontology concerning objects for linguistic description such as GOLD, Generic Ontology for Linguistic Description (Farrar and Langendoen, 2003). See GOLD web page (http://www.linguistics-ontology.org/gold.html) for more information.

axiomatizing the definitions (including the disambiguation of their terms) is still more of a research topic than a standard procedure for obtaining formal ontologies (see, however, Harabagiu *et al.*, 1999 and Chapter 3).

1.1.3   Scope

Three different levels of specificity for ontologies are recognized in ontological research and practice: upper-level, core (or reference), and domain ontologies. Foundational resources are sometimes confused with upper-level resources. They both concern the most general categories and relations which constitute the upper level of knowledge taxonomies. Foundational resources are further distinguished from upper-level by the additional requirement of providing a rich characterization, while upper-level resources include, for instance, simple taxonomies. They contrast with resources such as specialized lexicons or domain ontologies dealing with a specific domain of application that can be extremely restricted. The distance between upper and domain levels made it necessary to have an intermediate level: the *core* resources (see Figure 1.2). Core resources constitute the level at which is found intermediate concepts and links between foundational and domain resources. They can, however, vary greatly in content according to their main function: to provide a more specific but sound middle level or simply provide the mapping between the two levels. For example, MILO (MId-Level Ontology) is designed specifically to serve as the interface between upper and domain ontologies. Such mid-level ontologies can be considered as an extension of the upper ontology in the sense that they are supposed to be shared or linked to all domains. On the other hand, they also overlap greatly with a global resource since most of the terms at this level are

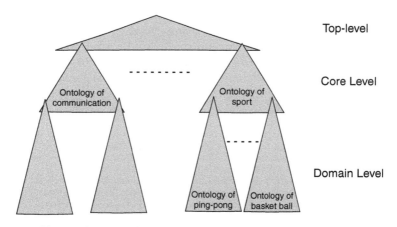

Figure 1.2 Scope of ontologies

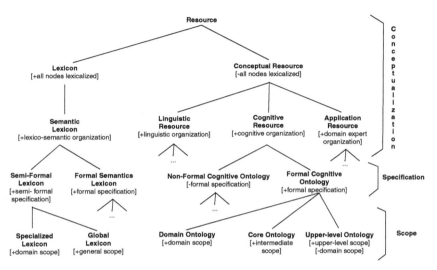

Figure 1.3 Ontolex resources taxonomy overview

linguistically realized, in comparison to many abstract and non-realized terms in upper ontology.[6]

More discussion on this issue is provided in the introductory Chapter 10 and in Chapter 13, where the notion of *global ontologies* is introduced for resources like WordNet, covering a broad scope while providing a good coverage by gathering all the entries a general purpose thesaurus could provide. Among traditional ontologies, CYC (Reed and Lenat, 2002) is also an example of global resource.

1.1.4   The ontolex interface

The previous sections allowed us to identify lexical resources and ontologies as objects of partially similar nature but differing with regard to their conceptualization, specification, and scope as illustrated in the taxonomy of Figure 1.3. These differences come from different research traditions. Ontologies and lexical resources, in their modern technical sense, historically belong to different applicative programs that have only recently been considered simultaneously.

---

[6] Note that the most recent version of IEEE upper ontology (www.ontologyportal.org) merged the original SUMO and MILO. Hence the distinction between upper and middle ontologies is blurred in this resource but the interface between upper ontology and lexicon is enhanced.

From an ontological viewpoint, the basic building blocks of ontologies are concepts and relations. Identifying these objects and deciding about their nature is a fundamental task of ontological analysis. A similar concern centred around terms and relations is found in lexical resources. These resources have sometimes been called *relational lexicons* (Evens, 1988) since the network of relations is supposed to contribute significantly to the meaning of the lexical entries. Concepts (or words) and relations are therefore the first two objects to consider while working with ontologies and lexical resources. This parallelism in their structure defines the ontolex interface.

Ontological analysis and construction handle concepts (for which words may or may not be available) that are grounded on knowledge representation arguments (homogeneity, clarity, compactness, etc.). On the other hand, lexical ontologies start from an existing and usually large vocabulary and come up with a sensible and useful organization for these terms. The work situated at the ontolex interface has therefore to find the best integration of both approaches. The exact combination of the conceptual information found in traditional ontologies and the lexical information is indeed the topic of most chapters of Parts III and IV of the present volume.

The ontolex interface also turns out to be extremely important in the design of multilingual resources. In the spirit of EuroWordNet (Vossen, 1998), these resources are typically constituted of several language-dependent monolingual resources mapped to an interlingua. Although this interlingua is generally unstructured (Vossen, 1998), giving it a structure is an important track of improvement followed in this domain (Hovy and Nirenburg, 1992) (see also Chapter 15). This structured interlingua might correspond to the conceptual level mentioned before. In addition to hold promise for language-engineering applications, this type of multilingual resource should facilitate the research on lexical universals and may also contribute to the recurrent universalists/relativists debate.

1.2   The content of ontologies

1.2.1   Concepts and terms

In an ontology, the nodes are of a conceptual nature and are called concepts, types, categories, or properties (see Guarino and Welty, 2000a). They are often characterized extensionally in terms of *classes* and correspond in this case to sets of instances or individuals. In ontologies directly derived from lexical resources, individuals (denoted by proper names and other named entities) are sometimes treated like other concepts. In some of these resources little attention has been given to the difference between classes and instances: they are both concept nodes of the resources and are represented in the same way.

Both classes and instances were entering in the same relation leading to the well-known **is-a** overload issue (see Chapter 3 for a detailed discussion of this issue). For example, until WordNet 2.0, each American president (e.g *Kennedy*) was given as a hyponym of *president*. Version 2.1 of WordNet added an **instance-of** relation for these cases. From a sound ontological perspective, a strong emphasis is put on the need for a clear distinction between these two components as made explicit by the distinction of an onomasticon, storing factual data, as a separate component of the Ontological Semantics (OntoSem) apparatus presented in Chapter 7 (see also Chapters 2 and 3).

The difference between a term-based lexicon and a concept-based lexicon is clear cut. However, the sense-based lexicon complicates the picture. In a sense-based lexicon like WordNet, the nodes of the resources are neither simple terms nor pure conceptual entities but word senses that correspond to a conventionalized use of a word, possibly coming from corpus-attested examples.[7] In WordNet, the nodes are *synsets*, i.e. sets of word senses that define sets of synonyms as made explicit in Chapter 2. Therefore, WordNet is primarily a lexicon since all its entries are linguistic expressions, but semantic structure defined by the synsets and their relations have frequently been used as a linguistic ontology (see Chapters 2 and 3 for issues with regard to this topic). The necessity of this intermediate semantic level is also discussed with more details in Chapters 14, 12 and 15.

1.2.1.1 The top-down approach to word senses   In formal ontologies, ambiguity of terms has to be resolved as much as possible before entering the formal specification phase. The objective is to reach high precision for the intended meaning of each term in order to avoid misunderstandings. A central task of ontology building is to track down and get rid of ambiguities from the knowledge domain and to build more precise and reliable formal ontologies through analysis. An essential step of the ontological analysis process consists in determining a backbone taxonomy that provides the main categories and their taxonomic architecture organized along an **is-a-kind-of** relation. The top level of this backbone introduces, for example, the distinctions between objects, processes and qualities, between artefact and natural objects. Applying these structures to lexicons constitutes a 'top-down' approach to word senses since they will be strongly determined by the position of their attachment in the taxonomy. This approach is exemplified in Chapters 2 and 3.

1.2.1.2 The bottom-up approach to word senses   In spite of its usefulness for knowledge representation, the top-down approach meets its limit when focus is put on natural language. Languages have productive mechanisms

---

[7] In Fellbaum, 1998: 24, synsets are described as lexicalized concepts.

to derive new meanings. It is important to bear in mind that neither regular polysemy (Copestake and Briscoe, 1995; Apresjan, 2000) nor creative use (Pustejovsky, 1995) can be exhaustively listed. The notion of word sense as a discrete semantic unit is itself put in question (Kilgariff, 1997). In the context of this book, we avoid this thorny issue with a data-driven approach. In the development of NLP and ontologies whether word senses really exist, or not, is not essential; but the frequent references to word senses in major existing resources makes them important elements to be considered. However, given the bottom-up approach, one still needs to deal with the different granularity among various resources. An interesting proposal for answering this issue is proposed in Chapter 15, where a method is proposed to have some control on the level of granularity of the sense introduced in the final resource.

1.2.2   Relations

In ontologies, concepts are integrated into a coherent whole with relations. The nature and the number of relations have been the subject of many studies in the field. In ontology, relations are conceptually driven and take concepts as arguments. On the other hand, lexical resources are concerned with the organization of lexicalized items. The relations they feature have only an indirect conceptual nature such as **antonymy**, which is primarily a relation between word *forms* and not between concepts or word meanings (Fellbaum, 1998: 49).[8] Relations with the same name in formal and linguistic ontologies might appear to be quite different under closer scrutiny. Moreover, the research issues involving these relations are quite different from the formal-ontology and lexical-resource perspectives. For formal ontologists it is important to clarify the nature and the formal properties of the relations: to which kind of entity do they relate (classes or individuals), are they reflexive, symmetric, transitive, and so on? For example, formal ontologists have focused attention on the **is-a** relationship overload. This relation has been used extensively but was often only loosely defined and merely corresponded to the intuitions triggered by its natural language expression **is-a**. On the other hand, relations of lexical resources hold between word senses (e.g. **hypernymy**) or even simply words in the case of lexical relations like **antonymy**. For lexical resources, the focus in recent studies is not on precise definitions for these relations, but more on the methods for discovering them automatically and for their application in extracting lexical knowledge. It is important to note that a general classification of these relations as either paradigmatic or syntagmatic is common to both conceptual and lexical approaches.

---

[8] In this case it is the conceptual opposition that can be associated with the lexical **antonymy**.

1.2.2.1 Paradigmatic relations   Paradigmatic relations hold between elements of the same nature that belong to a common paradigm. We restrict ourselves to terms that can be replaced in a given context as in Example 1.1. They belong typically to the same syntactic category as opposed to items related through syntagmatic relations.

(1.1) a. A(n) animal/dog/cat/dalmatian crossed the road.
       b. He ate/devoured the small rabbit.

In Cruse, 1986, paradigmatic relations are associated with congruence relations between classes such as **identity, inclusion, overlap,** and **disjunction**. Indeed the best-known paradigmatic relations in the lexical domain are **synonymy, antonymy, meronymy, hypernymy,** and **hyponymy**. In ontologies, related conceptual relations of **conceptual opposition, part-of, is-a-kind-of** are formally defined. However, more relations can be thought of, for example the relations among the siblings in a taxonomy are sometimes good candidates (e.g. red/black/blue, or cat/dog). Such richness in paradigmatic relations (Murphy, 2003) leads to the proposal of a very general *principle of relation by contrast* that covers paradigmatic relations. Huang *et al.*, 2007 proposes a specific relation called **paranymy** to cover paradigmatic relations among concepts belonging to the semantic classification.

Until recently, these relations have been the ones most widely studied and applied. Many NLP uses of ontologies restrict themselves to the use of a simple taxonomy. Relations have received different names according to the framework considered. This terminological profusion suggests different concerns and perspectives. For example, the highly debated **hypernymy** (and **hyponymy** its inverse) relates lexical entities but has been often used as a straightforward relation between concepts. The relation between concepts is also called **is-a** relation although **is-a-kind-of** is less ambiguous and favoured by ontologists who equate it with **subsumption**.

1.2.2.2 Syntagmatic relations   As mentioned above, *syntagmatic relations* hold between entities of different natures; the items related by these relations co-occur frequently but cannot be replaced by one another. They are often lexicalized by words having different syntactic categories. In lexical semantics, syntagmatic relations are more related to studies of syntax/semantic interface focusing on predication and thematic roles. Syntagmatic relations include relations between endurants (objects, agents) and perdurants[9] (including events and processes) at the lexical level (noun/verb relation), or, for example, between a category and its attributes (noun/adjective relation

---

[9] The term *occurent* is also used.

at the lexical level). Many of these relations have linguistic counterparts as *case relations*. They have been studied in depth by Fillmore to develop his Case Grammar (Fillmore, 1968) and they constitute the majority of FrameNet (Baker *et al.*, 1998) relations (see also Chapter 4).

While WordNet and most recent ontological-based works have focused on paradigmatic relations,[10] syntagmatic relations received less attention for resource developers while their importance for NLP applications gradually appeared as essential.

Even though its development is quite recent, FrameNet, as well as the related theory of Construction Grammar, is now subject to the same attention given to WordNet by computational linguists and ontology builders. This complementarity between syntagmatic and paradigmatic relations in WordNet and FrameNet and their efficient combination is an important element of this applied research area.

The syntagmatic/paradigmatic distinction partially overlaps with the division proposed in Nirenburg and Raskin, 2001 between syntax-driven and ontology-driven lexical semantics. The former corresponds to syntagmatic relations whose study had been bound tightly to the syntax/semantics interface (Levin, 1993). The latter, although putting a strong emphasis on paradigmatic relations (and in particular taxonomies and meronymies), includes also relations belonging to the syntagmatic class (e.g. **participation** of objects into processes).

1.3   Theoretical framework for the ontologies/lexicons interface

The fields involved in knowledge representation, regardless of whether they have a declared objective of psychological adequacy or not, already have a rich heritage. Several approaches can be broadly distinguished: philosophical studies tracing back to Aristotle, psychological studies focusing on the mental representation of knowledge, and linguistic studies. The topic of the interface between ontologies and lexical resources is therefore a re-examination of traditional issues of psycho-linguistics, linguistics, artificial intelligence, and philosophy in the light of recent advances in these disciplines and in response to a renewed interest in this topic due to its relevance for the Semantic Web major applications.

---

[10] To be fair, WordNet does host some syntagmatic relations such as **cause** from the beginning. However, the coverage of these syntagmatic relations is not comparable with the extensive hierarchical network in WordNet made up of paradigmatic relations (see Chapter 2 for a quantitative presentation of the relation in WordNet.). Moreover, the initial design of WordNet with a distinct structure for each syntactic category precluded the development of cross-category relations such as the ones present in EuroWordNet (Vossen, 1998).

Overall, the importance of a multidisciplinary approach is recognized for lexical resources development[11] and knowledge representation as acknowledged by many influential contributions to the field (Hobbs *et al.*, 1987; Sowa, 2000; Pustejovsky, 1995; Nirenburg and Raskin, 2004; Guarino, 1998b).

This section explains how such a rich ground is an opportunity for the current research in NLP, knowledge representation, and lexical semantics. We are particularly interested in the interface between formal ontology and lexical resources or linguistic ontologies. Here formal ontologies are understood as ontologies motivated by philosophical considerations, knowledge representation efficiency, and re-usability principles. Lexical resources or linguistic ontologies have structure motivated by natural language and more particularly the lexicon.

1.3.1   The cognitive ground

1.3.1.1 Categorization   Studies on categorization received a lot of attention from the cognitive side. The componential semantics (Katz and Fodor, 1963) in which the category of a word is defined as a set of features (syntactic and semantic) that distinguishes this word from other words in the language is one of the most influential accounts available. It is striking that this model fits extremely well with Formal Concept Analysis (FCA). Developed by Ganter and Wille (1997) and first applied to lexical data in Priss, 1998 and 2005, this framework is nowadays in use in several ontological approaches (illustrated, for example, in Chapter 6 of this volume). However, componential semantics has been limited by various developments centred on the notion of prototypicality (Rosch, 1973, 1978). It has been empirically established that the association of words and even concepts with a category is a scalar notion (*graded membership*). The problem of category boundaries, of their existence and of their potential determination, is therefore a serious one. Contextual factors have been said to influence these boundaries. Another issue is the use of a feature list that has been said to be far too simplistic and that raises the question of the definition of the features themselves. However, to see a parallel in the definition of categories from philosophy see section 1.3.2.

Besides the issue of prototypicality, another common ground is the investigation of the models for concept types (sortal, relational, individual, and functional concepts), category structure, and their respective relationships to 'frames'. There is wide converging evidence that language has a great impact on categorization. When there is a word labelling a concept in a certain language it makes the learning of the corresponding category by children much faster and easier.

---

[11] WordNet was originally intended for a psycho-linguistic experiment.

There is much more to say about categorization, but we point the reader to Wierzbicka, 1990, Croft and Cruse, 2004: 77–92, Murphy, 2003, and Schalley and Zaefferer, 2006, in which these approaches and their limitations are discussed at length.

1.3.1.2 Predication   In linguistics, a large body of work is focused on predication since it directs sentence interpretation. These works have been pioneered by Fillmore (1976) who proposed that we should analyse words in relation to each other according to the frame or script in which they appear. The study focuses on relations expressed by grammar case (Fillmore, 1968). In this domain essential contributions on argument structure (Grimshaw, 1990), thematic roles, selectional restrictions (Dowty, 1990), and type coercion (Pustejovsky, 1995) have been made in recent years. This field of research produced resources such as FrameNet (Baker *et al.*, 1998) and VerbNet (Kipper *et al.*, 2000).

1.3.1.3 Conceptual and semantic level: Are they identical?   Many proponents of the cognitive approach to languages postulate that semantics is equated with the conceptual level. Jackendoff explains that surface structures are directly related to the concepts they express by a set of rules. These concepts include more information associated with world knowledge (or encyclopedic knowledge). Since, according to him, it is impossible to disentangle purely semantic from encyclopedic information without losing generalizations (Jackendoff, 1983), semantic and conceptual levels must form a single level.

However, Levinson (Gumperz and Levinson, 1996; Levinson, 1997, 2003) advanced serious arguments, involving in particular pragmatics, in favour of the distinction between semantic and conceptual representations. These differences are explained by different views on language inherited from different theoretical perspectives. While Jackendoff focuses on Chomsky's I(nternal)-language, Levinson insists on the importance of the social nature of language and therefore takes care of the rather neglected E(xternal)-language in Jackendoff's account. Language as primarily a tool for communicating rather than a tool for representing knowledge (in someone's mind) corresponds to these different perspectives.

From an applicative viewpoint, Bateman (1997) argues, on methodological grounds, for the need of an interface ontology between the conceptual and surface levels. He specifies that such a resource should neither be too close to nor too far from the linguistic surface and details the General-Upper-Model (Bateman *et al.*, 1995) as an example of such a balanced interface ontology. This is also the line followed by Nirenburg and Raskin (2004) and exemplified in Chapter 7 of this volume. Pustejovsky and his colleagues, on the other hand, follow the direction of a single structure, though highly dynamic, as in the generative lexicon (Pustejovsky, 1991, 1995).

1.3.2   The philosophical ground

Determining a system of ontological categories in order to provide a view as to *What kinds of things exist?* is one of the essential tasks of metaphysics. It is also probably philosophy that offers the highest number of (sometimes contradictory) propositions regarding this issue, from Aristotle to contemporary authors. These proposals can differ strongly both on the nature of the ontological categories (*How exactly are the categories delineated?*) and on actual ontological decisions (e.g *What are artefacts, organizations, holes...?*). In this context the focus has been mainly on the upper level of the knowledge architecture and in finding an exhaustive system of mutually exclusive categories (Thomasson, 2004). The lack of consensual answers on these matters has resulted in a certain scepticism with regard to the determination of such an ontological system. However, recent approaches aiming at taking the best of philosophy while avoiding its pitfalls are rendering philosophical considerations worth the exploration.

   The crucial aspect where philosophy can help the ontology builder might not be the position of such and such a concept in a 'perfect' taxonomy, but rather the methodology for making such decisions. The second important aspect is grounded on Strawson's distinction between *revisionary* and *descriptive* metaphysics. For Strawson (adopting a descriptivist stance), the material accessible to the philosopher is not the real world but how the philosopher perceives and conceptualizes it. Contrarily, a revisionary approach uses rigorous paraphrases for supposedly imperfect common-sense notions. See, for example, a discussion about the difficulties that such a revisionary approach meets when trying to deal with objects as simple as holes (Casati and Varzi, 1996). Revisionary approaches tend to discard natural language and common-sense intuitions as serious sources for ontological analysis. On the other hand, the descriptivist stance is presented to be safer philosophically. It also provides a solid methodological starting point for practical ontological research. More precisely, by allowing different ontologies (as different descriptions of the world) to co-exist, it is able to avoid never-ending ontological considerations on the real nature of the objects of the world.

   This move leads to the distinction between Ontology as a philosophical discipline and ontologies as knowledge artefacts we are trying to develop (Guarino, 1998b). Modern ontology designers are not looking for a perfect ontology but consider many potential ontologies concerning different domains and capturing different views of the same reality.

To succeed in this task, philosophical works try to determine a set of fundamental categories. In Thomasson, 2004 three main methods have been summarized:

- *The feature negation method*: This method ensures exhaustiveness and mutual exclusivity. This method can divide any category into two others by distinguishing the things having a certain feature from those not having it. The feature system can be developed in a multi-dimensional fashion forming a matrix (potentially very rich) more than a tree. The two main philosophical issues with this approach are (a) the negative characterization of many concepts that might end up in the same category without sharing any intrinsic property and (b) the inadequacy of many feature/category pairs established by linguistic tests.
- *The absurdity detection method*: This method, originating with Husserl and Ryle (Ryle, 1971), consists of testing an expression (grammatical context) in which a concept can be employed without exhibiting an absurdity. For example, *this house is brown* is correct while *this hypothesis is brown* is absurd, thus exhibiting the different nature of these two concepts. This method can be used to prove that two elements belong to the two categories, but cannot prove that two candidates belong to the same category, since a new dividing context may always be found.
- *The method of distinguishing Identity and Existence conditions*: This method is a variation and an extension of the previous one. Instead of considering expressions, it is the objects denoted that are examined. According to Frege (1884), *names* are different from other terms by their condition of identity added to their criteria of application (that corresponds to the previous method). Names are associated with *sorts* of thing (*sortal term*). Armed with these names, it is possible to distinguish different categories of *objects* as correlates of names, thus distinguishing ontological categories. Then, the application conditions and identity criterion are tested on the sortals. The second essential ingredient for identifying the categories are the identity conditions. On this issue it is Quine's recommendation 'No entity without identity' (Quine, 1960) that forces us to know how to identify (and therefore distinguish) a given entity from another one before bringing it to existence. For example, an ANIMAL is distinguished from the COLLECTION-OF-PARTICLES constituting it because they each have a different *Identity Condition* (IC). All the particles are involved in the identity of the collection but not of the animal for which the IC has something to do with its DNA. Loosing a leg or a hair does not affect the identity of an animal but it does affect the identity of the corresponding collection of particles (which becomes a new collection of particles).

The *OntoClean* methodology (Guarino and Welty, 2000a, 2002a), widely accepted and now commonly applied to various practical situations, draws upon the last method and proposes a powerful methodology for building and maintaining ontologies. From the traditional philosophical investigations, *OntoClean* proposed a set of useful meta-properties that apply to the categories (called properties); these meta-properties include the identity condition (Guarino and Welty, 2002b). As emphasized earlier, the objective of this methodology is not to propose *the* only set of acceptable categories, but to help ontology builders and maintainers to make explicit their ontological commitments. This helps to discover ontological issues early in the building process rather than suffering from it once the ontology is developed. Said differently, *OntoClean* does not tell the designer which are the hypothetical 'perfect categories', but helps to make explicit the consequences of the choices made during conceptualization and specification. Chapters 3 and 10 of this book present some details of this approach.

1.3.3   The lexicographic ground

Lexicography, the discipline dealing with dictionaries, is traditionally split into the practical aspects, the craft of creating dictionaries, and the more theoretical lexicology. However, serious lexicography works generally combine practical and theoretical aspects. Since traditional dictionaries are the ancestors of our computational lexical resources, it might not be so surprising that early lexicography studies have already met with most of the difficulties that modern approaches are facing nowadays. Such early studies included the characterization of the different types of dictionaries (Shcherba, 1995), which appears quite in line with the discussions of the previous sections as illustrated in the following list of essential distinctions that operate among dictionaries:

- Encyclopedic vs general dictionaries. Encyclopedias emphasize the importance of proper nouns and show that many of them must be included in general dictionaries. Under this distinction, Shcherba also discusses the words that receive quite different entries in dictionaries and encyclopedias because of their respective level of specificity.
- Form-based (*ordinary*) from meaning-based (*ideological*) dictionaries. In the latter, the importance of synonymy and other relations was emphasized and exemplified through Roget's thesaurus.
- *Defining* from *translating* dictionaries where the complex nature of the relation between lexical entries across languages is emphasized.

Practical lexicography is restricted by the fact that lexica are essential resources which in turn require deployment of significant resources to develop.

For instance, timely development of a dictionary often requires deliberation of economy and exclusion of non-essential entries. However, far from being simply a burden, these constraints force the lexicographer to meaningful choices in order to include only lexical information corresponding to the general language and rejecting the rest into encyclopedias and specialized lexicons.

The importance of the distinction between lexical and encyclopedic knowledge is also fundamental for Nunberg and Zaenen, 1992. They explain that when language is taken as a social artefact in which cultural context is an active element of its definition, many regularities from encyclopedic knowledge deserve to be integrated in dictionaries.

Despite its practical orientation, lexicography can greatly benefit from linguistic theory as advocated in Apresjan, 2000, where four trends of modern linguistic theory are taken to be of immediate relevance for 'systematic lexicography': (a) the search for a common-sense picture of the world, (b) the shift from study of separate words to larger lexicographic types, (c) the meticulous study of separated word senses in all of their linguistically relevant aspects, (d) the convergence of grammatical and lexicological studies towards an integrated theory of linguistic description. All these elements also constitute the ground for the generative lexicon theory (Pustejovsky, 1991, 1995) that is presented in the next section.

1.3.4   The linguistic ground and contemporary lexical semantics

The frameworks presented in the previous sections largely included linguistic considerations and contributions from linguistics. However, the goal was generally not the study of language or the development of natural language systems. With regard to the philosophical ground, natural language semanticists and philosophers of language have been deeply interested in natural language ontology, or to which ontological categories the study of natural language commits. The work on tense and aspect (Dowty, 1977) but also on plurals (Bach, 1986a; Link, 1983) or mass/countable nouns provides research materials for a field that has sometimes been called natural language metaphysics (Bach, 1986b; Dölling, 1993). Although such crucial studies formed a firm theoretical ground allowing future advances, this body of research had little direct impact on the development of practical resources.

An important exception to this is the generative lexicon of James Pustejovsky (1991, 1995). The generative lexicon is a ground-breaking contribution to the study of lexicon and its relation with ontology. It combines the philosophical ground with a rich lexical-semantic theory featuring a sophisticated account for predication. The generative lexicon addresses two serious issues encountered by traditional resources. First, they are generally based on sense-enumeration and attempt to include a list of word senses. Pustejovsky argued convincingly that word senses are infinite since language producers can easily create new senses for a word. For example, coercion operated by the predicate alters the semantic type of a given argument. In this context the lexical entries are more dynamic and correspond to combinations of several aspects of meaning, the *qualia roles* inspired from Aristotle's *mode of explanations*. For nouns, the different aspects of meaning are *constitutive* (what are the parts of this object), *formal* (what is this object, the classical taxonomy), *agentive* (what is its origin) and *telic* (what is its intended function). The multidimensional view of meaning is sometimes captured by allowing for massive multi-inheritance in the hierarchy. However, such practice is considered precarious from a knowledge representation viewpoint since the structure becomes murky, and it is more difficult to preserve the consistency of the whole. The generative lexicon resolves this dilemma and sanctions a multidimensional view of meaning by maintaining a sound knowledge organization through the use of different relations rather than a single entangled tree. For example, inheritance is not allowed along all the dimensions and only careful orthogonal inheritance is allowed (Pustejovsky and Boguraev, 1993).

The generative lexicon has received a lot of attention, and some practical resources implement its principles into real-scale lexicons such as SIMPLE (Lenci *et al.*, 2000) including an extended qualia structure (Busa *et al.*, 1999) that is necessary to characterize precisely how each quale contributes to the typing of a concept. This powerful research on predication and coercion so far suggests that the four qualia aspects do not exhaust all the aspects of meaning coercion. For example, Asher and Denis (2004) proposed that we should generalize the idea of the generative lexicon to an arbitrary set (and not only the four qualia) of relations contextually triggered (including discourse information).

This section closes this brief presentation of the theoretical background supporting this volume. Before presenting in detail the structure of the book, the next section emphasizes the bidirectional nature of our enterprise and the centrality of NLP.

1.4   From ontologies to the lexicon and back

An essential view defended in this book is the bidirectionality of the relation between ontologies and lexical resources. We reject the primacy of ontological research over lexical research or vice versa. We argue for a balanced combination following clear principles backed by theoretical investigations. We consider both how ontological methodology and knowledge can enhance lexical resources and how these resources can in turn benefit ontologies.

1.4.1   From ontologies to lexicons

This direction concerns the ontological enhancement of lexical resources by using them as consistent knowledge sources for knowledge engineering applications. It includes checking the knowledge structure of lexical resources and suggests improvements of these resources (see Chapter 3). This direction is also concerned with the axiomatization of the glosses found in lexical resources (Harabagiu *et al.*, 1999; Gangemi *et al.*, 2003a). Some contributions presented here (see Chapters 3) argue for performing this integration as a preliminary step and only in a second step inputting lexical data in the ontology. However, other proposals apply more straightforwardly formal tools such as Formal Concept Analysis on natural language resources (see Chapter 6) or use directly conventionalized linguistic objects such as the Chinese writing system as potential linguistic ontologies (see Chapter 8).

1.4.2   From lexicons to ontologies

The other direction (from lexical resources to ontological knowledge) has been so far primarily concerned with the population by lexical terms of ontological resources. This process is an efficient way of building vast ontologies of common-sense or domain knowledge (according to the vocabulary included). Several experiments of this kind are represented in this book, either for populating an existing upper level (see Chapter 2) or for creating complete domain ontologies (Chapter 17). The existing lexical resources might also be used as guidelines during the construction of the ontology.

A general result of the contributions presented in this book is the improvement of the two types of resources by providing systematic links between them. Several models are compared in Chapter 10, and some promising solutions are presented in Chapters 12 and 13.

1.4.3   The centrality of natural language processing

According to the advocated bidirectionality, NLP is seen both as an application and as a tool for the ontolex interface (as emphasized in Chapters 7, 10, and 16). Several chapters illustrate the use of NLP techniques for building ontologies (semi-automatically). The techniques used range from syntactic parsing and semantic analysis to term and relation extraction. Chapter 6 points towards a deeper use of syntactic and semantic analysis for improving the ontology acquisition results. But NLP also makes use of the ontologically enhanced lexical resources for a variety of classical NLP tasks. Such applications include information retrieval and question-answering (see Chapter 15 and 16), co-reference resolution, and more globally semantic analysis for deep-language understanding (Chapter 7).

1.5   Outline of chapters

The book is divided into four parts. The first part is composed of five chapters. Chapters 2, 3 and 4 introduce essential resources of our field and expose different approaches of the combination between formal ontologies and WordNet or FrameNet. The part is concluded by a roadmap for the ontolex interface that provides perspectives for future work in the field (Chapter 5).

The second part, also composed of five chapters, concerns the discovery and representation of conceptual systems. This part of the book shows the variety of methods that can be used for unveiling ontological knowledge as well as the variety of representations. The sources for unveiling knowledge might be surprisingly rich as exhibited in this section, from automatic learning techniques coupled to formal representation tools (such as Formal Conceptual Analysis in Chapter 6) to the investigation of a 3,000-year old body of knowledge such as the Chinese writing systems described in Chapter 8. This chapter investigates further the notions of conceptualization and specification delineated in the general introduction in order to explain the different ways taken first for establishing a shared understanding of a domain (conceptualization) and then for specifying it in a given language (formal or not). The representation of a knowledge system is also addressed with the firm position of Chapter 7 defending a structure for semantic, ontological, and factual information. This chapter also shows how such architecture can be used in a practical treatment of lexical and compositional semantics of events of change. Finally, Chapter 9 proposes an ontological framework for cognitive linguistics.

The third part of the book, composed of six chapters, addresses explicitly the theoretical and practical problems encountered when interfacing ontologies and lexical resources. Chapter 10 provides a methodology classification that is also used for positioning the remaining chapters of this part. The other chapters include the presentation of SINICA-BOW (Chapter 11) an English–Chinese bilingual resource that combine a lexical resource (WordNet) and an ontology (SUMO). Chapter 12 discusses, on the one hand, the traditional model of semantic lexicons in which senses are assigned to lexical items and the set of senses is mostly open-ended. On the other hand, ontologies are said to provide formal class definitions for sets of objects, which can be seen as a 'sense' for those lexical items that express such objects. The model described in this chapter aims at merging these two disparate views into a unified approach to lexical semantics and ontology-based knowledge representation. Then Chapter 13 concerns the combination of linguistic ontologies having different granularity. This work tries to go a step further in the direction of the interoperability of specialized linguistic ontologies, by addressing the problem of their integration with global ontologies. This scenario offers some simplifications with respect to the general problem of merging ontologies, since it enables us to define a strong precedence criterion so that terminological information overshadows generic information in the case of conflicts.

The last part of the book concerns more explicitly NLP issues. The contributions (eight chapters) show the bidirectional nature of NLP at the interface between ontologies and lexical resources. NLP is used both for learning ontological knowledge and uses this knowledge in applications such as question answering, information retrieval or anaphora resolution.

Chapter 15 presents the Omega ontology, a shallow, lexically oriented term taxonomy. The chapter explains how such a resource is useful in a wide variety of applications such as question answering and information integration. Chapter 16 is devoted to the acquisition of lexico-semantic knowledge for question answering and evaluates the benefits of this acquisition. Chapter 17 is concerned with the semi-automatic construction or improvement of existing resources based on text or traditional resources.

2   Formal ontology as interlingua: the SUMO and WordNet linking project and global WordNet

Adam Pease and Christiane Fellbaum

2.1   WordNet

WordNet[1] is a large lexical database for English. With its broad coverage and a design that is useful for a range of natural-language processing applications, this resource has found wide general acceptance. We offer only a brief description here and refer the reader to Miller, 1990 and Fellbaum, 1998 for further details. WordNet's creation in the mid-1980s was motivated by current theories of human semantic organization (Collins and Quillian, 1969). People have knowledge about tens of thousands of concepts, and the words expressing these concepts must be stored and retrieved in an efficient and economic fashion. A semantic network such as WordNet is an attempt to model one way in which concepts and words could be organized.

The basic unit of WordNet is a set of cognitively equivalent synonyms, or synset. Examples of a noun, verb, and adjective synset are { *vacation, holiday* }, { *close, shut* }, and { *soiled, dirty* }, respectively. Each synset represents a concept, and each member of a synset encodes the same concept. Differently put, synset members are interchangeable in many contexts without changing the truth value of the context. Each synset also includes a definition, or 'gloss', and an illustrative sentence.

The current version of WordNet (3.0) contains over 117,000 synsets that are organized into a huge semantic network. The synsets are interlinked by means of bidirectional semantic relations such as hyponymy, meronymy, and a number of entailment relations. For example, the relation between *oak* and *tree* is such that *oak* is encoded as a hyponym (subordinate) of *tree* and *tree* is encoded as a hypernym (superordinate) of *oak*. *Leaf* and *trunk* are meronyms (parts) of *tree*, their holonym. Meronyms are transitive, so linking *leaf* and *trunk* to *tree* means that *oak* (and *beech* and *maple* etc.) inherits *leaf* and *trunk* as parts by virtue of its relation to *tree* (Miller, 1990, 1998). Concepts expressed by other parts of speech (verbs, adjectives) are interlinked by means of additional relations (Fellbaum, 1998).

---

[1] Available freely online at http://wordnet.princeton.edu

2.1.1   Types and instances

In earlier versions of WordNet, all subordinates (hyponyms) of a given synset were encoded as **kinds-of**, or Types. For example, *mountain peak* is a Type of *topographic_point* and *town* is a Type of *municipality*. The current version further differentiates hyponyms by means of the Instance relation (Miller and Hristea, 2006). Instances are always Named Entities, and they are the leaves of trees, i.e., they never have any subordinates. For example, *Aconcagua* is not a Type but an Instance of a *mountain peak* and *Princeton* is an Instance of a *town*. While the distinction among Types and Instances is a valuable addition to WordNet, other distinctions are lacking. For example, WordNet designates nouns like *brother* and *architect* as Types of *persons*, in the same way that *dwarf, midget* is a kind of *person*. Yet the relation between *dwarf* and *person* on the one hand, and *architect* and *person* on the other hand is not the same. This can be seen by the fact that somebody can refer to the same person as both a *dwarf* and an *architect*, violating the rule that nouns with the same superordinates cannot refer to the same entity (e.g., *ash* and *oak* are both subordinates of *tree* and thus an *oak* can never be an *ash*). Rather, *architect* is a Role that a person assumes. Roles often refer to professions or functions associated with a person or temporary states (stage-level predicates) (Carlson, 1980) like *patient* and *customer*.

2.1.2   Formal vs linguistic relations

One could include in WordNet not just its current roughly one dozen semantic links, but all the hundreds of relations that are found in a formally specified logical theory like SUMO, such as **part-of, beforeOrEqual, authors** etc. Having done that, the question would be how to relate informal linguistic notions with more formal ontological relations.

Some WordNet relations, like **part-of**, would appear to be similar. However, **part-of** relations concern not only classes, but also instances. For instance, the synset { *lock* } part of the synset { *door* }, means that locks can be or often are parts of doors (a modal relation between classes or types), and the synset { *Pillar of Hercules* } part of { *Gibraltar* } means that a particular rock is part of a particular island in this case. In contrast, SUMO's **part** relation is logically specified with axioms that limit it to a relation between instances, and a relation between classes would be specified with a more complex axiom, likely involving SUMO modal relations or normative attributes.

By keeping ontological relations in the formal ontology, and linguistic relations in the lexicon, one can avoid merging two different levels of analysis and yet still capture the information that is needed about both formal concepts and linguistic tokens. A formal ontology such as SUMO also contains formal rules that specify complex relations that cannot be captured explicitly as simple links in a graph.

What is needed is an interlingual ontology that accommodates not only English WordNet but all wordnets (Elkateb *et al.*, 2006; Vossen, 1998).

2.1.3   *Lexical vs conceptual ontologies*

WordNet is often called an ontology, although its creators did not have in mind a philosophical construct. WordNet merely represents an attempt to map the English lexicon into a network by means of a few semantic relations. Many of these relations are implicit in standard lexicographic definitions.

The lexicon can be defined as the mappings of concepts onto words. A structured lexicon like WordNet can reveal whether the mapping is arbitrary or follows certain patterns and principles according to which concepts get labelled with a word. WordNet shows that the lexicon obeys clear patterns of semantic organization (Fellbaum, 1998) (compare Levin's 1993 syntactically based patterning of the verb lexicon).

But there are structural gaps where the geometry of the relations would require a word, yet where the language does not have one. People intuitively distinguish the class of wheeled vehicles (like cars and motorbikes) from vehicles that run on rails (trains, trams), yet English does not have a simple word for these concepts. Fellbaum (1998) argues for the existence of specific gaps on the basis of syntactic evidence that distinguishes verb classes.

A look at the lexicons of other languages quickly reveals crosslinguistic differences in lexicalization patterns; a well-known case is kinship relations (e.g. Kroeber, 1917). Languages do not seem to label concepts arbitrarily. Instead, the labeled concepts (words) follow patterns that are revealed by the fact that words can be related to one another via a few relations like hyponymy (Fellbaum, 1998). Nevertheless, the concept-word mappings of any given language are to some extent accidental; existing words do not fully reflect the inventory of concepts that is available. That inventory can be represented in a non-lexical ontology such as SUMO.

2.1.4   *SUMO*

The Suggested Upper Merged Ontology (SUMO)[2] (Niles and Pease, 2001) is a formal ontology stated in a first-order logical language called SUO-KIF (Genesereth, 1991; Pease, 2003). It contains some 1,000 terms and 4,000 axioms

---

[2] Ontologies, tools and mappings to WordNet are available freely online at www.ontology portal.org.

(which are any logical formulae) using those terms in SUO-KIF statements. The axioms include some 750 rules. SUMO is an upper ontology, covering very general notions in common-sense reality, such as time, spatial relations, physical objects, events and processes. SUMO is capped at roughly 1,000 terms in order to keep it manageable and easily learned. There is no objective test for a concept being considered 'upper level' or 'domain level', so this cutoff is purely arbitrary.

To explain the metrics above we describe a 'term' as a named concept in the ontology, which has an associated definition in logic. An axiom is any statement in logic. A rule is a particular kind of axiom that has two parts: an antecedent and a consequent. If the conditions of the antecedent are true, then the consequent must also be true. 'If an entity is a man, then he is mortal' is an example of a rule, albeit one stated in English, rather than logic.

SUMO has been extended by lower-level ontologies. A Mid-Level Ontology (MILO) has several thousand more terms with associated definitions for concepts that are more specific than the ones in SUMO, and yet are general enough not to be considered part of a topic-specific domain ontology. Domain ontologies cover over a dozen specific areas including world government, finance and economics, and biological viruses. Together with SUMO and MILO they comprise roughly 20,000 terms and 70,000 axioms. Note that in this chapter we will refer broadly to the entire collection of SUMO and its extensions as 'SUMO'.

In addition to the mappings to WordNet and linguistic paraphrases in multiple languages discussed in more detail below, the SUMO family of products includes an open-source ontology development and inference system called Sigma (Pease, 2003). SUMO is also the basis for some current work in language understanding (Pease, 2003; Pease and Fellbaum, 2004).

A formal ontology is distinguished from other ontological efforts in that it contains first-order logical rules which describe each of the terms. For example:

```
(<=>
    (earlier ?INTERVAL1 ?INTERVAL2)
    (before
        (EndFn ?INTERVAL1)
        (BeginFn ?INTERVAL2)))
```

is part of the description of the relation **earlier**. It states that 'interval 1 precedes interval 2' means that the ending time of interval 1 is before the starting time of interval 2. The axiom is bidirectional, as indicated by '<=>', which means that the axiom also says that if the end of interval 1 is before the start of interval 2 then interval 1 is earlier than interval 2. The ontology also has axioms that define the meaning of **before**, **EndFn** etc.

Where in a semantic network or a frame-based ontology one would largely have to use natural language definitions to express the meaning of a word or concept, in a formal ontology it is solely the axioms as mathematical statements that give the terms their meaning. One could replace all the term names with arbitrary unique symbols and they would still have the same meaning. This entails that the meaning of the terms can be tested for consistency automatically with an automated theorem prover, rather than the ontologist having to rely completely on human inspection and judgment.

WordNet includes the word *earlier*, but it does not include formal axioms such as the one shown above that explains precisely to a computer what *earlier* means. Nothing in WordNet would allow a computer to assert that the end of one event is before the start of another if one event is earlier than the other.

Because the names of terms in SUMO are just convenient labels, nothing guarantees that the name of a term is going to parallel conventional usage in English. SUMO does not contain semantic relations among words of the kind found in WordNet, such as synonymy. Having two symbols that are logically equivalent is a redundancy in any mathematical theory. SUMO does contain links between formally axiomatized concepts and various labels, which include lexicalized items in different human languages, as well as locally evocative terms or phrases appropriate in a more restrict application context. For example, there is no need in SUMO to create formal terms **Above** and **HigherThan** with the same axiom:

```
(=>
    (orientation ?OBJ1 ?OBJ2 Above)
    (not
        (connected ?OBJ1 ?OBJ2)))

(=>
    (orientation ?OBJ1 ?OBJ2 HigherThan)
    (not
        (connected ?OBJ1 ?OBJ2)))
```

They would be logically redundant terms. However, SUMO can and does relate formal terms to linguistic elements appropriate in different contexts, including relating the formal term **Above** to the English WordNet synset containing the words *above*, *higher_up*, *in_a_higher_place*, *to_a_higher_place*, the Tagalog word *itaas*, the German *oberhalb* etc.

2.2   Principles of construction of formal ontologies and lexicons

Because a lexicon must accurately reflect the inventory and use of words in a given language, lexicographers do not have licence to judge whether a word has a rightful place in the lexicon. A word deemed redundant cannot be eliminated (rather, it might be treated as a synonym). And words cannot be considered to be 'missing' from the lexicon of a particular language, either, as argued by Zaefferer and Schalley, 2003. A structured lexicon like WordNet includes strings to fill 'lexical gaps' justified on structural or syntactic grounds (Fellbaum, 1998).

In contrast to a lexicon, an ontology is an engineered product. There are many ways to name, categorize, and define concepts, especially general notions in the realm of metaphysics (Loux, 2002). The absence of a word in a particular language does not prohibit creation of a term to cover a useful concept in an ontology. Similarly, the presence of a word does not entail inclusion of a term with the same name in an ontology. Every lexicalized concept should be covered by a term, but duplicate lexicalization for the same concept (synonymy) belongs in the lexicon and is not needed in a formal ontology.

In a formal ontology, the meaning of the terms only consists of the formal mathematics used to define those terms. The names of the terms could be replaced by arbitrary unique character strings and their meaning would still be the same. This independence from language gives some confidence in SUMO as a starting point for a true interlingua. While language serves as a starting point for many formalizations, it is only just that. In a lexicon, the meanings of words are determined by their use, while in a formal ontology meaning is determined only by the formal axioms. A word is coined to label a concept. The word, whether written or spoken, forms an index into the meanings. Many taxonomies, frame systems, and other informal ontologies combine the linguistic and the formal aspects, with some properties (most commonly type–instance and class–subclass relations) expressed formally, and more complex information, such as the example axiom for *earlier* given in the section above, left implicit in the name of the term or in natural language definitions.

There have been attempts to state principles for organizing ontology (Guarino and Welty, 2000b). While there is universal agreement that such principles exist, specific proposals differ. One principle is parsimony, or simplicity, which argues for inclusion of only those terms that are needed to cover the topics or domains of interest. Two terms in an ontology should not have the same formal definitions. There is no proper notion of a synonym in a formal ontology, because the names of concepts are not important.

2.3   Mappings

We have mapped SUMO to WordNet in two phases. The first phase (Niles and Pease, 2003) consisted of mapping just SUMO itself, consisting of approximately 1,000 formally defined terms. Each synset in WordNet 1.6 was examined manually, one at a time, and a particular SUMO term was chosen as the closest equivalent. Three types of mappings were employed: rough equivalence, subsuming, and instance.

In a second phase, we looked at mapping all the word senses that occurred three or more times in SemCor (Miller *et al.*, 1993), a version of the Brown Corpus which was manually annotated with WordNet synsets. For each synset we also created a new concept in the MILO if one did not already exist in SUMO, and linked the synset to the new, more specific term.

Since a fundamental aspect of WordNet is the grouping of words in synsets, there are many cases in which a WordNet synset has several synonymous words that map to a single SUMO term. For example, the synset { *artificial_satellite, orbiter, satellite* } *man-made equipment that orbits around the earth or the moon* maps to the formally defined term of ARTIFICIALSATELLITE. The mapping is an 'equivalence' mapping since there is nothing that appears to differentiate the linguistic notion from the formal term in this case.

A more common case of mapping is a 'subsuming' mapping. For example, { *elk* } *large northern deer with enormous flattened antlers in the male; called elk in Europe and moose in North America* maps to the SUMO term HOOFEDMAMMAL.

WordNet is considerably larger than SUMO and so many synsets map to the same more general formal term. As an example of an 'instance' link, the synset { *george_washington, president_washington, washington* } *first President of the United States; commander-in-chief of the Continental Army during the American Revolution (1732–1799)* is linked to the SUMO term HUMAN. Because WordNet discriminates among different senses of the same linguistic token (polysemy), the synset { *evergreen_state, wa, washington* } *a state in northwestern United States on the Pacific* is linked via an 'instance' relation to the different term STATEORPROVINCE.

In current work, we are updating the links to point to more specific terms in the domain ontologies, when available. We have also added many links to synsets that are new to WordNet 2.1 (and later, 3.0) from 1.6. We further created three new types of links that are the negations of the original links. However, only the addition of the 'negated subsuming' link appears to be needed at this time. As an example, the synset { *concealing, concealment, hiding* } *the activity of keeping something secret* has a 'negated subsuming' link to DISSEMINATING.

One of our recent tasks was to explore automatic additions of links from SUMO to synsets that are new to WordNet 2.1 (and later, 3.0). Evidence to date is that the hypernym links in WordNet, although very different from SUMO's subclass links at the higher levels of the ontology and lexicon respectively, are far more reliably similar near the leaf levels of each structure.

Consider the synset { *morphogenesis* } *differentiation and growth of the structure of an organism...* This synset entered WordNet in version 1.7 and was not initially mapped to SUMO. It has a hypernym link to { *growth* } *the process of an individual organism growing organically...* That synset has a 'subsuming' link to the SUMO term GROWTH, which is a formally defined subclass of a PROCESS. Adding a subsuming link from GROWTH to { *morphogenesis* } was reasonable in this case and was done automatically. Further experiments will be needed to determine the reliability of this method, but initial results are promising.

A limitation of the current linking approach is that a single mapping from a lexical entity to a formal term does not fully capture the meaning of some lexical items, even if there is the option of linking to or creating a very specific formal term. The verb synset { *continue* } *exist over a prolonged period of time; 'The bad weather continued for two more weeks'* cannot be expressed as a single term, because it can refer to many unrelated types of **Process**(es). It expresses a temporal relation to an earlier point in time, referenced in the context of previous sentences. One would need a more complex relation structure to express the semantics of this lexical item. Note, however, that the existence of such problematic cases does not negate the utility and, we would contend, the necessity of expressing the relations in simpler cases.

We therefore conclude that a full semantic inventory of language is beyond what has currently been attempted here. The authors are aware that a much richer corpus is needed, such as the PhraseBank proposal as described in Pease and Fellbaum, 2004, which would capture a logical semantics for complex template linguistic expressions, rather than individual lexical items. At least some of this need may be addressed by integrating with FrameNet (Fillmore *et al.*, 2003). Because SUMO and WordNet are fully related, and significant parts of WordNet and FrameNet have been related, this may be possible in the future.

2.4   Interpreting language

Relating language and ontology is a necessity if we wish to create a deep semantic interpretation of language as in the Controlled English to Logic Translation (CELT) system (Pease and Murray, 2003). To take an example from Parsons, 1990, let us say we wish to interpret the sentence 'Brutus stabbed Caesar with a knife on Tuesday.' There are many issues with the interpretation, especially the possibility of a Davidsonian (Davidson, 1967a) semantic interpretation as shown in Parsons and as performed in CELT. The logical form below is output from CELT interpreting Parson's example sentence.

```
(exists (?S ?K ?T)
  (and
    (instance ?S Poking)
```

```
(instance ?K Knife)
(instance ?T Tuesday)
(agent ?S Brutus)
(patient ?S Caesar)
(time ?S ?T)
(instrument ?S ?K)))
```

The SUMO-WordNet mappings provide the relation between the English root word *stab* and the formal SUMO term of POKING. Note that this is a 'subsuming' mapping in the current version, since there is no direct SUMO equivalent to *stabbing*. They provide a mapping to KNIFE and axioms that state that a KNIFE has the capability of being used as an INSTRUMENT in a CUTTING event. Note that the SUMO terms being referred to here are not words. They are formal terms with definitions in first-order logic. Note also that the relationship between KNIFE and CUTTING is not just a link, but a logical axiom suitable for use in theorem proving. Specifically,

```
(=>
    (instance ?X Knife)
    (capability Cutting ?X instrument))
```

Contrast the form above with what we would have to generate if there were no formal ontology with a mapping to a lexicon, for example:

```
(exists (?S ?K ?T)
  (and
     (instance ?S stabs)
     (instance ?K knife)
     (instance ?T Tuesday)
     (agent ?S Brutus)
     (object ?S Caesar)
     (on ?S ?T)
     (with ?S ?K)))
```

There would be no logical definition of *stabs* or any of the other predicates or terms to explain the meanings to a machine. A human would have to interpret the meaning of the terms in the logical form, leaving us about where we started in having an English sentence that has to be interpreted by a human, rather than understood by a machine.

2.5   Global WordNet

As the English WordNet gained wide acceptance in the natural language processing community, researchers in other countries began to construct word-nets in their languages. Vossen (1998) coordinated the effort to create eight

European wordnets that follow a common design and are interlinked via an Interlingual Index (ILI). At the time of writing, wordnets exist in over forty languages spoken around the world (Singh, 2002; Sojka *et al.*, 2004, 2006). Besides the obvious advantage for NLP applications in a given language, interconnected wordnets hold great potential for crosslinguistic applications. Furthermore, the construction of wordnets in typologically and genetically unrelated languages sheds light both on the commonalities and the differences in the ways languages map concepts onto words. To facilitate the construction of international WordNets and to enable their mapping, Vossen (1998) conceived of the Interlingual Index, or ILI.

2.5.1   *The Interlingual Index*

When EuroWordNet – the first international set of wordnets – was begun, it soon became clear that words and synsets could not just be translated from the English wordnet into the European languages; this became even more obvious for the more recent wordnets in Indian and Asian languages. Not only are there language-specific 'lexical gaps', seemingly accidental holes where a word in one language has no correspondence in another language, but there are differences in the ways languages structure their words and concepts. Vossen (1998) discusses the case of *spoon* in English and Dutch. Dutch has no exact equivalent for English *artefact*, which serves as a superordinate to a large class of synsets. As a result, the hierarchy where Dutch *lepel* ('spoon') is embedded is flatter than that of *spoon*.

EuroWordNet comprises three modules to which the individual languages refer. These are the Top Concept Ontology, the Domain Ontology, and the Interlingual Index (ILI). The ILI initially consisted of all English WordNet (1.5) synsets. Each international wordnet either links its synsets to the matching synsets in the ILI or adds a synset that is not yet in the ILI. The ILI thus becomes the superset of all concepts in all wordnets.

Equivalence relations between the synsets in different languages and Princeton WordNet are made explicit in the ILI. Each synset in the language-specific wordnet has at least one equivalence relation to an entry in the ILI. Thus, synsets linked to the same entry in the ILI can directly map the corresponding synsets and words, allowing for a variety of crosslinguistic applications. ILI entries are also linked to the Top Concept Ontology and the Domain Ontology. For further details and discussion see Vossen, 1998.

As pointed out earlier, lexical ontologies are limited in how they can express word meanings through relations in a graph, plus definitions in natural language. Similarly, much of the meaning of each term in the ILI is given by its name and the English definition, taken from the Princeton WordNet or newly created for a language-specific synset. The model is therefore limited to users who are reasonably fluent in English in addition to the target language. The lack of mathematical axioms defining terms in the ILI means that it cannot be shown mathematically to be consistent or correct. Finally, the meaning of the terms has to rely on a human interpretation of linguistic definition, rather than on a precise mathematical specification. While two people may disagree on aspects of a definition expressed in natural language, there can be no disagreement between two mathematically competent people about the meaning of a mathematical formula, other than whether it faithfully reflects some view of reality.

Many wordnets have been linked to English WordNet and thus also to SUMO. The formal and language-independent nature of SUMO holds some promise in enabling creators of new wordnets to verify these cross-language links by testing them against a formal, logical definition, rather than WordNet's definitions and semantic relations. Given the utility that has been gained from just having a lightweight interlingua of just over 100 terms for EuroWordNet (Vossen, 1998), a more extensive, precise, and language-independent formal ontology holds considerable promise.

2.6   SUMO translation templates

In an effort to make SUMO more understandable to a wider community, we have created a system that performs rough natural language paraphrasing of the formal axioms that are stated in first-order logic. While it is awkward and does not present an advance in the study of language generation, this system nevertheless allows SUMO users who do not understand formal logic to have a better idea of the axiomatic semantics of the terms. Because the SUMO terms are stated as English words or phrases, having translations of the terms is also required for non-English speakers whether or not they are conversant with logic. There are currently translation templates for English, German, Czech, Italian, Hindi, Chinese (traditional characters and pinyin), and Romanian. Partial translation sets have been created for Tagalog and Cebuano. Korean, Estonian, and Hungarian are under development.

Acknowledgment

This work has been sponsored by the United States Central Intelligence Agency and US Army CECOM. Ian Niles conceived of the SUMO-WordNet mapping project and did almost all of the original mappings.

3   Interfacing WordNet with DOLCE: towards OntoWordNet

Aldo Gangemi, Nicola Guarino, Claudio Masolo, and Alessandro Oltramari

3.1   Introduction

The number of applications where WordNet is being used as an ontology rather than as a mere lexical resource seems to be ever growing. However, WordNet is only really serviceable as an ontology if some of its lexical links are interpreted according to a referential semantics that tells us something about (our conceptualization of) 'the world'. One such link is the hyponym/hypernym relation, which corresponds in many cases to the usual subsumption **is-a** relation between concepts. An early attempt at exploring the semantic and ontological problems lying behind this correspondence is described in Guarino, 1998b.

In recent years, we have developed a methodology for testing the ontological adequacy of taxonomic links called OntoClean (Guarino and Welty, 2002a, 2002b), which was used as a tool for a first systematic analysis of WordNet's upper-level taxonomy of nouns (Gangemi *et al.*, 2001). OntoClean is based on an ontology of properties (unary universals), characterized by means of metaproperties. We complemented OntoClean with an ontology of particulars called DOLCE (Descriptive Ontology for Linguistic and Cognitive Engineering), which is presented here in some detail, although in an informal way. This ontology plays the role of a first reference module within a minimal library of foundational ontologies that we developed within the WonderWeb project.[1]

This chapter is structured as follows. We discuss in the next section some ontological inadequacies of WordNet's taxonomy of nouns. Then we introduce the basic assumptions and distinctions underlying DOLCE, and discuss the preliminary results of an alignment work aimed at improving WordNet's overall ontological (and cognitive) adequacy, and facilitate its effective deployment in practical applications.

---

[1] http://wonderweb.semanticweb.org/

3.2   WordNet's preliminary analysis

3.2.1   Main problems found

3.2.1.1 Confusing concepts and individuals   The first critical point
was the confusion between concepts and individuals. For instance, if we look
at the hyponyms of the Unique Beginner { *event* }, we will find the synset
{ *fall* } – an individual – whose gloss is *the lapse of mankind into sinful-
ness because of the sin of Adam and Eve*, together with conceptual hyponyms
such as { *social_event* } and { *miracle* }. Under { *territorial_dominion* } we
find { *Macao* } and { *Palestine* } together with { *trust_territory* }. The latter
synset, defined as *a dependent country, administered by a country under the
supervision of United Nations*, denotes[2] a general kind of country, rather than a
specific country as those preceding it. If we go deeper in the taxonomy, we find
many other examples of this sort. For instance, the hyponyms of { *composer* }
are a mixture of concepts and instances: there are classes corresponding to different special fields, such as { *contrapuntist* } or { *songwriter* }, and examples
of famous musicians of the past, such as { *Bach* } and { *Beethoven* }.

Under { *martial_art* }, whose top hypernym is { *act* }, we find { *karate* }
and { *kung fu* }, but these synsets do not stand for concepts, they represent
individuals, namely particular examples of martial arts.

If we look through { *organization* }, under the branch whose root
is { *group* }, we find conceptual hyponyms such as { *company* },
{ *alliance, federation* }, { *committee* }, together with instances like
{ *Irish_Republican_Army* }, { *Red Cross* }, and so on.

We face here a general problem: the confusion between concept and
individual is nothing but the product of a 'lacking in expressiveness'. In
fact, if there was an **instance-of** relation, we could distinguish between
a concept-to-concept relation (subsumption) and an individual-to-concept one
(instantiation).

3.2.1.2 Confusing object-level and metalevel   The synset { *abstraction* } seems to include both object-level concepts, such as { *set* }, { *time* }, and
{ *space* }, and metalevel concepts such as { *attribute* } and { *relation* }. From
the corresponding gloss, an abstraction *is a general concept formed by extracting common features from specific examples*. An abstraction seems therefore
intended as the result of a psychological process of generalization, in accordance with Locke's position (Lowe, 1998). This meaning seems to fit the latter
group of terms ({ *attribute* }, { *relation* }, and possibly some hyponyms of

---

[2] In the text body, we usually do not report all the synonyms of a synset (or their numeration), but
only the most meaningful ones.

{ *quantity* }), but not the former. Moreover, it is quite natural to consider attributes and relations as metalevel concepts, while set, time, and space seem to belong to the object domain.

3.2.1.3 OntoClean constraints violations
A core aspect of Onto-Clean is the analysis of subsumption constraints induced by the identity, rigidity, and unity metaproperties. In our analysis, we only found rigidity violations. We suspect that there are two reasons why we did not observe other kinds of violation: on the one hand, we limited our analysis to the upper levels, where the criteria of identity and unity are very general; on the other hand, WordNet tends, notoriously, to multiply senses, so the chances of conflict are relatively limited.

The most common violation we registered is bound to the distinction between roles (like Student) and types (like Person). Roles are anti-rigid: every instance of a student can possibly be a non-student. Types, on the other hand, are rigid: every instance of a person must be a person. Therefore, roles cannot subsume types. Let us see a clarifying example.

In its first sense, { *person* } (which we consider as a type) is subsumed by two different concepts, { *organism* } and { *causal_agent* }. { *organism* } can be conceived as a type, { *causal_agent* } as a formal role. The first subsumption relationship is correct, while the second one shows a rigidity violation. We propose therefore to drop it. Someone could argue that every person is necessarily a causal agent, since 'agentivity' (capability of performing actions) is an essential property of human beings. { *causal_agent* } should therefore be intended as a synonym of 'intentional agent', and considered as rigid. But, in this case, it would have only hyponyms denoting things that are (essentially) causal agents, including animals, spiritual beings, the personified { *fate* }, and so on. Unfortunately, this is not what is the case in WordNet: { *agent* }, one of the hyponyms of { *causal_agent* }, is defined as: *an active and efficient cause; capable of producing a certain effect; (the research uncovered new disease agents)*. { *causal_agent* } subsumes roles such as { *germicide* }, { *vasoconstrictor* }, { *antifungal* }. Instances of these concepts are not causal agents essentially. This means that considering { *causal_agent* } as rigid would introduce further inconsistencies. These considerations allow us to add a pragmatic guideline to our methodology: when deciding about the formal metaproperty to attach to a certain concept, it is useful to look at all its children.

3.2.1.4 Heterogeneous levels of generality
Going down the lower layers of WordNet's top level, we register a certain 'heterogeneity' in their intuitive level of generality. It seems that this fact can be explained by the difference between types and roles. For example, among the hyponyms of { *entity* } there are types such as { *physical_ object* }, and roles such

as { *subject* }. The latter is defined as *something (a person or object or scene) selected by an artist or photographer for graphic representation*, and has no hyponyms (indeed, almost any entity can be an instance of { *subject* }, but none is necessarily a subject). For { *animal* } (subsumed by { *life_form* }) this heterogeneity becomes clearer. Together with concepts such as { *chordate* }, { *larva* }, { *fictional_animal* } etc., we find apparently more specific concepts, such as { *work_animal* }, { *domestic_ animal* }, { *mate* }, { *captive* }, { *prey* }, etc. We are induced to consider the former as types, the latter as roles. Although problematic on the side of ontological distinctions among event-classes, the hyponyms of { *phenomenon* } represent another relevant example of heterogeneity. At the same taxonomic level there are reasonably general synsets like { *natural_phenomenon* } and { *process* } together with a specific concept like { *consequence* }, which could be modelled as a role (every event can be the consequence of a previous event, but it seems that this is not an essential characteristic of the event itself).

3.3   The DOLCE upper ontology

3.3.1   *Basic choices*

The ontology we present here is a first reference module of the WonderWeb library of foundational ontologies. In contrast with *lightweight* ontologies, which focus on a minimal terminological structure (often just a taxonomy) fitting the needs of a specific community, the main purpose of foundational ontologies is to negotiate meaning, either for enabling effective cooperation among multiple artificial agents, or for establishing consensus in a mixed society where artificial agents cooperate with human beings. The WonderWeb vision is to have a library of such ontologies, reflecting different ontological choices. The idea is to make the rationales and alternatives underlying such choices as explicit as possible, as a result of a careful isolation of the fundamental ontological options and their formal relationships.

As reflected by its acronym, DOLCE has a clear cognitive orientation, in the sense that it aims at capturing the ontological categories underlying natural language and human common sense. Hence, we do not intend DOLCE's categories to account for the intimate nature of the world, but we rather see them as cognitive artefacts ultimately depending on human perception, cultural imprints and social conventions.

DOLCE is an ontology of particulars, in the sense that its domain of discourse is restricted to them. The fundamental ontological distinction between universals and particulars can be informally understood by taking the relation

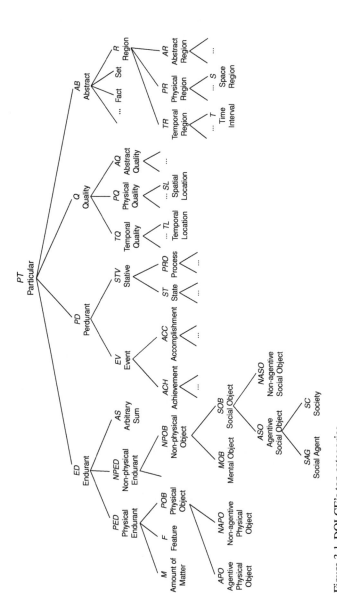

Figure 3.1 DOLCE's top categories

of instantiation as a primitive: particulars are entities that have no instances;[3] universals are entities that do have instances. Properties and relations (corresponding to predicates in a logical language) are usually considered as universals. Since their domains of discourse are disjoint, we take the ontology of universals as formally separated from that of particulars. Of course, universals do appear in an ontology of particulars, insofar as they are used to organize and characterize them: simply, since they are not in the domain of discourse, they are not themselves subject to being organized and characterized (e.g., by means of metaproperties). An ontology of unary universals has been presented in Guarino and Welty, 2000a.

A basic choice we make in DOLCE is the so-called multiplicative approach: different entities can be co-located in the same space-time. The reason why we assume they are different is because we ascribe to them incompatible essential properties. The classical example is that of the vase and the amount of clay: necessarily, the vase does not survive a radical change in shape or topology, while, necessarily, the amount of clay does. Therefore the two things must be different, yet co-located: as we shall see, we say that the vase is constituted by an amount of clay, but it is not an amount of clay.[4] Certain properties a particular amount of clay happened to have (when it was shaped by the vase-master) are considered as essential for the emergence of a new entity; in language and cognition, we refer to this new entity as a genuinely different thing: for instance, we say that a vase has a handle, but not that a piece of clay has a handle.

3.3.2   The top categories

The taxonomy of the most basic categories of particulars in DOLCE is depicted in Figure 3.1. They are assumed to be mutually disjoint, and cover the whole domain of particulars. At the metalevel, they are considered as rigid properties, according to the OntoClean methodology that stresses the importance of focusing on these properties first. In the following, we shall keep the discussion to an informal, introductory level; the reader can refer to Masolo *et al.*, 2003 for a formal axiomatization.

3.3.2.1 Endurants and perdurants   A fundamental distinction we assume is that between enduring and perduring entities. This is almost identical, as we shall see, to the distinction between so-called continuants

---

[3] More exactly, we should say that they cannot have instances. This coincides with saying that they have no instances, if – as we do – we include possibilia (possible instances) in our domain of discourse.

[4] One of the purposes of OntoClean is indeed to help the user evaluating ontological choices like this one.

and occurrents (Simons, 1987), which is still being debated both in the philosophical literature (Varzi, 2000) and within ontology standardization initiatives.[5]

Again, we must stress that this distinction is motivated by our cognitive bias: we do not commit to the fact that both these kinds of entity really exist, and we are indeed sympathetic with the recent proposal made by Peter Simons, that enduring entities can be seen as equivalence classes of perduring entities, as the result of some kind of abstraction mechanism (Simons, 2000).

Classically, the difference between enduring and perduring entities (which we shall also call endurants and perdurants) is related to their behaviour in time. Endurants are always wholly present (i.e., all their proper parts are present) at any time they are present. Perdurants, on the other hand, just extend in time by accumulating different temporal parts, so that, at any time they are present, they are only partially present, in the sense that some of their proper parts (e.g., their previous or future phases) may be not present. For instance, the piece of paper you are reading now is wholly present, while some temporal parts of your reading are not present any more. Philosophers say that endurants are entities that are in time, while lacking however temporal parts (so to speak, all their parts flow with them in time). Perdurants, on the other hand, are entities that happen in time, and can have temporal parts (all their parts are fixed in time).

This different behaviour affects the notion of change in time. Endurants can *genuinely* change in time, in the sense that the very same whole endurant can have incompatible properties at different times; perdurants cannot change in this sense, since none of their parts keeps their identity in time. To see this, suppose that an endurant has a property at a time t, and a different, incompatible property at time t': in both cases we refer to the whole object, without picking up any particular part. On the other hand, when we say that a perdurant has a property at t, and an incompatible property at t', there are always two different parts exhibiting the two properties.

Another way of characterizing endurants and perdurants has been proposed recently by Katherine Hawley: something is an endurant if and only if (a) it exists at more than one moment and (b) statements about what parts it has must be made relative to some time or other (Hawley, 2001). In other words, the distinction is based on the different nature of the parthood relation when applied to the two categories: endurants need a time-indexed parthood, while perdurants do not. Indeed, a statement like 'this keyboard is part of my computer' is incomplete unless you specify a particular time, while 'my youth is part of my life' does not require such specification.

---

[5] See, for instance, the extensive debate about the 3D vs the 4D approach at www.suo.ieee.org

In DOLCE, the main relation between endurants and perdurants is that of participation: an endurant 'lives' in time by participating in some perdurant(s). For example, a person (endurant) may participate in a discussion (perdurant). A person's life is also a perdurant, in which a person participates throughout its duration. In the following, we shall take the term *occurrence* as synonym of perdurant. We prefer this choice to the more common *occurrent*, which we reserve for denoting a type (a universal), whose instances are occurrences (particulars).

3.3.2.2 Qualities and quality spaces   Qualities can be seen as the basic entities we can perceive or measure: shapes, colours, sizes, sounds, smells, as well as weights, lengths, electrical charges etc. *Quality* is often used as a synonym of *property*, but this is not the case in DOLCE: qualities are particulars, while properties are universals. Qualities *inhere* to entities: every entity (including qualities themselves) comes with its own exclusive qualities, which exist as long as the entity exists. So we distinguish between a QUALITY (e.g., the colour of a specific rose) and its 'value' (e.g., a particular shade of red). The latter is called QUALE, and describes the position of an individual quality within a certain conceptual space (called here quality space) (Gärdenfors, 2000). So, when we say that two roses have (exactly) the same colour, their two colours have the same position in the colour space (they have the same colour quale), but still they are numerically distinct qualities. Each quality is an instance of a quality type (e.g., colour, size, smell, etc.), and each quality type is associated to a quality space. Quality types are universals, quality spaces are abstract particulars (see below). This distinction between qualities and qualia is inspired by Goodman, 1951 and the so-called trope theory (Campbell, 1990). Its intuitive rationale is mainly due to the fact that natural language – in certain constructs – seems often to make a similar distinction. For instance, when we say the colour of the rose turned from red to brown in one week or the room temperature is increasing, we are not speaking of a certain shade of red or a specific thermodynamic status, but of something else that keeps its identity while some of its properties change. On the other hand, when we say that red is opposite to green or red is close to brown we are not referring to qualities, but to regions within a quality space. The specific shade of red of our rose – its colour quale – is therefore a point (or an atom, mereologically speaking) in the colour space.

Each quality type has an associated quality space with a specific structure. For example, lengths are usually associated to a metric linear space, and colours to a topological 2D space. The structure of these spaces reflects our perceptual and cognitive bias.

Under this approach, we can explain the relation existing between 'red' intended as an adjective (as in this rose is red) and 'red' intended as a noun (as in red is a colour): the rose is red because its colour is located in the red region within the colour space (more exactly, its colour quale is a part of that region).

Space and time locations as special qualities   In our ontology, space and time are considered as quality types like colour, weight, etc. The spatial (temporal) individual quality of an entity is called spatial (temporal) location, while its quale is called spatial (temporal) region. For example, the spatial location of a physical object is just one of its individual qualities: it belongs to the quality type space, and its quale is a region in the geometric space. Similarly for the temporal location of an occurrence, whose quale is a region in the temporal space. This allows a homogeneous approach that remains neutral about the properties of the geometric/temporal space adopted (for instance, one may assume a circular time). Notice that quality regions can have qualities themselves (for instance, the spatial location of a certain object can have a shape).

Direct and indirect qualities   We distinguish in DOLCE between direct and indirect *quality inherence*. The main reason for this choice comes from the symmetric behaviour of perdurants and endurants with respect to their temporal and spatial locations: perdurants have a well-defined temporal location, while their spatial location seems to come indirectly from the spatial location of their participants; similarly, most endurants (what we call physical endurants, see below) have a clear spatial location, while their temporal location comes indirectly from that of the perdurants they participate in. Another reason for this distinction concerns complex qualities like colours, which – according to Gärdenfors – exhibit multiple dimensions (hue, luminosity, etc.). We model this case by assuming that such dimensions are qualities of qualities: each colour quality has a specific hue that directly inheres to it.

3.3.2.3 Abstract entities   The main characteristic of abstract entities is that they have neither spatial nor temporal qualities, and they are not qualities themselves. The only class of abstract entities we consider in the present version of DOLCE is that of quality regions (or simply regions). Quality spaces are special kinds of quality regions, being mereological sums of all the regions related to a certain quality type. The other examples of abstract entities reported in Figure 3.2 (sets and propositions) are only indicative.

3.3.3   *Further distinctions*

Before discussing further distinctions within the basic DOLCE categories, let us introduce informally some useful definitions based on three notions:

mereological invariance (obvious for time-indexed parthood), unity (discussed informally in Guarino and Welty, 2002a and formalized in Gangemi *et al.*, 2001), and ontological dependence (adapted from Thomasson, 1999).

An endurant is *mereologically constant* if and only if all its parts remain the same during its life, and *mereologically invariant* if and only if they remain the same across all possible worlds. For example, as we shall see, amounts of matter are taken as mereologically invariant (all their parts are essential parts).

A particular x is an *essential whole* if there is a suitable relation R such that, necessarily, x is a maximal mereological sum of entities that are all bound by R. For example, a piece of matter is a topological whole, whose parts are bound together by a relation of topological connection; a bikini is a functional whole, whose parts are bound together by a functional relationship.

A particular x is *specifically constantly dependent* (SCD) on another particular y if and only if, at any time t, x cannot be present at t unless y is also present at t. For example, a person might be specifically constantly dependent on her/his brain.

A particular x is *generically constantly dependent* (GCD) on a property Φ if and only if, at any time t, x cannot be present at t, unless a certain instance y of Φ is also present at t. For example, a person might be generically constantly dependent on the property of having a heart.

3.3.3.1 Kinds of endurant Within endurants, we distinguish between physical and non-physical endurants, according to whether they have direct spatial qualities. Within physical endurants, the main categories are amounts of matter, physical objects, and features.

Amounts of matter The common trait of amounts of matter – *stuff* referred to by mass nouns like *gold*, *iron*, *wood*, *sand*, *meat*, etc. – is that they are endurants with no unity (none of them is an essential whole). They are also mereologically invariant, since they change their identity when they change some of their parts.

Physical objects The main characteristic of physical objects is that they are endurants with unity. However, they have no common unity, since different subtypes of objects may have different unity criteria. Different from amounts of matter, (most) physical objects change some of their parts while keeping their identity; therefore they can have temporary parts. Often objects (indeed, all endurants) are ontologically independent from occurrences (discussed below). However, if we admit that every object has a life, it is hard to exclude a mutual specific constant dependence between the two. Nevertheless, we may still use the notion of dependence to (weakly) characterize objects as being not specifically constantly dependent on other objects.

Features   Typical examples of features are 'parasitic entities' such as holes, boundaries, surfaces, or stains, which are generically constantly dependent on physical objects (their hosts). All features are essential wholes, but, as in the case of objects, no common unity criterion may exist for all of them. However, typical features have a topological unity, as they are singular entities. Some features may be relevant parts of their host, like a bump or an edge, or places like a hole in a piece of cheese, the underneath of a table, the front of a house, which are not parts of their host. It may be interesting to note that we do not consider body parts like heads or hands as features: the reason is that we assume that a hand can be detached from its host (differently from a hole or a bump), and we assume that in this case it retains its identity. Should we reject this assumption, then body parts would be features.

The agentive/non-agentive distinction   Within physical objects, special recognition is given to those to which we ascribe intentions, beliefs, and desires. These are called agentive, as opposed to non-agentive. Intentionality is understood here as the capability of heading for/dealing with objects or states of the world. This is an important area of ontological investigation that we have not properly explored yet, so our suggestions are still rather preliminary.

In general, we assume that agentive objects are constituted by non-agentive objects: persons are constituted by organisms, robots are constituted by hardware, and so on. Among non-agentive physical objects we have, for example, houses, body organs, pieces of wood, etc. Non-physical objects are divided into social objects and mental objects according to whether or not they are generically dependent on a community of agents. A private experience, for instance, is an example of a mental object. Social objects are further divided into agentive and non-agentive. Examples of agentive social objects are social agents like 'the president of United States': we may think that the latter, besides depending generically on a community of US citizens, depends also generically on 'Barack Obama qua legal person' (since the president can be substituted), which in turn depends specifically on 'Barack Obama qua human being'. Social agents are not constituted by agentive physical objects (although they depend on them), while they can constitute societies, like Cambridge University, Mercedes-Benz, etc. Examples of non-agentive social objects are laws, norms, shares, peace treaties, etc., which are generically dependent on societies.

3.3.3.2 Kinds of perdurant   Perdurants (also called occurrences) comprise what are variously called events, processes, phenomena, activities, and states. They can have temporal parts or spatial parts. For instance, the first movement of (an execution of) a symphony is a temporal part of it. On the other side, the playing by the left side of the orchestra is a spatial part. In both cases, these parts are occurrences themselves. We assume that objects cannot be parts of occurrences, but rather they participate in them.

In DOLCE we distinguish among different kinds of occurrences mainly on the basis of two notions, both extensively discussed in the linguistic and philosophic literature: homeomericity and cumulativity. The former is discussed, for instance, in Casati and Varzi, 1996; the latter has been introduced in Goodman, 1951, and refined in Pelletier, 1979.

Intuitively, we say that an occurrence is homeomeric if and only if all its temporal parts are described by the very expression used for the whole occurrence. Every temporal part of the occurrence 'John sitting here' is still described by 'John sitting here'. But if we consider 'a walk from Ponte dei Sospiri in Venice to Piazza S. Marco', there are no parts of such an event that constitute a walk from these two places. In linguistic as well as in philosophical terminology, the notion of the homeomericity of an occurrence is often introduced with respect to a property characteristic of (or exemplified by) the occurrence itself. If such property holds for all the temporal parts of the occurrence, then the occurrence is homeomeric. In our axiomatization, this presupposes a finite list of occurrence-types (occurrents) that are declared in advance.

An occurrence-type is stative or eventive according to whether it holds of the mereological sum of two of its instances, i.e. if it is cumulative or not. A sitting occurrence is stative since the sum of two sittings is still a sitting occurrence. Within stative occurrences, we distinguish between states and processes according to homeomericity: sitting is classified as a state but running is classified as a process, since there are (very short) temporal parts of a run that are not themselves runs. Finally, eventive occurrences (events) are called achievements if they are atomic, and accomplishments otherwise.

3.3.3.3 Kinds of quality   We assume that qualities belong to disjoint quality types according to the kinds of entity they directly inhere to. That is, temporal qualities are those that directly inhere to perdurants, physical qualities those that directly inhere to physical endurants, and abstract qualities those that directly inhere to non-physical perdurants. We are aware that, unfortunately, this terminology is very problematic: for instance, it should be clear that abstract qualities are not abstracts, since they have a temporal location.

3.4   Mapping WordNet into DOLCE

Let us consider now the results of integrating the WordNet 1.6 top concepts into our upper level. According to the OntoClean methodology, we concentrated first on the so-called backbone taxonomy, which only includes the rigid properties. Formal and material roles were therefore excluded from this preliminary work. Comparing WordNet's unique beginners with our ontological categories, it becomes evident that some notions are very heterogeneous: for example, { *entity* } looks like a 'catch-all' class containing concepts hardly classifiable elsewhere, like { *anticipation* }, { *imaginary_place* }, { *inessential* }, etc. Such synsets have only a few children and these have already been excluded in our analysis. Some examples of our merging work are sketched in Figure 3.2. Some problems encountered for each category are discussed below.

3.4.1   Endurants

{ *entity* } is a very confused synset. A lot of its hyponyms have to be rejected: in fact there are roles ({ *causal_agent* }, { *subject_4* }), unclear synsets ({ *location* })[6] and so on. This Unique Beginner maps partly to our AMOUNT OF MATTER and partly to our PHYSICAL OBJECT category. Some hyponyms of { *physical_object* } are mapped to our top concept FEATURE. By removing roles like { *arrangement* } and { *straggle* }, { *group* } appears to include AGENTIVE SOCIAL OBJECT ({ *social_group* }, { *ethnic_group* }), NON-AGENTIVE SOCIAL OBJECT ({ *circuit* }), AGENTIVE PHYSICAL OBJECT ({ *citizenry* }) and NONAGENTIVE PHYSICAL OBJECT({ *biological group* }, { *kingdom* }, { *collection* }).

{ *possession_1* } is a role, and it includes both roles and types. In our opinion, the synsets marked as types ({ *asset* }, { *liability* }, etc.) should be moved towards lower levels of the ontology, since their meanings seem to deal more with a specific domain – the economic one – than with a set of general concepts. This means that the remainder branch has also to be eliminated from the top level, because of its overall anti-rigidity (the peculiarity of roles).

3.4.2   Perdurants

{ *event_1* }, { *phenomenon_1* }, { *state_1* }, and { *act_1* } are the Unique Beginners of those branches of WordNet denoting perdurants. In particular,

---

[6] Referring to { *location* }, we find roles ({ *there* }, { *here* }, { *home* }, { *base* }, { *whereabouts* }), instances ({ *earth* }), and geometric concepts like ({ *line* }, { *point* }, etc.)

ENDURANT
  PHYSICAL ENDURANT
    AMOUNT OF MATTER
      { *body substance* }
      { *chemical element* }
      { *mixture* }
      { *compound, chemical compound* }
      { *mass_5* }
      { *fluid_1* }
    PHYSICAL OBJECT
      AGENTIVE PHYSICAL OBJECT
        { *life form, organism* }...
        { *citizenry* }
        { *sainthood* }
        { *ethnic group* }
      NON-AGENTIVE PHYSICAL OBJECT
        { *body of water, water* }
        { *land, dry land, earth* } ...
        { *body, organic structure* }
        { *artifact, artefact* }
        { *biological group* }
        { *kingdom* }
        { *collection* }
        { *blackbody, full radiatior* }
        { *body_5* }
        { *universe, existence, nature, creation* }
    FEATURE
      { *edge_3* }
      { *skin_4* }
      { *paring, parings* }
      { *opening_3* }
      { *excavation, hole in the ground* }
  NON-PHYSICAL ENDURANT
    MENTAL OBJECT
      { *cognition* }
      { *motivation* }
    SOCIAL OBJECT
      NON-AGENTIVE SOCIAL OBJECT
        { *rule, script* }
          { *law* }
        { *circuit_5* }
      AGENTIVE SOCIAL OBJECT
        { *social group* }

PERDURANT
  EVENTIVE
    ACCOMPLISHMENT
      { *accomplishment, achievement* }
  STATIVE
    STATE
      { *condition, status* }
      { *cognitive state* }
      { *existence* }
      { *death_4* }
      { *degree* }
      { *medium_4* }
      { *relationship_1* }
      { *relationship_2* }
      { *conflict* }
    PROCESS
      { *decrement_2* }
      { *increment* }
      { *shaping* }
      { *activity_1* }
      { *chelation_1* }
      { *execution* }
QUALITY
  PHYSICAL QUALITY
    { *position, place* }
    { *chromatic colour* }
  TEMPORAL QUALITY
    { *time interval, interval* }
ABSTRACT
  QUALITY REGION
    { *space_1* }
    { *time_1* }
    { *time interval, interval* }
    { *chromatic colour* }
  SET
    { *set_5* }
  PROPOSITION
    { *statement_1* }
    { *symbol* }

Figure 3.2 WordNet's top level cleaned

the hyponyms of { *state_1* } seem to fit well with our STATE category, as the children of { *process* } (a subordinate of { *phenomenon* }). For the time being, we restrict the mapping of our ACCOMPLISHMENT category to the homonymous synset of WordNet. { *event_1* } is too heterogeneous to be clearly partitioned in terms of our approach: to a great extent, however, its hyponyms could be added to lower levels of the taxonomy of occurrences.

3.4.3   Qualities and abstracts

{ *abstraction_1* } is the most heterogeneous Unique Beginner: it contains ABSTRACTS such as { *set_5* }, QUALITY REGIONS such as { *chromatic_colour* }, QUALITIES (mostly from the synset { *attribute* }), and a hybrid concept ({ *relation_1* }) that contains social objects, concrete entities (as { *substance_4* } – *The stuff of which an object consists*), and even meta-level categories. Each child synset has been mapped appropriately. { *psychological_feature* } contains both mental objects ({ *cognition* } – *The psychological result of perception, and learning and reasoning*) and events ({ *feeling_1* }). We consider { *motivation* } as a material role, so to be added to lower levels of the taxonomy of mental objects.

The classification of qualities deals mainly with adjectives. This chapter focuses on the WordNet database of nouns; nevertheless our treatment of qualities foreshadows a semantic organization of the database of adjectives too, which is a current desideratum in the WordNet community.[7]

3.4.4   OntoWordNet

The work underlying the OntoWordNet project is rooted in early proposals about upper levels of lexical resources (Guarino, 1998b). More recent presentations can be found in this volume. The program of OntoWordNet includes:

1. Re-engineering WordNet lexicon as a formal ontology, and in particular:
   1.1 to distinguish synsets that can be formalized as classes from those that can be formalized as individuals;
   1.2 to interpret lexical relations from WordNet as ontological relations.
2. Aligning WordNet's top-level to the ontology by allowing re-interpretation of hyperonymy if needed.
3. Consistency check of the overall result and consequent corrections.
4. Learning and revising formal domain relations (from glosses or from corpora).

The first point corresponds to the restructuring task mentioned in Section 10.2, while points (2) and (3) deal with populating an ontology. Point

---

[7] Although some WordNet-based resources actually support structured arrangement of adjectives, e.g. GermaNet (see http://www.sfs.uni-tuebingen.de/lsd/).

(4) addresses the orthogonal issue of *constraint density* (axiomatizing the glosses).

The OntoWordNet project relies on the OntoClean methodology (Guarino and Welty, 2004). This methodology consists in determining the meta-properties of the given property. Very roughly, a *rigid* property is a property that is essential to all its instances while a *non-rigid* property is not and an *anti-rigid* one is essential to none of them. Some properties (called sortals) carry an *identity* criterion. A property ϕ can be said to be *dependent* on a property ψ if for all instances of ϕ some instance of ψ must exist (without being a part or a constituent).[8] Finally, another metaproperty we will use in Section 10.5 is *unity*: 'a property ϕ is said to carry *unity* (+**U**) if there is a *common* unifying relation R such that all the instances of ϕ are essential wholes under R. A property carries *anti-unity* (~**U**) if all its instances can possibly be non-wholes' (Gangemi *et al.*, 2001).

In the second step of the methodology, one checks that a series of constraints on these metaproperties are satisfied. For example, unitary properties cannot subsume anti-unitary ones, and properties subsuming rigid property must be rigid themselves. Other constraints follow automatically from these. For example, roles cannot subsume types. More precisely, from Guarino and Welty, 2000a roles are *non-rigid*, they do not supply their *identity criterion* but might carry one, and they are *dependent* on other properties. Types, on the other hand, are *rigid* and supply their own *identity criterion*. (The first version of OntoWordNet required the removal of roles from the ontology while the new version softens this constraint and requires one only to label roles in order to separate them from types.)

This constraint checking is a crucial aspect of the OntoWordNet project. It is at this step that the lexical resource benefits from some ontological cleaning. OntoWordNet does not simply populate the top-level ontology by attaching WordNet terms under ontology concepts. It determines which constraints have to be satisfied for integrating a WordNet synset in an ontology in order to preserve its properties. OntoWordNet also claims that WordNet itself benefits from the reorganization and from the application of the constraints. A full description of these constraints can be found in the Chapter 3. Note that the restructuring has been systematically performed only up to the third (somewhere fourth) upper level of WordNet. The current OntoWordNet comprises now a restructured and cleaned upper level, and a bare copy of WordNet at the lower levels (without any OntoClean check).

---

[8] For a detailed account, see Guarino and Welty, 2000a. For an overview of OntoClean, see Guarino and Welty, 2004.

Finally, the axiomatization of WordNet glosses (in the spirit of eXtended-WordNet as described in Section 10.4.4) is an active area of research for the OntoWordNet project as shown in Gangemi *et al.*, 2003a.

3.5   Conclusion

The final results of our mapping are sketched in Figure 3.2. As one can see, a substantial taxonomy rearrangement has been performed. The application of OntoClean's taxonomy evaluation methodology provided a first guideline, while the explicit distinctions of DOLCE helped clarify the meaning of WordNet senses. We believe that strong (and explicit) ontological distinctions should also help reduce the risk of classification mistakes in the ontology development process, and simplify the update and maintenance process.

WordNet is largely used mainly because of its coverage, and has proved to be a key resource in many strategic applications. What we are curious to see now is whether a principled restructuring like the one we have proposed will have some positive impact on the performance of these applications.

4   Reasoning over natural language text by means of FrameNet and ontologies

Jan Scheffczyk, Collin F. Baker, and Srini Narayanan

4.1   Introduction

Combining large lexical resources with world knowledge, via ontologies, is a crucial step for reasoning over natural language, particularly for the Semantic Web. Concrete NLP applications include semantic parsing, text summarization, translation, and question answering. For example, questions like 'Could Y have murdered X?' require several inference steps based on semantic facts that simple lexicons do not include. An essential ingredient is so-called open-world semantics offered by state-of-the-art Description Logic (DL) reasoners, e.g., FaCT (Horrocks, 1998) or Racer (Wessel and Möller, 2005).

The FrameNet lexicon (Ruppenhofer *et al.*, 2006a) has a uniquely rich level of semantic detail, which is based on frame semantics (and not on open-world semantics). Therefore, we are building bindings from FrameNet to multiple ontologies. For a specific application, we choose an appropriate ontology and build the binding for this application. Thus, we enable reasoners to make inferences over natural language text.

In this chapter, we report on the first steps towards this goal:[1] we have automatically translated a crucial portion of FrameNet to OWL DL, and we show how state-of-the-art DL reasoners can make inferences over FrameNet-annotated sentences. Thus, annotated text becomes available to the Semantic Web, and FrameNet itself can be linked to other ontologies. While our OWL translation is limited to facts included in FrameNet, links to ontologies make world knowledge available to reasoning over natural language text. Therefore, we link FrameNet to the Suggested Upper Merged Ontology (SUMO). This groundwork gives a clear motivation for the design of further ontology bindings and defines the baseline for measuring their benefits.

This chapter proceeds as follows: in Section 4.2, we briefly introduce FrameNet – a lexical resource for English. We present our design decisions for linking FrameNet to ontologies in Section 4.3. Section 4.4 describes our

[1] Part of this work was funded by the German Academic Exchange Service (DAAD). The FrameNet project is funded by the AQUINAS project of the AQUAINT program.

53

formalization of FrameNet and FrameNet-annotated sentences in OWL DL. In Section 4.5, we show how our OWL DL representation can be used by the DL reasoner Racer in order to implement tasks of a question-answering system, based on reasoning. In order to include world knowledge into the reasoning process, we link FrameNet to SUMO, which is shown in Section 4.6. We discuss the role of reasoning in NLP applications in Section 4.7. Section 4.8 concludes and sketches directions for future research. We do not claim to have a fully fledged system that is able to perform reasoning on natural language text. Rather, our research is targeted at providing a suitable basis for such a system and at identifying approaches for the different subtasks.

4.2   An introduction to the FrameNet lexicon

FrameNet is a lexical resource for English that contains highly detailed information on the syntax and semantics of lexical units (roughly equivalent to word senses in a dictionary); this information is derived from the manual annotation of sentences from a large text corpus. The FrameNet lexicon currently contains more than 780 frames, covering roughly 10,000 lexical units; these are supported by more than 135,000 FrameNet-annotated example sentences.

The theoretical basis of the FrameNet project is frame semantics (Fillmore, 1976; Fillmore *et al.*, 2003; Narayanan *et al.*, 2003). A semantic frame (hereafter, simply frame) represents a set of concepts associated with an event, a relation, or a state, ranging from simple (Attack, Placing) to complex (Revenge, Criminal_process). Causatives, inchoatives, and statives are placed in distinct frames; e.g., *I detached the trailer from the car*, *The trailer detached (itself) from the car*, and *The trailer is detached from the car* would be in separate frames.

For each frame, a set of roles, called frame elements (FEs), is defined, about ten per frame. We say that a word can evoke a frame, and its syntactic dependents can fill the FE slots. For each frame, a set of lexical units is also defined, which may be single words or multiword expressions; e.g., the Revenge frame can be evoked by the noun *vengeance*, the adjective *vengeful*, the verb *avenge* or the multiword verbs *get back* and *get even*. The annotations themselves and the lexical entries, representing generalizations from them, are distributed and widely used in NLP research, and comparable resources are being developed for Spanish, German, Japanese, and other languages. The annotated examples are also used as training data for frame and FE recognizing systems (Litowski, 2004; Erk and Padó, 2005, 2006a).[2]

---

[2] For further information on FrameNet, including a browsable version of the lexicon and a graphical browser for the frame relations, please see http://framenet.icsi.berkeley.edu.

Semantic relations between frames are captured in frame relations, each with accompanying FE-to-FE mappings. The most important of these for our present purposes are:

- Inheritance: All of the core FEs of the parent frame are mapped to corresponding FEs in the child frame. The child frame is a subtype of the parent frame.
- Using: Some of the core FEs of the parent frame are mapped to FEs in the child frame, but not all. The child frame uses the parent as semantic 'background' information.
- Perspective on: Like Using, except that the child frame differs from the parent in that certain of the child FEs are profiled and others deprofiled, which is not true of the parent. The parent represents a 'non-perspectival' view of the situation. For example, the frame Employment_start represents the start of some kind of employment in the abstract (it contains no lexical units), while its child frames Get_a_job (containing the verb *sign on*) and Hiring (containing the verb *hire*) represent the situation from the point of view of the employee or the employer, respectively. We say the Get_a_job has a *Perspective on* relation to Employment_start.
- Subframe: The child frames represent subevents of the complex event denoted by the parent frame. At least some of the FEs are bound between the parent and children. For example, the Employment_scenario has three subframes: Employment_start, Employment_continue, and Employment_end.

Figure 4.1 shows a portion of the Attack frame, which *inherits* from the more general frame Intentionally_affect (which, in turn, inherits from the frames Transitive_action and Intentionally_act). In addition, Attack has a **perspectiveOn** relation to the frame Hostile_encounter. The FEs of the Attack frame are mapped to their corresponding FEs in connected frames. For example, the FE Assailant is mapped to the FE Agent in the Intentionally_act frame.

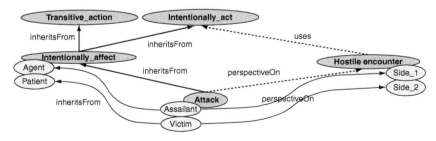

Figure 4.1 Abridged example frame Attack and some connected frames

Due to FrameNet's rich semantics, our bindings of FrameNet to ontologies are more complex than bindings of other lexicons, e.g. WordNet (see Chapters 2, 3, and 11). Also, creating the bindings themselves is not as automatizable as in other approaches.

4.3   Linking FrameNet to ontologies for reasoning

NLP applications using FrameNet require knowledge about the possible fillers for FEs. For example, a semantic frame parser needs to know whether a certain chunk of text (or a named entity) might be a proper filler for an FE – so it will check whether the filler type of the FE is compatible with the type of the named entity. Therefore, we want to provide constraints on fillers of FEs, so-called *semantic types*.

Currently, FrameNet itself has defined about forty semantic types that are ordered by a subtype hierarchy. For example, the Assailant FE and the Victim FE in the Attack frame both have the semantic type Sentient, which in turn is a subtype of Living_thing, and then Physical_object and Physical_entity. FrameNet semantic types are quite similar to the semantic concepts (often called classes) defined in ontologies like SUMO (Niles and Pease, 2001) or Cyc (Lenat, 1995). Compared to ontology classes, however, FrameNet semantic types are much more shallow, have fewer relations between them (only subtyping), and are not context specific. Naturally, a *lexicographic* project like FrameNet focuses on modelling language rather than world knowledge.

In order to improve the utility of FrameNet for NLP applications, we want to employ the semantic types from existing large ontologies such as SUMO or Cyc; in this way, we will gain a number of advantages:

- AI applications can use knowledge provided by ontologies.
- We can provide context-specific semantic types suitable for particular applications by bindings to different domain ontologies.
- We can use ontologies to query and analyse FrameNet data.
- Ontologies benefit from FrameNet, supplementing their ontological knowledge with a frame lexicon and annotated example sentences.

Compared to other lexicon-ontology bindings like the WordNet-SUMO binding described in Chapter 2 or the Cyc lexicon (Burns and Davis, 1999), our bindings offer a range of advantages due to specific FrameNet characteristics: FrameNet models semantic and syntactic valences plus the predicate-argument structure. FrameNet includes many high-quality annotations, providing training data for machine learning. In contrast to WordNet synset annotations, our annotations include role labelling. Frame semantics naturally provide crosslinguistic abstraction plus normalization of paraphrases and support for null instantiation. However, FrameNet has much less coverage than WordNet. Notice that a detour via WordNet would introduce additional noise through the lookup of lexical units (Burchardt *et al.*, 2005). In addition, WordNet synset relations are not necessarily compatible with FrameNet relations.

The bindings from FrameNet to ontologies should be described in the native language of the target ontologies, i.e., KIF (for bindings to SUMO), CycL (for bindings to Cyc), or OWL (for bindings to OWL ontologies). This allows the use of standard tools like reasoners directly, without any intermediate steps. Also, arbitrary class expressions can be used and ad hoc classes can be defined if no exact corresponding class could be found in the target ontology. While FrameNet records language-specific framings, ontologies are typically concerned with non-linguistic categorization. Finally, the binding should be as specific as possible for the application at hand. For example, in a military context we would like to bind FEs to classes in an ontology about weapons of mass destruction or terrorism instead of using a binding to SUMO itself, which only provides upper-level classes.[3]

A vital precondition for any such bindings is, however, to have FrameNet available in an appropriate ontology language (e.g., KIF, CycL, or OWL). A representation of FrameNet in an ontology language bears the additional advantages of formalizing certain properties of frames and FEs, enabling us to use ontology tools to view, query, and reason about FrameNet data. For querying, one could, for example, use the ontology query language SPARQL. Next, we describe a formalization of a portion of FrameNet in OWL DL, which easily generalizes to more expressive ontology languages like KIF or CycL.

4.4   Formalizing FrameNet in OWL DL

Our major design decisions for representing FrameNet as an ontology are:

1. to represent frames, FE filler types, and semantic types formally as classes,
2. to model relations between frames and FEs via existential property restrictions on these classes,[4] and
3. to represent frame realizations and FE fillers in FrameNet-annotated texts as *instances* of the appropriate frame and FE filler classes, respectively.

Building on Narayanan *et al.*, 2003, we have chosen OWL DL as the representation language mainly because better tools are available for it (particularly for reasoning) than for OWL Full or other similarly expressive languages.

---

[3] For examples of SUMO domain ontologies, see www.ontologyportal.org.
[4] Notice that FEs are actually relations, but our OWL DL translation models FE filler types instead. Existential property restrictions between FE filler types stand for relations between FEs.

Our representation differs from many WordNet OWL representations, which represent synsets as *instances* and, hence, cannot use class expressions for ontology bindings.[5] Instead, WordNet bindings to SUMO employ a proprietary mechanism, which cannot be used 'out of the box' by ontology tools like reasoners (see Chapter 2).

In order to keep the size of our ontology manageable, we have chosen to split it into the *FrameNet Ontology* and *Annotation Ontologies*. The FrameNet Ontology includes FrameNet data like frames, FE filler types, semantic types, and relations between them. Annotation Ontologies represent FrameNet-annotated sentences and include parts of the FrameNet Ontology that are necessary.

4.4.1   The FrameNet Ontology

Figure 4.2 shows a simplified excerpt of the FrameNet Ontology. The subclasses of the Syntax class are used for annotations and are connected to frames and FE fillers via the **evokes** and **fillerOf** relations, respectively. Frames and FE fillers are connected via binary relations, e.g., the *perspectiveOnF* property or the *feFiller* property, which connects a frame to its FE fillers. Consider our example frame Attack, which inherits from the frame Intentionally_affect

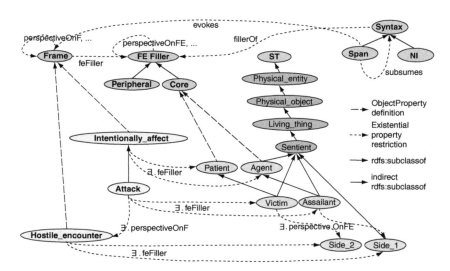

Figure 4.2 Part of the FrameNet Ontology for the Attack frame and some connected frames

5 See, for example, http://www.w3.org/2001/sw/BestPractices/

and uses the frame Hostile_encounter. We model frame and FE inheritance via subclassing and other frame and FE relations via existential property restrictions (owl:someValuesFrom). Thus, the class Attack is a subclass of Intentionally_affect. In addition, we require that an instance of class Attack has at least one instance of class Hostile_encounter connected via the *perspectiveOnF* property. The FE filler types of Attack are connected via an existential restriction on the *feFiller* property. FE relations are modelled similarly to frame relations.

Recall that class restrictions are inherited. Therefore, the class Attack inherits the restrictions $\exists.feFiller$ Patient and $\exists.feFiller$ Agent from the class Intentionally_affect. These restrictions are, however, subsumed by the restrictions on the Attack class itself, because Victim is a subclass of Patient and Assailant is a subclass of Agent. Of course, OWL inheritance requires proper inheritance on the FrameNet data. We have implemented rigorous formal quality management for FrameNet that takes care of proper inheritance and other quality requirements (Scheffczyk and Ellsworth, 2006).

Notice that our formal representation is incomplete. We would love to say that, for example, an instance of Intentionally_affect has exactly one instance of type Patient connected via the *feFiller* property:

Intentionally_affect *feFiller* 1 Patient

This requires, however, so-called qualified cardinality restrictions (QCR) – a non-standard extension to OWL.[6] One might be tempted to work around this issue by requiring something like

Intentionally_affect *feFiller* 2   or
Intentionally_affect *feFiller* $\leq$ 2

This does not, however, work in our case due to inheritance: the Attack frame may have more than just two FEs. Indeed, we could define subproperties for the *feFiller* property (and *all* other properties), which would, however, clutter up our data significantly.[7] Therefore, we live with this incomplete modelling unless QCRs are accepted as a standard.

Our semantic type hierarchy is modelled as a simple subclass hierarchy. Semantic types are attached to FE filler types via subclass relationships. So, the classes Agent, Victim, Assailant, and Side_1 are all subclasses of the class Sentient. We use this simple mechanism also for linking FrameNet to other ontologies (see Section 4.5). So we can use arbitrary OWL DL class expressions for our bindings and at the same time achieve a homogeneous formal representation that OWL tools can make use of.

[6] See http://www.w3.org/2001/sw/BestPractices/OEP/QCR/
[7] Even now, the FrameNet Ontology reaches a critical size of 100,000 triples.

One could use the FrameNet Ontology for querying and reasoning over FrameNet itself. For reasoning over natural language text, however, we must find a way to incorporate this text into the FrameNet Ontology. We do this by means of *Annotation Ontologies*, which we generate from FrameNet-annotated text.

4.4.2   Annotation Ontologies

FrameNet-annotated text provides textual realizations of frames and FEs, i.e., the frames and FEs cover the semantics of the annotated sentences. In ontological terms, FrameNet-annotated text constitutes instances of the appropriate frame and FE filler classes, respectively. From an annotated sentence, we generate an Annotation Ontology, which includes parts of the FrameNet Ontology and fulfils all of its class restrictions. In other words, the FrameNet Ontology provides a formal specification for Annotation Ontologies.

Consider an example sentence, which we derived from an evaluation exercise within the AQUINAS project called 'KB Eval', where sentences for analysis were contributed by various members of the consortium.

S *48 Kuwaiti jet fighters managed to escape the Iraqi invasion.*[8]

This sentence has three annotation sets:

1. The target word *invasion* evokes the Attack frame, where *Iraqi* fills the Assailant FE. The Victim FE has no filler, i.e., it is null instantiated.
2. The target word *escape* evokes the Avoiding frame, with FE fillers *48 Kuwaiti jet fighters* → Agent, *the Iraqi invasion* → Undesirable_situation.
3. The target word *managed* evokes the Successful_action frame, with FE fillers *48 Kuwaiti jet fighters* → Protagonist, *to escape the Iraqi invasion* → Goal.

From these annotations, we first create a syntactic dependency graph and generate the appropriate frame instances and FE fillers as shown in Figure 4.3. A Span represents a chunk of text that can evoke a frame or provide a filler for an FE. We derive Spans, syntactic subsumption, and the relations to frames and FEs based on the annotations. For example, *invasion* evokes the Attack frame. Thus we (1) generate a Span that represents the text *invasion* and place it properly into the Span dependency graph, (2) generate the frame instance Attack$_S$ (of class Attack), and (3) connect the Span to Attack$_S$ via the *evokes* property. We proceed similarly with the FE filler *Iraqi* → Agent. Here we generate the FE filler Agent$_S$, connect it to its frame instance Attack$_S$ via the *feFiller* property, and connect the Span representing *Iraqi* to Agent$_S$ via

---

[8] In the sequel, we index the instances emerging from a sentence by its identifier, here S.

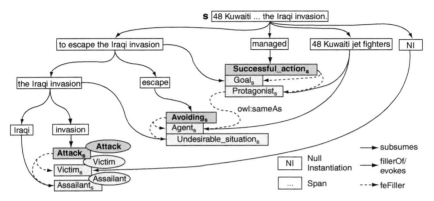

Figure 4.3 Annotation Ontology for: *48 Kuwaiti jet fighters managed to escape the Iraqi invasion.* (Step 1)

the *fillerOf* property. Finally, we identify FEs that are evoked by the same Span via owl:sameAs. We can do this purely based on syntactic evidence. For example, the FE fillers Protagonist$_S$ and Agent$_S$ are identified because they are both filled by the Span representing the text *48 Kuwaiti jet fighters*. This significantly aids reasoning over FrameNet-annotated text.[9]

The second step in generating an Annotation Ontology is to satisfy the class restrictions of the FrameNet ontology, i.e., to generate appropriate instances and to connect them properly. Thus, for a frame instance i of class C_i we

1. travel along each existential class restriction on a property pr to a class C_j ($\exists.pr\ C_j$),
2. generate an instance j of class C_j,
3. connect the instances i and j via the property pr, and
4. proceed with instance j.

Figure 4.4 illustrates this algorithm for our example frame instance Attack. We generate the frame instance Hostile_encounter$_S$ and its FE instances Side_1$_S$ and Side_2$_S$, and connect Attack$_S$ to Hostile_encounter$_S$ via *perspectiveOnF*. Similarly, we connect Assailant$_S$ to Side_1$_S$ and Victim$_S$ to Side_2$_S$ via *perspectiveOnFE*. In addition, we identify the connected FE instances via owl:sameAs, which expresses the semantics of FE mappings: the Victim in an Attack *is* the Side_2 in a Hostile_encounter, i.e., their fillers are the same.

In addition to the class restrictions, we also travel along the inheritance hierarchy, which could be useful, e.g., for paraphrasing. Therefore, we generate the

---

[9] Alternatively, we could formalize a SWRL rule *fillerOf(s, a)* ∧ *fillerOf(s, b)* → *owl:sameAs(a, b)*. We do not do so because not all reasoners provide a SWRL implementation.

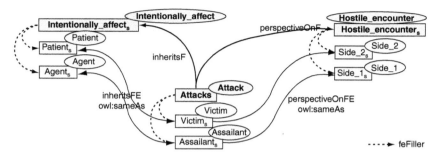

Figure 4.4 Connecting the Attack instance (Step 2 of Annotation Ontology generation)

frame instance Intentionally_affect$_S$ and its FEs. The act of attacking someone is also an act of intentionally affecting the person (in a more general sense). We connect the instances via the somewhat artificial properties *inheritsF* and *inheritsFE* because there is no other way to relate particular instances in OWL.

Figure 4.4 shows only a small fraction of the generated ontology. Because the size of the ontologies is crucial for DL reasoners, we limit the number of generations. Also, Annotation Ontologies do not import the whole FrameNet Ontology but include only those classes that we generate instances for, i.e., classes connected to the evoked frame classes.

Next, we show a simple example, illustrating the use of Annotation Ontologies for reasoning.

4.5   Reasoning over FrameNet-annotated text

We have investigated the potential of DL reasoners in question answering, which is a challenging application area for ontology text representation. For our current experiments, we use Racer[10] (Wessel and Möller, 2005). Given a FrameNet-annotated question, we let Racer perform various reasoning tasks in order to identify frames and FE fillers in potential answer sentences that ought to be compatible with the frames and FE fillers in the question. If Racer succeeds, then the Spans bound to these FE fillers contain the answer, otherwise the question cannot be answered from the text. Notice that our approach assumes that another approach, e.g., a question type analyzer or text matcher, determines whether identified FE fillers are really compatible. Also, we require that both the question and potential answers already have FrameNet annotations.

---

[10] See www.racer-systems.com

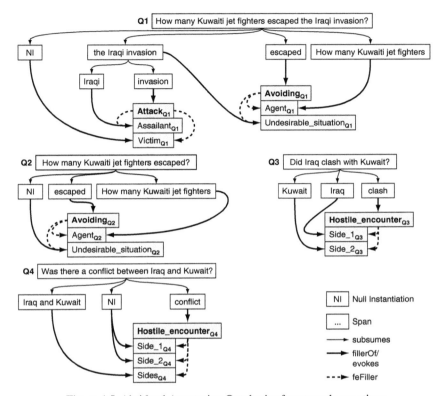

Figure 4.5 Abridged Annotation Ontologies for example questions

Consider four example questions.

Q1 *How many Kuwaiti jet fighters escaped the Iraqi invasion?*

Q2 *How many Kuwaiti jet fighters escaped?*

Q3 *Did Iraq clash with Kuwait?*

Q4 *Was there a conflict between Iraq and Kuwait?*

Partial Annotation Ontologies for these questions are illustrated in Figure 4.5.

Given the Annotation Ontology of the question, we let Racer perform the following queries, which can be formalized in nRQL.[11] In the following, we will use question Q1 as an example of how the algorithm works.

---

[11] We have to use multiple queries because class and instance queries cannot be intermixed in Racer.

(4.1) For the question, get the evoked frame instances, their FE fillers, and Spans.

$\text{Avoiding}_{Q1} \rightarrow \text{Undesirable\_situation}_{Q1} \rightarrow$ the Iraqi invasion
$\rightarrow \text{Agent}_{Q1}$ $\rightarrow$ How many ...
Attack_{Q1} $\rightarrow \text{Assailant}_{Q1}$ $\rightarrow$ Iraqi
$\rightarrow \text{Victim}_{Q1}$ $\rightarrow$ [null instantiated]

(4.2) For each frame instance and FE filler, determine the direct classes.

Avoiding_{Q1} $\rightarrow \text{Avoiding}$
$\text{Undesirable\_situation}_{Q1} \rightarrow \text{Undesirable\_situation}$
Agent_{Q1} $\rightarrow \text{Agent}$
Attack_{Q1} $\rightarrow \text{Attack}$
Assailant_{Q1} $\rightarrow \text{Assailant}$
Victim_{Q1} $\rightarrow \text{Victim}$

Notice that we get only one class because in this question a Span is the filler of at most one FE.

(4.3) For each of the frame classes, obtain frame instances f that are different from the ones in the question. Similarly, we look for corresponding FE fillers fe that are connected to the frame instance f via the *feFiller* property.

Avoiding $\rightarrow \text{Avoiding}_S$
$\text{Undesirable\_situation} \rightarrow$ $\text{Undesirable\_situation}_S$
Agent $\rightarrow$ Agent_S
Attack $\rightarrow \text{Attack}_S$
Assailant $\rightarrow$ Assailant_S
Victim $\rightarrow$ Victim_S

(4.4) Get the Spans of the FE instances above and determine whether they are compatible with the Spans of the corresponding FEs in the question (we mark success by $\checkmark$ and failure by $\times$).

$\text{Undesirable\_situation}_S \rightarrow$ the Iraqi invasion $\checkmark$
Agent_S $\rightarrow$ 48 Kuwaiti jet fighters $\times$
Assailant_S $\rightarrow$ Iraqi $\checkmark$
Victim_S $\rightarrow$ [null instantatiated]

Since Racer is a reasoner (and not an NLP tool), checking the compatibility of Spans is limited to checking syntactic equality. Therefore, the Span *48 Kuwaiti jet fighters* does not match the Span *How many Kuwaiti jet fighters*. Racer can, however, determine the Spans that are supposed to be compatible in order to yield an answer. Then Span compatibility can be determined by other NLP tools such as question type recognizers.

Question $Q2$ is simpler than $Q1$ because we are asking for only one frame in which one FE is null instantiated. In this case, our approach only using a reasoning engine yields the final answer:

Undesirable_situation$_S$ → the Iraqi invasion $\checkmark$

Agent$_S$ → 48 Kuwaiti jet fighters $\times$

Notice that here the Span *the Iraqi invasion* is in fact compatible with the corresponding null-instantiated Span from the question. If we are asking for a null-instantiated FE, we only check whether the corresponding FE has a proper filler.

Question $Q3$ leverages our ontology structure in that it asks for the more general event of a Hostile_encounter. Our approach proceeds as follows:

(4.5) Get evoked frames instances, FEs, and Spans:
Hostile_encounter$_{Q3}$ → Side_1$_{Q3}$ → Iraq
→ Side_2$_{Q3}$ → Kuwait

(4.6) Determine the direct classes for frame/FE instances:
Hostile_encounter$_{Q3}$ → Hostile_encounter
Side_1$_{Q3}$ → Side_1
Side_2$_{Q3}$ → Side_2

(4.7) Obtain corresponding frame/FE instances:
Hostile_encounter → Hostile_encounter$_S$
Side_1   →   Side_1$_S$
Side_2   →   Side_2$_S$

(4.8) Determine compatible Spans:
Side_1$_S$ → Iraqi $\times$
Side_2$_S$ → [null instantatiated] $\times$
Racer can infer the above because Side_1$_S$ is the same as Assailant$_S$ and Side_2$_S$ is the same as Victim$_S$. However, the Span *Iraqi* is not compatible with *Iraq* and the null-instantiated Span in the sentence is not compatible with the Span *Kuwait*. We should be able to determine that the adjective *Iraqi* is compatible with the noun *Iraq* by using the corresponding WordNet synsets: { *Iraqi* } should be connected to { *Iraq* } via the **pertainym** relation. From the fact that the Kuwaiti jet fighters escaped the Iraqi invasion, we could infer that there was a clash between Iraq and Kuwait, which clearly needs world knowledge not present in FrameNet and, thus, gives good motivation for our links to SUMO (see Section 4.6).

Question $Q4$ is even more problematic than $Q3$ because in $Q4$ the FE Sides is annotated, which is in an **Excludes** relation to both FEs Side_1 and Side_2. In FrameNet we find, however, no formal relation saying that the FEs Side_1 and Side_2 'make up' the FE Sides; also, it is unclear how the Span *Iraq and Kuwait* should be distributed to Side_1 and Side_2. Therefore, using only FrameNet, Racer would infer the correct answer for this example, but it would do so for *any* conflict.

Our example shows that in principle we can employ a DL reasoner for querying the FrameNet Ontology and Annotation Ontologies. However, even using a state-of-the-art DL reasoner like Racer, inference performance is not satisfying. For our small example, Racer takes several seconds for the final query. This is because we are dealing with a large amount of data: the FrameNet Ontology contains about 100,000 triples, Annotation Ontologies contain on the order of 10,000 to 30,000 triples, depending on the complexity and the amount of annotated text (even though we do not import the whole FrameNet Ontology). Moreover, checking Span compatibility requires other external tools. On the other hand, determining the direct classes of the frame instances and FE fillers (Step 2) and getting the other instances of their classes (Step 3) can be done by a DL reasoner, especially since these tasks can require querying other ontologies.

Using Annotation Ontologies, DL reasoners can make basic inferences on natural-language text, which is, however, limited to the facts formalized in FrameNet itself. Recall that we only translated FrameNet and did not add further knowledge in the form of semantic relations, axioms, or inference rules because FrameNet is a lexicographic project. Rather, we want to use the knowledge formalized in ontologies by linking FrameNet to these knowledge sources. In a first account, we have linked FrameNet to SUMO, which is described next.

4.6   Linking FrameNet to SUMO

We have aligned the FrameNet semantic types with SUMO, thus asserting SUMO axioms on semantic types for free. Based on this general-domain alignment, we have developed a semi-automatic approach to link FEs to SUMO classes, taking advantage of pre-existing mappings from WordNet to SUMO (see Chapter 2). This allows us to develop *domain-specific* links from FEs to SUMO by examining annotated examples from a particular domain. Thus, we can provide restricted, ontology-based types on the fillers of FEs, which should help semantic parsers both with word-sense disambiguation of predicators and identifying which pieces of a sentence fill FEs. By relating FrameNet and SUMO, we have realized significant benefits, such as identifying areas which can be improved in both products.

In this section, we describe the general-domain alignment of semantic types with SUMO. Further details can be found in Scheffczyk *et al.*, 2006, which also includes our approach to linking FEs to SUMO for specific domains.

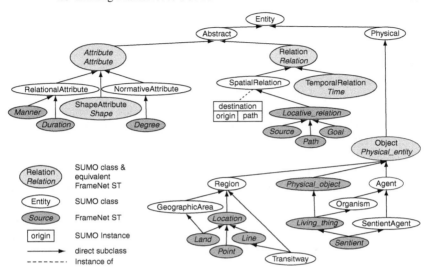

Figure 4.6 Alignment of a portion of the FrameNet semantic types with SUMO

Figure 4.6 shows the alignment of a portion of the FrameNet semantic type hierarchy to SUMO.[12] The SUMO class hierarchy is slightly different from the semantic type hierarchy because the former follows knowledge-engineering principles rather than linguistic principles. For example, SUMO distinguishes between physical and abstract entities. Also, the level of detail is different between SUMO classes and semantic types.

FrameNet has defined semantic types that best cover the most general and common FE fillers. Semantic types are not intended to correspond to WordNet synsets or SUMO classes, but many of the semantic types we formed, in fact, do correspond naturally. The most important semantic types that do *not* correspond to SUMO classes are Source, Path, and Goal. We use Source to mark FEs whose fillers relate themes of processes to their origins. Similarly, Goal relates to destination relations and Path to path relations. We distinguish between Locative_relations and Locations; Locations are often used as the range of Locative_relations. Relations in the Source and Goal class have Point as their range. Relations in the Path class have Line as their range. Point and Line do *not* mean geometric figures but locations (which may be construed as geometric figures).

---

[12] Other semantic types – including Event and State – are linked straightforwardly to SUMO.

Our alignment preserves the hierarchies of both SUMO and semantic types. The bindings are, however, of various kinds:

- Some semantic types have equivalent SUMO classes, such as Shape, Time, Relation, or Physical_entity. In such cases, we identify the semantic type with its corresponding SUMO class.
- Some semantic types, e.g., Sentient, correspond to the intersection of multiple SUMO classes. A Sentient being is something alive that is able to reason. In SUMO, a SENTIENTAGENT does not need to be alive; e.g., ORGANIZATIONS are also SENTIENTAGENTS. So we use multiple inheritance to SENTIENTAGENT and ORGANISM.
- Some semantic types, such as Line, have a broader meaning than some SUMO classes. LINE is an arbitrary linear region, whereas TRANSITWAY is used for transportation. Therefore, we make TRANSITWAY a subclass of LINE.
- For some semantic types we find classes in SUMO with a broader meaning, but instances of them are closely related. For example, for the semantic type *classes* Source, Path, and Goal, we find closely related relation *instances* like origin, path, and destination.

If we do not find an equivalent SUMO class for a semantic type, we refine its semantics, i.e., we express in SUO-KIF what distinguishes the semantic type from its SUMO superclass. Also, we define relations between semantic types themselves.

For example, a Locative_relation r relates at least two physical objects:

$$r : \texttt{Locative\_relation} \quad \Rightarrow \quad \begin{aligned} &\texttt{domain}(r, 1, \texttt{Physical}) \land \\ &\texttt{domain}(r, 2, \texttt{Physical}) \end{aligned}$$

Given a Goal relation *rel* as filler of an FE of some process p, we can conclude the following: The relation **rel** relates some patient *thm* of the Motion process p to its destination *dest*, which also is a filler of **rel**. The destination *dest* itself will be of type Point. Finally, **rel** invokes a Locative_relation *lr* at the end of p:

$$\begin{aligned} &\texttt{rel} : \texttt{Goal} \land \\ &\texttt{feFiller}(p, \textbf{rel}) \end{aligned} \Rightarrow \begin{aligned} &\exists\, dest, thm, lr \bullet \\ &p : \texttt{Motion} \land dest : \texttt{Point} \land \\ &lr : \texttt{Locative\_relation} \land \\ &\texttt{feFiller}(lr, dest) \land \texttt{feFiller}(lr, thm) \land \\ &lr(thm, dest, (\texttt{EndFn}(\texttt{WhenFn}\ p))) \land \\ &rel(thm, dest, p) \land \\ &\texttt{patient}(p, thm) \land \texttt{destination}(p, dest) \end{aligned}$$

The semantics of Source and Path relations are expressed similarly. Notice that these fairly complex alignments between FrameNet and SUMO do not point out flaws or errors. Rather, they reveal modelling choices taken due to different methodologies.

In FrameNet, we distinguish countable entities (Physical_object) from non-countable entities (Material). Therefore, for every Physical_object, a Counting process has the capability to count the Physical_object and vice versa. Similarly, for every Material, a Measuring process has the capability to measure the Material and vice versa.

$$o:\texttt{Physical\_object} \leftrightarrow \texttt{capability(Counting, patient, } o\texttt{)}$$
$$m:\texttt{Material} \qquad\quad \leftrightarrow \texttt{capability(Measuring, patient, } m\texttt{)}$$

Through SUMO semantic types, FrameNet data receive a deeper level of formal semantics. For example, in the Placing frame, we have annotations such as the following:

$$[_{\text{AGENT}} \text{ She}] \text{ PUT } [_{\text{THEME}} \text{ two pieces}] [_{\text{GOAL}} \text{ under the grill}] [_{\text{PURPOSE}} \text{ to toast}].$$

Leaving aside the Agent, Theme, and Purpose FEs, the semantic type on the Goal FE is specified as Goal. So we can conclude about a Putting process P and a Goal relation rel:

$$\texttt{rel:Goal} \land \texttt{feFiller(P, rel)} \land \texttt{P:Putting}$$

The axiom for Goal relations yields:

$$\exists\, dest, thm, lr \bullet dest:\texttt{Point} \land lr:\texttt{Locative\_relation} \land$$
$$\texttt{feFiller(}lr, dest\texttt{)} \land \texttt{feFiller(}lr, thm\texttt{)} \land$$
$$lr(thm, dest, (\texttt{EndFn(WhenFn P)})) \land \texttt{rel(}thm, dest, \text{P}) \land$$
$$\texttt{patient(P, }thm\texttt{)} \land \texttt{destination(P, }dest\texttt{)}$$

Thus, there must be a Locative_relation lr in the context that relates thm and $dest$, which should be given as a second annotation. Given such an annotation, the existentially quantified variables lr, thm, and $dest$ can be instantiated with the locative relation, theme, and destination mentioned in the sentence. Otherwise, this instructs a frame parser to create a proper Locative_relation annotation. Even without this annotation for the Locative_relation lr, one could instantiate the filler for thm given a link from the Motion frame (which the Putting frame uses) to the TRANSLOCATION Process in SUMO.

4.7   Discussion

We envision DL inference as a component of a lexical semantic reasoner. The DL component has to be integrated with other inferencing techniques for temporal, spatial, and event structure inference to adequately model the different dimensions of lexical semantics. For example, a model of predication must have the ability to capture linguistic aspects (modelling actions, state changes, resources, and event structure). This requires extensions to model situations, variables, and fluents and unification, which leads to full first-order logic. The price for this expressiveness is, of course, less effective inference. An alternative approach is to not lose the efficiency of the DL reasoner for certain purposes, but to integrate it to special purpose representation and reasoning mechanisms for aspect and event structure, such as Narayanan, 1999.

In previous work (Narayanan and McIlraith, 2003), we successfully explored one method of accomplishing this integration. We used an extension of OWL (OWL-S) that has a rich process ontology and was designed to model transactions and services on the Web.[13] Especially, OWL-S has an expressive process-model ontology that provides a declarative description of the properties of the events we wish to reason about. The process-model ontology makes fine-grained distinctions relevant to reasoning about event structure, and the DL reasoner is able to perform consistency checks on the ontology.

As part of the integration, we implemented an OWL-S interpreter that translates OWL-S markups to the simulation and modelling environment KarmaSIM (Narayanan, 1999), which is able to reason effectively about events. This allows the system to integrate interactive simulations and use a variety of analysis techniques to model the temporal evolution of events and to perform inference related to linguistic aspects. We believe this mode of using OWL ontologies as structured interfaces (with special-purpose ontologies) and using the DL reasoner for consistency checks will carry over to integrating with spatial and temporal reasoners.

4.8   Conclusion and outlook

Our research is targeted at providing bindings of the FrameNet lexicon to multiple ontologies, in order to provide ontological filler types for FEs and to gain from the world knowledge formalized in ontologies. As a first step, we have translated a crucial portion of FrameNet to OWL DL. The FrameNet Ontology provides a formal specification of FrameNet itself by means of ontology classes and existential restrictions on these classes. Annotation Ontologies are generated for specific FrameNet-annotated sentences, thus filling and satisfying the FrameNet Ontology. Thus, FrameNet and annotated sentences become available for reasoning. Also, our OWL DL translation provides a solid basis for binding FrameNet to arbitrary OWL ontologies by using OWL itself for specifying the bindings. The resulting homogeneous ontology has a number of advantages over using proprietary techniques for specifying ontology bindings,

---

[13] See www.daml.org/services/

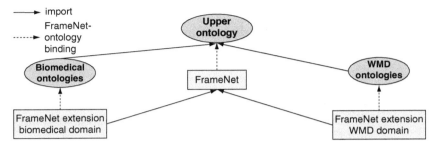

Figure 4.7 Architecture for domain-specific frame lexicons

particularly when it comes to tool support. As a second step, we have aligned
FrameNet semantic types with SUMO classes, thereby gaining from SUMO's
rich axiomatization.

In the future, we will concentrate on enhancing the bindings between
FrameNet and ontologies, in order to improve frame parsing and to improve
reasoning on natural language text. Also, we have begun to develop special-
domain FrameNets with tight filler-type constraints for FEs, rich axiomatization, and links to domain-specific ontologies. One example is BioFrameNet
for the domain of bio medicine (Dolbey *et al.*, 2006). Further experiments
in semantic parsing should evaluate the usefulness of this approach for automatic frame recognition and role (i.e., FE) labelling. An issue that needs to
be resolved is related with the different ontology languages we used (OWL
DL and SUO-KIF). This can be done by translating OWL DL to SUO-KIF or
portions of SUO-KIF to OWL DL.

Domain-specific lexical resources that are linked to domain-specific ontologies – under the umbrella of an upper lexical resource (like FrameNet), an
upper ontology (like SUMO), and modelled using a common formal language
(like OWL DL) – seem to be a reasonable approach to NLP (see Figure 4.7).
Thus, in the long run, we see FrameNet as a backbone of several domain-
specific frame lexicons that, in turn, are linked to domain-specific ontologies.
Even though the domain-specific frame lexicons will have links to ontologies, FrameNet itself also needs these links in order to support inferences on
frames that are not included in the domain-specific frame lexicons, such as the
Avoiding frame.

5   Synergizing ontologies and the lexicon: a roadmap

Alessandro Oltramari, Aldo Gangemi,
Chu-Ren Huang, Nicoletta Calzolari, Alessandro Lenci,
and Laurent Prévot

5.1   Formal mappings between ontologies

The establishment of mappings with precise semantics between formal ontologies constitutes one of the central tasks in research on ontology. This requirement affects primarily ontologies and their reciprocal understandability in shared environments like the Semantic Web, providing also a solid infrastructure for the interoperability of *ontolex* resources.

Suppose that a naive agent, human or artificial, wants to know the meaning of the word 'thesaurus'. A query submitted to WordNet returns the gloss: *a book containing a classified list of synonyms*. Navigating through the upward hierarchy, our agent might discover that a { *book* } is an { *artefact* }, and then a { *physical object* }. This result is trivial, indeed. But what about the 'content' of the book? Does it make sense to refer to contents as mere physical objects? To us, as human beings, this is obviously not the case. However, we know this is 'obvious' because of our (relatively) huge background world knowledge. Is there a conceptual model that can help a naive agent (e.g. a personal software agent that needs to be trained) to shape this knowledge? SUMOwn, Cycwn and DOLCEwn (respectively, the integration of SUMO, Cyc and DOLCE with WordNet) can be exploited for this task. For example, SUMOwn represents *book* as a CONTENTBEARINGPHYSICAL, namely something physical that 'contains' some information about a given topic; Cycwn gives a similar conceptualization by linking *thesaurus* to OBJECT-TYPE entities, those collections of things that are partially like a physical object. The DOLCEwn approach is a bit different: the content of the book and its physical support are 'split' into two different concepts, respectively NONPHYSICALENDURANT and PHYSICALENDURANT, mutually interconnected by a formal relation of **dependence** (in the spirit of the 'multiplicative approach' mentioned in Chapter 3).

Although it is important for a human user to access these data in natural language, artificial agents need machine-understandable (formal) languages. This is the main reason why we need to enable machines to access competing conceptualizations of lexical entries via formal mappings, i.e. within CON-TENTBEARINGPHYSICAL, OBJECT-TYPE, NONPHYSICALENDURANT, and PHYSICALENDURANT. To achieve this task, more careful formal connections between existing ontologies have to be conducted, in line, for example, with Masolo *et al.*, 2003. If the need for semantic interoperability and ontology-reuse have fostered the development of technological infrastructures, a number of software tools for *semi-automatic mapping* have been created in particular to support ontology integration (Choi *et al.*, 2006). There are mainly three different *perspectives* according to which ontological integration can be considered: (1) mapping global and local ontologies; (2) mapping between local ontologies; (3) ontology merging and alignment. The role of mappings between global and local ontologies is to clarify the semantic structure of the local ontology by means of an integrated global ontology as reference: LSD (Learning Source Description) (Doan *et al.*, 2003) and MOMIS (Mediator Environment for Multiple Information Resources) (Beneventano *et al.*, 2003) are two widely used ontology integration systems for the first perspective. Concerning mappings between local ontologies, where the mutual independence of the local ontologies represents the richness to be preserved by the ontology-mapping technique, several instruments have been developed recently: CTXMATCH, an algorithm for discovering semantic mappings across hierarchical classifications using logical deduction (Bouquet *et al.*, 2003), GLUE, which exploits machine-learning techniques to create mappings (Doan *et al.*, 2002), OMEN (Ontology Mapping Enhancer), which uses Bayesian nets to discover ontological mappings (Mitra *et al.*, 2005), OKMS, an ontology-based knowledge management system (Maedche *et al.*, 2003), among others. Finally, the third perspective deals with the creation of a unified ontology through a complex merging process, where human intervention is a substantial requirement, as for example in PROMPT (Noy and Musen, 2000) or CHIMAERA (McGuinnes *et al.*, 2000). Besides ontology-based application systems, this technological framework can also be seen as the 'natural' starting point for mapping ontolex resources: nevertheless, the specific semantic heterogeneity of these hybrid systems needs to be carefully studied to promote the engineering of a new and more suitable generation of integration technologies.

5.2   Evaluation of ontolex resources

There are many proposals for ontologies and ontolex resources evaluation as the topic becomes of central importance, illustrated for example by the creation of a specific workshop EON (Evaluation of Ontologies for the Web). The evaluation principles include principally formal evaluation, lexical coverage, task adequacy, and economic sustainability, and are developed in Gangemi *et al.*, 2006. As for task adequacy, also called application-based evaluation, many different tasks can be conceived, including NLP ones such as information retrieval, question answering (QA), anaphora resolution, or temporal indexing.

Before detailing this application-based evaluation and the formal evaluation, we will discuss lexical coverage and economic sustainability.

Lexical or conceptual coverage should, a priori, be the most direct evaluation principle. As long as a list of basic conceptual atoms can be agreed upon, coverage can be easily calculated. However, in practice, since lexical resources are very expensive to build, different tasks often share the same lexical resource. This makes the evaluation based on lexical coverage trivial. In addition, there is no consensus on the exact list of basic concepts that must be covered. Hence evaluation on lexical coverage alone has not been adopted for ontolex interfaces.

Economic sustainability, on the other hand, presupposes longer-term applications that can be commercialized, which will hopefully be in the near future for ontolex interfaces.

We now turn to the other types of evaluation, one based on ontological principles, and the other based on application. In particular, the application-based evaluation of the ontolex interface typically involves evaluating the performance of a system integrating the ontolex resource based on an example NLP task. This is crucial as it is currently the most effective way to show the contribution of the ontolex interface to language and knowledge engineering.

5.2.1   Ontology-driven formal evaluation

The focus here is on the way a user can understand whether the structure of a lexicon fits some suitable ontological principles or not. Such a test enables and facilitates the possible interfacing between that computational lexicon and a foundational ontology (point 3 of the classification developed in Chapter 10, p. 186).

Ontology-driven restructuring of computational lexicons mentioned earlier and developed in Chapter 3 is a relevant point which partially overlaps but does not merely correspond to ontology-evaluation methods.[1] Methodologies like *OntoClean* are the most effective in this context (see Chapters 3 and 10). Nevertheless, they have two major problems: their demand for massive human intervention and the need of philosophical training (most parts of the adopted

---

[1] For a comprehensive list of references in the field, see http://ontology.buffalo.edu/ evaulation.html

criteria come from the insights of analytic philosophy). It is without doubt that the ontolex community needs a wider analysis of the metalevel restructuring of lexical resources. Actually, there are no contending approaches that now challenge Guarino and Welty's OntoClean framework.

5.2.2 *Application-based evaluation*

This type of evaluation consists in fixing for a given application a set of parameters while varying the resource used to achieve the task. Such a type of evaluation is illustrated by Welty *et al.*, 2003, where the same QA task has been conducted with different versions of a resource (more or less conforming to formal principles) and where the results are compared.

The current crucial issue in the domain of evaluation is to determine whether the ontologies that receive a positive formal evaluation are also those who perform well on various tasks. More precise results will allow us to determine objectively which formal properties (if any) it is essential to preserve for a given NLP task. For example, a resource for question answering might not need to feature the same qualities as one for word-sense disambiguation, malapropism detection (Hirst and St-Onge, 1998), or associative anaphora resolution (Poesio *et al.*, 1997; Meyer and Dale, 2002).

5.3   Bridging different lexical models and resources

Computational lexicons reflect the multifariousness of lexical resources (Cole *et al.*, 1997): they can largely 'differentiate upon the explicit linguistic information they expose, which may vary in format, content granularity and motivation (linguistic theories, task or system-oriented scope, etc...)' (Pazienza and Stellato, 2006b). The development of meta-models for linguistic features is a crucial step towards their full interoperability. For example, both WordNet and FrameNet now exist in OWL (Web Ontology Language). More precisely OWL-WordNet is the topic of the W3C (World Wide Web Consortium) task force 'WNET';[2] FrameNet as it is illustrated in Chapter 4 has also been ported for a large part into OWL format.

On-the-fly resource re-engineering is a clean method, well-suited to small projects and lightweight tools. On the other hand, the availability of completely re-engineered resources is an advantage within large projects or more complex tools. Hence, it is not surprising that W3C decided to start a project on 'Porting WordNet to the Semantic Web'.

---

[2] 'Porting WordNet into Semantic Web', part of 'the Semantic Web Best Practices and Deployment' working group.

The way Princeton WordNet has been re-engineered by the WNET task force can be considered good practice for wordnets in general. The WNET task force has produced a standard conversion of WordNet to the RDF/OWL representation language in use in the Semantic Web community. Such a standard representation is useful in providing application developers with a high-quality resource, as well as to promote interoperability. Important requirements in this conversion process are that it should be complete and should stay close to the wordnet-like conceptual model.

The steps taken to produce the conversion included the following design decisions:

- the composition of class hierarchy and properties;
- the addition of a suitable OWL semantics;
- the chosen format of the URIs (Uniform Resource Identifier);
- a strategy to incorporate OWL and RDFS semantics in one schema such that both RDFS and OWL infrastructures can interpret the information correctly;
- the description of the two versions that are provided (Basic and Full) to accommodate different usages of WordNet.

We mention here only the most relevant issues that have arisen for translating WordNet's conceptual model to OWL semantics; the details of the work can be found in Gangemi *et al.*, 2003b.

The WNET task force defined characteristics for each of the seventeen WordNet relationships (hyponymy, entailment, similarity, member meronymy, substance meronymy, part meronymy, classification, cause, verb grouping, attribute), such as (anti-)symmetry, inverseness, and value restrictions on the lexical groups (e.g. nouns, verbs) that may appear in relations. Most of these informally stated requirements can be formalized in OWL and are present in the conversion.

Although WordNet and FrameNet, for example, were built following distinct models, nowadays it appears evident that one can benefit from the other in terms of knowledge coverage, content explicitness, linguistic phenomena comprehension, etc. Following this path a tool has been developed, 'WordNet Detour of FrameNet',[3] which supplies a first step towards such an integration: using a specific algorithm (Burchardt *et al.*, 2005), this tool can associate WordNet synsets with frames, frame elements and lexical units, ranking the results by assigning weights to the discovered connections.

Other relevant initiatives are: the Lexical Markup Framework (LMF) proposal drafted by the ISO TC37 SC4 committee (Francopoulo *et al.*, 2006), the Expert Advisory Group on Language Engineering Standards (EAGLES project) (Calzolari *et al.*, 2002), currently active proposals such as LIRICS

---

[3] See the website: http://www.coli.uni-saarland.de/~albu/cgi-bin/FN-Detour.cgi

(Linguistic Infrastructure for Inter-operable Resources and Systems),[4] and the Japanese funded 'Developing International Standards of Language Resources for Semantic Web Applications', focused on Asian languages (Takenobu *et al.*, 2006).

Of course the ontolex world needs more than this to be effective: dedicated interfaces, agreement on the OWL models of the most important computational lexicons, testing in multi-agent systems and many others. Moreover, the migration to open-source of current commercial resources like EuroWordNet (Vossen, 1998) and SIMPLE (Lenci *et al.*, 2000) is another crucial issue. Concerning multilinguality, does the structural arrangements of words in one language make sense in another language? Does it allow equally well for inferencing? Both successful alignments and misalignments can provide valuable information for the constructions of ontolex resources.

5.4   Technological framework

Research scientists studying and implementing ontolex resources do definitely need standard platforms and compatible formats for developing and sharing their work. It is easy to notice that this requirement originates from both the two converging sides of 'knowledge technology', namely linguistic resources and computational ontologies. The heterogenity of linguistic information, structure, conventions, and cultural heritage have led to a multitude of lexical systems so far; in this sense, for example, the MANAGELEX project (Vertan *et al.*, 2005) has been created to face the need of standardization for NLP: it is a lexicon-management tool that permits us to read, create, convert, and combine lexicons, sharing linguistical information across systems. A similarly urgent issue has also characterized ontologies, at least until Protégé appeared[5] in the community. Now Protégé[6] is the *de facto* standard for implementing ontologies: it supports a range of different language formats (OWL, RDF, XML, DAML) and – mostly relevant for our present topic – it allows for a huge number of different extensions and plug-ins. Among these, Pazienza and Stellato's OntoLing can be considered as the 'killer-application' for building up ontolex resources: it allows us to import a computational lexicon into the ontology, enabling the semi-automatic process of integration with a given ontology.[7] In terms of the methodological options we showed that OntoLing can help to restructure a computational lexicon,[8] to populate an implemented

---

[4] See the official website of the project, http://lirics.loria.fr/
[5] http://protege.stanford.edu/
[6] See, however, SwoopSwoop www.mindswap.org/2004/SWOOP/ which is a light-weight ontology editor with less features than Protégé but also useful for a variety of simpler tasks.
[7] We will see a concrete example in Chapter 10.
[8] OntoClean can also be implemented in Protégé and used in combination with OntoLing.

ontology, and to align the two. Another Protégé plug-in worth mentioning in our framework is PROMPT which allows for automated merging, comparing ontologies and provides an interface to help users to do these tasks manually.

Together with well-established 'inference engines' or 'reasoners' like Racer,[9] Pellet,[10] and FaCT,[11] OntoLing and Protégé represent the real technological framework for the present and new-frontier ontolex resources, indeed for the creation of the basic infrastructure of the ontolex world.

---

[9] http://www.sts.tu-harburg.de/~r.f.moeller/racer/
[10] http://www.mindswap.org/2003/pellet/
[11] http://www.cs.man.ac.uk/~horrocks/FaCT/

Part II

Discovery and representation
of conceptual systems

6   Experiments of ontology construction with Formal Concept Analysis

SuJian Li, Qin Lu, and Wenjie Li

6.1   Introduction

Ontologies are constructs of domain-specific concepts, and their relationships are used to reason about or define that domain. While an ontology may be constructed either manually or semi-automatically, it is never a trivial task. Manual methods usually require that the concept architecture be constructed by experts who consult dictionaries and other text sources. For example, the Upper Cyc Ontology built by Cycorp was manually constructed with approximately 3,000 terms (Lenat, 1998). Automatic and semi-automatic methods require two separate steps in which the first step acquires domain-specific terms followed by the second step of identifying relations among them from available lexicons or corpora. As lexicons are a good resource and are helpful for ontology construction, Chapters 5 and 15 discuss the problems involving ontology construction and lexicons. To use the available corpus resource, a common approach for automatic acquisition employs heuristic rules (Hearst, 1992; Maedche and Staab, 2000). However, such a method can only acquire limited relations.

One new approach in the automatic construction of ontologies (Cimiano *et al.*, 2004) is FCA (Formal Concept Analysis), a mathematical data analysis approach based on the lattice theory. Because formal concept lattices are a natural representation of hierarchies and classifications, FCA has evolved from a pure mathematical tool to an effective method in computer science (Stumme, 2002), such as in the automatic construction of an ontology (Cimiano *et al.*, 2004). The focus of this work is on how to use FCA to construct a domain-specific ontology based on different Chinese data sources. To achieve this goal, two experiments are conducted using two different Chinese data sources: one is lexical-based and the other is corpus-based. These experiments aim at addressing the attribute selection issue in ontology construction as well as efficiency tradeoffs. Results show that when using the lexicons provided by HowNet with sememes as attributes, granularity of the sememes used in the construction of HowNet is very important. When the data source is a corpus, selecting the appropriate context words with careful selection of the POS (Part-of-Speech) types plays a very important role for performance. Attribute-selection algorithms purely based on statistics, without regard to syntax or semantics, can result in an ontology that is hard to interpret.

This chapter is organized as follows: Section 6.2 introduces basic concepts and related works. Section 6.3 describes the dataset selection and design of experiments. Section 6.4 presents the experimental results, analysis, and discussion. Section 6.5 offers concluding remarks and suggested future research.

6.2   Basic concepts and related work

6.2.1   Ontology definitions

Philosophically, the term 'ontology' refers to the study of the existence and form of entities, their categories, and relationships. The same term is used similarly in computer science except that the focus is on the representation and construction of formal ontologies mentioned in Chapters 2 and 9 for various knowledge domains. Currently, there is no uniform definition of what constitutes a formal ontology. Gruber (1995) defines an ontology as 'a specification of a conceptualization' with the difference between an ontology and a conceptualization being that an ontology is language-dependent while a conceptualization is language-independent. In Gruber's definition, the subject of ontology is the study of the categorization of entities that either do or may exist in a domain. An alternative view sees an ontology as a catalogue of the types of things assumed to exist in a domain of interest D from the perspective of a person who uses a language L when talking about D. Most simply, an ontology describes a hierarchy of domain concepts related by subsumption where one concept simply subsumes another (Guarino, 1998b).

Sowa (2000) makes the distinction between a formal and an informal ontology. An *informal ontology* may be specified by a catalogue of types that are classified as undefined or defined only by means of statements in a natural language text. In contrast, a *formal ontology* is specified by a collection of names for formal concepts and relation types organized in a *partial ordering* by the type–subtype relation. In this work, we define *ontology* as follows:

> **Definition 1** *An **ontology**, denoted by **O**, is defined by a quadruplet, O = (L, D, C, R), where L is a specified language, D is a specific domain, C is the set of concepts, and R is the set of relations between concepts.*

Thus, in this work the term 'ontology' refers to a formal ontology.

Given that any ontology construction method will apply to a specific domain D in a particular language L, the primary construction task is to determine how to obtain C and then build R, although ontology construction methods may indeed be dependent on either L, D, or both.

In the ontology-learning framework of the Semantic Web, Maedche and Staab (2000) define an ontology with eight elements $< Lex, C, C_H, R, R_H, F, G, A >$, in which Lex denotes a set of strings that describes lexical entries for concepts and relations, C and C_H denote concepts and taxonomic relations, respectively, R and R_H denote other relations among concepts and their relation types, F and G are the mappings of lexical entries to C and R, respectively, and A is a set of axioms to describe any additional constraints on the ontology. This definition describes a more comprehensive framework than what is given in Definition 1. The concept in Definition 1 is similar to the concept definition given above, except that lexical items and concepts they represent are merged as one item in Definition 1. Also, both taxonomic relations and other relations are merged as one element. No axioms are defined in Definition 1, making it a simpler model.

6.2.2   FCA overview

FCA is a formal data analysis and knowledge representation technique. It can be used to automatically construct formal concepts as a lattice for a given context, thereby replacing the time-consuming manual construction of an ontology. FCA takes two sets of data, the *object set* and the *attribute set*, and locates a binary relationship between the data of the two sets. It then constructs a so-called *formal concept* lattice that contains a concept inclusion ordering according to a *formal context*. The definition of *formal context* and the definition of *formal concept* in terms of formal context in FCA are given below (Ganter and Wille, 1997).

> **Definition 2** *A **formal context** is a triple (G, M, I) where G is a set of objects, M is a set of attributes, and I is the relation of $G \times M$.*

> **Definition 3** *A **formal concept** of a formal context (G, M, I) is a pair (A, B) where $A \subseteq G$, $B \subseteq M$, $Intent(A) = B$ and $Extent(B) = A$, where*
>
> $$Intent(A) := \{m \in M | (g, m) \in I, \forall g \in A\}$$
>
> *and*
>
> $$Extent(B) := \{g \in G | (g, m) \in I, \forall m \in B\}.$$

In a pair *(A,B)* of a formal concept, *A* is the *extent* and *B* is the *intent*. Formal concepts satisfy the *partial ordering relationship*, as denoted by $\subseteq$, with regard to inclusion of their extents or inverse inclusion of their intents, formulated as follows:

$$(A_1, B_1) \leq (A_2, B_2) \Leftrightarrow A_1 \subseteq A_2 \text{ and } B_2 \subseteq B_1$$

A formal concept (A_1, B_1) in the concept lattice contains more attributes than its super-concept (A_2, B_2). On the other hand, the more attributes a formal concept is associated with, the fewer the objects it contains. Thus, a formal concept in the lattice is associated with fewer objects and more attributes than its super-concept.

It is possible that some selected attributes can describe the characteristics of objects. Yet their existence or removal does not affect the construction of the concept lattice. These attributes are called reducible attributes and can be written as a combination of other attributes. Formally, if $m \in M$ is an attribute and $X \subseteq M$ is a set of attributes with $m \notin X$, but $Extent(m) = Extent(X)$, then the formal concept $(Extent(m), Intent(Extent(m)))$ will be the infimum of the formal concept $(Extent(x), Intent(Extent(x)))$, where $x \in X$. Suppose the set $(M - \{m\})$ is P. P is also the infimum-dense of (G, M, I). According to the Basic Theorem of concept lattices, (G, M, I) is isomorphic to $(G, P, I \cap (G \times P))$, i.e. $(G, M, I) \cong (G, P, I \cap (G \times P))$. The attribute m here is then a reducible attribute. For a detailed presentation of this proposition, please refer to Ganter and Wille, 1997.

An ontology basically consists of a set of concepts, which can be described by the so-called objects and a set of relations. The simplest and most fundamental relation of these concept objects is the taxonomic relation, which is binary and satisfies the partial ordering property. Thus, FCA is a natural tool for ontology construction. FCA allows each lexical term to be mapped onto an object in FCA. This means that a term along with its respective set of attributes is included in a node as a *formal concept* in the FCA lattice. It is then possible to identify the taxonomic relation between terms by following the partial ordering relationships in the concept lattice.

It should be noted that in the case of a lexical term being associated with different concepts (multiple senses), it should be associated with a different set of attributes. Thus, in this chapter, the lexical terms and concepts are used interchangeably. Take the three concepts associated with the terms 计算机(computer), 微型机(microcomputer), and 大型机(mainframe) as examples. Suppose, 机器(machine), 大(large), and 小(small) are identified as attributes to describe them and the acquired concept lattice is shown in Figure 6.1. The cross '×' in the lattice for a term *T*(row) by an attribute *A*(column) simply indicates that the attribute *A* is identified for *T*. The subsumption relation of the attributes for the terms *computer* and *mainframe* show that *computer*

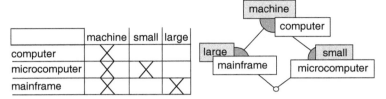

Figure 6.1 A sample concept lattice

and *mainframe* must present some kind of taxonomic relation. It also implies that the attributes 'large' and 'small' provide a firm basis for distinguishing between the terms *microcomputer* and *mainframe*.

Applying the FCA model to an ontology requires two mapping steps. First, formal concepts in FCA are mapped to concepts in the concept set C. Then the partial ordering relationship in FCA is mapped to R, for a specific language L and a specific domain D. How to make use of the partial-ordering relation to acquire relations between terms is the key in ontology construction using the FCA model.

The open-source software ConExp[1] (Concept Explorer) is a publically available Java visualization tool for FCA modelling written in JAVA that can generate concept-oriented views of the data (Serhiy, 2000). ConExp takes concept lattice data to display the concepts and the partial ordering relations in a graph. It provides the function to edit the lattice as well as the function to remove reducible attributes. The visual method to observe the structure of these partial ordering relationships is quite useful to see whether an ontology is built properly.

6.2.3   Related work

FCA is an effective tool for constructing formal ontologies. It allows terms and associated concepts (described, in turn, by a set of attributes) to be represented by objects. Most work on the use of FCA in ontologies has focused on the selection of formal objects and attributes. In Haav, 2003, a text describing a certain entity was seen as an object. In this view, an object can be any domain-specific text that uses domain-specific vocabulary to describe domain-specific entities and, thus, Haav defined attributes of the object as noun phrases in a domain-specific text. On the basis of noun phrases, an ontology for the domain of real estate was constructed. Jiang and Ogasawara (2003) used FCA to construct a context-based ontology of a clinical domain. They used

---

[1] http://sourceforge.net/projects/conexp

medical documents as formal objects, and attributes were compound medical phrases extracted using an NLP module. Of the medical concept relations extracted, 57.7% were found to be positive. FOGA (Fuzzy Ontology Generation frAmework), proposed by Quan *et al.* (2004), incorporated fuzzy logic into FCA in order to form a fuzzy-concept lattice for identifying topics of documents. Documents served as formal objects and research topics (terms) as attributes. Under these conditions, the relationship between an object and an attribute is not, as is usually the case, a binary value, but a membership value between 0 and 1. In this work, only one main topic is returned for each document, although one document often has more than one topic.

There are also works which take words or terms as objects. In Cimiano *et al.*, 2003, verb–object dependencies were extracted from texts where the headword of a grammatical object was considered an FCA object and the corresponding verb together with the postfix 'able' were used as attributes. In Marek *et al.*, 2004, only adjectives were chosen as attributes because for the chosen set of object terms, such as *river, lake, pond*, etc., adjectives are more discriminating. The ability of attributes to distinguish between objects, for example, because they exhibit certain word-type preferences, is a basic criterion for choosing them as attributes. Priss (2005) gave a good summary on the linguistic application of FCA and hypothesized that lexical databases could be represented or analysed using FCA.

6.3   Dataset selection and design of experiments

The construction of an ontology using FCA involves first identifying terms associated with certain concepts to serve as formal objects in FCA and then identifying the most appropriate set of attributes to describe these objects. The relations between concepts can then be extracted through the FCA concept lattice. If the concepts are predetermined, the most important issue is the selection of an appropriate attribute set. Of course, the selection of attributes is dependent on the data source used.

Generally speaking, data sources are either lexical or corpus based. The advantage of using a lexical base is that each term already exists and can be easily matched to an attribute set compiled by experts. The advantage of a corpus-based approach is that it is free of human bias because attributes are selected based on real data. However, the quality of the corpus-based approach depends on the availability of a representative large-scale domain corpus.

6.3.1   Dataset selection

The objective of this work is to evaluate the effectiveness of FCA in the construction of an ontology using different data sources, especially with regard to the selection of attributes. The chosen domain is Information Technology with a given set of IT terms as the concept terms, denoted as T. This hand-picked set of forty-nine domain-specific terms T (see Appendix) are then used as formal objects in FCA no matter what data source is used for attribute selection. For purposes of comparison, two different Chinese data sources are used. One is lexical and the other is corpus based.

It is ideal if we can automatically construct an ontology according to the available data resources compiled by experts. A lexical base that contains lexical terms and explanatory notes can serve as such a resource. The lexical base collects a repository of words and can be seen as a machine-readable dictionary that provides an index into human knowledge. However, a dictionary often gives independent definitions of concepts without explicitly indicating their relationships with other concepts. FCA can be used to model a lexical knowledge base and construct it as an ontology with clear structures.

A lexical base, denoted as LB, consists of a set of terms with a detailed explanation for each of them as expressed below:

$$LB = \{< t_i, e_i > \,|\, 1 \leq i \leq n\}$$

where t_i is a term and e_i is the corresponding verbal explanation or definition normally used in the so-called informal ontology to define t_i. To construct the formal context of FCA, each t_i serves as a formal object, and attributes can be extracted from e_i. The HowNet (Dong and Dong, 1999) Lexicon is chosen as the lexical base. Terms in HowNet are described formally by sememes (the smallest semantic unit), which can serve as attributes in FCA. For example, 部件(part) is a sememe and 显示器(monitor) is a term defined by a set of sememes such as 'computer', 'part', or 'look'. The HowNet version 2000 used in the experiments contains 1,667 sememes and 68,630 concepts.

The corpus-based experiment uses a large-scale corpus collected from some Chinese newspapers. The corpus consists of 97 million words and has been segmented and tagged (Yu *et al.*, 2001). Each sentence with n words takes the form '$w_1/p_1, w_2/p_2, w_3/p_3, \ldots, w_n/p_n$', where w_i is a word and p_i is the corresponding POS tag of w_i. The selection of attributes is purely statistical. The attributes are the words which co-occur with the IT terms with a certain statistical significance. A word bi-gram co-occurrence database is established by collecting and sorting all word bi-gram co-occurrences in the corpus within a context window of $[-5, 5]$.

It may be obvious that both HowNet and the selected corpus are not prime sources of IT domain-specific data, but the goal of this work is not to construct a full IT ontology. Rather, the goal is to investigate how different data sources can affect the construction of an ontology for a given set of terms/concepts. Two general-purpose data sources are quite suitable for this purpose, and in any case, the selected terms are the most representative IT domain terms that are often used in general contexts.

As the forty-nine concept terms forming the object set have already been selected, the next step is to select the attribute set. Because of the use of different data sources, different attribute sets must be selected so that the construction of formal concept contexts may take place.

6.3.2   Experiment 1: data source from HowNet with sememes as attributes

The HowNet lexicon is a typical lexical base. Each term in its lexicon has a set of descriptive sememes used to define and discriminate the terms. Because HowNet is a general-knowledge data source, many of its terms are not relevant to IT and, thus, are not considered in the selection process. Only IT terms are selected as objects in FCA, and their corresponding sememes serve as attribute candidates. The relationship between an object and an attribute is represented by a binary membership value. If an IT term t_i is defined by a sememe s_j, the membership value $\mu(i_i, s_j)$ is 1. Otherwise, it is 0.

Among all the relevant sememes, only those sememes having discriminative power are selected to differentiate concepts represented by these terms. The discriminating power is calculated through Information Gain (IG) for each sememe s_i according to the following formula:

$$IG(s_i) = E(S - s_i) - E(S)$$
$$E(S) = \sum(P_j log P_j)$$

where $E(S)$ is the entropy of all terms according to the sememe set S of HowNet. $E(S - s_i)$ is the entropy after s_i is deleted from S. P_j is the probability of each class of terms that are split by the sememe set S using FCA. All of the sememes in HowNet, whose information gain is less than a threshold N_{IG}, are filtered out. The attribute set is composed of the remaining sememes. The threshold N_{IG} is a parameter determined experimentally.

Figure 6.2 shows an example of a formal context in the form of a matrix using a selected nine terms from T, {操作系统 (operating system), 存储器(memory), 电脑(PC), 工作站(workstation), 计算机(computer), 显示器(monitor), 软件(software), 硬件(hardware), 中央处理器(CPU) }. Terms in the first column correspond to objects and the sememes in the first row correspond to attributes. An '×' entry indicates a membership value of 1.

Figure 6.3 shows the corresponding concept lattice as depicted using ConExp. The concept lattice displays the extension of formal concepts represented by these IT terms and the partial ordering relationships between these formal concepts. To interpret the relationships of any two terms, two kinds of binary relations, **is-a** and **equivalent** are defined. **is-a** relations are

	computer	software	part	heart	control	store	look
操作系统	X	X			X		
存储器	X		X			X	
电脑	X						
工作站	X						
计算机	X						
显示器	X		X				X
软件	X	X					
硬件	X		X				
中央处理器	X		X	X			

Figure 6.2 Example of concept context from HowNet

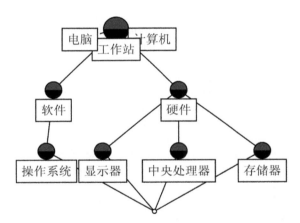

Figure 6.3 The corresponding concept lattice of Figure 6.2

subclass/superclass relations. For example, 'A **is-a** B' means that term A is a subclass of term B. 'A **equivalent** B' means that A and B are semantically equivalent. Objects with fewer attributes are superclasses of objects with more attributes. For simplicity of illustration, only superclass/subclass relations are shown. Attribute values are not displayed. For example,计算机(computer) is the superclass of 硬件(hardware), because the attribute set of 计算机(computer) has only one attribute {('computer')} which is contained in the attribute set {'computer', 'part'}, of 硬件(hardware). Again, 硬件(hardware) is the superclass of 硬盘(hard disk) because the attribute set of 硬件(hardware), {'computer', 'part'}, is contained in {'computer', 'part', 'store'} which is the attribute set of 硬盘(hard disk). Two objects described by the same set of attributes are considered equivalent. For example, 电脑(computer) and 计算机(computer) are considered equivalent because they are described by the same set of attributes, 'computer'. Thus, the concept lattice visually displays the subsumption relationships between terms. The relations between different terms are represented in the form of a triplet $< t_i, t_j, R(t_i, t_j) >$, where t_i and t_j are any two terms and $R(t_i, t_j)$ represents the relation. Figure 6.3 gives the results, such as $<$ 电脑(computer), 计算机(computer), **equivalent**$>$, $<$硬件(hardware), 电脑(computer), **is-a**$>$, and so on. From the concept lattice, these concept relations can be identified.

6.3.3   Experiment 2: data source from corpus using context verbs as attributes

Due to the lack of an IT-domain corpus, an annotated large-scale general news corpus is used as already explained in Section 6.3.1. It is easy to see that the content words in the context of a given term usually play an important role in describing a term semantically. Content words can be identified from POS tagging information in the corpus. In principle, nouns, adjectives, and verbs are all content words and can be considered as attribute candidates. However, because all of the selected IT terms are already nouns, and if nouns are chosen as attributes, it is very likely that the attribute set will contain terms which can form anfractuous relations, thereby making it difficult to acquire explicit hierarchical relations. Adjectives are also not a good choice for attributes because they are not often used to modify IT terms. Even when used, adjectives do not show patterns favouring certain IT terms over other general terms and are, therefore, lacking distinguishing power. Verbs, on the other hand, describe the functions of the concept terms and are, thus, better able to differentiate different terms. For this reason, verbs are selected as attributes in this work. The issue at hand becomes how to select the verbs for inclusion in the attribute set. This chapter takes verbs using a simple context window without consideration of syntax or semantics. Only co-occurrence statistics for concept terms and verbs are used.

The co-occurrence statistics are represented by a triplet $< t_i, v_j, n_{ij} >$, where t_i represents a term in T, v_j is a co-occurring verb, and n_{ij} indicates their co-occurring frequency. As the number of co-occurring verbs is very large, different criteria for extracting appropriate verbs can be adopted. Here, two methods are tested for extracting the term-attribute pairs:

- Method 1: Weak Frequency (WF)

    After the collection of statistics, all the triplets are sorted in descending order according to n_{ij}. The system has a threshold parameter N_1 below which the co-occurrence is considered statistically insignificant. The selection algorithm picks all t_i, v_j, n_{ij} with $n_{ij} \geq N_1$. If a term t_i in T still does not occur in the selected set after this process, the algorithm goes further down the sorted list to select the first v_j, until all the terms in T have occurred at least once. Then all the verbs in the selected set are included in the attribute set.

• Method 2: Strong Frequency (SF)

Similarly, all the triplets $< t_i, v_j, n_{ij} >$ are sorted in descending order according to n_{ij}, and those triplets are extracted with $n_{ij} \geq N_2$ where N_2, is a threshold parameter. The verbs in these triplets are selected in the attribute set.

A top word list is used to eliminate some very general verbs, such as 是(is) and 成为(become), both of which have very little or no discriminating power in any specific domain unless further syntactic analysis is conducted.

The relationship between a term and a verb is represented by a binary membership value, $\mu(t_i, v_j)$. For each triplet $< t_i, v_j, n_{ij} >$ occurring in the selected attribute set, the membership value $\mu(t_i, v_j)$ is set to 1; otherwise, it is 0. Figure 6.4 shows the formal context using the same nine terms again, similar to what was shown in Figure 6.3. Figure 6.5 shows the corresponding concept lattice. The reducible attributes are already eliminated by ConExp. Generally speaking, terms used in the predicative contexts that display the greatest variety are more likely to be general terms. The more general the meaning of a term is, the more verbs it collocates with. In Figure 6.5, the nodes in the lower levels are actually superclasses of those in the upper levels. That is, the subsumption relation between the objects in Figure 6.5 are inverse to those in Figure 6.3, yet the formal concepts still satisfy the relationship of partial ordering. For example, the term 计算机(computer) co-occurs with all the attributes in Figure 6.4, including 使用(use), 存储(store), 拷贝(copy), and so

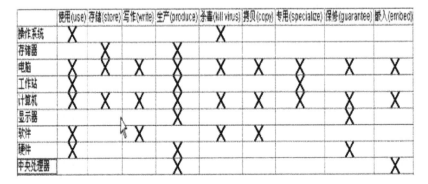

Figure 6.4 An example of concept context from corpus

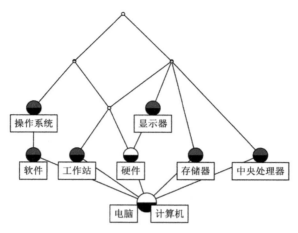

Figure 6.5 The corresponding concept lattice of Figure 6.4

on. The more specific term 存储器(memory), co-occurs with fewer attributes 存储(store) and 生产(produce). According to the concept lattice in Figure 6.5, results such as < '计算机(computer)', '电脑(computer)', **equivalent** >, < '硬件(hardware)', '计算机(computer)', **is-a** > are obtained.

6.4   Evaluation and discussion

6.4.1   Evaluation

In Experiment 1, thirty-three attributes are extracted based on the descriptive sememes for those forty-nine terms in T taken from HowNet. These attributes are listed in the Appendix, and the concept lattice generated is shown in Figure 6.6. In Experiment 2, using the same set, verbs that co-occur within the context windows of $[-5, 5]$ are extracted as discussed in Section 6.3.3. The thresholds N_1 and N_2 are set to 10 and 20, respectively. Using Method 1, 1,094 co-occurrence pairs are extracted from the corpus, among which there are 326 distinct verbs. After being filtered by the stop word list and removing reducible attributes, only sixty-eight verbs are left for inclusion. These verbs are listed in the Appendix, and the concept lattice generated is shown in Figure 6.7. In Experiment 2, using Method 2, 405 co-occurrence pairs are extracted, among which there are 234 distinct verbs. The concept lattice is similar to Figure 6.7 and is not shown here.

Currently, there are no uniform, widely used methods to evaluate an ontology. Most researchers evaluate their ontologies with respect to the lexical part as well as taxonomic part in a separate analysis (Cimiano *et al.*, 2003; Jiang and

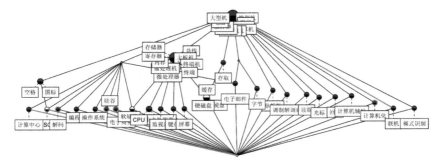

Figure 6.6 Lattice generated in Experiment 1

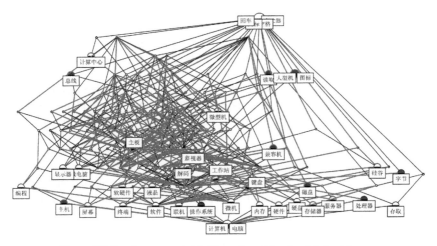

Figure 6.7 Lattice generated in Experiment 2 using Method 1

Ogasawara, 2003). Cimiano *et al.* (2003) compared their ontology with a standard domain ontology, treating it as a semiotic sign system, and comparisons were conducted in terms of Lexical Overlap (LO) and taxonomic similarity with respect to Semantic Cotopy (SC). In Jiang and Ogasawara, 2003, medical phrases and attribute implication pairs were evaluated manually using the ratio of answers.

In this work, the terms given in T are considered domain-specific terms. That is, the correctness of the objects are not in question. The evaluation focuses on the validity of the automatically generated taxonomic relationship between these terms using simple statistical methods. This evaluation is done manually with reference to the links of two terms t_i and t_j in each concept lattice, represented by relation R of either **equivalent** or **is-a**, and partial ordering the superclass (the reverse is subclass relations, so it is not double listed) by a triplet $< t_i, t_j, R(t_i, t_j) >$. Five researchers in the IT field manually evaluated the eligibility of these triplets to mark them either as correct (YES) or incorrect (NO). In Experiment 1, 43.2% of the 1,118 triplets received YES evaluations. In Experiment 2, 56.2% of the seventy-three relations are considered correct using Method 1 while 38.46% of the relations are correct using Method 2. Results show that Method 1 (WF) obtains more attributes and relations, with a much better performance than Method 2 (SF).

6.4.2   Discussion

The automatic identification of the relations between domain-specific concepts is the main task at hand when constructing an ontology. Due to the lack of other reference data, comparisons can only be made between the results of the two experiments discussed in this work. Here, the comparisons are made from results between Experiment 1 and Method 1 in Experiment 2 (hereafter, Experiment 2 means using Method 1).

In principle, attributes in the attribute set should be independent of each other. In reality, however, it is very difficult to select independent attributes. For example, in HowNet, both 计算机(computer) and 软件(software) are sememes, and yet they are semantically related. In fact, it is impossible to avoid dependent attributes where one attribute is the subtype of another attribute (its parent attribute). Subtype attributes are important without which it is difficult to distinguish some terms. However, when a concept is associated with the subtype attribute, its association to its parent attribute should be made explicit to maintain consistent subsumption relations.

Attributes may have other relations. For example, attributes 设计(design) and 开发(develop) selected in Experiment 2 are semantically related because design is normally required for a development. However, there is no easy way to describe the relations of two related verbs. One possible solution is to use the corpus or other resources to cluster verbs to reduce related attributes.

As mentioned earlier, thirty-three and sixty-eight attributes are selected for Experiment 1 and Experiment 2, respectively. Comparing the two lattices in Figure 6.6 and Figure 6.7, it can be seen that Experiment 1 produces a relatively flat and less intricate concept lattice with fewer levels of hierarchy than that of Experiment 2. This is because the two attribute sets possess different degrees of granularity. Obviously, the granularity of the sememes is not refined to the extent of having enough discriminating power to differentiate concept terms. Even at the same level of hierarchy, more terms belong to the **equivalent** class in Experiment 1 of eighty-six instances than Experiment 2 of twelve instances. For example, in HowNet, both 终端(terminal) and 存储器(memory) are described by the same attribute set 部件(part), 计算机(computer), and are, thus, equivalent. A finer granularity should, however, be added with two more sememes 显示(display) and 存储(storage) so that 终端(terminal) can be distinguished by using the sememes {'部件(part)', '计算机(computer)', '显示(display)'}, whereas 存储器(memory) can be distinguished by sememes {'部件(part)', '计算机(computer)', '存储(store)'}.

Besides the **equivalent** relationships, the number of **is-a** relationships exhibit a similar pattern. Experiment 1 has thirty-two **is-a** relationships whereas Experiment 2 has sixty-one. It is not difficult to understand that HowNet, being a manually constructed lexicon, is not tailored to the IT domain and has a lot of limitations as a resource for ontology construction. A great deal of additional labour is required to modify HowNet so that sufficient information can be provided for domain-specific research and applications.

When using the statistical approach in Experiment 2, the process is basically automatically saving a great deal of manual labour and time. This is because the techniques of segmentation and POS tagging are available and are relatively mature. If the corpus is domain-relevant and reasonable in size, the results should be quite reliable. In addition, the availability of a large-scale domain-relevant data source ensures that subjectivity is reduced to a minimum. Even in the case of a general-purpose corpus, like the one used in this work, the result is still better than that of a manually constructed lexicon resource.

For both the manually constructed ontology using HowNet and the automatically generated ontology based on a corpus, the obtained ontology still needs manual fine tuning because some of the data is incorrect from a semantic point of view. For example, in Experiment 1, the term 存储器(memory) is described by {'部件(part)', '计算机(computer)'} and the term 硬盘(hard disk) is described by {'部件(part)', '计算机(computer)', '存储(store)'}. Therefore, it is wrong for memory to be found within the superclass of hard disk. Experiment 2 exhibits similar problems, too.

Even though the ratio of correct relations (answer 'YES') in Experiment 2 (56.2%) is higher than that of Experiment 1 (43.2%), it cannot be interpreted blindly that the lexically based one is not as good as the corpus-based one. By examining the various ways of constructing an ontology, it can be seen that the more important issue in manual construction is the granularity of the attributes and the correct mapping of these attributes to their terms. On the other hand, it is more important to determine the types of attributes for consideration using the statistical approach. By looking at an example in Experiment 2, where the term 微机 (micro computer) is described by 开发(develop), 应用(apply), 控制(control), 设计(design), one may question how useful these attributes are even if their discriminating power is higher than those found in Experiment 1. If these verb attributes are changed to their corresponding nouns (development, application, control, and design), the noun set only represents the predicate nature of the term and, thus, relationships such as part-of still may not necessarily be captured. This gives rise to the issue of algorithm design for attribute selection. In language understanding, verbs are not the only type of words to describe concepts because concepts are in many situations described by nouns and adjectives. Thus, the use of nouns and noun phrases is inevitable. Furthermore, more comprehensive algorithms should look into the context of the terms both syntactically and semantically so that subject and object relationships can be properly identified.

6.5   Conclusion and future work

In this chapter, two kinds of data sources have been explored to investigate the selection of attribute sets for ontology construction through the use of the FCA model and its related visualization tools. Two experiments were conducted, one using the manually constructed HowNet lexicon with sememes as attributes and the other using a large-scale corpus and a set of statistically chosen context verbs. A number of useful findings were made. First, when using a lexicon, both the choice of sememes and their granularity are very important, as is the correct mapping of the terms to the set of attributes. In the corpus-based statistical approach, methods to select the appropriate context words and their types are influential in the results, and a purely statistical method without consideration of syntax and semantics can produce an ontology that is difficult to interpret. It is also important to point out that the use of a good visualization tool is very helpful in tuning **is-a** and **equivalent** relations of the ontology and in examining the appropriateness of the proposed partial ordering relations.

Both data resources in this work can only be said to be domain relevant, and not domain specific. This was due to limited resources as well as keeping the comparison meaningful. In future work, more comprehensive attribute-selection algorithms will be investigated taking into consideration various knowledge, such as different word types and syntactic and semantic cues. Additional language- and document-specific knowledge should also be explored. The FCA model is a good method to identify partial ordering relationships, in which ontology construction is more suitable for identifying taxonomic relations. Investigations should also be conducted on methods to identify other types of relations.

Acknowledgement

This work is partially supported by The Research Grants Council of Hong Kong (reference number: CERG PolyU 5190/04E and 5181/03E), the NSFC Project (Reference number: 60603093), and the National 973 Programme (Reference number: 004CB318102).

Appendix

The Selected IT terms

ASCII, CPU, 编程(programming) 操作系统(operating system), 存储器(memory), 存取(storing) 大型机(mainframe computer), 单板机(single board computer), 电脑(computer) 电子商务 (e-business), 电子邮件(email), 调制解调器(modem) 读取(reading), 服务器(server), 工作站(workstation) 光标(cursor), 硅谷(Silicon Valley), 缓存(cache) 回车(return), 寄存器(register), 计算机(computer) 计算机辅助(computer aided), 计算机化(computerization), 计算中心(computing centre) 显示器(monitor), 兼容机(compatible machine), 键盘(keyboard) 解码(decoding), 空格(space), 联机(online) 模式识别(pattern recognition), 内存(memory), 屏幕(screen) 软硬件(hardware and software), 数字计算机(digital computer), 图标(icon) 微处理机(microcomputer), 微处理器(microprocessor), 微电脑(microcomputer) 微机(microcomputer), 微型机(microcomputer), 硬磁盘(hard disk) 硬盘(hard disk), 中央处理器(CPU), 终端(terminal) 终端机(terminal), 主板(mainboard), 字节(byte) 总线(bus)

Selected attributes from HowNet

Symbol, computer, software part, Heart, compile control, Store, simple affair, commercial, facilities communicate, information, tool take, Mark, aim at place, ProperName, order help, Ize, InstitutePlace display, musictool, translate relate, perception, pattern machine, Look, unit

Attributes selected from the corpus

开发(exploit), 管理(manage), 应用(apply) 发展(develop), 联网(online), 控制(control) 显示(display), 设计(design), 建设(construct) 处理(process), 研究(research), 操作(operate) 制造(make), 实现(implement), 研制(manufacture) 生产(produce), 通信(communicate), 服务(serve) 培训(train), 联想(associate), 销售(sell) 奔腾(Pentium), 检索(retrieve), 查询(query) 运行(run), 制作(do), 并行(parallel) 引进(introduce), 活动(activity), 专用(for a special purpose) 排版(typeset), 安装(install), 分析(analyse) 自动化(automate), 出口(export), 存储(store) 组装(assemble), 监控(watch), 开办(launch) 接收(receive), 投资(invest), 连接(link) 进口(import), 设立(set up), 预装(preinstall) 借助(in virtue of), 改善(improve), 改造(reconstruct) 合成(synthesize), 组成(make up of), 打印(print) 同步(synchronize), 发布(publish), 指挥(command) 取代(replace), 代替(substitute), 开通(open up) 创造(create), 清除(clear), 共享(share) 联接(join), 扩大(enlarge), 试验(test) 上网(be on line), 数字化(computerize), 选用(choose) 独立(independent), 调控(adjust)

7 Ontology, lexicon, and fact repository as leveraged to interpret events of change

Marjorie McShane, Sergei Nirenburg, and Stephen Beale

7.1 Introduction

A semantically insightful way to describe events of change is in terms of their preconditions and effects. For example, if a car accelerates, the value of the 'speed' attribute as applied to the car's motion is higher in its effect than it had been in the precondition of the acceleration event; and if the importance of a certain political theory increases, the value of the modality 'saliency' scoping over that political theory is higher in its effect than it had been in the precondition of the increase event. Consider the following examples of change events drawn from the Wall Street Journal corpus covering 1987, 1988, 1989:

1. Other food stocks rallied in response to the offer for Kraft. Gerber Products **shot up** $4\frac{3}{8}$ to $57\frac{3}{4}$, CPC International **rose** $2\frac{1}{4}$ to $55\frac{1}{2}$, General Mills **gained** $2\frac{1}{8}$ to $54\frac{1}{2}$, Borden **rose** $1\frac{3}{4}$ to $56\frac{1}{2}$, Quaker Oats **went up** $1\frac{3}{8}$ to $56\frac{3}{8}$ and H.J. Heinz **went up** $1\frac{3}{8}$ to $47\frac{3}{4}$.
2. This development follows recent proposals from Saudi Arabia, Kuwait, the United Arab Emirates and Qatar that the current OPEC production ceiling of 16.6 million barrels a day should be **increased** by 900,000 barrels a day.
3. In 1985, 3.9 million women were enrolled in four-year schools. Their number **increased** by 49,000 in 1986.
4. Interco **shot up** 4 to $71\frac{3}{4}$ after a Delaware judge barred its poison pill defense against the Rales group's hostile $74 offer.
5. An index of longterm Treasury bonds compiled by Shearson Lehman Brothers Inc. **rose** by 0.79 point to 1262.85.
6. Stocks of copper in New York's Commodity Exchange warehouses as of the close of business Monday **fell** another 2,250 tons to 52,540 tons. 'Keep your eye on the premium of December over March,' said William O'Neill, research director for Elders Futures Inc. 'The way the premium goes, the market will go.' He said that if the premium continues to **increase**, the market will **go higher**...

For a text processor to glean from such contexts the same information that humans would, it must be able to, among other things:

a. recognize different lexical ways of expressing the same or very similar meanings, like *shot up, rose, gained, went up* in (1);[1]
b. recognize different syntactic means of expressing the same relationship: the amount by which something rises can be expressed either by a direct object (*rose $2\frac{1}{4}$ to $55\frac{1}{2}$* in (1)) or by a prepositional phrase (*rose by 0.79 point* in (5)); (2) uses the passive voice in *the production ceiling should be increased*, while (6) uses the middle voice in *the premium continues to increase*;
c. recognize phrasal entities, like *shot up* and *went up* in (1), and *go higher* in (6);
d. carry out word-sense disambiguation, both for events and for their associated arguments: the spatial meanings of *shot up* and *rose* in (1), (5) and (6) must be excluded; *premium*, in (6), can have a dozen different meanings, but here it refers to the amount at which something is valued above its par value;
e. calculate a third property value based on two given values: the starting value for each of the stocks mentioned in (1) can be calculated based on the amount of change, the direction of change (increase), and the final value; the final value for the number of barrels in (2) and the number of women in four-year schools in (4) can be calculated based on starting values, amount of change and direction of change (increase);
f. restore elided information: the values provided in (1) and (4) are in dollars per share; the measurement unit of 1262.85 and 0.79 in (5) is points; the premium referred to in (5) is for copper, as implied by the preceding context;
g. understand non-literal language: in (1), *Gerber Products shot up* means that the price per share for the company called Gerber Products shot up (likewise for the other companies listed in (1) and (4)); in (6), *stocks of copper ... fell* means that the value of stocks of copper fell.

If a system could do all the types of processing listed above, it should be able to perform the same sorts of tasks after reading such texts as a human could, such as answering the following questions:[2]

---

[1] These can be called near-synonyms, a term borrowed from Graeme Hirst (Hirst, 1995). Within OntoSem, if near-synonyms are not distinguished by property values, it is typically because, for the given domain, we do not yet have sufficient resources to pursue fine semantic distinctions.

[2] Although the current version of the 1980s' corpus from which we drew these examples does not include datelines, we expect most news articles, emails, etc. that we process to include text or metadata indicating the date. Specifying the date, or somehow grounding the question in a given time period, would be expected in a question-answering application.

- What was the price per share of Gerber Products and CPC International before an offer was made to buy Kraft?
- How many barrels of oil a day does Saudi Arabia think OPEC should be able to produce?
- How many women (or 'female students' or 'co-eds') were enrolled in four-year schools in 1986?

Without semantic processing, a system must essentially operate at the level of text strings, extracting only the information that is supplied explicitly, in the local context, and in the expected lexico-syntactic form(s). With semantic processing and a multifaceted knowledge base like the one we will describe, a system can have access to information that is overt or implied, supplied in any of an array of lexico-syntactic forms, and supplied either in a local or non-local context. In this chapter, we seek to show how this latter approach promises significant returns in one semantic realm: events of change.

7.2   A snapshot of OntoSem

OntoSem is a text-processing environment that takes as input raw text and carries out its tokenization, morphological analysis, syntactic analysis, and semantic analysis to yield **text-meaning representations (TMRs)**. Text analysis relies on:

- The OntoSem language-independent **ontology**, which currently contains over 8,000 concepts, amounting to over 140,000 RDF (Resource Description Framework) resource-property-value triples (Java *et al.*, 2006). The meta-vocabulary of the ontology is comprised of about 350 basic properties (relations and attributes). The number of concepts is intentionally restricted, such that a given ontological concept is typically used, with necessary local modifications, in the lexical descriptions of many words and phrases, not only synonyms.
- Entries in an OntoSem **lexicon** for each language processed contain, among other information, syntactic and semantic zones (linked through special variables) as well as procedural-semantic attachments, which we call *meaning procedures*. The semantic zone most frequently invokes ontological concepts, either directly or with modifications, but can also describe word meaning extra-ontologically, for example, in terms of parameterized values of modality, aspect, time, or combinations thereof. The English lexicon currently contains about 35,000 senses, not counting word forms productively analysed on the fly using lexical rules (taking those forms into account significantly increases the number of understood senses in our lexicon).
- A **fact repository**, which is a persistent knowledge base of what logicians call assertions. It contains real-world facts represented as numbered

remembered instances of ontological concepts: e.g., SPEECH-ACT-3186 is the 3,186th instantiation of the concept SPEECH-ACT in the world model constructed during text processing.

• The OntoSem text **analysers**, covering everything from tokenization to extended TMR creation (extended TMRs differ from basic TMRs in that they reflect the results of procedural semantic reasoning).

• The TMR language, which is the **metalanguage** for representing text meaning and is compatible with the metalanguage of the ontology and the fact repository.

The OntoSem environment can actually accomplish, with varying degrees of precision, all the types of processing listed in (a)–(g) of Section 7.1; naturally, lexical coverage is not complete, and cases of ellipsis and non-literal language are especially challenging.[3]

The core of semantic analysis, as we view it, is creating an unambiguous, language-independent representation of text meaning. Our preferred approach to creating applications is to store information extracted from TMRs in the fact repository, then to query the fact repository as needed. Just as the relationships between *types* of objects and events are stored in the ontology (the descriptive component of the knowledge base), the relationships between *instances* of objects and events are stored in the fact repository (the assertion component of the knowledge base). The fact repository, in fact, stores what have recently become known as object and entity profiles. The information in the fact repository both supports the processing of any given text (being a substrate of computer-tractable knowledge) and is supplemented by information from that text. The metalanguage and inventory of properties are the same in the ontology and the fact repository. The knowledge stored in the fact repository is decoupled from the form in which it is expressed in text; it can even be extracted from multilingual sources.

7.3   Motivation for pursuing deep analysis of events of change

A key to successfully populating the fact repository is resolving each expression to its context-free anchor. The most obvious example is finding the real-world referents (not just textual coreferents) for pronouns, but relevant phenomena extend much further. To cite just a few examples:

---

[3] Although space does not permit a substantive justification for this claim, we can point interested readers to recent publications that provide more details: for example, Nirenburg and Raskin, 2004; Beale *et al.*, 2003; McShane *et al.*, 2005, and the publications are available at the ILIT web site: http://ilit.umbc.edu.

- relative time expressions like *two weeks from Thursday* should, if possible be resolved to a specific date, just as *two hours ago* should be resolved to a specific time;
- approximations like *around 50 pounds* should be resolved to actual ranges;
- calculations, like *She is 3 inches taller than Harry*, should be carried out (how tall *is* she?).

These and other related types of processing are carried out in OntoSem using procedural semantic routines called meaning procedures (McShane *et al.*, 2004). Their results add another layer of knowledge to text-meaning representations. That is, the process of generating TMRs is actually composed of two steps: first, the basic semantic dependency structure is established, including the resolution of syntactic and semantic ambiguity, which yields a basic TMR; then specialized reasoners about language and the world are launched in order to further concretize the TMR. The resulting TMRs – called extended TMRs – show calculated, specific values wherever possible. It is these values that are used to populate the fact repository. The result is that the information in the fact repository is truly divorced from the idiosyncrasies of its source text and from any particular natural language.

Events of change provide an interesting case study for discussing semantic analysis and the use of the fact repository as a query space for applications. At the **ontological level**, events of change need not be listed individually, as is typically done in ontologies and wordnets, but can rather be explained in the lexicon (and, subsequently, in the TMR and fact repository) in terms of their preconditions and effects. At the **lexical level**, the implied information lurking in expressions about events of change must be interpreted differently based on the actual syntactic and semantic input; automating this process requires close lexical specification of relevant lexemes. At the **procedural semantic level**, the actual value of some property before or after an event of change often must be calculated based on the start value or end value in conjunction with the amount and direction of change. At the **fact repository level**, the anchor upon which a calculation must be carried out is often not provided in the local context but, instead, is either an aspect of general knowledge or is supplied elsewhere in the text. In the next section, we will consider *increase* and its synonyms and hyponyms as representatives of events of change. We will describe their lexical and runtime treatment, as well as the TMRs and the fact repository knowledge that they produce.

7.4   *Increase*

Increase and other semantically similar words expressing change are typically recorded in ontologies and wordnets as concepts; after all, they are events, like *run* or *eat*, and could thus be argued to have ontological status. However, are they *really* like *running* or *eating*? We suggest that they are not, primarily because whenever a verb of change is used, the questions 'which property value changed?', 'in which direction?', and 'by how much?' insinuate themselves into the context. In fact, the comparative values of some property (or properties) in the precondition and effect *constitute* the meaning of verbs of change.

This interpretation of change events has led us to conflate the notion 'event of change' into a single ontological concept, CHANGE-EVENT, which is quite high on the tree of inheritance: its parents are PHYSICAL-EVENT and MENTAL-EVENT, which themselves are children of EVENT. As a high-level ontological concept, CHANGE-EVENT does not have very constrained property values. The main work of interpreting CHANGE-EVENTs, therefore, lies in the further specification of their preconditions and effects. All lexical items that convey change events are mapped to CHANGE-EVENT and are further described in the lexicon using preconditions, effects, and, if needed, other property values: for example, the extent and speed of change is different in *shoot up* than it is in *increase*. This information is housed in the lexicon because the form of lexical input, including the arguments and adjuncts of verbs of change, must be considered when positing an interpretation for any given verb of change in a given context.

In the following subsections, we describe four types of semantic contexts requiring different interpretations of *increase* and its synonyms/hyponyms. Specifically, we consider these verbs as applied to **scalar attributes** (7.4.1), **modalities** (7.4.2), **count nouns** (7.4.3), and **non-count nouns** (7.4.4). For brevity's sake, for each subtype we present just one lexical sense of just one verb (*increase*): for example, we discuss the intransitive *the weight of the elephant increased*, but not the corresponding transitive *they increased the weight of the elephant* or the nominal *the increase in the weight of the elephant*, all of which are treated similarly. All in all, we currently have eighteen senses of *increase*. A summary of the first six is provided in Figure 7.1 for orientation. The other twelve senses include six transitive senses and six nominal senses. For all senses except v4, the synonyms that are treated similarly are *grow, escalate, rise, climb,* and *go up*. The hyponyms that are also treated similarly but include additional semantic features are *soar, jump, skyrocket, shoot up, inch up,* and *creep up*: for example, *skyrocket* has the additional features (SPEED $(>= .9)$), (INTENSITY $(>= .9)$). Factoring in all the relevant lexemes and syntactic configurations, over 500 lexico-syntactic input combinations are covered by this microtheory of increase events (and a similar number are covered by the corresponding treatment of decrease events).

7.4.1   *Increase with scalar attributes*

Among the properties defined in the PROPERTY branch of the OntoSem ontology are SCALAR-ATTRIBUTEs, a sample of which includes COMPLEXITY,

Sense	Description of Sense	Example
v1	Intransitive. Subject is a SCALAR-ATTRIBUTE whose RANGE goes up.	The height <the height of the tree, the tree's height> increased ((by) z) (from x) (to y).
v2	Intransitive. Subject is a word expressing an ontological semantic modality whose value goes up.	The importance <the importance of the plan, the plan's importance> increased.
v3	Intransitive. Subject is a count noun whose CARDINALITY goes up.	Mosquitoes <cases of the flu> increased ((by) z) (from x) (to y).
v4	Intransitive. Subject is a non-count noun whose AMOUNT goes up.	Potable water increased ((by) z) (from x) (to y).
v5	Intransitive. Subject is a noun-noun compound in which the second noun denotes an EVENT and the first noun denotes the count-noun THEME of that EVENT, whose CARDINALITY goes up.	Cigarette smoking increased ((by) z) (from x) (to y).
v6	Intransitive. Subject is a noun-noun compound in which the second noun denotes an EVENT and the first noun denotes the non-count-noun THEME of that EVENT, whose amount goes up.	Tofu production increased ((by) z) (from x) (to y).

Figure 7.1 Summary of the intransitive senses of *increase*

COST, INTENSITY, USEFULNESS, RAPIDITY, AGE, and ABSTRACTNESS. While SCALAR-ATTRIBUTEs can take various types of OBJECTs or EVENTs as their domain, they all take a numerical value, or range of values, as their range. That value can either be a real value or a point on the abstract $\{0,1\}$ scale. For example, *expensive* is lexically described as .8 on the scale of COST. (Of course, one could quibble about whether *expensive* should be rendered as .7, .8, between .7 and .9, etc., but lingering over such questions does not support practical solutions.) Automatic reasoning systems can interpret these abstract values relative to the ontologically listed normal range of property values listed for a concept: for example, an expensive car is a car whose COST is around .8 of the maximum COST listed for cars. During lexicon acquisition we attempt to be consistent in our interpretation of points on the abstract scale: just as *expensive* is .8 on the scale of COST, *tall* is .8 on the scale of HEIGHT and *heavy* is .8 on the scale of WEIGHT. Likewise, *very* consistently shifts the given value by .1 towards the extreme of the scale, and *extremely* shifts it by .2, so *very heavy* will be .9 on the scale of WEIGHT and *extremely heavy* will be 1

```
(increase-v1
  (def  "of scalar attributes: the value of the range is greater in the effect than in
         the precondition of the event")
  (ex   "The weight of the elephant increased ((by) 500 lbs.) (from 1000 lbs.) (to
         1500 lbs.)")
  (syn-struc
    ((subject ((root $var1) (cat n)))
     (root $var0) (cat v)
     (pp ((root $var2) (cat prep) (root by) (prep-head-opt +) (opt +)
          (obj ((root $var3) (cat n)))))
     (pp ((root $var4) (cat prep) (root from) (opt +)
          (obj ((root $var5) (cat n)))))
     (pp ((root $var6) (cat prep) (root to) (opt +)
          (obj ((root $var7) (cat n)))))))
  (sem-struc
    (CHANGE-EVENT
     (PRECONDITION (value refsem1))
     (EFFECT (value refsem2))
     (CHANGE-IN-VALUE ((value ^$var3) add)))
    (refsem1 (SCALAR-ATTRIBUTE  (RANGE (value ^$var5))))
    (refsem2 (SCALAR-ATTRIBUTE  (RANGE (value ^$var7))))
    (< (value refsem1.RANGE) (value refsem2.RANGE))
    (^$var2 (null-sem +)) (^$var4 (null-sem +)) (^$var6 (null-sem +)))
  (meaning-procedure
    (seek-specification (value refsem1) (value ^$var1))
    (seek-specification (value refsem2) (value ^$var1))
    (fill-in-missing-values-for-increase-v1)))
```

Figure 7.2 The first verbal sense of *increase*

(see McShane *et al.*, 2004 for further discussion of modifications to scalars). For change events, it is the relative values of scalar attributes that are most important: if the size of something increases, the value of its range is higher in the effect of the change event than in its precondition. Let us consider how one of the verbal senses for *increase* (*increase-v1* in Figure 7.2) supports such an interpretation, after some background is provided on the formalism used in OntoSem.

Lexicon entries are written using an extended variety of LFG in LISP-compatible format. Elements of the syntactic structure (*syn-struc*) and semantic structure (*sem-struc*) are linked using variables, and the same variables are referred to in the *meaning-procedure* zone. The caret ($^$) preceding variable names in the sem-struc indicates 'the meaning of (the variable)'. *Refsem* is a reserved term used for certain coreference needs within an entry. Onto-logical concepts are written in SMALL CAPS. The optionality of categories is indicated by *(opt +)*, noted at the level of the head of the category. The feature *(prep-head-opt +)* indicates that if the PP is overt, its preposition may be elided (to account for the difference between *The cost increased $10* and *The cost increased by $10*). The descriptor *(null-sem +)* indicates that no compositional meaning should be attributed to the prepositions since their meaning – or, more precisely, function – has already been taken care of in the semantic description.

Let us start by considering a sentence in which none of the optional PPs is overt in the context, such as *The weight of the elephant increased.* The meaning of *increase* can be rendered, 'the value of the range of WEIGHT is greater in the effect than in the precondition of *increase*'. This information is captured in the sem-struc statement:

$$(<(\text{value refsem1.RANGE}) (\text{value refsem2.RANGE}))$$

Refsem1 and refsem2 refer to some SCALAR-ATTRIBUTE, whose specific meaning can only be understood after the subject of the clause has been semantically analysed. The procedural semantic routine that seeks the meaning of certain elements of input and uses that meaning to interpret other elements of input is called *seek-specification*. The call to this routine, which is listed in the *meaning-procedure* zone of the entry, essentially says 'Seek the meaning of the SCALAR-ATTRIBUTE referred to by refsem1 and refsem2 using the meaning of $var1 as an input parameter.' Assuming that the subject of the sentence is *the weight of the elephant,* as in our example, the analyser will select the sense of the word *weight* in Figure 7.3.[4]

This sense indicates that the word *weight* instantiates the ontological concept WEIGHT whose DOMAIN is the meaning of $var2, which in our example instantiates the concept ELEPHANT. The result of the *seek-specification* meaning procedure, therefore, is replacement of the SCALAR-ATTRIBUTE instantiated by *increase* with WEIGHT (DOMAIN ELEPHANT) in the TMR. The TMR

---

[4] One bit of lexical complexity is worth mentioning. Some words that map to SCALAR-ATTRIBUTEs have two different interpretations: one in which the range of the attribute is unspecified, and the other in which the range is understood as having a high value. For example, height can mean either 'distance from the base of something to the top' or 'the condition or attribute of being relatively or sufficiently high or tall'. Under the first interpretation, the range of HEIGHT is unspecified, whereas under the second interpretation it is, say, $(> .7)$. If one says *I was surprised by the height of that steeple,* the interpretation is (HEIGHT $(> .7)$), whereas if one says *The height of the tree increased,* the initial and ending HEIGHTs remains unspecified. We are working on developing heuristics for such disambiguation in the context of our larger work on semantic disambiguation (see, e.g., Beale *et al.*, 2003 for an overview of disambiguation in OntoSem).

```
(weight-n1
  (def "indicates physical heaviness")
  (ex "the weight (of the child)")
  (syn-struc
    ((root $var0) (cat n)
     (pp ((root $var1) (cat prep) (root of) (opt +)
          (obj ((root $var2) (cat n)))))))
  (sem-struc
    (WEIGHT
      (DOMAIN (value ^$var2)))
    (^$var1 (null-sem +))))
```

Figure 7.3 The first nominal sense of *weight*

resulting from the input sentence *The weight of the elephant increased* will be as shown in 7.4.[5]

This text-meaning representation was generated from input in which none of the optional PPs for *increase* were overt: that is, there was no indication of the elephant's starting weight, ending weight or change in weight. However, as shown in the 'example' field for *increase-v1*, any combinations of PPs can be overt: *The weight of the elephant increased ((by) 500 lbs.) (from 1,000 lbs.) (to 1,500 lbs.)*. When such optional information is present, it is used in two ways. First, it directly fills slots in the *sem-struc* (e.g., the value of a *to*-PP fills in the RANGE of refsem2), which is then rendered as a more information-rich TMR. Second, if at least two of the three values are provided or can be recovered from the context, the full template of values (the value before the increase, after the increase, and the amount of increase) can be filled in. This is the ideal situation for one of the main applications of OntoSem: populating the fact repository with real-world facts, both explicit in the text and inferred with a high degree of confidence.

Consider the TMR for the input *The weight of the elephant increased by 500 lbs. to 1,500 lbs.* in Figure 7.5. Since we have two values (end value and amount of change), we can calculate the starting value (the RANGE of WEIGHT-3). The meaning procedure called to do this is descriptively named *fill-in-missing-values-for-increase1*. It is actually a multi-part routine (whose full call is not presented here) that does several things: if two values are present,

[5] '(< find-anchor-time)' is a call to a meaning procedure that seeks the anchor time in a dateline or other text source. Since the anchor time cannot be resolved in our short context, the reference to the meaning procedure (which means 'prior to the anchor time' and reflects the past tense of the verb) remains in the TMR.

CHANGE-EVENT-1
    textpointer   increased
    PRECONDITION   WEIGHT-1
    EFFECT   WEIGHT-2
    TIME   (< find-anchor-time)
    (< WEIGHT-1.RANGE WEIGHT-2.RANGE)
WEIGHT-1
    textpointer   weight
    DOMAIN   ELEPHANT-1
    PRECONDITION-OF   CHANGE-EVENT-1
WEIGHT-2
    textpointer   weight
    DOMAIN   ELEPHANT-1
    EFFECT-OF   CHANGE-EVENT-1
ELEPHANT-1
    textpointer   elephant
    DOMAIN-OF   WEIGHT-1 WEIGHT-2

Figure 7.4 The TMR for *The weight of the elephant increased*

it calculates the third; if only the amount of change is present, it seeks out the initial or final value from the preceding context (more specifically, the TMR for the preceding context) and, if successful, uses the now-known two values to calculate the third one. Notice that the *fill-in-missing-values-for-increase1* has a different status than *seek-specification*: whereas *seek-specification* is essential to interpreting the actual textual input, *fill-in-missing-values-for-increase1* attempts to go beyond the input in order to arrive at a fuller representation of all available meaning for the fact repository. Although we have been talking about the example of weight throughout, we must emphasize that this sense of *increase* covers input in which the subject refers to any scalar attribute.

One final note is worth mentioning before we leave the topic of scalar attributes. *Increase* is a particularly complex example since one cannot record beforehand which scalar attribute is in question: that must be compositionally determined. However, for many other lexemes, the relevant scalar attribute can be lexically encoded: e.g., *to accelerate* refers to increasing the value of VELOCITY, *to smooth out* refers to increasing the value of SMOOTH-NESS, and *to dry* refers to decreasing the value of WETNESS. The description of such lexemes and their representation in TMR are very similar to the case of *increase* except that the *seek-specification* procedural routine is not required.

CHANGE-EVENT-2
textpointer	increased
PRECONDITION	WEIGHT-3
EFFECT	WEIGHT-4
CHANGE-IN-VALUE	+ 500 (MEASURED-IN POUND)
TIME	(< find-anchor-time)
(< WEIGHT-3.RANGE	WEIGHT-4.RANGE)

WEIGHT-3
textpointer	weight
DOMAIN	ELEPHANT-2
PRECONDITION-OF	CHANGE-EVENT-2

WEIGHT-4
textpointer	weight
DOMAIN	ELEPHANT-2
RANGE	1500 (MEASURED-IN POUND)
EFFECT-OF	CHANGE-EVENT-2

ELEPHANT-2
textpointer	elephant
DOMAIN-OF	WEIGHT-3 WEIGHT-4

Figure 7.5 The TMR for *The weight of the elephant increased by 500 lbs. to 1,500 lbs.*

7.4.2   *Increase with modalities*

Modalities express an attitude on the part of the speaker towards the content of a proposition.[6] Within OntoSem, they are treated as extra-ontological aspects of meaning. The modalities currently used in OntoSem are: *epistemic, belief, obligative, permissive, potential, evaluative, intentional, epiteuctic, effort, volitive,* and *saliency.* The scale for the values of each modality is {0,1}, with any decimal value or range in between being valid. Examples of lexical items whose meanings are conveyed by values of modality are: *must* – obligative 1; *might* – epistemic .4 <> .6; *important* – saliency .8; *loathe* – evaluative 0. Modalities are defined for *type, scope, value,* and *attributed-to,* with the latter defaulting to the speaker if not overtly specified. For example, one sense of *importance* is described as in Figure 7.6.[7]

---

[6] There is often semantic ellipsis of part of the proposition: e.g., if one says that honour is important, the proposition is a person's having the attribute of being honourable.

[7] Another sense of *importance* is 'high level of importance', in which the value for saliency would be (> .7). Cf. footnote 4.

```
(importance-n1
 (cat n)
 (def "some unspecified value of the modality 'saliency'")
 (ex "the importance of taking vitamins")
 (comments "This sense is used primarily in contexts of comparison and events
   of change; the sense 'highly important' is the default otherwise.")
 (syn-struc
  ((root $var0) (cat n)
   (pp ((root $var1) (cat prep) (root of) (opt +)
       (obj ((root $var2) (cat n)))))))
 (sem-struc
  (modality
   (type saliency)
   (scope (value ^$var2)))
  (^$var1 (null-sem +))))
```

Figure 7.6 The first nominal sense of *importance*

Values for modality are compared in inputs like the following, extracted from a corpus: *The importance of this issue ⟨ The need for help, The emphasis on health care, Efforts by insurers ⟩ increased*. The lexical sense of *increase* that covers such inputs is shown in Figure 7.7.

This sense assumes, as appears to be justified from a small corpus study, that PP adjuncts indicating exact values will not typically be used with modals (modifiers like *a lot* and *significantly* will be treated compositionally and need not be referred to in the entry for *increase*).[8] Apart from its relative simplicity due to a lack of optional PPs, *increase-v2* is actually quite similar to *increase-v1*, the differences reducing to those listed in Figure 7.8. The analysis of an input like *The importance of diplomacy increased* will produce the TMR as in Figure 7.9.

The semantic analyser can disambiguate between *increase-v1* and *increase-v2* because each sense imposes semantic constraints on ^$var1: in *increase-v1*, it must be a SCALAR-ATTRIBUTE and, in *increase-v2*, it must be a type of modality.

7.4.3   *Increase with count nouns*

Ellipsis in language is widespread, which poses well-known problems for NLP (McShane, 2005). However, some cases of ellipsis are predictable and can be

---

[8] If a PP that indicates the starting value, ending value or amount of change should happen to be used with *increase-v2*, its meaning can be arrived at compositionally, though disambiguation of the preposition(s) in question will need to be carried out. The main reason for listing optional PPs explicitly in certain senses of *increase* is to circumvent the need for run-time disambiguation of prepositions.

```
(increase-v2
  (def "used with modalities: the value of the modality increases")
  (ex "The importance of diplomacy has increased.")
  (syn-struc
    ((subject ((root $var1) (cat n)))
     (root $var0) (cat v)))
  (sem-struc
    (CHANGE-EVENT
      (PRECONDITION (value refsem1))
      (EFFECT (value refsem2)))
    (refsem1 (modality))
    (refsem2 (modality))
    (< (value refsem1.value) (value refsem2.value)))
  (meaning-procedure
    (seek-specification (value refsem1) (value ^$var1))
    (seek-specification (value refsem2) (value ^$var1))))
```

Figure 7.7 The second verbal sense of *increase*

	increase-v1	increase-v2
Which sem-struc element requires procedural-semantic specification?	SCALAR-ATTRIBUTE	The type of modality
What changes from the precondition to the effect of the CHANGE-EVENT?	The range of the SCALAR-ATTRIBUTE	The value of the modality

Figure 7.8 Comparing *increase-v1* and *increase-v2*

handled using a combination of static resources and programs that use them. Consider the following corpus excerpts:

- After that **the mosquitoes increased** and there was a considerable amount of fever in October and November.
- Following cessation of wolf control in 1960 **wolves increased** and attained densities of approximately 16 wolves/1000 km^2 by 1970.
- As Figure 2 shows, **total accidents increased** modestly from 1993 through 1997.

CHANGE-EVENT- 3
textpointer	increased
PRECONDITION	modality-1
EFFECT	modality-2
TIME	(< find-anchor-time)
(< modality-1.value	modality-2.value)

modality-1
textpointer	importance
SCOPE	DIPLOMATIC-EVENT-1
TYPE	saliency
PRECONDITION-OF	CHANGE-EVENT-3

modality-2
textpointer	importance
SCOPE	DIPLOMATIC-EVENT-1
TYPE	saliency
EFFECT-OF	CHANGE-EVENT-3

DIPLOMATIC-EVENT-1
textpointer	diplomacy
scope-of	modality-1 modality-2

Figure 7.9 The TMR for *The importance of diplomacy increased*

The implications of the above three sentences are, respectively, that the number of mosquitoes, the number of wolves, and the number of accidents increased, even though there is no explicit reference to *number* in any of the contexts. The pivotal clue that underpins the automated interpretation of such contexts is the recognition that the subject NP is a count noun – regardless of whether it refers to an ontological OBJECT (MOSQUITO, WOLF) or EVENT (ACCIDENT).

In OntoSem, count and non-count are not defined lexically, they are defined ontologically. Count nouns are mapped to concepts which are in the domain of CARDINALITY, whereas non-count nouns are mapped to concepts which are in the domain of AMOUNT. Roughly speaking, MATERIAL and INTANGIBLE-OBJECT are defined for AMOUNT, whereas all other OBJECTs and EVENTs are defined for CARDINALITY. The semantic analyser will select *increase-v3* (Figure 7.10) only in those contexts in which the subject maps to an entity whose ontological mapping is in the domain of CARDINALITY.

Note that no meaning procedure is required to seek the specification of the property in question: the property CARDINALITY is asserted to be the

```
(increase-v3
  (def "used with count nouns")
  (ex "The mosquitoes increased")
  (syn-struc
    ((subject ((root $var1) (cat n)))
      (root $var0) (cat v)
      (pp ((root $var2) (cat prep) (root by) (prep-head-opt +) (opt +)
            (obj ((root $var3) (cat n)))))
      (pp ((root $var4) (cat prep) (root from) (opt +)
            (obj ((root $var5) (cat n)))))
      (pp ((root $var6) (cat prep) (root to) (opt +)
            (obj ((root $var7) (cat n)))))))
  (sem-struc
    (CHANGE-EVENT
      (PRECONDITION (value refsem1))
      (EFFECT (value refsem2))
      (CHANGE-IN-VALUE ((value ^$var3) add)))
    (refsem1
      (set
        (element-type (value ^$var1))
        (CARDINALITY (value ^$var5))))
    (refsem2
      (set
        (element-type (value ^$var1))
        (CARDINALITY (value ^$var7))))
    (< (value refsem1.CARDINALITY) (value refsem2.CARDINALITY))
    (^$var2 (null-sem +)) (^$var4 (null-sem +)) (^$var6 (null-sem +)))
  (meaning-procedure (fill-in-missing-values-for-increase-v3)))
```

Figure 7.10 The third verbal sense of *increase*

one in question for all inputs whose ^$var1 refers to a count OBJECT or EVENT. The TMR produced for the input *The mosquitoes increased* is shown in Figure 7.11.

7.4.4 *Increase with non-count nouns in N-N compounds*

A similar type of semantic ellipsis can occur with non-count nouns: an *amount* of something can be referred to without the word *amount*, as in *Potable water increased*. For the sake of variety, let us consider a lexical sense of increase that treats implied amounts but in a slightly more complex syntactic structure – one

CHANGE-EVENT- 4

textpointer	increased
PRECONDITION	SET-1
EFFECT	SET-2
TIME	(< find-anchor-time)

(< set-1.CARDINALITY set-2.CARDINALITY)

set-1

ELEMENT-TYPE	MOSQUITO-1
PRECONDITION-OF	CHANGE-EVENT-4

set-2

ELEMENT-TYPE	MOSQUITO-1
EFFECT-OF	CHANGE-EVENT-4

MOSQUITO-1

textpointer	mosquitoes
CARDINALITY	(> 1)
element-of	set-1 set-2

Figure 7.11 The TMR for *The mosquitoes increased*

in which the subject is a noun-noun compound. The configuration in question is illustrated by examples like the following: *Wine consumption ⟨ Calcium intake, Cocaine use ⟩ increased*. Here, the first noun in each N-N compound has two notable properties: it is the THEME of the EVENT referred to by the second noun of the compound, and its AMOUNT is understood to increase. The lexical sense that covers such contexts is *increase-v6*, as shown in Figure 7.12.

The *syn-struc* of this entry explicitly requires an N-N compound as its subject. The *sem-struc* says that there is a CHANGE-EVENT, through which the AMOUNT of ^$var1 (WINE) in the PRECONDITION is less than in the EFFECT. The *sem-struc* also asserts that ^$var1 (WINE) is the THEME of ^$var2 (DRINK), and that ^$var2 itself must be an EVENT. This latter semantic constraint supports disambiguation between *Wine consumption increased (increase-v6)* and *Wine vinegar increased*. The latter would be covered by *increase-v4*, a sense, not shown here, that expects the subject to be a non-count entity.

Increase-v6 as applied to the input *Wine consumption increased* yields the TMR shown in Figure 7.13.

7.5   Content divorced from its rendering

One of the main emphases of OntoSem text processing is separating content from form. For practical purposes, *The price increased by $2.00 to $22.00* and *The price increased by $2.00 from a starting price of $20.00* are synonymous,

```
(increase-v6
  (def "intransitive; the subject is a N-N compound in which the first N is a non-
    count noun")
  (ex "Wine consumption increased ((by) 10%) (from 10 glasses per month) (to
    11 glasses per month)")
  (syn-struc
    ((subject
        (n ((root $var1) (cat n)))
        (n ((root $var8) (cat n))))
      (root $var0) (cat v)
      (pp ((root $var2) (cat prep) (root by) (prep-head-opt +) (opt +)
          (obj ((root $var3) (cat n)))))
      (pp ((root $var4) (cat prep) (root from) (opt +)
          (obj ((root $var5) (cat n)))))
      (pp ((root $var6) (cat prep) (root to) (opt +)
          (obj ((root $var7) (cat n)))))))
  (sem-struc
    (CHANGE-EVENT
      (PRECONDITION (value refsem1))
      (EFFECT (value refsem2))
      (CHANGE-IN-VALUE ((value ^$var3) add)))
    (^$var8 (sem EVENT)
      (THEME (value ^$VAR1)))
    (refsem1
      (AMOUNT
          (DOMAIN (value ^$var1))
          (RANGE (value ^$var5))))
    (refsem2
      (AMOUNT
          (DOMAIN (value ^$var1))
          (RANGE (value ^$var7))))
    (< (value refsem1.RANGE) (value  refsem2.RANGE))
    (^$var2 (null-sem +))  (^$var4 (null-sem +))  (^$var6 (null-sem +)))
    (meaning-procedure (fill-in-missing-values-for-increase-v6)))
```

Figure 7.12 The sixth verbal sense of *increase*

and a human reader/listener who recalls the information later will likely
not remember in which form it was presented. Similarly, we would want
reasoning-oriented NLP systems to extract and record the same information
from two synonymous texts regardless of the form in which the information was expressed in each source. In the example just cited, the analysis
requirement is calculating the missing value from the 'start-change-end' value

CHANGE-EVENT-5
        textpointer   increased
        PRECONDITION   AMOUNT-1
        EFFECT   AMOUNT-2
        TIME   (< find-anchor-time)
        (< AMOUT-1.RANGE AMOUNT-2.RANGE)
AMOUNT-1
        DOMAIN   WINE-1
        PRECONDITION-OF   CHANGE-EVENT-5
AMOUNT-2
        DOMAIN   WINE-1
        EFFECT-OF   CHANGE-EVENT-5
WINE-1
        textpointer   wine
        DOMAIN-OF   AMOUNT-1 AMOUNT-2
        THEME-OF   DRINK-1
DRINK-1
        textpointer   consumption
        THEME   WINE-1

Figure 7.13 The TMR for *Wine consumption increased*

triple – all of whose values are equally accessible to any human interpreter of such a text.[9]

Another requirement of a sufficient NLP system is keeping a record of crucial bits of information presented elsewhere in a communication. A human reader/listener is expected to keep track of non-local information and, over the course of an article, description, etc., construct a unified mental model from its facts. Any approach to NLP that is strictly sentence-based, clause-based or based on the physical proximity of information is bound to miss crucial connections.

A third requirement of a truly intelligent NLP system is making use of what is understood to be general world knowledge. For example, if a newspaper reports that a presidential candidate in some country is even younger than John F. Kennedy was when he ran for president, the reader would be expected to know that JFK was in his early forties when he was elected president of the United States (or, more broadly, to understand that he was young for a president).

[9] For a discussion of paraphrase at the level of TMR, see McShane *et al.*, 2005.

Yet another challenge for an optimal, reasoning-oriented NLP system is to extract information from multilingual sources and merge it into unified knowledge structures. Such a multilingual application – unlike, for example, machine translation – cannot pass ambiguity, underspecification, ellipsis, etc., on to the end user to resolve.

Finally, an intelligent NLP system should be able to carry out reasoning beyond that needed for the interpretation of textual input. It is to such reasoning that we now turn.

7.6   NLP with reasoning and for reasoning

At present, the quality of automatic reasoning for real-world problems is insufficiently high and its coverage insufficiently broad at the level of both system components and knowledge elements. A central contributing factor is brittleness due to (a) the insufficiency of factual, heuristic, and other necessary types of knowledge in current reasoners, (b) a relatively narrow inventory of reasoning methods (deduction is still the main reasoning tool of choice), and (c) the need to find a balance between completeness and soundness of reasoning systems, on the one hand, and their efficiency and utility, on the other.

We have already shown that reasoning is needed for the semantic analysis of text and the piecing together of knowledge elements both from different portions of texts and from different texts altogether. Once a set of such structures is created and stored, it can support further reasoning, since reasoning is almost universally understood as operations that take structured data as input and generate other structured data (see, for example, the JTP system (Fikes *et al.*, 2003)). Without the availability of structured data, like the fact repository we have been discussing, the reasoning enterprise would not be able to relate to the real world. Moreover, in a realistic application, the data must be ample and dynamic, meaning that its knowledge resources must be constantly and promptly augmented. If knowledge is generated largely by people, this latter condition makes it more difficult to expect utility in real-world applications. The knowledge-generation process must be automated, which is why we are pursuing 'smart' automatic augmentation of the fact repository from TMRs.

The areas of general reasoning and NLP are often, though clearly not always, separated in the reasoning community. That is, the history of automated reasoning has shown an unfortunate bifurcation: the separation of language understanding from other aspects of reasoning, which predates even the inception of AI. One of the first acute observations on this split was made by Yehoshua Bar Hillel in the 1950s:

The evaluation of arguments presented in a natural language should have been one of the major worries of logic since its beginnings. However ... the actual development of formal logic took a different course. It seems that ... the almost general attitude of all formal logicians was to regard such an evaluation process as a two-stage affair. In the first stage, the original language formulation had to be rephrased, without loss, in a normalized idiom, while in the second stage, these normalized formulations would be put through the grindstone of the formal logic evaluator ... Without substantial progress in the first stage even the incredible progress made by mathematical logic in our time will not help us much in solving our total problem (Hillel, 1970, pp. 202–3).

Once one substitutes 'knowledge representation language' for 'normalized idiom' and 'reasoner' for 'formal logic evaluator', we can see that the current state of affairs is quite similar to that of almost half a century ago.

There are many reasons why such an extension of the purview of reasoning has not really occurred, an important one being that the task of extracting text meaning has been considered too complicated to succeed. However, just as in the area of reasoning, after a long period of intensive theoretical work, many people in NLP have come to realize that application-oriented work requires various kinds of simplification, coarsening of the grain size of description and inferencing, and concentration on the main bulk of knowledge. Theory-oriented work, by contrast, justifiably ponders over difficult cases, paradoxes, and counterexamples.

Both deductive and abductive logical approaches have been applied to NLP. Deductive approaches tend to focus on small, well-defined phenomena – often just one or two rules – and generally do not support the broad-coverage extraction and manipulation of meaning in practical systems (a typical recent contribution is Condoravdi et al., 2003). Abductive approaches, by contrast, have been applied to larger, real-world tasks: typically, an abductive model-based reasoner is supported by (1) an ontology featuring co-occurrence properties (e.g., agents, themes, or instruments of events), (2) knowledge about typical sequences of events (scripts), and (3) the agents' goals and plans (Hobbs et al., 1990, 1997). The grain size of such knowledge is coarser than that used in a typical lexical database reasoner and the results are seldom provably correct, but they represent the most probable conclusion that can be drawn based on the available data.

7.7   Conclusion

We began this discussion with a set of examples that involved events of change – specifically, events conveying increases and decreases of property values. We showed that a variety of lexical and syntactic means could be used to convey essentially the same information, and described the OntoSem methods of capturing such meaning using a language-independent metalanguage grounded in an ontology. We then turned to larger issues of reasoning, including the almost universal need for the input of reasoning systems to be statements in an unambiguous metalanguage. The NLP community has not yet developed methods of providing this kind of input large-scale. Using OntoSem, we are working towards that goal, interpreting the fact repository both as a target of structured knowledge from NLP and as a source of structured knowledge to support better NLP. Supporting reasoning capabilities is one of the central reasons for pursuing deeper semantic analysis than might otherwise be deemed necessary. Some of these reasoning capabilities must, in fact, be used in the semantic analysis process itself.

7.7.1 *Comparing OntoSem resources with others*

The chapters in this volume reflect two currently dominant currents in NLP: (1) building resources is a method- and resource-driven undertaking and (2) applications are developed to leverage available resources rather than resources being developed to serve the needs of independently acknowledged applications. We comment on both of these as a means of orienting OntoSem with respect to outside resources and systems.

Most work on developing knowledge resources for NLP over the past ten years has involved automatic methods and already existing resources. Projects have included learning ontologies or wordnets from corpora (e.g., Aramaki *et al.*, 2005), automatically merging ontologies or wordnets (e.g., Chapter 10, Pustejovsky *et al.*, 2002), and generating wordnets in one language by bootstrapping from another language. Such approaches typically have two goals: the first (and in many cases foremost) goal is to develop methods – hone algorithms, test machine-learning engines, etc.; the second is to create large knowledge bases to be used in applications. Although the benefits of such approaches are much discussed, not so the drawbacks: for example, the quality and depth of knowledge offered by the base resources is, across the board, not sufficient to support truly sophisticated applications, and automatic processes launched on those resources – as through merging – only aggravate this problem. In sum, for short-term applications and for long-term applications in which either the depth of semantic analysis is not crucial or errors do not carry a high cost, the resources thus generated are appropriate. However, this description does not cover all applications.

The OntoSem group, by contrast, has a different sphere of interests and, accordingly, different methods for building resources. We are pursuing the rigorous semantic interpretation of language to support high-end applications, with special areas of interest being disambiguation, the detection and resolution of elided and underspecified structures, and reasoning about language and the world. As such, the quality of our static resources needs to be very high, and the only currently feasible method for acquiring them is manually (we are currently experimenting with bootstrapping our current resources using machine-learning techniques and expect to report results shortly).

An example of a current OntoSem application is medical simulation and tutoring, for which the OntoSem ontology must support both the interactive simulation and the natural language dialogue that permits intelligent agents (virtual patients, virtual diagnosticians, and the virtual tutor) to communicate with human users. Related ontology expansion involves not only recording dozens of property values for each object and event (using multivalued selectional restrictions in the ontology), but also extensive domain and workflow scripts. When we began expanding our general-purpose ontology into the medical domain, we attempted to exploit the Unified Medical Language System (UMLS) metathesaurus and semantic network (see Nirenburg *et al.*, 2005 and cf. Pustejovsky *et al.*, 2002) but soon abandoned the effort because the results we were able to present to physicians for their validation were too noisy (recall that UMLS was created by librarians for librarians).

This is not to say that we do not use outside resources – we do, but to inform rather than displace the manual acquisition process. For example, the lexicon acquisition process regularly involves checking WordNet and dictionary.com for synonyms and hyponyms, and the anatomical aspect of our medical ontology building has been facilitated by the University of Washington's Foundational Model of Anatomy.[10] We have found that pruning or cleaning a noisy resource is no less work than building a resource from scratch, and our acquisition methodolgy reflects this experience.

We have reported elsewhere on the benefits of creating resources to serve applications rather than the other way around (McShane *et al.*, 2004; Nirenburg *et al.*, 2004). However, even if one must develop an application using extant resources, it is essential to understand what those resources actually provide. An often misinterpreted resource, it seems, is WordNet (and its progeny). Developers of WordNet do not oversell its content: 'WordNet is often called an ontology, although its creators did not have in mind a philosophical construct. WordNet merely represents an attempt to map the English lexicon into a network by means of a few semantic relations ... A full semantic inventory of language is beyond what has currently been attempted here. The authors are aware that a much richer corpus is needed ... which would capture a logical semantics for complex template linguistic expressions, rather than individual lexical items' as described in Chapter 2. In short, WordNet is not propounded to be the ultimate NLP lexicon: it is a useful, available tool for some types of applications. However, it seems to be misinterpreted by many as the last word in lexicons for NLP. A case in point is Chapter 10, which discusses methods

---

[10] Available at http://sig.biostr.washington.edu/projects/fm/FME/index.html

of merging ontologies and lexical resources. Although that survey includes several types of ontologies, the only types of lexical resources considered are those having the structure and content of a wordnet, the reason being that 'nowadays in the literature "WordNet" is the de facto standard for interfacing' (Chapter 10). The key word here is 'nowadays'. We would suggest the need for the community to consider not only the present and very near future when formulating approaches to developing and using resources for NLP: the longer term goal of developing truly intelligent agents is no less compelling a window of opportunity.

8   Hantology: conceptual system discovery based on orthographic convention

Ya-Min Chou and Chu-Ren Huang

8.1   Introduction: hanzi and conventionalized conceptualization

Two theoretical approaches to the ontolex interface are the direct approach of the discovery of conceptual systems and the indirect approach of the ontologization of lexical knowledge bases (LKB). The indirect approach has been adopted the most, since a structured LKB containing essential building blocks of ontology already allows studies to focus on the formalization, consistency, and completeness of the ontology itself. On the other hand, the direct approach, especially the discovery of the conventionalized human conceptual system(s), can deal with the important cognitive issues of how concept systems are formed by humans. In addition, since any such conventionalized system is already attested by shared human use, it should be robust in both theoretical explanation and applications. However, except for manual and empirical work (e.g. Wierzbicka, 1996), such approaches are rare due to the fact that shared human concept systems are rarely documented when it was conventionalized. In this chapter, we demonstrate the feasibility of the direct conceptual system approach with the construction of an ontology based on the conventionalized semantic-based orthographic system of Chinese.

Hanzi, or Chinese characters, offer a rare case of an orthographically conventionalized human concept system. The hanzi writing system represents and classifies lexical units according to semantic classes. This linguistic ontology is robust enough to have endured over 3,000 years of use by the Chinese people, regardless of its glyphic variations, such as greater and lesser seals, or the modern traditional/simplified contrast. It also has undergone adaptation by neighbouring languages, for example, kanji in Japanese. This robust and richly encoded ontology is fully and explicitly studied in this chapter. We map the ontology underlining hanzi to SUMO (Suggested Upper Merged Ontology) for systematic and theoretical discussion. The result is fully encoded in OWL (Web Ontology Language) to render it shareable and accessible for future Semantic Web applications. We call this ontology Hantology, an abbreviation for Hanzi Ontology.

8.1.1   Overview: hanzi as a conventionalized human concept system

Can an ontology be psychologically real as a shared conceptual system of a group of people? This is a critical issue that comprehensive 'linguistic ontologies', such as WordNet (Niles and Pease, 2003), poses. Since it is impractical to test experimentally the psychological reality of the expert-annotated lexical semantic relations of WordNet individually or collectively, the proof has to rely indirectly on applications. However, the popular and successful applications of WordNet in NLP research, in contrast with its infrequent use in psycholinguistic studies, give ambivalent indications. Given the challenge of ensuring the psychological reality of ontology, it seems like one possible way is to capture a conceptual system that has already been conventionalized and attested to by shared use. We observe that there is indeed a human-language writing system that has conventionalized a system of semantic classification. The richly structured and robust system has been used continuously for over 3,000 years and has been adopted by neighbouring languages; it is the writing system of Chinese characters (hanzi, also known as kanji in Japanese). We develop a linguistic ontology to represent the knowledge structure of Chinese characters' radicals, orthographic forms, variants, and derived words. In this chapter, we focus mainly on the knowledge structure of Chinese characters' radicals, the significance of which in representing semantic taxonomy was first documented by Xyu Shen (Xyu, 121/2004).

It is important to note that the Chinese writing system consists of a family of glyphs. Because of both historical changes and regional variations, allographs can occur at both the synchronic and diachronic levels. The best known allographs are the current contrast between simplified and traditional characters (such as between 庆 and 慶, to celebrate). This is not unlike the center/centre contrast between American and British orthographies. However, more drastic graphic differences can be detected due to over 3,000 years of using the same system: each modern character can be traced back to an allograph of the oracle bone engraving over 3,000 years ago, though only trained eyes can read them. Remarkably, both the external character semantic classification system and the internal component composition of each glyph have remained largely intact. This can even be said of the semantic classification of the languages that borrowed characters as part of their writing systems, such as Japanese kanji. Hantology aims to first encode then discover this extremely rich and robust conceptual system that underlies 3,000 years of Chinese culture as well as some of its neighbouring cultures.

8.1.2   Logographic semantic classification of Chinese characters

Generally speaking, each Chinese character corresponds to a morpheme, instead of a word in the language. Since archaic Chinese is predominantly

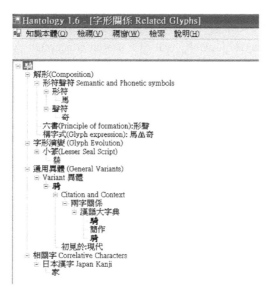

Figure 8.1 Illustration of radical plus phonetic part composition 騎 (qi2)

mono-morphemic, and even modern Chinese has a strong tendency of using mono-morphemic words,[1] there is a high degree of overlap between a character and a word, which causes conceptual confusion. Chao (1968) termed a character as a 'sociological word', since it is perceived as the basic unit of language by Chinese speakers yet can be shown to be different from a linguistic word.

When describing the two component parts of a Chinese character as a radical part and a phonetic part, it is important to bear in mind that a character represents a morpheme which necessarily contains both a linguistic form and the meaning it represents. The Chinese writing system is special because unlike most writing systems in the world, it uses meaning as the primary criterion of rendering the representation instead of the more apparent approach of describing linguistic forms. It is also important to note that the internal composition of Chinese characters is traditionally classified into six different principles, with a vast majority (over 80%) formed by the form-and-sound (xing2sheng1 形聲) principle. The form-and-sound principle composes a character by complementing the 'semantic' form

---

[1] According to the study of the Sinica Corpus (Huang *et al.*, 1998), mono-morphemic words compose only 20% of all word types yet represent 50% of all word tokens.

(xing2) with a 'phonetic' form (sheng1), which is the basis of the radical plus phonetic parts analysis. Among the remaining characters, which do not describe the spoken linguistic form, and hence do not have a phonetic part, it is still possible to identify the radical part as indicating their primary semantic classification. Therefore, it is not true that all Chinese characters can be analysed to have a radical and a phonetic part. A more precise description is that a Chinese character typically has a radical representing its semantic classification, and very often it has a phonetic part indicating phonological association.

The meaning-based representational system of Chinese characters can be illustrated with a small subset of a set of characters sharing the radical 馬 *ma3*. In these examples, 馬 *ma3* is a radical denoting 'horse': 驪, 'a kind of horse'; 驫, 'many horses'; 騎, 'to ride a horse'; 驍, 'a good horse'; 驚, (referring to a horse) 'to be startled'. These Chinese characters shown above show that characters sharing the same radical indeed share the same concept, but each has a different relation to the basic concept represented by the radical. At least two of them, namely, 'to ride a horse' and (referring to a horse) 'to be startled', cannot be described by the **is-a** relation in a taxonomy. Huang *et al.* (2008) show that there is indeed a complex conceptual system underlying the clustering of characters sharing the same radical. We will illustrate in the next section that when an appropriate formal representation is chosen, the semantic classification encoded by the character system can be exploited in the construction of an ontology.

8.1.3   *Bootstrapping conceptual representation with Chinese radicals*

Any formal account of a conceptual system must solve the dilemma of choosing a representational framework. Since a representational framework is itself built upon certain conceptualizations, any choice is potentially an a priori distortion of the account. A possible solution to this dilemma is the adoption of a shared upper ontology that is conceptually complete and yet general and robust enough to cover the different conceptual systems under consideration. We have adopted SUMO for the purpose of this study. All concepts expressed in Chinese characters are mapped to SUMO representation in the hope that the mapping can be transformed to a specialized ontology at a later date.

Adopting the SUMO representation has another immediate benefit. Semantic classification information can be formally represented and used in inference. For instance, all characters containing the 魚 'fish' radical can be assigned to this SUMO's concept with the same knowledge. Applying the linking between SUMO and WordNet (Chapter 2) and Sinica BOW (Chapter 11), the following inference is possible. Such inference can be done in English when a word is annotated as a hyponym of fish in WordNet. In Chinese, when the ontology of the radical system is explicitly represented as in Hantology, the same inference can be achieved without externally represented knowledge from a wordnet.

8.2   General framework

We elaborate the theoretical motivation as well as the overall design of Hantology (Chou, 2005) in this section. Hantology is proposed as a system of explicit encoding for conceptual knowledge encoded in Chinese orthography. It serves a dual purpose: it is an exercise in the discovery of a conventional system of conceptualization as well as a formal and explicit representation of linguistic information, treating characters as fundamental linguistic units in Chinese and important resources for natural language processing. The focus of Hantology is on a felicitous and robust encoding of the linguistic and conceptual knowledge encoded in the Chinese writing system through the decomposition and composition of Chinese characters.

The linguistic knowledge encoded in Hantology includes orthographic forms, phonological forms, senses, glyph variants, historical changes, and morphosyntactic generations (i.e., word and compound formation). As discussed above, the most important feature of the Chinese writing system is that each character is an extension of its radical component. In glyph form, a character necessarily contains a radical and optionally contains other parts, such as the phonetics parts. In terms of the meaning, the basic meaning of a character is an extension or association with the meaning of a radical as a semantic symbol (意符 yi4fu2). In this view, these meaning-bearing radicals become the representational core of ontology for the Chinese writing system. In this study, we adopt the 540 radicals from Xyu, 121/2004 *ShuoWenJieZi*. In order to enable computational applications, the concepts indicated by each radical are analysed and mapped into SUMO. Adopting SUMO allows Hantology to integrate and share information with other linguistic ontologies, such as WordNet and the Academia Sinica Bilingual Ontological Wordnet (Sinica BOW, Chapter 11). The meaning(s) of each Chinese character are formally encoded by mapping to SUMO nodes. Meanings of morphosyntactically derived words are also mapped to SUMO and encoded.

Since some meanings of a character are dependent on its pronunciation, the relation between pronunciation and sense is also described. In Chinese writing, it is possible to have glyph variants for the same character. However, it is very often the case that not all variants can represent the full range of meanings of that particular character. Hence, the relations among different character variants are described in terms of the different linguistic contexts in which each variant is used. Lastly, to make the information encoded by Hantology computable and easily sharable, we construct a model expressed by Web Ontology Language-Description Logic (OWL-DL). In terms of linguistic metaknowledge, this model integrates the General Ontology for Linguistic Description (Farrar and Langendoen, 2003).

In sum, Hantology makes substantial contributions in the following areas: first, the proposal and construction of this new linguistic ontology describes the knowledge structure of the Chinese writing system and Hantology is the first linguistic ontology of an ideographic writing system. Hantology's approach significantly augments knowledge available to the glyph-based Chinese encoding systems and, in addition, allows this systemic knowledge to be applied to facilitate NLP.

Second, Hantology proposes a linguistic context for describing the relation of character variants. Chinese character variants are an important characteristic of Chinese texts (Hsieh and Lin, 1997). Unfortunately, the relations of variants have not been properly represented to date. Whether two glyph forms can be free variants for the same character often depends on morpholexical contexts. For instance, the two glyph forms 姊 and 姐 are considered free variants for the character representation of the meaning 'elder sister'. However, only 姐 (the second glyph form) is allowed in the word 小姐 'Miss'. To ensure their proper representation, we propose a linguistic context for describing the relation of variants. Evaluation results show that this linguistic context provides a significant improvement over previous counterparts.

Third, a knowledge-based framework to describe language changes and variations is proposed in this chapter. A language inevitably changes over time. These changes are compounded by regional variations. The range of changes and variations of Chinese is probably the richest among all languages, because its writing system represents the longest unbroken written record among languages in the world, and it is also the shared written form for all Sinitic languages.[2] Hantology is the first linguistic ontology to describe the variation of languages. The aspects of variation described by Hantology include orthographic form, pronunciation, sense, lexicalization, and variants. This approach can systematically illustrate the development of the Chinese writing system. Hantology's treatment of historical changes and regional variations is detailed in Chou and Huang, 2006.

Last, but not least, the problem of missing (or unencoded) characters and retrieval of character variants are solved (Juang *et al.*, 2005). An inherent

[2] The Sinitic languages are more traditionally referred to as Chinese dialects, even though each of them is mutually unintelligible to the others. Most of them, such as Cantonese, Hakka, Shanghainese, or South-Min, have at least 1,000 years of history.

disadvantage of the Chinese writing system, when adapted for computation, is its large and open character set. Unlike alphabetical languages that have a small and finite set of characters, the Chinese character set can range from more than 5,000 to over 100,000, depending on how historical and regional variants are dealt with. Given the computer's architectural restriction of encoding only a finite set of characters, it is possible to encounter unencoded characters that the computer does not recognize and cannot represent or process. We propose to change the approach to the representation of Chinese characters fundamentally. Hantology allows the direct description of the glyph form as well as the linguistic contents it represents, without having to specifically encode each character in the system. This approach allows for all possible and principled changes and variations.

8.3   Conceptualization and classification of the radicals system

Since the invention of Chinese characters marks the beginning of conventionalized writing for the Chinese language, there is no documentation of the principles governing their construction. Fortunately, a classical text that is reasonably close to the origin of the Chinese characters exists to aid us in this matter. 'The Explanation of Words and the Parsing of Characters' *ShuoWenJieZi* (Xyu, 121/2004) is a text in which Xyu Shen identifies 540 radicals (bu4shou3, literally 'head of classification') for hanzi. Although later studies, which include excavated data, necessitate revisions of the *ShuoWenJieZi* system and interpretation, it remains the most widely accepted system that also appears to be the closest to the original interpretation.

8.3.1   *Mapping radical-based semantic classes to SUMO*

In order to ensure that we can felicitously discover the original conceptualization of Chinese characters, we have taken the complete set of radicals of the *ShuoWenJieZi* as basic meaning-bearing atoms. For formal representation, as well as ease of comparative study, they are mapped to the upper ontology of SUMO. The conceptual classification of each radical is determined by two sources of information. The first is the definition and explanation given in *ShuoWenJieZi*. However, this source may contain errors caused by the author's idiosyncratic interpretation or the lack of data. For instance, *ShuoWenJieZi* gives a distinctive account of the two bird-related radicals. It is said that 鳥 (114 derived characters) refers to long-tailed birds, while 隹 (38 derived characters) refers to short-tailed birds. However, when these 152 bird-related characters are examined, this generalization cannot be attested, therefore, we must conclude that the concept for both radicals is simply BIRD.

The second, and in fact more authentic and reliable piece of evidence is the distribution of the family of derived characters according to their radical. In other words, we are taking a data-driven descriptive approach and trying to determine the conceptual system supporting the set of concepts that are attested to be related or derived from the same basic concept represented by the radical. The most productive radical among the 540 radicals is 水 'water', from which 467 characters have been derived. It is important to note that some radicals have allographs and may represent more than one concept and, hence require multiple inheritances, as allowed by SUMO. An example is 雨 'rain' which will be linked both to the ontology node of 'water' and also to 'weather process'. While Sinica BOW is used in order to look up the SUMO correspondences for some characters (see Chapter 11), most mapping tasks require human verification.

8.3.2 Discovery of the conceptual system encoded by radicals

The radical system of Chinese orthography is often intuitively taken as a taxonomy, especially in learning, and is often criticized for its exceptions. Take the 艸 cao3 'grass' radical, for example. It is generally accepted that 艸 represents the concept PLANT.[3] However, basic meanings of many of the 444 characters containing the grass radical are clearly not a kind of plant. These 'exceptional' characters include 花 hua1 'flower', 藥 yao4 'medicine', 芳 fang1 '(of plants) fragrant'. We (Chou and Huang, 2005) made the first observation that these semantic associations are the rules rather than exceptions based on complete mapping between radicals and ontology nodes. The conceptual links are clear and intuitive: a flower is a part of a plant, a major function of plants is to be used as (herbal) medicine, and being fragrant is an important description of plants.

After exhaustively examining all mappings of the basic meaning of the 444 characters containing the semantic symbol 艸 to the three conceptual locations on an ontology, we found that there are four productive relations described by the radical, and there are no exceptions. As seen in Figure 8.3, being a kind of plant (e.g., orchid), being a part of a plant (e.g., leaves), being a description of a plant (e.g., fallen (leaves)), and being the usage of a plant (e.g., medicine) are our classifications for the represented conceptual system. The concepts of most radicals that represent concrete objects can be classified into name, part, description, and usage. Following the same method, a slightly different set of conceptual systems can be discovered based on the radical 金 jin1, which stands for the basic concept METAL.

---

[3] Note that the grass radical 艸, when realized as a component of a character, is represented as the double cross on top of a character, such as in 藥, 花, and 芳.

Figure 8.2 shows that the conceptual system based on the concept METAL shares two conceptual classes as the conceptual system headed by the concept PLANT: name and usage. The name class includes different kinds of metal, such as copper (銅 tong2) and silver (銀 yin2), while the usage class contains man-made objects, such as bell (鐘 zhong1). In addition, a third class of 'origin' links to the conceptual system, describing how metal products are made, such as 鑄 (zhu4 'cast'). When the two conceptual systems based on two different basic concepts are both taken into consideration, a possible formal account based on Aristotle's Four Causes emerges. Aristotle's Four Causes of Knowledge have been made directly relevant to computational linguistics by the Theory of Generative Lexicon (Pustejovsky, 1995), which will be adopted in our account. Pustejovsky posits that regular polysemy of lexical meaning can be derived and predicted from a basic meaning through conceptually motivated coercion based on our knowledge of the basic meaning.

The four aspects of Pustejovsky's Qualia structure are: formal, constitutive, telic, and agentive. In addition to the **is-a** taxonomic relation of name, we can see that the telic aspect is attested as usage by both radicals examined, and that the formal aspect is attested by the description. The constitutive aspect, on the other hand, is only attested by the conceptual system of 'plant'. The lack of the constitutive aspect for the conceptual system of metal can be explained, since a metal is mass matter that does not have naturally delineated parts. In addition, the agentive aspect is only attested by the conceptual system, since the description of how a thing comes to be is crucial and salient for man-made objects.

Our recent works (e.g., Huang *et al.*, 2008) have elaborated on the general description of Chinese character orthography as explicitly encoding a generative lexicon. In sum, we take Xyu's 540 radicals as conceptual primitives, which anchor conceptual structures. Concepts are conventionalized by the orthography of their relatedness to a basic concept. In other words, a character containing a certain radical encodes its conceptual relatedness to that conceptual primitive. Our in-depth study also showed that the conceptual relatedness is motivated by human experience. Hence, in addition to the four causes encoded in Pustejovsky's Qualia, the basic meaning of a character is often derived from event-based shared experience. Figure 8.2 illustrates the complexity of a radical-headed conceptual structure based, again, on 金 (jin1 'metal').[4]

---

[4] We have constructed over twenty radical-based conceptual structures covering a wide range of concepts, such as artefact, heavenly bodies, metal, body parts, living organisms, etc. Hence, the conceptual structure discovery approach driven by radicals as conceptual primes is well attested. In-depth accounting of the ontological nature of these conceptual structures, however, requires a separate study.

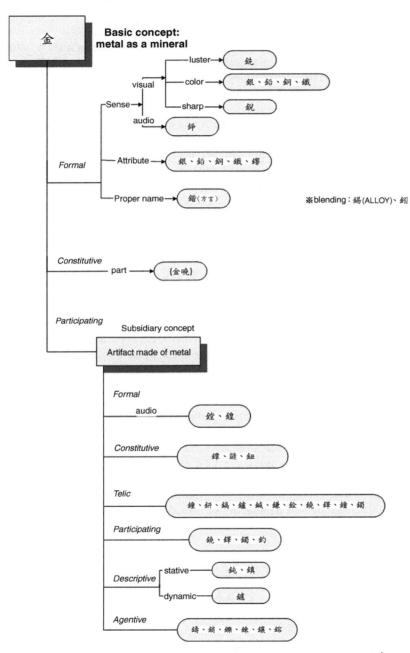

Figure 8.2 Conceptual system represented by the semantic radical 金 (jin1)

8.4   The ontology of a radical as a semantic symbol

One illuminating discovery that we made while trying to map radicals to ontology nodes is that each radical actually represents a cluster of concepts that can be associated with the core meaning by a set of rules. Take the 艸 (cao3 'grass') radical, for example: it is generally accepted that 艸 represents the concept PLANT.

There is no doubt that the 444 characters containing the semantic symbol 艸 are all related to the concept PLANT; however, what is surprising is that the conceptual clustering is not simply a taxonomic classification. As seen in Figure 8.3, there are four productive relations described by the radical: being a kind of plant (e.g., *orchid*), being a part of a plant (e.g., *leaves*), being a description of a plant (e.g., *fallen (leaves)*), and being the usage of a plant (e.g., *medicine*). The concepts of most radicals that represent concrete objects can be classified into name, part, description and usage. For example, the concepts represented by the radicals 馬 (horse), 牛 (cow), and 木 (wood) also could be divided into the same four classes.

We have observed that this principle is similar to the Theory of Generative Lexicon, where formal, constitutive, telic, and agentive represent the four aspects of the Qualia structure of a word that describe motivated semantic changes and coercions (Pustejovsky, 1995). It is interesting to note that all except the agentive aspect were attested with the conceptual clustering of Chinese characters derived from the 'grass' radical. Since Pustejovsky's agentive aspect is strongly associated with artefacts and other human creations, it is not unreasonable that the radicals based on natural objects lack any obvious semantic extension on how they were created. In addition, the descriptive attributes can be subsumed by the formal aspect of the Qualia structure.

Indeed, the agentive aspect is attested by a different radical that is conceptually associated with man-made objects. The radical that we take as an example is 金 (jin1 'metal'). Since metals are not useful to humans in their natural form, they are shaped by humans to become different tools. In the conceptual clusters classified according to the semantic radical 金 (jin1 'metal'), a substantial subset is defined by how a metal object is made, as in Figure 8.4.

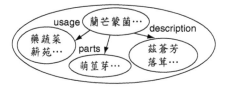

Figure 8.3 Conceptual classes represented by the semantic radical 艸 (cao3)

Figure 8.4 Conceptual classes represented by the semantic radical 金 (jin1)

It is interesting that no instantiation of the constitutive aspect for the semantic radical 金 exists, which can be easily explained by the fact that metal in its
natural form is a mass and does not have any components. Hence, we show
that the seeming idiosyncrasies in the conceptual clustering under each radical
are actually dependent on the knowledge acquired through human experience.
Hence, we contend that the conceptual structure of encoding by semantic
radicals in the Chinese writing system supports Pustejovsky's Theory of Generative Lexicon and Qualia structure. The same principles were used to derive
Chinese characters 3,000 years ago suggesting that there is cognitive validity
to this model.[5]

8.5   The architecture of Hantology

As mentioned above, each radical is the head of a semantic class cluster. Hence,
each radical forms a small ontology itself, governing all the concepts and
words derived from it. Each concept then can be mapped to a SUMO ontology
node and a matrix system linking two sets of hierarchically ordered ontology,
as shown in Figure 8.5.

Hantology is designed to handle both diachronic changes and synchronic
variations. Orthography as a conventionalized representation of language tends
to be less volatile than spoken language. The stability of the Chinese character
orthography is even more remarkable, since it is driven by semantic, not phonological representation. Hence, throughout the history of Chinese character
orthography, the most salient changes and variations are glyphic transformations, while the radical-based internal conceptual organization remains
intact.

An illustrative example of such glyphic transformation is the adoption of
simplified characters by the People's Republic of China (PRC) in the 1950s.
Near homomorphism is maintained between the simplified character set and
the traditional character set. Such near homomorphism is also maintained
between any two diachronically consecutive systems, all the way to when

---

[5] It should be noted that the Generative Lexicon Theory adopts the basic concepts from Aristotle's
Four Causes of Knowledge, a theory that is nearly as old as the Chinese writing system.

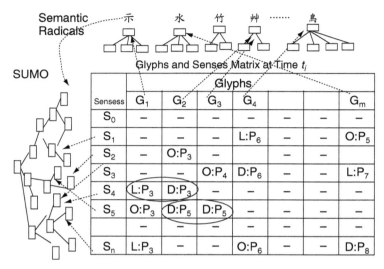

Figure 8.5 Mapping Hantology to SUMO at time t_i

Qin2shi3huang2 (秦始皇, the first emperor) unified all variants of Chinese writing systems towards the end of the third century BC. Regular mappings, though not near homomorphism, can be traced all the way back to the original oracle bone scripts (甲骨文 jia3gu3wen2), dating back to as early as the fifteenth century BC.

The near homomorphism of the diachronic changes allows us to propose a unified system of representation. According to Chou and Huang (2006), each time-specific Hantology representation, such as the one given in Figure 8.5, is a snapshot of the state of Chinese character ontology anchored by the radical-driven ontology given that particular time or ontology. Note that in this figure, each radical heads a small ontology. In addition, the system anchored by 540 radicals remains pretty much intact since it was first proposed by Xyu Shen in AD 121. In sum, the stability of the radical-based ontological structure underlines Hantology's design for representing the historical depth of conceptual systems represented by Chinese characters.

The fact that changes and variations are manifested as glyphic transformation, and that orthography tends to be conservative, gives rise to the predominance of character variants in the study of Chinese orthography. On the one hand, since each transformed glyph still represents the same content, they can be treated as variants of the old form. On the other hand, due to the conservativeness of orthographic convention, it is not uncommon that both new and old forms co-exist and become variants in the same system.

In the representation of character variants, it is crucial to be able to describe both the anchored form-meaning mapping and the contrasts in different glyph forms.

In Hantology, the radical ontology is denoted by the clustering of concepts related to the head concept, which can be mapped to the shared upper ontology of SUMO. Of critical importance is the fact that the linguistic coding space is a matrix with both a sense dimension and a glyph dimension. Figure 8.5 shows some of the possible relations among the characters. In this figure, 'O' stands for the original meaning, 'D' stands for the derived meaning, 'L' stands for the loaned meaning, and 'P' stands for pronunciation. As postulated in Chou and Huang 2006, each specific temporal-regional variant of the Chinese character system will be fully represented by a different instance of Figure 8.5. Hence, by comparing these homomorphic systems, the historical changes of the characters can be described by either global changes from system to system, general changes from domain ontology to domain ontology with the same radical, or local changes based on a character/glyph form.

Character variants pose a great challenge to the design of encoding systems for the computer, including Unicode (Hsieh and Lin, 1997; Juang *et al.*, 2005). Since these systems are based on the one-code-per-form principle, two different codes must represent two different characters. However, for the Chinese writing system, where different character forms may be the variants of the same character this assumption is too strong. For example, 説 and 說 are two variants of the same Chinese character but are encoded with different Unicode codes. Actually, 説 and 說 differ from each other only in the direction of two of the strokes.

Variants are the main reasons that computer applications are not able to process Chinese characters properly. It is important to note that the difficulty of the character variants problem lies in the fact that different glyph forms are variants only given certain context of the meaning they represent. This is where previous approaches fail, since they tackle this issue as a strict issue of form variants. Hantology is better equipped to solve the character variants problem, since it is a complete representational system of all character-encoded linguistic information (Chou, 2005). This framework consists of several dimensions including sense, pronunciation, time, place, and constraints of derived words.

(1) Sense dimension: Each Chinese character represents a range of senses. Two characters can only be variants given certain senses. In other words, for all of the senses of character A, there may be a subset of senses where it is possible to freely substitute character A with character B; however, they are not substitutable for other senses and hence no variants are given those senses. The sense dimension stipulates the most important information, i.e., the set of senses under which the characters can be considered variants.

(2) Pronunciation dimension: A change in meaning is very often signalled by different pronunciations, especially in different tones, of the same character form.

(3) Time dimension: Since meaning changes over time, it is obvious that variant relation must be given a time frame in order to establish identity of meaning. It is important to describe the dynamic features of this variant relation.

(4) Location dimension: Chinese dialects are sometimes called Sinitic languages since many of them are mutually unintelligible. For the writing system, this means that dialectal differences may be realized as different characters in writing. Consequently, variants may be subject to the regions where the character is used.

(5) Word formation constraints: A Chinese word is composed of one or more morphemes, each represented by a character. A word presents the most immediate context of a character; hence, word-formation information can be treated as conditions to character variants. For example, whether a specific variation is allowed or not allowed depends on the words it occurs in. From the more practical language-technology perspective, mapping characters to the words they occur in allows direct NLP applications.

Recall that Figure 8.5 represents a complete character system in terms of a form-sense matrix, given a specific time and region. Hence, the historical or regional variants relations can be fully represented when complete systems for each historical period as well as regional variants are composed. In Figure 8.5, the symbol of a circle indicates that there is a variant relation between two

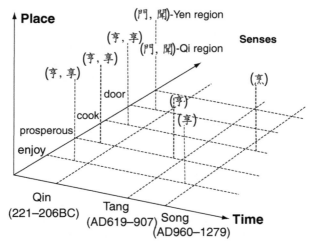

Figure 8.6 Character variants: temporal and locational dependencies

specific glyphs. For instance, G2 and G1 are different glyphs representing the same sense S4 at time t_i. In addition, G2 and G3 also are variants in the sense S5 at time t_i. However, although G3 and G4 can represent the same sense S3, they are not variants, since they have different linguistic forms in terms of pronunciations. Once all such matrixes are available, full representation and full explication of variants can be achieved formally. Figure 8.6 illustrates the interaction among sense, time, and place. On the one hand, 門 and 聞 were variants of the concept DOOR in the Yen region, but on the other hand, 聞 did not have the 'door' meaning in the Qi region. Chinese characters can generate words. In the modern Chinese language, most words consist of two characters. To reject this feature, the words generated from each character are described in Hantology.

8.6   OWL encoding of Hantology

The Semantic Web initiative not only underlines the need for automatic semantic processing on the Web but also highlights the crucial role ontology plays as the infrastructure of a system of knowledge representation. The fact that there is a widely used linguistic ontology with overt encoding of semantic classes should be significant for Semantic Web applications. Hence, it is worthwhile to convert Hantology to a formal representation that can be accessed in the Semantic Web. Since OWL (Web Ontology Language) has been designated as the Web Ontology Language for W3C, we adopt OWL-DL to formally represent Hantology. The name space of Hantology on the web is http://www.ntu.edu.tw/2005/Hantology.owl\#. We give a semantic model of the part of Hantology that describes glyphs as an example in Figure 8.7. The successful implementation is significant in two ways. First, converting Hantology to a formal representation allows us to check the consistency of the ontology. Second, it facilitates exchange and processing of texts represented in Chinese characters as well as allowing Web-based applications. For instance, since Japanese texts are also encoded in Chinese characters (i.e., kanji), Hantology can serve as an infrastructure for exchanging Japanese to Chinese information. The Japanese kanji system can be captured in the same radical-anchored ontology as in Figure 8.5.

Another application for the OWL-DL encoding is the implementation of resolution of character variants as discussed in the last section. It is not easy for any encoding-based system to deal with the equivalence or difference of the semantic content of two similar glyph forms. Given the infrastructure of comparison between different variations- or changes-based ontologies, adopting OWL-DL allows a solution to the formal representation of this problem. OWL-DL has an inference function that will allow computers to identify Chinese characters properly as character variants without having to have all variant

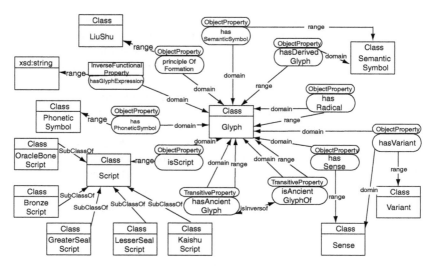

Figure 8.7 OWL semantic model of glyph in Hantology

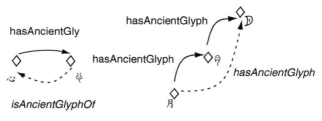

Figure 8.8 Ancient glyphs and inferred glyphs

pairs hand-annotated. Given two glyphs that are diachronically related, the two predicates *hasAncientGlyph* and *isAncientGlyphOf* can be applied. Since both *hasAncientGlyph* and *isAncientGlyphOf* have inversed and transitive features, variant relations can be inferred without being explicitly marked, an important feature given the time-depth of over 3,000 possible diachronic variations. An illustrative example, Figure 8.8, which describes historical variants of the character 心 (xin1 'heart') and 月 (yue4 'moon'), is given above. In both cases, we mark the relation between modern forms and the three-thousand-year-old oracle bone script forms.

It is important to note that the same set of glyph variations can be interpreted differently, given the context of use. Linguistically, as possibly represented in the proposed ISO Lexical Markup Framework (LMF) standard, these glyph variants can be described as either orthographic differences or font differences. If they are viewed diachronically as counterparts in different

If hasGlyphyInUnicode(G_k, $Unicode_i$) and hasGlyphyInUnicode
(G_k, $Unicode_k$)
then $Unicode_i = Unicode_j$

for example :
If hasGlyphyInUnicode(G_i, 說) and hasGlyphyInUnicode(G_i, 説)
then 說 = 説

If hasGlyphyInUnicode(G_j, 研) and hasGlyphyInUnicode(G_j, 研)
then 研 = 研

If hasGlyphyInUnicode(G_k, 眾) and hasGlyphyInUnicode(G_k, 衆)
then 眾 = 衆

Figure 8.9 Example for the translation mechanism

time-specific writing systems, they are orthographic variants with the assumption that the orthographic systems have evolved. However, if they are viewed synchronically as alternative forms to represent the same character for visual effect, they are font variants. For instance, the Lishu writing of the Han dynasty in Xyu Shen's time, around the first century BC, is significantly different than most forms. On one hand, we can describe a copy of *ShuoWenJieZi* as being written in the Lishu orthography. On the other hand, due to the ingenious work of modern font companies, we can also convert any modern text to Lishu with one keystroke for presentational or artistic purposes. This, then, is simply font variations.

A particularly tricky problem involving characters given Unicode is the variations between different linguistic and geo-political influences. Unicode allows a certain degree of autonomy over coding spaces among participating national groups. As a result, some variant characters are given two coding spaces in two different numbers. One famous example is the Chinese character 説 (shuo1 'to speak'), which is given two different Unicode numbers, with the two top right strokes either turning inwards or outwards, since these two variants were encoded independently by the Chinese and Japanese national groups. Computers will not be able to identify that these are the same characters. With our OWL-DL description, we can solve these idiosyncratic encoding problems by stipulating the identity relations between the relevant Unicode coded characters, as given in Figure 8.9.

8.7   Summary

Hantology is an explicit representational framework of the conceptual system encoded by Chinese characters and anchored by the 540 radicals representing basic concepts. On the one hand, the conceptual system is described by organizing radical-encoded character groups according to SUMO ontology. On the other hand, the orthographic forms, senses, variants, and word formation of each character are recorded in a database, which will be later translated into formal representations in OWL-DL. At this point, more than 3,000 most frequently used characters are hand-coded and will soon be available for public access.

8.7.1   The Knowledge Structure of Chinese Radicals

The complete knowledge structure anchored by 540 radicals is in essence an upper ontology for the Chinese language, as conventionalized by its orthography. As illustrated by Figure 8.5, there are two ways to view this conventional conceptual system: We can either take each radical as a root or take a unified view based on an upper ontology. Following Prévot *et al.*'s (Chapter 10) classification of approaches to the ontolex interface, the radical-driven view requires future work of ontology alignment, while the SUMO-driven view populates the ontology with a radical-based lexicon. Figure 8.10 shows the result after populating the SUMO concept of ANIMAL with Chinese

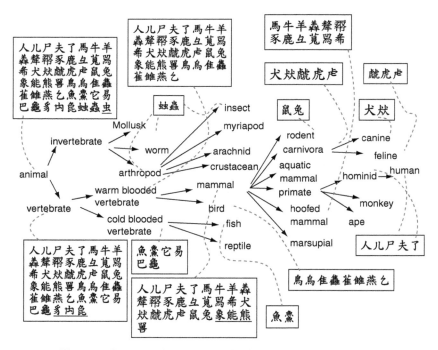

Figure 8.10 Knowledge structure of animal-related radicals

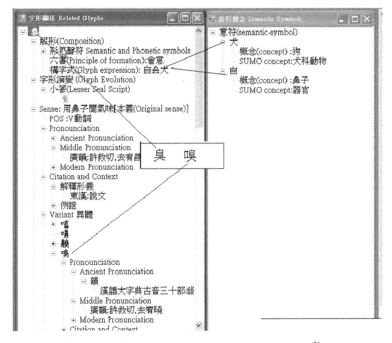

Figure 8.11 The glyphs and variants knowledge for 臭

orthography data. We map all attested senses of Chinese characters to their corresponding SUMO nodes, as indicated by a linked box of characters in the figure.

8.7.2   Accessing Hantology

A Web-accessible prototype of Hantology can be found at http://hantology. ling.sinica.edu.tw. A user can browse by form, including the semantic components of a character, by meaning, or by variants.

To illustrate the major contents of Hantology, we use the character 臭 as an example. Figure 8.11 shows the glyphs, pronunciations, and variants for 臭. The principle formation is 會意(ideographic compound), one of the six criteria for character formation (六 書 liu4shu1). Glyph evolution shows the derivational history of the script. 臭 originated as a verb and referred to the act of smelling by nose. There are four variants for the sense of smell. 後作 in Figure 8.11 means 臭 and is replaced by 嗅 to express the sense of smelling later. The first citation appears in the period of 唐 (Tang dynasty, AD 619–907).

Figure 8.12 Radicals classification by SUMO

Figure 8.12 illustrates one of the features of our interface system. For this application, a user can query radicals using a SUMO-defined ontological concept. The figure shows that a query on the SUMO concept of FABRIC returns 11 radicals that either express the concept or have a sense dependent on that concept. A possible application of this feature is to execute a content-based search without a lexicon or segmentation for Chinese and Japanese. For such applications, conceptual distribution can be calculated by converting the frequency of characters in a plain text to radical frequency, and the radical frequency can be mapped to the distribution of SUMO concepts based on the Hantology record.

8.8   Conclusion

Hantology is a formal representation of the conventionalized conceptual system based on Chinese orthography. The representation captures the knowledge conventionalized and encoded by Chinese characters and aims to formalize it for use in language processing in the future. It is a well-established practice in computational linguistics to manipulate lexical- and inter-lexical-level knowledge, such as the very active research based on WordNet. However, the knowledge encoded on Chinese characters is intra-lexical and embedded in the orthography.

In this chapter, we dealt first with the issue of how to discover and capture the knowledge encoded in the orthography, and showed that the semantic symbols (意符 yi4fu2) represented by radicals do have explicit conceptual motivations. In fact, our research suggested that each semantic symbol can be considered as a basic concept governing a domain ontology, not unlike the Qualia structure of the generative lexicon. We are already undertaking a series of studies (e.g. Huang *et al.*, 2008) to discover and explicate the conceptual structure based on the basic concepts represented by the radicals. Such studies can supplement and contrast with the SUMO ontology populated with character-based lexical information already available from Hantology.

In terms of applications, Chou *et al.* (2007) argued that this conventionalized cluster of ontologies can be utilized in the multilingual processing of languages adopting Chinese character writing. In addition to exploring the possibility of representing a conceptual system that has been implicitly followed by speakers of the languages adopting this orthography, we also provide a formal way to represent variations and changes within this robust system. The historical depth of Hantology allows us to examine how knowledge systems evolve through time. In the future, we will explore how richly encoded knowledge at the basic writing level supports content processing of texts without having to involve the higher syntactic processes of segmentation, chunking, or parsing.

9 What's in a schema?

Aldo Gangemi

9.1   Introduction

This chapter presents an application of metamodelling[1] to the ontolex interface, intended here as the set of relations (e.g. annotation, reuse, mapping,
transformation, etc.) which can hold between the elements of an ontology, and
the elements of a lexicon.

The *c.DnS* ontology (Gangemi, 2008) is here extended to formally define
an Embodied Construction Grammar (ECG) (Feldman, 2006) ontology,[2] and a
semiotic façade,[3] called *Semion*, which is applied to define a FrameNet (Baker
et al., 1998) metamodel (*OntoFrameNet*[4]) and to introduce a formal method
for lexical information integration. This application is critical for the ontolex
interface, because it addresses sophisticated approaches to lexicon design and
linguistic theory and requires an understanding of the different notions of
schema (a.k.a. frame, knowledge pattern, etc.) across domains as different as
lexicon and ontology design.

In this chapter, schemata are considered as *invariances that emerge from
the co-evolution of organisms and environment, and that are exemplified by
neurobiological, cognitive, linguistic, and social constructs.* The ontologies
presented here are designed according to this assumption.

While specific relations between individual ontologies and lexica are
addressed in literature quite often (e.g. Gangemi *et al.*, 2003; Buitelaar *et al.*,
2007; De Luca *et al.*, 2007 and several chapters in this volume), it is far
less usual to propose a metamodel to formally describe the ontolex interface.
Metamodels have been proposed to abridge different lexical resources, starting with OLIF (McCormick *et al.*, 2004), and recently with reference to lexical

---

[1] A metamodel, broadly speaking, is a model that describes constructs and rules needed to create
specific models.
[2] See http://ontologydesignpatterns.org/ont/cdns/ECG.owl
[3] A façade is an architectural object: the frontage of a building, which is used metaphorically in
software engineering to talk of an object that provides a simplified interface to a larger body
of code (West *et al.*, 2008). Here façade means a semiotic metamodel that acts as a layer in
between heterogeneous lexical models and an ontology.
[4] See www.ontologydesignpatterns.org/ont/ofn/ofntb.owl

semantics, as in LMF (Francopoulo *et al.*, 2006), where an attempt has been made to informally align some lexica under the same metamodel.[5] Some steps towards linking lexica and ontologies have also been made in order to manage lexicon reuse in ontologies (Pazienza and Stellato, 2006a), multilinguality in ontologies (Peters *et al.*, 2007), as well as to make cookbook-like transforms between syntactic patterns and formal constructs (Cimiano *et al.*, 2007).

The research partly reported here aims at abstracting from individual interfaces, lexical standards or specific transformation methods, by providing a semiotic façade inbetween the intuitive semantics of different lexica and formal semantics.[6] A semiotic façade is an appropriate metamodel, because its constructs are intuitive enough in order to align the underlying assumptions of different lexical resources, but they can also be made formal by applying a *transformation pattern*[7] to a formal semantic construct. A notable advantage of this intermediate layer is that any interface or translation method can refer to a unique *façade* (West *et al.*, 2008), without worrying about the intended conceptualization of the data models used in the original lexical resources, or about how to access them. Moreover, developers of lexical resources can continue developing their resources without changing their workflow in order to stay tuned with, e.g., Semantic Web applications, which require different data models.

This chapter illustrates the semiotic intermediate layer with reference to a difficult problem: integrating the notions of a *schema* (Johnson, 1987), a *verb class* (Kipper *et al.*, 2000), and a *frame* (Fillmore *et al.*, 1988) in (cognitive) linguistics and construction grammar, which are at the basis of lexical resources such as the *Metaphor List* (Lakoff, 1994), *FrameNet* (Baker *et al.*, 1998), and *VerbNet* (Kipper *et al.*, 2000), with the formal notions of a *relation representation* (Foerster, 1974), a *frame* (Minsky, 1975; Brachman, 1977), an *intensional relation* (Guarino, 1998a), a *knowledge pattern* (Clark *et al.*, 2000), and a *content ontology design pattern* (Gangemi, 2005) in knowledge representation and ontology design.

I show that Semion, the semiotic façade presented here, is compliant with the intuitive social meaning underlying schemata and frames, while retaining the possibility of mapping them to formal notions, which grants desirable computational properties to lexical resources, specially in order to foster the achievement of a generalized *information integration*, which is a main

---

[5] See http://lirics.loria.fr/doc_pub/ExtendedExamplesOfLexiconsUsingLMF29August05.pdf

[6] Formal semantics is a theory of meaning based on a formal language, and on its interpretation given by assigning a denotation (e.g. a set extension) to each non-logical construct in that language.

[7] In ontology design, a transformation pattern is a formal guideline to transform a model into another (Presutti *et al.*, 2008).

challenge, e.g., for 'Web Science' (Berners-Lee *et al.*, 2006) and the *Linking Open Data* W3C project.[8]

In Section 9.2, the background of cognitive linguistics, schemata, and their ontology is presented. In Section 9.3, the *c.DnS* ontology is introduced and motivated with reference to the metamodelling task for this chapter. In Sections 9.4 and 9.5, the ECG and Semion ontologies are respectively sketched. In Section 9.6, the proposal is complemented with five applications of Semion for the formalization of FrameNet and VerbNet, for the integration of lexical resources, for the representation of schemata, and of schema occurrences as denoted by natural language sentences. In Section 9.7, the main points of the chapter are summarized with respect to ongoing and future work.

9.2   An ontology for cognitive linguistics

A somewhat 'underground' approach in cognitive science, which has been gradually emerging since the late 1980s, stresses the constructive, context-dependent (or situated) and action-oriented nature of cognition. No longer seen as faithful and exhaustive replicas of an 'absolute' reality, the representations with which the mind operates are conceived of as views on the world, emerging from active interaction with the (physical and cultural) environment, and relating only to those aspects which are salient for the perceiver/cognizer (Clark, 1993; Churchland *et al.*, 1994; Gallese and Metzinger, 2003). Focusing on the non-abstract nature of cognition, moreover, has led to a new emphasis on the gestaltic aspects of representations and thought, i.e. the need of taking into account 'the interconnected whole that gives meaning to the parts' (Light and Butterworth, 1992).

In cognitive linguistics, this approach has come to be known as the *embodiment* hypothesis, i.e. the idea that 'the structures used to put together our conceptual systems grow out of bodily experience and make sense in terms of it' (Lakoff, 1987). According to this hypothesis, language understanding and reasoning are carried out by means of basic (both motor and image) schemata and frames, while abstract reasoning is enabled by the use of spatial analogies or metaphors (Lakoff and Johnson, 1980; Lakoff, 1987; Johnson, 1987; Langacker, 1990; Talmy, 2003). Evidence on the use of image schemata such as PATH, SELF-MOTION, CAUSED MOTION, and CONTAINMENT, as soon as in early infancy, comes from developmental and neuropsychological studies (Mandler, 2004). Mathematical characterizations of similarly gestalt-oriented schemata have been proposed in catastrophe-theoretic semantics (Petitot-Cocorda, 1995; Wildgen, 2004). Other work also finds analogies between

---

[8] See http://esw.w3.org/topic/SweoIG/TaskForces/CommunityProjects/LinkingOpenData

schemata and neurobiological theories (Gallese and Lakoff, 2005; Rohrer, 2005). FrameNet implements some general schemata as non-lexical frames (Ruppenhofer *et al.*, 2006b).

While research greatly differs in depth (schemata are usually given as informal primitives) and precision (most approaches lack a formal semantics) across the different disciplines and individual authors, what clearly emerges from that heterogeneous literature is the need to establish some conceptual framework of reference to talk about the different approaches, the phenomena analysed, and the theories proposed.

An example of what that framework might look like is presented here by reusing the *Constructive Descriptions and Situations* ontology (hereafter *c.DnS*) (Gangemi, 2008) to formally represent some core notions introduced by cognitive linguistics and ECG (Chang *et al.*, 2002; Porzel *et al.*, 2006).

c.DnS is a constructivist ontology[9] that represents the aspects of the human cognitive ability to re-contextualize concepts, entities, and observable facts according to current needs. In the field of developmental psychology, this ability has been described in terms of *Representational Redescription*, 'a process by which (implicit) information that is in a cognitive system becomes progressively explicit to that system' (Karmiloff-Smith, 1994), allowing for greater flexibility. *Descriptions* in *c.DnS* are conceived as the social (communicable) counterpart of 'reportable' internal representations in Karmiloff-Smith's cognitive architecture, namely so-called E3 (explicit-3) internal representations.[10] In *c.DnS*, redescription originates from extensive reification, and from the representation of other cognitive processes described, e.g., by Gestalt psychology (Köhler, 1947), which allow us to refer synthetically to some commonly agreed context labels. This mechanism makes *c.DnS* a tool for representing social (hence, non-physical) objects such as information, frames, concepts, collectives, plans, norms, designs, diagnoses, situations, organizations, etc. (see Gangemi, 2008 for a detailed axiomatization).

c.DnS, however, can also be used as a formalism for representing the descriptive, communicable version of so called *schemata* (Johnson, 1987), *mental spaces* (Fauconnier, 1994; Turner, 2007), and *constructions* (Fillmore *et al.*, 1988; Croft, 2001; Feldman, 2006), which are among the fundamental entities that an ECG ontology is supposed to include (Chang *et al.*, 2002). Within *c.DnS*, schemata are the general structures, by which constructions (made up of information objects) are built, and give rise to mental spaces.

---

[9] The first-order logic version of the ontology is presented in Gangemi, 2008; an OWL (W3C, 2004) version of the ontology for application on the Semantic Web can be downloaded from http://ontologydesignpatterns.org/ont/cdns/cdns.owl and http://ontologydesignpatterns.org/ont/cdns/ground.owl

[10] Following the constructivist paradigm, internal representations are called here *internal constructs*.

c.DnS formalizes some foundational principles (relationality, situatedness, interpretability, containment, classification, taxonomy, etc.), and some of them are conceived as direct counterparts of some core cognitive schemata. For example, the containment, classification, and taxonomy principles are counterpart to (or an elaboration of) the CONTAINMENT schema; the relationality and situatedness principles are counterpart to the CONFIGURATION schema, etc. The principles are detailed elsewhere (Gangemi, 2008), and here they are implicitly introduced by means of the projections of the maximal *c.DnS* relation (Section 9.3).

In this chapter, schemata are formalized as kinds of descriptions that have a special place in the organization of conceptual spaces and linguistic constructions.

9.3   The *c.DnS* ontology

The core structure for the *c.DnS* ontology is represented as a relation with arity=8 (see Gangemi, 2008 for an axiomatization):

$$(9.1) \ c.DnS(d, s, c, e, a, k, i, t) \ \rightarrow \ D(d) \wedge S(s) \wedge C(c) \wedge E(e) \wedge \\ A(a) \wedge K(k) \wedge I(i) \wedge T(t)$$

where D is the class of *Descriptions*, S is the class of *Situations*, C is the class of *Concepts*, E is the class of *Entities*, A is the class of *Social Agents*, K is the class of *Collections*, I is the class of *Information Objects*, and T is the class of *Time intervals*.

c.DnS classes are structured as follows: E *is the class of everything that is assumed to exist in some domain of interest, for any possible world*. E is partitioned in the class SE of 'schematic entities', i.e. entities that are axiomatized in *c.DnS* (D, S, C, A, K, I), and the class $\neg SE$ of 'non-schematic entities', which are not characterized in *c.DnS* (T, as well as classes such as those introduced in Section 9.3.1). Schematic entities include concepts, roles, relationships, information, organizations, rules, plans, groups, etc. Examples of non-schematic entities include time intervals, events, physical objects, spatial coordinates, and whatever is not considered as a schematic entity by a modeller.

G is another subclass of E, and includes either schematic or non-schematic entities. Its definition is: *any entity that is described by a description in* *c.DnS*.[11] The formal definition of G will be given in Section 9.3.3.

In intuitive terms, *c.DnS* classes allow us to model how a social agent, as a member of a certain community, singles out a situation at a certain

---

[11] When an entity is *described* in *c.DnS*, it gets a 'unity criterion': a property that makes that entity an individual, distinct from any other one. For example, topological self-connexity, perceptual saliency, and functional role in a system are typical unity criteria.

time, by using information objects that express a descriptive relation that assigns concepts to entities within that situation. In other words, these classes express the constructivist assumption according to which, in order to contextualize entities and concepts, one needs to take into account the viewpoint for which the concept is defined or used, the situation that the viewpoint 'carves out' from the observable environment, the entities that are in the setting of the said situation, the social agents who share the viewpoint, the community of which these agents are members, the information object by which the viewpoint is expressed, and the time-span characterizing the viewpoint.

The key notion in *c.DnS* is *satisfiability* of a description within a situation. Situations (*circumstantial* contexts) select a set of entities and their relations as being relevant from the viewpoint of a description (*conceptual* context). In mainstream terms, a situation is the context in which a set of entities **count as** the concepts in the context of a description. The **countsAs** relation (Searle, 1995), originally defined as holding between an entity, a concept, and a generic context, is then revised in order to allow for two types of contexts, which are orderly paired to entities and concepts. For example, the relation:

$$(9.2) \quad countsAs(John, Student, University)$$

saying that John counts as a student in a university context, can be refined in *c.DnS* as:

$$(9.3) \quad c.DnS([John, JohnAtUniversity], [Student, University Rules])$$

That is that $(John \in E)$ in the circumstantial context of a university $(JohnAtUniversity \in S)$ is a student $(Student \in C)$ according to the conceptual context of the rules of that university $(UniversityRules \in D)$. The other classes in *c.DnS* represent two additional context types: informational and social.

Informational contexts are the ones encompassing the information objects that are used to express descriptions and concepts, for example the sentence

$$(9.4) \quad \text{John goes to the university}$$

in the context of a family conversation about John respecting course duties gets appropriate circumstantial and conceptual contexts, while a context like this résumé of a TV episode in which John is a policeman does not:

(9.5) John goes to the university and while undergoing an MRI, they discover that he has something metallic inside him which is preventing the MRI scan

Social contexts, like communities, groups, etc., are the ones encompassing agents that conceptualize entities. For example, the online community of death metal fans could fit the conceptual context of John as a university student, while a local group of knitted lace shawl makers is far less typical.

9.3.1   Physical Grounding of c.DnS

Some types of entities can be postulated in order to represent the physical grounding (i.e. the physical counterpart) of schematic entities:

$$(9.6)\quad grounded.DnS(d,s,c,e,a,k,i,t,ic,pa,ir,ag) \rightarrow c.DnS$$
$$(d,s,c,e,a,k,i,t) \wedge IC(ic) \wedge PA(pa) \wedge IR(ir) \wedge AG(ag)$$

where IC is the class of *Individual Constructs*, PA is the class of *Physical Agents*, IR is the class of *Information Realizations*, and AG is the class of *Aggregates*.

Intuitively, grounding classes allow us to represent (1) IC, physical and individualized counterparts to descriptions, concepts, or situations, (2) PA, physical counterparts to agents, (3) IR, physical counterparts to information objects, and (4) AG, physical counterparts to collections.

These additional classes ground *c.DnS* in physical reality. In other words, we are enabled to represent the fact that physical agents, as parts of agent aggregates, produce internal constructs of a context, by manipulating concrete realizations of information objects.

The grounding assumption can also be used to encode the embodiment hypothesis, i.e. that conceptualization grows out of bodily experience and reflects it.

On the other hand, grounding is not primary in *c.DnS*, because *c.DnS* assumes that conceptual systems are grown *while* interpreting an environment. Gibson (1979) puts it as a *co-evolutionary system*: 'The affordances of the environment are what it offers the animal, what it provides or furnishes, either for good or ill ... [they imply] the complementarity of the animal and the environment.' In *c.DnS*, a contextualized entity will only be such if experienced in a circumstantial context and interpreted in the conceptual context of an agent. The rationale is that circumstantial contexts emerge because they fit conceptual contexts, but concepts are evolved to appropriately interact with circumstances.[12]

---

[12] Cf. Gangemi, 2008 for a longer discussion; Gibson, 1979 is the natural starting point to these ideas; Gero and Smith, 2007 applies an interactionist approach to embodiment in the context of design; Quine (1951) is the originator of this kind of ontological relativism, and Searle (1995) defends the pragmatic view, by which entities created by cognitive systems are *epistemologically objective*, even if some of them are *ontologically subjective*, and even for those that can be considered *ontologically objective*, from this fact one cannot derive much more than 'they are what they are'.

In *c.DnS*, in order to accommodate different hypotheses (including the embodiment one), we simply need a commitment to whatever entities ($e_{1...n} \in E$) one wants or needs to assume as given, because the identity and unity of given entities is ultimately provided by the way they are situated and conceptualized in context.

To this purpose, the descriptive framework of *c.DnS* provides four context types (conceptual, circumstantial, informational, and social), which are summarized in the class diagram of Figure 9.1, together with the projections of the *grounded.DnS* relation, which are summarized in Section 9.3.3. The co-evolutionary-based interpretation of the embodiment hypothesis also supports validation of schemata. If conceptual systems are artefacts for successful interaction between our bodies and the environment, and environments share invariances, social construction of reality will reflect shared invariances

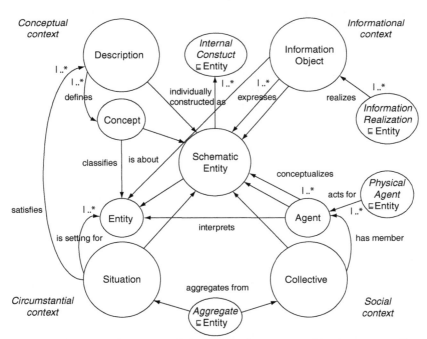

Figure 9.1 The contextual bindings for the representation of a conceptualization in *grounded.DnS* (following the OWL version of the ontology). Ovals denote classes, bold arrows denote subclass relations, regular arrows denote relations holding between members of the linked classes. The cardinality of a relation and its inverse is by default 0...*, except when indicated explicitly. Classes with names in italics are classes of grounded entities

in the conceptual systems of the agents' bodies, which have evolved appropriate ways of interacting with their environment. The quest for invariances in the world (Nozick, 2001) may then be coupled with a quest for conceptual invariances (Lakoff, 1990), which is a way of testing the validity of hypothetical *schemata* that are central in most cognitive linguistic proposals.

The quest for conceptual invariances is not exclusive to cognitive linguistics. Besides the philosophical and mathematical literature, which is naturally devoted to establishing or revising reusable structures that ultimately help us in organizing our knowledge, other areas of research have specifically addressed the task of describing and cataloguing schemata, patterns, frames, etc. as conceptual invariances for many different purposes. These areas of research range from cybernetics and artificial intelligence (Foerster, 1974; Minsky, 1975) and knowledge engineering (Clark *et al.*, 2000; Gangemi, 2005) to architecture and design (Alexander, 1979; Gero and Smith, 2007), linguistics (Fillmore, 1982), and cognitive sciences (Bartlett, 1932; Piaget, 1968; Rumelhart, 1980; Chi *et al.*, 1988; Mandler, 2004; Gallese and Metzinger, 2003).

Devising a common framework for all these heterogeneous approaches to schemata has not been attempted yet, and it is the focus of *c.DnS* metamodelling in Section 9.3.2 and projections (relations) in Section 9.3.3. Strictly speaking, a formal framework for ECG does not need a metamodel that acts as a hub or a *façade* to integrate different schematic notions. On the other hand, a desirable application and validation of ECG may use that framework in a strategic way. Examples include integration of heterogeneous lexical resources, modelling of NLP experiments, customized transformation of informal lexical knowledge into formal ontologies, etc.

A minimal axiomatization for *grounded.DnS* is given in Section 9.3.3, the ECG extension is described in 9.4, the semiotic extension is described in 9.5, and some examples are included in 9.6.

9.3.2   Metamodelling with c.DnS

Within this chapter, the *c.DnS* metamodel is positioned with reference to semiotics, cognitive linguistics, and formal semantics.

9.3.2.1 Semiotics   The expressive power of *c.DnS* lies at the level where semiotic activity of cognitive systems occurs: where agents encode expressions that have a meaning in order to denote or construct reference entities in the world. From this perspective (Peirce, 1958; Jakobson, 1990; Eco, 1975), the *c.DnS* informational context matches the *expression layer*, the circumstantial context matches the *reference layer*, the social context matches the *interpreter layer*, while all contexts together, and especially the conceptual one, match the *meaning* layer.

For example, I can represent statements such as

(9.7) When João says he's rich, he means he has a lot of friends.

which applies both referential and metalinguistic functions (Jakobson, 1990) in the same speech act (Searle, 1969); João is an agent in the social context, and uses contextualized information objects ('rich') that have a contextualized meaning ('having a lot of friends') and contextualized circumstances (João's linguistic act and his situation of having a lot of friends). This is the case for most linguistic acts that are implicit in lexica, thesauri, explanatory texts, web tags, etc. I will examine semiotic matching in Section 9.5.

When leveraging semiotics, *c.DnS* can be used to align and integrate models that have heterogeneous semantics and (implicitly) encode different linguistic acts, e.g. different lexical models: WordNet (Fellbaum, 1998), FrameNet (Ruppenhofer *et al.*, 2006b), VerbNet (Kipper *et al.*, 2000); different theories of meaning: frame semantics (Fillmore, 1982), semiotic theory (e.g. Eco, 1975), formal languages such as OWL (W3C, 2004); different texts: explanatory, metalinguistic; tagging (e.g. in Web2.0 applications (Gruber, 2007)) vs. topic assignment (e.g. in subject hierarchies (Welty, 1999)), etc.

A collection of examples for this integration task is collected under the LMM (Lexical MetaModel) umbrella[13] (Picca *et al.*, 2008), as a formal infrastructure for 'extreme information integration' over the Web.[14] Here I only show two examples that are relevant for this chapter: (1) integration of the FrameNet database schema under *c.DnS*, with a sample formalization of frames and their occurrences as *c.DnS* descriptions, and (2) integration of ECG framework under *grounded.DnS*.

9.3.2.2 Cognitive linguistics   From the point of view of cognitive linguistics, the basic intuition of *grounded.DnS* can be rephrased as follows: descriptions can be seen as corresponding to (the communicable version of) schemata, situations as corresponding to applied schemata (occurrences of schemata in the interaction between agents and environment), concepts as corresponding to aspects of schemata, and entities as corresponding to applied aspects of schemata (occurrences of aspects of schemata in the interaction between agents and environment, see Section 9.4).

For example, the FrameNet frame 'Desiring' can be formalized as a description, the frame element 'Event' can be formalized as a concept, an occurrence

---

[13] See http://ontologydesignpatterns.org/ont/lmm/opensourcex2lmm.owl
[14] Extreme information integration aims at creating knowledge bases from any information source, in a way that makes them interoperable.

of the frame in a real agent desiring some event, e.g. expressed by the sentence

(9.8) Susan really wishes that Marko would listen to her

can be formalized as a situation, and the desired event, e.g. expressed by the sentence

(9.9) Marko is listening to Susan

can be formalized as an entity (see Section 9.6).

9.3.2.3 Formal semantics From a formal perspective, the basic intuition of *c.DnS* can be interpreted in the context of a procedure of logical reification:[15] a *description* can be understood as the reification of (1) $\rho \in T$, with ρ being an intensional relation of any arity, either mono- or polymorphic, and T being an ontology (a typed logical theory), and (2) the axioms $\alpha_{1...n}$ that characterize ρ (i.e. the sub-theory $T_\rho \subseteq T$ with $\alpha_{1...n} \in T_\rho$).

On the other hand, *situations* result from reifications of (1) each of the individuals $r_{1...n} \in R^I$, R^I being the extensional intepretation of ρ, and of (2) the assertions $a_{1...n}$ that characterize r_i in accordance with the extensional interpretation of the axioms $\alpha_{1...n} \in T_\rho$. A *situation class* is consequently the reification of the set $\{r_1, ..., r_n\}$ where $r_i \in R^I$.[16]

c.DnS is able to formally represent the entire FrameNet knowledge base. This is ensured by the assumption that frames, schemata from cognitive linguistics, patterns from knowledge engineering, etc. can all be considered as n-ary relations, with typed arguments (either mandatory or optional), qualified cardinalities, etc. For example,

(9.10) $Desiring(x, y, e) \rightarrow Agent(x) \wedge Agent(y) \wedge Event(e)$

An occurrence of a frame is straightforwardly treated as an instance of an n-ary relation, e.g.:

(9.11) $Desiring(Susan, Marko, ListeningToHer)$

The logical representation of frames as n-ary intensional relations is elegant and clear, but hardly manageable by automated reasoners on large knowledge bases. A difficult design problem is constituted by the polymorphism of many n-ary relations, which can vary in the number of the arguments that can be

---

[15] See also Masolo *et al.*, 2004 for an alternative, but compatible axiomatization of a part of *c.DnS*.

[16] Notice that *reification* is used here in two different senses, as pinpointed in Galton, 1995: *type-reification* of classes to individuals, metaclasses to classes, etc., versus *token-reification* of tuples to individuals, sets of tuples to classes, etc.

taken by the relation. For example, the same frame Desiring can be assumed with four arguments:

$$(9.12) \quad Desiring(x, y, e, t) \rightarrow Agent(x) \wedge Agent(y) \wedge Event(e) \wedge$$
$$Time(t)$$

This problem was originally evidenced by Davidson with reference to a logic of events (Davidson, 1967b).

A formal semantics for frames that is also computationally manageable has been provided by description logics (Baader *et al.*, 2003). Due to their limited expressive power – e.g. they can only represent relations with arity=2 – that is balanced by desirable computational complexity properties, description logics represent frames as classes, with *roles* (binary relations) that link a class to the types of the arguments of the original n-ary relation. Those types are classes as well, so that a graph of frames emerges out of this semantics. The example in 9.12 can be re-engineered in DL as follows:

$$(9.13) \quad T \sqsubseteq \forall R_1.Agent, \ T \sqsubseteq \forall R_1^-.Desiring$$

$$(9.14) \quad T \sqsubseteq \forall R_2.Agent, \ T \sqsubseteq \forall R_2^-.Desiring$$

$$(9.15) \quad T \sqsubseteq \forall R_3.Event, \ T \sqsubseteq \forall R_3^-.Desiring$$

$$(9.16) \quad T \sqsubseteq \forall R_4.Time, \ T \sqsubseteq \forall R_4^-.Desiring$$

$$(9.17) \quad Desiring \sqsubseteq (=1R_1 \sqcap \ =1R_2 \sqcap \ =1R_3 \sqcap \ =1R_4)$$

The computational features of description logics make them a reasonable choice to formally represent linguistic frames, and this is the approach adopted in Chapter 4 of this book. On the other hand, even the description-logic solution hits the ceiling of formalizing the metalevel conceptualization of frames and schemata. For example, the intended semantics of FrameNet relations between frames, between frame elements, and between frames and frame elements, lexical units, and lexemes is hardly representable in a description logic.

Frames can be subframes of others, can have multiple linguistic units that realize them, multiple lexemes that lexicalize those units, can have frame elements that are core or peripheral, words can evoke frames, etc. Logically speaking, these are second-order relations, and cannot be rebuilt into regular description-logic semantics, which is basically first order. However, recent advancements in higher-order description logics (De Giacomo *et al.*, 2008) are very promising in order to represent the full range of frame-related relations. See also Section 9.6.1.

The ontology outlined here makes use of a stratified approach that takes advantage of the reified higher-order expressivity of *c.DnS*. The ontology is represented in both first-order logic and OWL-DL (Bechhofer *et al.*, 2004), the Web Ontology Language in its description logic variety.[17] Reification does not allow the same detail of representation and automated reasoning functionalities as the one enabled by a real higher-order logic, but the resulting 'signature' (the intensional classes and relations of a theory) can still be applied within an actual higher-order theory. Future work includes applying the *c.DnS* vocabulary to a higher-order description logic (De Giacomo *et al.*, 2008).

9.3.3   *Projections of the grounded.DnS Relation*

Some relevant projections of the *c.DnS* and *grounded.cDnS* relations can be defined as binary or ternary relations and axioms. Here I list, informally, the ones that I deem necessary in order to introduce a metamodel for the lexicon–ontology interface, and its application to frames and ECG. For a more complete axiomatization, and technical details on how *c.DnS* is applied in domain ontology projects, I refer to Gangemi, 2008.

The following is the signature of the projections:

$$(9.18) \quad \Pi_{g.cdns} = \{defines, usesConcept, satisfies, classifies,$$
$$about, describes, conceptualizes, redescribes,$$
$$expresses, memberOf, isSettingFor, deputes,$$
$$instantiates, covers, characterizes, unifies,$$
$$hasInScope, specializes, assumes, aggregates$$
$$From, individuallyConstructedAs, actsFor,$$
$$constructs, realizes, \}$$

The rationale for the introduction of projections is such that each projection implies the full *grounded.DnS* relation, according to the axiom schema in 9.19.

$$(9.19) \quad \pi(x_1 \ldots x_{n \geq 2} \mid x_i \in \{d, s, c, e, a, k, i, t, ic, pa, ir, ag\}) \rightarrow$$
$$grounded.DnS(d, s, c, e, a, k, i, t, , ic, pa, ir, ag)$$

Descriptions are schematic entities that reify (the intension of) n-ary relations; for example, the *give(x,y,z,t)* relation (some *x* gives some *y* to some *z* at time *t*) can be reified as *D(giving)*. The axioms of the original relation, e.g. domain restrictions, are reified accordingly, by using the *defines* or *usesConcept* relations. For example,

$$(9.20) \quad defines(giving, donor)$$

$$(9.21) \quad usesConcept(giving, timespan)$$

---

[17] The OWL-DL ontologies presented here can be downloaded from: http://ontology designpatterns.org/ont/cdns/index.html

In *c.DnS*, descriptions must be *conceptualizedBy* social agents, *internallyConstructedBy* some physical agent, and *expressedBy* some information object, i.e. they should be communicable (Masolo *et al.*, 2004). Examples of descriptions include theories, regulations, plans, diagnoses, projects, designs, techniques, social practices, etc. Descriptions can unify collections, and describe entities. For example,

(9.22) *unifies(giving, /donor collection/)*

(9.23) *describes(giving, /my recent birthday gift/, t_1)*

Descriptions, as any schematic entity, can be *specialized* (the reification of the formal subsumption relation) and *instantiated* (the reification of the formal inclusion relation) by other descriptions.

Situations are schematic entities that reify instances of n-ary relations; for example, the relationship implicit in the sentence

(9.24) Ali gave a puppet to Amélie on Sunday

can be formalized as

(9.25) *give(Ali, puppet, Amelie, Sunday)*

and can be reified as

(9.26) *S(/Ali gave a puppet to Amelie on Sunday/)*

Similar to conceptual axioms for descriptions, the assertional axioms for situations need also to be reified accordingly, typically as elementary situations that are part of the complete situation, e.g., if the assertional relation axiom *receives(Amelie, puppet)* is reified as the assertional class axiom *S(/Amelie receives a puppet/)*, the following holds:

(9.27) *hasPart(/Ali gave a puppet to Amelie on Sunday/, /Amelie receives a puppet/)*

In *c.DnS*, situations must *satisfy* a description and are *settingsFor* entities, e.g.:

(9.28) *satisfies(/Ali gave a puppet to Amelie on Sunday/, giving)*

(9.29) *settingFor(/Ali gave a puppet to Amelie on Sunday/, Ali)*

Examples of situations include facts, plan executions, legal cases, diagnostic cases, attempted projects, technical actions. Situations can *haveInScope* other situations. Situation classes project n-ary relation extensions into class extensions. For example, the *give(x,y,z,t)* relation can be projected as the situation class $Giving \subseteq S$, so that the following holds:

(9.30) *Giving(/Ali gave a puppet to Amelie on Sunday/)*

Concepts are schematic entities that reify (the intension of) classes; for example, the $Person(x)$ class can be reified as $C(person)$. Concepts are *defined* or *used* in descriptions, for example in order to reify the domains of n-ary relations. The axiom

(9.31) $give(x, y, z, t) \rightarrow person(x)$

can be reified as

(9.32) $D(giving)$
$\quad\quad C(person)$
$\quad\quad defines(giving, person)$

Concepts typically *classify* entities, e.g.

(9.33) $classifies(person, Ali)$

and can *cover* or *characterize* collections, e.g.

(9.34) $covers(person, personCollection)$

(9.35) $characterizes(person, Italians)$

Collections are schematic entities that reify the extension of classes; for example, the $\{x_1 \ldots x_n\}$ extension of class *Person* can be reified as $K(personCollection)$, so that

(9.36) $\forall(x)(Person(x) \rightarrow (memberOf(x, personCollection, t_1)))$

Collections are *coveredBy* or *characterizedBy* concepts, and can have members, e.g.

(9.37) $memberOf(Ali, personCollection, t_1)$

Collections capture the common-sense intuition underlying groups, teams, collections, collectives, associations, etc.

Social agents are schematic entities that personify other entities within the social realm: corporations, institutions, organizations, social relata of natural persons. For example, the natural person *Ali* can be personified as *A(AliAsLegalPerson)*. Social agents must be *introducedBy* descriptions, for example by legal constitutive rules (Searle, 1995); social agents are also able to *conceptualize* descriptions, to *redescribe* situations, and to *depute* concepts.

Information objects are schematic entities that 'naturalize' units of information: the character Q, the German word *Sturm*, the symbol $\otimes$, the text of *Dante's Comedy*, the image of *Francis Bacon's Study from Innocent X*, etc. Information objects *express* a schematic entity ($se \in SE$): a description, a concept, a situation, a collection, another information object, or even a social agent. For example, *expresses(Sturm,Storm)*. Information objects can also be *about* other entities, typically situations; for example,

(9.38)   *about('Ali gave a puppet to Amelie on Sunday', / Ali gave a puppet to Amelie on Sunday/)*

Internal constructs are non-schematic entities, assumed to be grounded in the physical world, which are *individualConstructionsOf* schematic entities, and in particular of descriptions and concepts. For example, Ali's embodied knowledge of the Ulysses Canto XXVI from the Comedy is an individual construct ($ic \in IC$) of an intended meaning ($se \in SE$) of the Canto, as expressed by the Canto's text ($i \in I$).

Physical agents are non-schematic entities, assumed to be grounded in the physical world, which *act for* social agents: organisms, robots, etc. For example, the physical agent $Ali \in PA$ can act for Ali as a legal person ($\in A$):

(9.39)   *actsFor(Ali, AliAsLegalPerson, t_1)*

Physical agents can *construct* internal constructions.

Information realizations are non-schematic entities, assumed to be grounded in the physical world, which *realize* information objects. For example,

(9.40)   *realizes(ComedyPaperCopy, ComedyText, t_1)*

Aggregates are entities (grounded or not, or mixed) which have as parts entities from either collections or situations. An aggregate *aggregates* those entities *from* their being members of a collection. For example,

(9.41)   *aggregatesFrom(personAggregate, personCollection, t_1)*
$\leftarrow$ *(Person(x)* $\leftrightarrow$ *(memberOf(x, personCollection)* $\leftrightarrow$
hasPart(personAggregate, x))

Based on these projections, axiom 9.43 formalizes the *grounded construction principle* underlying the intuition of the grounded version of *c.DnS*. Axiom 9.43 is quite complex; it expands the basic idea of an entity that is given a unity criterion by being *described* by a description, as encoded in the simple axiom 9.42.

(9.42) $G(x) \leftrightarrow E(x) \wedge \exists(y, t)(D(y) \wedge describes(y, x, t))$

(9.43) $G(x) \leftrightarrow \exists(d, s, c, a, k, i, t, c_1, pa, ir, ic, ag, d_1, s_1, t_1)(D(d) \wedge$
$S(s) \wedge C(c) \wedge A(a) \wedge I(i) \wedge K(kc) \wedge T(t) \wedge C(c_1) \wedge$
$PA(pa) \wedge IR(ir) \wedge IC(ic) \wedge D(d_1) \wedge S(s_1) \wedge T(t_1) \wedge$
$classifies(c, x, t) \wedge isSettingFor(s, x) \wedge defines(d, c) \wedge$
$satisfies(s, d) \wedge conceptualizes(a, d, t) \wedge unifies(d, kc) \wedge$
$constructs(pa, ic, t) \wedge individuallyConstructedAs(d, ic, t) \wedge$
$memberOf(a, kc, t) \wedge deputes(a, c_1, t) \wedge classifies(c_1, pa, t) \wedge$
$expresses(i, d, t) \wedge actsFor(pa, a, t) \wedge realizes(ir, i, t) \wedge$
$aggregatesFrom(ag, kc, t) \wedge hasPart(ag, pa, t) \wedge settingFor$
$(s, t) \wedge settingFor(s, pa) \wedge redescribes(a, s, t_1) \wedge settingFor$
$(s_1, pa) \wedge settingFor(s_1, ir) \wedge settingFor(s_1, ic) \wedge$
$conceptualizes(a, d_1, t_1) \wedge describes(d_1, d, t_1) \wedge satisfies$
$(s_1, d_1) \wedge hasInScope(s_1, s))$

Axiom 9.43 verbosely says that any ground entity x (i.e. an entity whose identity and unity are given through the interpretation of a situation, in which it is contextualized) entails the activation of a complex pattern of associations within a physical agent situated in a knowledge community:

- x is always classified at some time by at least one concept that is defined in a description, which results to describe x;
- x is always contextualized in a situation that satisfies the description;
- both the description and the situation of x are conceptualized by a social agent that is a member of a community whose members share some knowledge;
- the description is expressed by an information object that is realized by some information realization;
- the social agent that conceptualizes x's description redescribes x's situation by means of describing the description itself into another description. This is equivalent to having x's situation in the scope of the redescription situation; in practice, this means that the agent has some intention to describe x in a context, with some expectations, assumptions, goals, etc.;
- the social agent is acted for by at least one physical agent that is capable of constructing internal constructs for the schematic entities mentioned so far;
- the agent's community that shares the knowledge about x has a corresponding aggregate at some time, made up of physical agents;
- 'knowledge' in c.DnS is the set of schematic entities that are (partly or wholly) shared by a community, and (partly or wholly) individually constructed in the cognitive systems of the physical agents that are members of that community. For example, for an expert, having expertise (say practical knowledge) on something is represented as having the ability to apply internal constructs of descriptions to internal constructs of situations with (internal constructs of) some informational and social contexts. The degree

to which such internal constructs can be used to observe, reason, and efficiently act in context distinguishes agent capabilities in a community.

The pattern axiomatized in 9.43 is very general, and can be applied to many disparate phenomena: linguistic acts, planning, diagnosing, designing, etc. In this chapter, I am interested in how *c.DnS* can be used to create a façade for different lexical models.

9.4   Schemata, mental spaces, and constructions

An ECG ontology should include *schemata*, *mental spaces*, and *constructions* (Chang *et al.*, 2002) in its domain. The distinction holds, e.g., when comparing the term 'Alice in Wonderland' (a construction), the conceptualization (a mental space) that can be evoked by the term, and the frame (a schema) underlying the mental space, e.g. a frame for conceptualizing action in imaginary locations.

Within *c.DnS*, ECG primitives must be considered from both an individual and a social perspective, because internal constructs are individually constructed as dependent not only on internal and external sensory systems of a cognitive agent (Karmiloff-Smith, 1994), but also on distributed, collective knowledge. In turn, collective knowledge is said to be dependent on individual internal constructs (Section 9.3.3). I will then postulate both individual and collective (public, or at least reportable) versions of constructions, mental spaces, and schemata.

Following the RR framework proposed by Karmiloff-Smith, I assume four levels at which knowledge is present (and re-presented) with different degrees of explicitness and detail: Implicit (I), Explicit-1 (E1), Explicit-2 (E2), and Explicit-3 (E3). At level I, information is encoded in a procedural form, it has no component parts and, as a consequence, no intra- or inter-domain links within the system. At level E1, on the contrary, knowledge results from redescription of the information encoded at level I: it has component parts and possibly representational links; however, they are not yet available to conscious access and linguistic (semiotic) report. At level E2, it is hypothesized that representations gain conscious access and functionality, but still lack reportability. The latter obtains only at level E3, where representations are stored in a communicable format, e.g. akin to natural languages (Karmiloff-Smith, 1994).

Based on this assumption, schemata, mental spaces, and constructions should be present at various levels in the human cognitive system, i.e.:

1. as instances of neural activation patterns (event-like entities $n_{1...n} \in NE \subseteq E$) in (specific areas of) the perceptual or motor systems (level I knowledge). This is knowledge that is typically learnt from motor routines, or

inductively when an agent is exposed to a critical mass of inputs that contain invariances against transformations (Nozick, 2001), and constitute *affordances* for the agent's behaviour (Gibson, 1979). Examples include sound constructions, reactive mental spaces, motor schemata. An ontology specific for this level is proposed in Gallese and Metzinger, 2003;

2. as instances of functional internal constructs ($f_{1...n} \in FE {\subseteq} IC$), including both conscious and non-conscious non-semiotic formats, i.e. level E1 and E2 knowledge. Examples include phonetic constructions, non-mappable mental spaces, image schemata;

3. as instances of reportable entities ($r_{1...n} \in RE \subseteq SE$), including reportable formats, i.e. level E3 knowledge.[18] Examples include lexical constructs ($co_{1...n} \in I$), mappable (and reportable) mental spaces, and blendings (Turner, 2007) ($ms_{1...n} \in SE$), as well as reportable schemata ($sc_{1...n} \in D$).

A schema can then be represented: as an instance of a neural schema in the perceptual or motor system at level I,

(9.44) $NeuralSchema \subseteq NE$

as an instance of a functional schema at levels E1 or E2,

(9.45) $FunctionalSchema \subseteq FE$

or as an instance of a reportable schema at level E3,

(9.46) $ReportableSchema \subseteq (D \cap RE)$

A reportable schema is a description that is individually constructed as a functional schema and allows the primary organization of public (expressible) conceptualizations into social knowledge. The dependency of reportable on functional schemata, which in turn depend on neural schemata, is then a hypothesis for the grounding of intersubjective knowledge into invariances across the neural circuits of physical agents.

Similarly, a mental space can be represented as an instance of a neural space,

(9.47) $NeuralSpace \subseteq NE$

as an instance of a functional space,

(9.48) $FunctionalSchema \subseteq FE$

---

[18] The use of *knowledge* for E3 entities corresponds to the one defined in Section 9.3.3, as the set of schematic entities and their relations, which are available to a community. On the contrary, embodied knowledge in levels I and E1–2 is the grounding counterpart to schematic knowledge.

or as an instance of a reportable space,

(9.49) $ReportableSchema \subseteq RE$

A functional schema is probably akin to a 'perceptual symbol' (Barsalou, 1999). In this framework, a functional schema allows the primary organization of external, kinaesthetic and internal sensory data into efficient (affordance-oriented) internal constructs (Viezzer and Nieuwenhuis, 2005).

Finally, a construction can be represented as an instance of a neural construction,

(9.50) $NeuralConstruction \subseteq NE$

as an instance of a functional construction,

(9.51) $FunctionalConstruction \subseteq FE$

or as an instance of a reportable construction,

(9.52) $ReportableConstruction \subseteq (I \cap RE)$

A bipartite graph is obtained which is summarized in the diagram from Figure 9.2, where constructions *evoke* (in different senses according to the level) mental spaces, which are *structuredBy* schemata. The combination of three types of entities (Constructions, Mental Spaces, Schemata), and three levels (Neural, Functional, Reportable) produce nine classes, which constitute a proposal for an ECG ontology of *individual* knowledge. *Evoking* relations associate Constructions with Mental Spaces, e.g.

(9.53) $evokes\_r(x, y, t) \rightarrow ReportableConstruction(x) \land$ $ReportableMentalSpace(y) \land TimeInterval(t)$

(9.54) $ReportableConstruction(x) \rightarrow \exists(y, t)(evokes\_r(x, y, t))$

The *evokes_r* relation (but not the other evoking relations) is a subrelation of *expresses*:

(9.55) $evokes\_r(x, y, t) \rightarrow expresses(x, y, t)$

Reportable constructions get their intuition from the fact that they must be reportable, i.e. *realizedBy* some information realization, as it holds for all information objects, according to the grounded construction principle. This realization can be public: sounds, bytes, gestures, ink traces, etc., but at the individual level there is at least one realization as a functional construction, emerging in its turn from a neural construction (see axiom 9.59). A related assumption, i.e. that public and individual realizations of reportable constructions have a common counterpart, is critical, since it founds the possibility

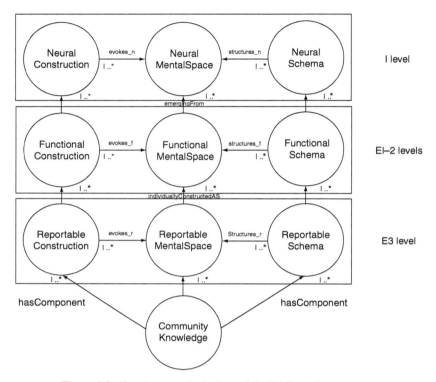

Figure 9.2 The classes and relations of the ECG ontology

of *shared meaning* across the agent members of a community. The assumption can be strong or weak depending on what degree of correspondance is assumed between functional and reportable constructions. Here I do not take any position about this.

Structuring relations associate Schemata with Mental Spaces, e.g.

(9.56) $structures\_r(x, y, t) \rightarrow ReportableSchema(x) \wedge$
$ReportableMentalSpace(y) \wedge TimeInterval(t)$

(9.57) $ReportableMentalSpace(y) \rightarrow \exists(x, t)(structures\_r(x, y, t))$

Structuring implies that all situations that satisfy a mental space, must also satisfy the structuring schema (the following example is for structuring applied to reportable spaces only):

(9.58) $structures\_r(x, y, t) \rightarrow \forall(s)(satisfies(s, y) \rightarrow satisfies(s, x))$

The axioms 9.56 and 9.58 about the structuring role of schemata over mental spaces, together with axiom 9.53 about the grounding of reportable constructions into functional constructions, make formally explicit the embodiment and cognitive invariance hypotheses: mental spaces can be communized because reportable constructions leverage schematic invariances.

The Reportable level is *individually constructed* at the Functional level; the relation is locally axiomatized, e.g. as follows:

(9.59) $ReportableConstruction(x) \rightarrow \exists(y,t)(Functional$
$Construction(y) \wedge individuallyConstructedAs(x,y,t))$

The Functional level *emerges* out of the Neural level, e.g.

(9.60) $emergingFrom(x,y,t) \rightarrow FunctionalConstruction(x) \wedge$
$NeuralConstruction(y) \wedge TimeInterval(t)$

(9.61) $FunctionalConstruction(x) \rightarrow \exists(y,t)(Neural$
$Construction(y) \wedge emergingFrom(x,y,t))$

The relation *emergingFrom* does not imply identity: functional entities at levels E1 and E2 are different (in format, hence in use and in underlying neural patterns) from the original I-level ones. However, evidence from neurophysiological and neuropsychological studies suggests that higher-order representations (e.g. recalled images) involve complex neural circuits, in which patterns located in the so-called association cortices 'recruit' other neural patterns from the early sensory cortices (Edelman, 1989; Damasio, 1994). Moreover, damage in the areas where non-verbal knowledge is stored causes drastic alteration of reasoning and linguistic performance (Bisiach, 1988). What emergence does imply, thus, is the necessary co-participation of a lower-level neural entity into the activation of a higher-order, constructed one.

Anyway, emergence of internal constructs from level I neural entities is far less clear in current research. (Gallese and Metzinger, 2003), based on empirical evidence from mirror neurons research results, is an interesting proposal for a *motor ontology* that is specific to nervous systems in creating embodied goals, actions, and 'intentional selves'. The authors also envision a theory of how such motor ontology could be gradually extended into the subjective and social domains.

Finally, simple componency relations associate individual knowledge with community knowledge, which results in a whole composed of some reportable entities (individual knowledge):

(9.62) $CommunityKnowledge(x) \rightarrow \exists(y_1,y_2,t,a_1,a_2)$
$(RE(y_1) \wedge RE(y_2) \wedge y_1 \neq y_2 \wedge A(a_1) \wedge A(a_2) \wedge a_1 \neq a_2 \wedge$
$conceptualizes(a_1,y_1) \wedge conceptualizes(a_2,y_2) \wedge$
$hasProperPart(x,y_1,t) \wedge hasProperPart(x,y_2,t))$

While reportable entities (RE) are dependent on functional and neural entities (FE, NE), coherently with the co-evolutionary assumption (cf. Section 9.3.2), there is a converse dependency of functional and neural entities on reportable entities too, because neural entities co-evolve with reportable entities, which, as schematic entities, are socially constructed. This converse dependency is in agreement with constructivist, socio-historical theories of cognitive development (Vigotsky, 1962) and with recent data on the role played by social interaction on the development of cognitive and linguistic skills (Tomasello, 2003).

9.5   An embodied semiotic metamodel

This section introduces *Semion*, an ontology that represents a semiotic pattern that dates back at least to Peirce (1958) and Saussure (1906), and adapts it to *c.DnS* and the ECG ontology.

Peirce used a peculiar terminology, and the versioning of his theory is not trivial. Semion encodes a pattern that basically conveys his mainstream ideas: meaning as a role, indirectness of reference, and the dialogic nature of thinking. These ideas have slowly found their way into the literature, and can be formalized by using *c.DnS* as a backbone.

Expressions are information objects used to express a meaning in context at some time. *c.DnS* has contextualization as a primitive assumption in the grounded construction principle, therefore each extension of it assumes a multifaceted contextualization as depicted in Figure 9.1. The Expression class (which Peirce called 'representamen', and Saussure 'signifiant') is minimally axiomatized by assuming that an expression is an information object that expresses some schematic entity at some time, and is about some entity at that time:

$$(9.63) \quad Exp(e) =_{df} ReportableConstruction(i) \land \exists(se, x, t)(SE$$
$$(se) \land expresses(e, se, t) \land E(x) \land T(t) \land isAbout(e, x, t))$$

Meanings are schematic entities that are expressed by an expression in context at some time. The Meaning class (which Peirce called 'interpretant', and Saussure 'signifié') is minimally axiomatized by assuming that a meaning is a schematic entity that is expressed by some information object at some time, and allows the interpretation of some entity at that time:

$$(9.64) \quad Mea(m) =_{df} SE(m) \land \exists(i, e, t)(I(i) \land expresses(i, m, t) \land$$
$$E(e) \land T(t) \land interpretedAs(e, m, t))$$

References are entities that an expression is about at some time. The Reference class (which Peirce called 'object') is minimally axiomatized by assuming that a reference is an entity that an information object is about at some time, and which is interpreted according to a schematic entity at that time:

$$(9.65) \quad Ref(r) =_{df} E(r) \wedge \exists(i, se, t)(I(i) \wedge isAbout(i, r, t) \wedge \\ SE(se) \wedge T(t) \wedge interpretedAs(r, se, t))$$

Interpreters are agents that conceptualize a meaning at some time in an ideal dialogic context with other agents. The Interpreter class is axiomatized by assuming that an interpreter is a physical or social agent, which conceptualizes a schematic entity in the context of a situation at some time, which also involves another agent:

$$(9.66) \quad Int(a) =_{df} (A(a) \vee PA(a)) \wedge \exists(se, s, t, a_1)(SE(se) \wedge \\ conceptualizes(a, se, t) \wedge S(s) \wedge T(t) \wedge settingFor(s, a) \wedge \\ settingFor(s, se) \wedge settingFor(s, t) \wedge A(a_1) \wedge settingFor \\ (s, a_1))$$

The situation of an interpreter conceptualizing a meaning evoked by an expression, in a context involving another interpreter conceptualizing the same expression, is called here *linguistic act (LingAct)*. It is related to the notion of *speech act* from Searle, 1969, and to the notion of *social act* from Reinach, 1983 and Smith, 1990. Linguistic acts are implicit in the grounded construction principle, where the interpretive activity of an agent generates two situations: the observable one and the linguistic one, which includes the agent in the loop (cf. Section 9.3.3). The *LingAct* class is axiomatized by assuming that a linguistic act is a situation, in which two agents conceptualize two meanings for a same expression at two given time spans, and refers to two entities (the two agents, meanings, time spans and entities respectively are not necessarily different).[19] Before introducing the class of linguistic acts, the maximal Semion relation is shown, which leverages the grounded construction principle and the previous definitions:

$$(9.67) \quad semion(a, e, m, r, l, t, a_1, m_1, r_1, t_1) =_{df} (Int(a) \wedge Exp(e) \wedge \\ Mea(m) \wedge Ref(r) \wedge S(l) \wedge T(t) \wedge A(a_1) \wedge Mea(m_1) \wedge T(t_1) \wedge \\ Ref(r_1) \wedge conceptualizes(a, m, t) \wedge expresses(e, m, t) \wedge \\ interpretedAs(r, m, t) \wedge conceptualizes(a_1, m_1, t_1) \wedge \\ isAbout(e, r, t) \wedge expresses(e, m_1, t_1) \wedge isAbout(e, r_1, t_1) \wedge \\ settingFor(l, a) \wedge settingFor(l, a_1) \wedge settingFor(l, t) \wedge \\ settingFor(l, t_1) \wedge settingFor(l, m) \wedge settingFor(l, m_1) \wedge \\ settingFor(l, r) \wedge settingFor(l, r_1) \wedge settingFor(l, e))$$

---

[19] In the dialogic view of semiotics, even an interpreter alone has an 'internal conversation'.

An instance of the Semion relation is an occurrence of the semiotic pattern in a community of agents that share some common knowledge.

Since schematic entities in *c.DnS* have individual counterparts in the ECG ontology ($RE \subseteq SE$), and communized knowledge is made up of reportable entities (axiom 9.62), Semion acquires an embodied grounding by formally associating meanings with reportable entities (axiom 9.68).

$$(9.68) \quad semion(a, e, m, r, l, t, a_1) \rightarrow \exists(re)(RE(re) \wedge m = re)$$

Now, the *LingAct* class is introduced directly by assuming the Semion relation:

$$(9.69) \quad LingAct(l) =_{df} S(l) \wedge \exists(a, e, m, r, t, a_1, m_1, r_1, t_1)(semion$$
$$(a, e, m, r, l, t, a_1, m_1, r_1, t_1))$$

The Semion approach is pragmatic, in the spirit of Peirce's: a meaning can be *any* schematic entity, including expressions, concepts, descriptions, collections, or situations. Therefore, any linguistic act is easily representable by specializing the axiom 9.64. For example, the act performed by lexicographers, by which expressions have other expressions as their meanings, specializes ($Mea \subseteq SE$) as $Mea \subseteq I$. Cognitive theories of meaning, which defend the individual dimension of meaning, can be represented by specializing the axiom 9.64 as $Mea \subseteq RE$. Frame semantics (Section 9.6.1) can be represented by specializing 9.64 as $Mea \subseteq (D \cap ReportableSchema)$. Extensional formal semantics can be represented by specializing axiom 9.64 as $Mea \subseteq K$, etc.

Moreover, indirectness of reference can be defended or not in some theory of meaning, but in Semion, any such theory can be represented: if some form of conceptualism is taken, the **isAbout** relation can be used with a dependence on a meaning as a mediator; in some form of referentialism, it can be applied directly.

Semion-based models, as exemplified in Section 9.6.1, can be transformed into (formal) ontologies by applying a transformation pattern. Since *c.DnS* leverages logical reification, its de-reification is already a transformation pattern; whenever a customization is needed, different patterns can be defined and applied, and the formal choices made are then explicitly represented. See Section 9.6.3 for an example.

Since any kind of linguistic act (e.g., explanatory text, lexicographic metalanguage, document tagging or indexing, etc.) can be represented as an instantiation of the *LingAct* class, the coverage of Semion is very broad, and ready to apply within an extreme information integration task, for example over the Semantic Web by using its OWL version.[20]

---

[20] See www.ontologydesignpatterns.org/ont/cdns/semion.owl

9.6   Applying Semion to FrameNet and related resources

In this section, I exemplify the application of Semion to FrameNet. Section 9.6.1 describes a part of the FrameNet metamodel based on Semion, and how it allows us to create a formal version of FrameNet, called OntoFrameNet. In Section 9.6.2 the same procedure is applied to VerbNet. In Section 9.6.3 Semion is applied to mapping and transformation examples. In Section 9.6.4 some examples from schematic and non-schematic containment-oriented frames are modelled. In Section 9.6.5 a grounding example is given by providing a model of a situation that satisfies the said frames.

9.6.1   OntoFrameNet

FrameNet is a lexical knowledge base, which consists of a set of *frames*, which have proper *frame elements* and *lexical units*, expressed by *lexemes*. Frame elements are unique to their frame, and can be optional. An occurrence of a frame consists in some piece of text whose words can be normalized as lexemes from a lexical unit of a frame, and which have semantic roles dictated by the elements of that frame. A frame can occur with all its roles filled or not. Frames can be *lexicalized* or not. The non-lexicalized ones typically encode *schemata* from cognitive linguistics. Frames, as well as frame elements, are related between them, e.g. through the **subframe** relation. FrameNet contains more information, related to parts of speech, *semantic types* assigned to frames, elements, and lexical units, and other metadata.

A complete re-engineering of FrameNet (version 1.2) as a *c.DnS* plugin can be found in the OWL version of OntoFrameNet.[21] Another OWL version is presented in Chapter 4 of this book, which translates the first-order fragment of FrameNet 1.3 into an OWL TBox (the conceptual part of an ontology).

A critical difference between the two is that in the first-order translation neither the inter-frame and inter-frame-element relations can be formalized, nor the relations between lexemes and lexical units, lexical units and frames, word and frames, etc. In exchange, the full automated reasoning power implemented for description logics can be used. On the contrary, OntoFrameNet is based on *c.DnS*, therefore all FrameNet data are put in the same domain of quantification, by using a reified higher-order approach. This transformation allows us to preserve the original schema of the knowledge base, without any loss of information. The only problem is that the automated reasoning over OntoFrameNet occurs mainly at the OWL ABox level, the assertional part of an ontology

---

[21] See www.ontologydesignpatterns.org/ont/ofn/ofntb.owl

(Baader *et al.*, 2003). There are several reasons why the second approach is better in my opinion. Firstly, the formal semantic assumptions made in order to transform the first-order FrameNet fragment into an OWL TBox are not explicit, and the consequent reasoning is exploited on a case-by-case basis. Secondly, too much information is lost in the process, which characterizes FrameNet relevant (although informal) semantics (Frame Semantics (Fillmore *et al.*, 1988)). Thirdly, the OntoFrameNet approach exploits Semion as a semiotic façade that can be shared with other resources and data sets (WordNet, VerbNet, etc.), thus facilitating advanced forms of information integration and ontology matching.

That façade is not available when a direct translation to a TBox is performed. Incidentally, this is also the reason why I abandoned a similar approach with WordNet (see, e.g., Gangemi *et al.*, 2003) and moved to a reified strategy in a porting commissioned by W3C (Assem *et al.*, 2006).[22] Fourthly, ongoing work on using HiDL-Lite (De Giacomo *et al.*, 2008) will allow us to obtain the best of both worlds: a *c.DnS*-like vocabulary and a truly higher-order automated reasoner. Fifthly, by using the full set of semiotic ontologies in the LMM umbrella (Picca *et al.*, 2008),[23] a custom translation of selected parts of OntoFrameNet to a TBox can be performed with an explicit semantics (cf. Section 9.6.3 below).

The backbone of FrameNet is the notion of a *Frame*. As the authors pragmatically state (Ruppenhofer *et al.*, 2006b),

with enough time to make a truly in-depth analysis of the data, and enough data to make an exhaustive account of the language, then undoubtedly each lexical unit could be given its own unique description in terms of the frames and/or subframes which it evokes. The situation is, in a sense, worse than the question suggests: it is not that every word has its own frame, but every sense of every word (i.e., every lexical unit) has its own frame. It is a matter of granularity. Instead, we are sorting lexical units into groups in the hope that they permit parallel analyses in terms of certain basic semantic roles, i.e., the frame elements that we have assigned to the frame. This allows us (1) to make the sorts of generalizations that should be helpful to the users mentioned above and (2) to provide semantically annotated sentences that can exemplify paraphrase relations within given semantic domains.

In practice, FrameNet is trying to find schematic invariances in the conceptual structures of linguistic usage, in order to reduce the complexity of making explicit all the schemata applicable to each word sense. This hypothesis is compatible with the cognitive linguistics paradigm, with intensional relations in formal semantics, as well as with the *c.DnS* reified relational

---

[22] See www.ontologydesignpatterns.org/ont/lmm/wn202lmm.owl
[23] See www.ontologydesignpatterns.org/ont/dul/FormalSemantics.owl
    www.ontologydesignpatterns.org/ont/lmm/ofn2lmm.owl

ontology. The core OntoFrameNet metamodel consists of the following relation (9.70):

$$(9.70) \quad FrameNetRel(f, fe, st, lu, l) \rightarrow Frame(f) \wedge FE(fe) \wedge$$
$$hasFE(f, fe) \wedge SemanticType(st) \wedge hasSemType$$
$$(fe, st) \wedge LexicalUnit(lu) \wedge hasLU(f, lu) \wedge$$
$$Lexeme(l) \wedge hasLexeme(lu, l)$$

For example:

$$(9.71) \quad FrameNetRel(F\_Desiring, FE\_Event\_3363, StateOf$$
$$Affairs, LU\_desire.v\_6413, LEX\_desire\_10357)$$

The projections of the frame relation characterize its arguments further: for each frame there are one or more elements, but each element is unique to one frame. For each frame there are one or more lexical units (senses), but each unit is unique to a frame. For each frame, frame element or lexical unit there should be a semantic type (in the core relation, only the type of the frame element is mandatory). Moreover, several relations create further ordering between frames, and between frame elements. Unfortunately, FrameNet data are not complete: for example, many frame elements are still missing a semantic type.

In OntoFrameNet, besides formalizing the metamodel and creating inverse projections where needed, some additions have been implemented; for example, a *generic* frame element has been created for sets of frame elements with the same name: in this way it is possible to run more sophisticated queries in order to measure frame distance (e.g. finding those sharing two generic frame elements except Space and Time). Moreover, situations corresponding to occurrences of frames in the interaction with the environment, as expressed by textual sentences (e.g. those annotated in PropBank with frames and frame elements), have been given room in a newly created class (*FrameOccurrence*).

The alignment is summarized as follows, and a shortened axiomatization is presented in axioms 9.72 ff. *Frames* are aligned as meanings in Semion, and since frames have a relational structure (as conceptual contexts), they are more specifically aligned as descriptions (reified intensional relations). Moreover, from ECG, one can also give frames a (cognitive) schema status, so that frames are also aligned as reportable schemata. The relations between frames have been aligned consequently: the frame **inheritance** relation as *c.DnS* specialization, the **subframe** relation as proper part, etc.

The **evokes** relation between lexemes or lexical units, and frames is aligned to the **evokes_r** relation. *Frame elements* are 'FEin' a frame, and are aligned as meanings, and as concepts (uniquely) defined in a frame. *Lexical units* are aligned as meanings, and as descriptions, expressed by a specific aggregate of lexemes, which is also a reportable construction. *Lexemes* are aligned as expressions, and as reportable constructions. *Occurrences* of frames are aligned as reportable mental spaces that are expressed (evoked_r) by reportable constructions (as sentences).

(9.72) $Frame \subseteq (Mea \cap D \cap ReportableSchema)inheritsFrom$
$(f_1, f_2) \rightarrow specializes(f_1, f_2) \wedge$

(9.73) $Frame(f_1 \wedge Frame(f_2)isSubFrameOf(f_1, f_2) \rightarrow is$
$ProperPartOf(f_1, f_2) \wedge$

(9.74) $Frame(f_1 \wedge Frame(f_2)$

(9.75) $evokes(x, y) \rightarrow evokes\_r(x, y)$

(9.76) $hasFE(f, fe) \rightarrow defines(f, fe) \wedge F(f) \wedge FE$
$(fe)FE(fe) =_{df} Mea(fe) \wedge C(fe) \wedge \exists!(f)$

(9.77) $(Frame(f) \wedge defines(f, fe))GenFE(gfe) =_{df} Mea$
$(gfe) \wedge C(gfe) \wedge \exists(fe)(FE(fe) \wedge specializes(fe, gfe) \wedge$

(9.78) $\neg\exists(f)(Frame(f) \wedge defines(f, gfe)))LexicalUnit(lu) \rightarrow$
$Mea(lu) \wedge D(lu) \wedge \exists(ag, l, t)(Aggregate(ag) \wedge Lexeme(l) \wedge$
$hasProperPart(ag, l) \wedge$

(9.79) $expresses(ag, lu, t))$

(9.80) $Lexeme(le) \rightarrow ReportableConstruction(le)$

(9.81) $SemanticType \subseteq (Mea \cup C)FrameOccurrence(fo) =_{df}$
$S(fo) \wedge ReportableMentalSpace(fo) \wedge \exists(f, ag, lu, t)$
$(Frame(f) \wedge Aggregate(ag) \wedge satisfies(fo, f) \wedge$
$ReportableConstruction(le) \wedge$

(9.82) $hasProperPart(ag, le) \wedge evokes\_r(ag, fo, t))$

Superficially, the linguistic act involved in FrameNet consists in a *metalinguistic* function (Jakobson, 1990), typical of lexica, dictionaries, etc., in which an agent assigns meanings to expressions, and the observable situation of the act is a linguistic situation. On the other hand, frame semantics tries to reach out to language usage, not only to an abstract characterization of linguistic items; as a matter of fact, frame occurrences, as denoted by annotations made over the PropBank corpus, are real-world situations (explanatory, expressive, etc.), not metalinguistic ones. This hybrid nature of frame semantics distinguishes it from, e.g., WordNet-based annotations of corpora, where real-world situations cannot be denoted in a relational way.

While other lexical resources, such as WordNet and VerbNet, have not the same groundedness as FrameNet, nonetheless they are widely used and contain a lot of reusable content that can be combined effectively with FrameNet. Additional alignments from other resources to Semion show how to use it as a semiotic façade.

9.6.2   OntoVerbNet

VerbNet (Kipper *et al.*, 2000) has a different metamodel from FrameNet; it is focused on verb syntax and semantics, rather than frame semantics, which abstracts out of parts of speech. A new metamodel (called OntoVerbNet) has been created, which is shown partly in the maximal semantic relation 9.83 (some names from the original relational database schema have been changed for readability):

$$
\begin{aligned}
(9.83) \quad & VerbNetRel(vn, fr, pr, ar, ca) \rightarrow VNClass(vn) \wedge \\
& VNFrame(fr) \wedge hasFrame(vn, fr) \wedge Predicate(pr) \wedge \\
& hasPred(fr, pr) \wedge \\
& Argument(ar) \wedge hasArg(pr, ar) \wedge \\
& Category(ca) \wedge hasType(ar, ca)
\end{aligned}
$$

$$
(9.84) \quad VNClass(vn) \rightarrow \exists(v)(Verb(v) \wedge hasMember(vn, v))
$$

For example:

$$
\begin{aligned}
(9.85) \quad & VerbNetRel(battle\_36.4, fr_{8.1}, social\_interaction, \\
& Actor1, animate)
\end{aligned}
$$

$$
(9.86) \quad hasMember(battle\_36.4, argue)
$$

The OntoVerbNet interpretation over VerbNet represents different lexical semantics for each 'verb class', trying to catch the basic semantic structure of VerbNet, consisting of typed arguments holding for a predicate in a 'frame' that contributes to the complete semantics of a verb class; frames also have syntactic constructs applicable to the verb, to which the frame is applied.

In the example 9.85, the verb class *battle* has a frame (including both syntactic and semantics specifications), with some predicates (*social_interaction*, *conflict*, *about*), each having arguments (e.g. *Actor1*), with a category (e.g. *animate*). One or more verbs are members of the verb class. For each verb class, more than one frame for a verb class, predicate for a frame, and argument/category for a predicate can be asserted.

VerbNet relies on a small number of primitives (about 100 predicates, 70 arguments, and 40 categories in version 2.1) to account for the semantics of verbs. No assumption of uniqueness of arguments or predicates for a frame are made. The VerbNet approach is therefore closer to traditional linguistic theories, and it is not trivial to match it to FrameNet construction grammar. Here some alignment suggestions are shown[24] which can help to achieve that task, and demonstrate the role of Semion as a semiotic façade.

(9.87) $VNClass \subseteq (Mea \cap D)subClass(x, y) \rightarrow specializes$
$(x, y) \wedge VNClass(x) \wedge$

(9.88) $VNClass(y)$

(9.89) $VNFrame \subseteq (Mea \cap D)hasFrame(vn, fr) \rightarrow$
$hasProperPart(vn, fr) \wedge$

(9.90) $VNClass(vn) \wedge VNFrame(fr)$

(9.91) $Predicate \subseteq (Mea \cap D)hasPredicate(fr, pr) \rightarrow$
$hasProperPart(fr, pr) \wedge$

(9.92) $VNFrame(fr) \wedge Predicate(pr)$

(9.93) $Argument(ar) \subseteq (Mea \cap C)$

(9.94) $Argument(ar) \rightarrow \exists(pr)(usesConcept(pr, ar))hasArg$
$(pr, ar) \rightarrow usesConcept(pr, ar) \wedge$

(9.95) $Predicate(pr) \wedge Argument(ar)$

(9.96) $Category \subseteq (Mea \cap C)hasType(ar, ca) \rightarrow specializes$
$(ar, ca) \wedge$

(9.97) $Argument(ar) \wedge Category(ca)$

(9.98) $Verb \subseteq ExphasMember(vn, v) \rightarrow expresses(v, vn) \wedge$

(9.99) $Verb(v) \wedge VNClass(vn)$

In practice, a VerbNet predicate is comparable to a FrameNet frame, but it is not unique to a verb class, while a VerbNet argument is comparable to a FrameNet frame element, but again it is not unique to a predicate. The semantic part of VerbNet frames is comparable to a composition of FrameNet frames. These differences are due to the fact that VerbNet focuses on verb classes rather than on conceptual structures.

On the other hand, based on OntoFrameNet and OntoVerbNet, it is easier to compare the two lexical knowledge bases on a formal basis, e.g. by restricting the matching to VerbNet arguments against FrameNet generic frame elements, or by finding recurrent arguments in VerbNet predicates, and trying to approximate core predicate structures.

---

[24] See www.ontologydesignpatterns.org/ont/lmm/ovn2lmm.owl

Now, since FrameNet frames can be matched against VerbNet predicates, one can check the consistency between core frame elements and arguments shared across the predicates that hold for different verb classes. Moreover, FrameNet frames can be matched against VNFrames: we will check the consistency of the about 100 predicates from VerbNet as a top-level for FrameNet frames.

VerbNet arguments seem to match frame elements: in that case, argument categories can be matched to or used to populate FrameNet semantic types for frame elements when missing. Whatever matching pattern is taken, one will know what entities are involved in the matching, and what consequences will be derived. For example, VerbNet arguments are not unique to predicates, while frame elements are unique to frames, therefore it is more appropriate to match OntoVerbNet arguments with OntoFrameNet generic frame elements.

Additional metamodels can be added in order to increase the matching redundancy. WordNet is a first-class candidate because it is extensively used, its metamodel is already built, and an alignment would be straightforward, e.g. the Synset class can be aligned as in axiom 9.100, and it can be used to feed argument and frame element with semantic types of a finer granularity. VerbNet categories can then be matched against synsets, and possibly proposed as an alternative top-level for synsets, comparable to WordNet *lexical names*, also known as 'super-senses'. The following sample axioms make it viable to map VerbNet categories to super-senses, synsets to super-senses, and therefore synsets to categories:

(9.100) $Synset \subseteq (Mea \cap C)$

(9.101) $SuperSense \subseteq (Mea \cap C)$

(9.102) $\forall(x)(SuperSense(x) \rightarrow \exists(y)(Synset(y) \wedge specializes(x, y))$

(9.103) $\forall(x, y, z)((mappableTo(x, y) \wedge specializes(z, x)) \rightarrow specializes(z, y))$

How Semion supports well-founded mappings and transformations is explained shortly in Section 9.6.3.

9.6.3   Mapping and transformation patterns

Comparison between Semion-based elements can be formalized by defining appropriate relations, which are used as *mapping patterns* between elements from different lexical resources:

(9.104) $mappableTo(x, y, r_1, r_2) \rightarrow Mea(x) \wedge Mea(y) \wedge$
$Resource(r_1) \wedge Resource(r_2) \wedge belongsTo(x, r_1) \wedge belongs$
$To(y, r_2)$

(9.105) $mappableConcept(x, y, r_1, r_2) =_{df} mappableTo(x, y, r_1,$
$r_2) \wedge C(x) \wedge (C(y)$

(9.106) $mappableConceptFN2VN(x, y, r_1, r_2) =_{df} mappable$
$Concept(x, y, r_1, r_2) \wedge (r_1 = FrameNet) \wedge (r_2 =$
$VerbNet)(GenFE(x) \wedge Argument(y)) \vee (SemanticType$
$(x) \wedge Category(y))$

For example, based on the mapping pattern in 9.106, one can safely assert that a certain generic frame element abstracted from FrameNet, e.g. ofn:Agent, is mappable to a VerbNet argument, e.g. ovn:Agent:

(9.107) $mappableConceptFN2VN(Agent, Agent, FrameNet,$
$VerbNet)$

I finally include the encoding of a sample transformation pattern that constrains what Semion construct (e.g. a $Mea \cap C$) can be transformed to what formal semantic construct (e.g. a $Class$):

(9.108) $\forall(x, y)(transformableTo(x, y) \rightarrow ((Mea(x) \wedge C(x)) \rightarrow$
$Class(y))$

When adopting axiom 9.108, we accept that any lexical element y can only be encoded as any ontology element that has $Class$ semantics, e.g. an owl:Class (in the Web Ontology Language). In addition, we know that all FrameNet, VerbNet, or WordNet elements that are aligned to $(Mea \cap C)$ must be encoded as classes, so that formal operations on them will be founded on a shared semantics.

Appropriate recipes including transformation patterns can be used to manage large integration scenarios on heterogeneous lexical knowledge.

9.6.4   Containment-related schemata from FrameNet

In Gangemi, 2008 the *containment* frame, inspired by the CONTAINER schema (Johnson, 1987), is associated with the containment principle underlying the *c.DnS* **memberOf** relation, holding between entities and collections (cf. Section 9.3.3).

FrameNet version 1.2, for example, includes four containment-related schemata, represented as *frames*: F-Containment, F-Containment-relation, F-Containing, and F-Containers. Semion and OntoFrameNet are used in order to formalize these schemata and apply them to real-world frame occurrences. The following is a summary of the four frames in terms of their frame elements:

(9.109) F-Containment: {FE-Container, FE-Boundary, FE-Interior, FE-Exterior, FE-Portal}

(9.110) F-Containing: {FE-Contents, FE-Container}

(9.111) F-Containment-relation: {FE-Profiled-region, FE-Landmark, FE_Trajector }

(9.112) F-Containers: {FE-Container, FE-Content, FE-Use, FE_Construction, FE-Part, FE-Descriptor, FE-Relative-location, FE_Material, FE-Owner, FE-Type}

Following the transformation pattern applied to OntoFrameNet, the formalization of the schemata is straightforward (FrameNet name prefixes have been removed for simplicity).

(9.113) $Frame(ContainmentSchema), FE(Container), defines$
$(ContainmentSchema, Container), FE(Boundary),$
$defines(ContainmentSchema, Boundary), FE$
$(Interior), defines(ContainmentSchema, Interior), FE$
$(Exterior), defines(ContainmentSchema, Exterior),$
$FE(Portal), defines(ContainmentSchema, Portal)$

The ContainmentSchema (9.113) introduces the basic building blocks of many schemata, and can be used to provide a cognitive basis to intensional relations such as **membership** and **part** (Gangemi, 2008).

(9.114) $Frame(ContainingSchema), FE(Container), uses$
$(ContainingSchema, Container), FE(Content), defines$
$(ContainingSchema, Content)$

ContainingSchema is the minimal schema for containment, and if matched to the ContainmentSchema (e.g. by assuming $Boundary \approx Container$ and $Interior \approx Content$), it results in a **subFrameOf** it.

(9.115) $Frame(TrajectorLandmarkSchema), FE(Profiled$
$Region), FE(Landmark), FE(Trajector), defines$
$(TrajectorLandmarkSchema, Profiled$
$Region), defines(TrajectorLandmarkSchema,$
$Landmark), defines(TrajectorLandmarkSchema,$
$Trajector)$

(9.116) $Frame(ContainersSchema), FE(Type), FE(Use), FE$
$(Construction), FE(Content), FE(RelativeLocation),$

$FE(Part)$, $FE(Descriptor)$, $FE(Container)$, FE
$(Material)$, $FE(Owner)$, $defines(Containers Schema,$
$Type)$, $defines(Containers Schema, Use)$, $defines$
$(Containers Schema, Construction)$, $defines(Containers$
$Schema, Content)$, $defines(Containers Schema, Relative$
$Location)$, $defines(Containers Schema, Part)$, $defines$
$(Containers Schema, Descriptor)$, $defines(Containers$
$Schema, Material)$, $defines(Containers Schema,$
$Container)$, $defines(Containers Schema, Owner)$

FrameNet assumes that frame elements in different frames are different by default. For example, FrameNet does not make an identity assumption between Container defined in the ContainmentSchema and Container used in the ContainersSchema, or between Content defined in the ContainingSchema and Content used in the ContainersSchema.

A possible matching between these schemata can only be made between generic frame elements. For example, by using the generic level, we can hypothetically infer that, since the ContainersSchema has localizations of both Content and Container generic frame elements, which are also localized in the ContainingSchema, then ContainersSchema is a specialization of ContainingSchema.

Moreover, we may want to support more complex inferences. For example, a *superordination* relation among concepts can be introduced, by which a concept – when reused – always carries other concepts with it, and then it can be applied to Container as defined in the ContainmentSchema:

(9.117) $superordinatedTo(x, y, z) \rightarrow C(x) \wedge C(y) \wedge Frame(z)$

(9.118) $superordinatedTo(Container, \{Boundary, Interior,$
$Exterior, Portal\}, ContainmentSchema)$

This will cause the use of Container in the ContainingSchema to inherit the concepts subordinated to Container from the ContainmentSchema.

Descriptions, hence also schemata and frames, can define or use either *required* or *optional* concepts. For example, ContainmentSchema defines the frame element Portal with the *optional* parameter

(9.119) $parametricallyDefines(Containment Schema, Portal,$
$optional)$

while ContainersSchema defines the following concepts as optional: Type, RelativeLocation, Material, and Owner.

The optional parameter, a second-order property that is represented in *c.DnS* through reification, is used to restrict the scope on how many entities of a situation are checked against a description.

9.6.5   Sentences, situations, and schemata: an example

Provided with this background, the use of *c.DnS* is now exemplified with respect to occurrences of schemata and frames. Given the example sentence s,

> (9.120) Chuck's money is in his waterproof leather suitcase hidden in the company's backroom

s is annotated with FrameNet frame elements: ['Owner' Chuck's] ['Content' money] ['Container' is in his ['Construction' waterproof] ['Material' leather] suitcase]. Then, the reference (*Ref* in Semion) of s is represented as a situation and as a reportable mental space CMS (for Chuck's Money Situation) that satisfies the ContainersSchema (9.121):

> (9.121) $classifies(Construction, waterproof, time_{cms}) \models$
> $E(money_{cms}), E(suitcase_{cms}), E(backroom_{cms}),$
> $E(leather_{cms}), A(Chuck), E(waterproof), T(time_{cms})$
> $S(CMS), ReportableMentalSpace(CMS)$

> (9.122) $settingFor(CMS, \{money_{cms}, suitcase_{cms},$
> $leather_{cms}, waterproof, Chuck, backroom_{cms}, time_{cms}\})$

> (9.123) $classifies(Container, suitcase_{cms}, time_{cms})$

> (9.124) $classifies(Material, leather_{cms}, time_{cms})$

> (9.125) $classifies(RelativeLocation, backroom_{cms}, time_{cms})$

> (9.126) $classifies(Owner, Chuck, time_{cms})$

> (9.127) $classifies(Content, money_{cms}, time_{cms})$

> (9.128) $classifies(Construction, waterproof, time_{cms})$

> (9.129) $\models satisfies(CMS, ContainersSchema)$

The inference holds because all non-optional frame elements from ContainersSchema classify some entity from CMS at the same time.

The reference of s can be represented as a situation on the assumption that a sentence constitutes a unity criterion for a set of entities under a certain interpretation. By hypothesis, we know that the unity criterion underlying that sentence is the reportable mental space that is expressed by s (cf. Section 9.6.1), and which is structured by a reportable schema.

From the examples, CMS satisfies the ContainersSchema and the schemata specialized by it: ContainmentSchema, ContainingSchema.

Since s can be represented as a (complex) reportable construction, as well as its component phrases, words, morphemes, etc., it is now possible to assert explicit relations between s, the reportable mental space it evokes, and the schemata that provide a structure to that space. A sample of such representation is provided below. Firstly, a sample of the constructions needed to represent the sentence is included here (RC stands for ReportableConstruction, Sen for Sentence, Ph for Phrase, W for Word:

(9.130) $Sen(x) \rightarrow RC(x) \wedge \exists(y)(Ph(y) \wedge partOf(y, x))$

(9.131) $Ph(x) \rightarrow RC(x) \wedge \exists(y)(W(y) \wedge partOf(y, x))$

(9.132) $W(x) \rightarrow RC(x)$

Secondly, words can be axiomatized with reference to morphemes, morphemes to phonemes, and so on. Hence, these classes can be assigned to the constructions from s:

(9.133) $Sen(s), W(money), Ph(Chuck's), Ph(is\,in\,his\,water$
$proof\,leather\,suitcase), Ph(hidden\,in\,the\,company's$
$backroom), W(waterproof), W(leather), W(suitcase),$
$etc.$

Finally, the association between a reportable construction, a mental space (RMS), and a schema can be exemplified as follows,

(9.134) $RMS(rms_s)$

(9.135) $evokes\_r(s, rms_s, time_{cms})$

(9.136) $isAbout(s, CMS, time_{cms})$

(9.137) $satisfies(CMS, rms_s)$

and, since CMS also satisfies the ContainersSchema, we can infer that:

(9.138) $structures\_r(x, y, t)(ContainersSchema, rms_s, time_{cms})$

The pile including Semion with ECG ontology and $c.DnS$ has been exemplified as a formal proposal to represent how constructions are shared based on a common grounding, and embodied into the neural systems of the agents from a community. When the situations (frame occurrences) that a construction is about can satisfy both reportable mental spaces and schemata, the **structures_r** relation can be inferred automatically. This is purely representational, but contributes to the construction of a common framework to discuss and integrate the theories, resources, and experiments aiming at a cognitively founded, rich explanation of semiotic phenomena at the ontolex interface.

9.7 **Conclusion**

I have presented a formal framework to represent (some) primitives from Embodied Construction Grammar, and have used them to design Semion, a semiotic ontology, which has been applied to FrameNet and related resources, thus contributing a foundation to the ontolex interface. The framework enables a linguist or a knowledge engineer to represent frames, frame elements, constructions, mental spaces, and schemata, to map and transform them, to apply them to realistic modelling situations as conveyed by natural language sentences (or other encodings), and to reason on them with inference engines and knowledge-management tools.

I have specialized the *c.DnS* ontology, and in particular the notions of Description, Concept, Information object, Situation, and the relations holding between them. An ECG-related ontology for constructions, mental spaces, and schemata has been introduced, with axioms to represent the relations between the public (social), private (cognitive), and grounded (neural) entities involved in the theory. This layered approach is an advantage compared to the existing literature, where a huge amount of evidence on the validity of ECG is sometimes hampered by a lack of design at both the theoretical and the experimental level. A formal-ontology framework for ECG can be a useful tool for formulating research hypotheses, creating experimental settings, and deploying ECG resources in information and communication technology. A first example of how to do it is shown with FrameNet and related resources and corpora.

Future work will investigate on the one hand basic research areas, including the representation of metaphors and conceptual integration (Turner, 2007). On the other hand, research will also focus on the pragmatical aspects of information integration by providing façades for existing resources, based on Semion. Another area that can benefit from a semiotic façade is the design of NLP experiments, which are often silent on which commitments to what entities are being made.

While the classification of entities by means of schematic concepts has been done manually in the examples from this chapter, ongoing work within the EU NeOn[25] project, aimed at building a robust platform for knowledge management and ontology engineering for industrial, business, and organizational tasks, aims at exploring the feasibility of semi-automatic annotation of constructions with schematic structures, and to match them to ontology design patterns (Gangemi, 2005) from existing repositories. In addition, a new repository of patterns[26] (Presutti and Gangemi, 2008) will be partly populated with

[25] See www.neon-project.org
[26] See www.ontologydesignpatterns.org

frames and schemata after they are re-engineered by applying the methods presented here.

Acknowledgements

I thank Carola Catenacci, who substantially contributed to the early drafts of this work, as well as Alfio Gliozzo and Davide Picca, who have co-authored the LMM metamodel, an inspiration (and an applicative context) for Semion.

Part III

Interfacing ontologies and lexical resources

10   Interfacing ontologies and lexical resources

Laurent Prévot, Stefano Borgo, and
Alessandro Oltramari

10.1   Introduction

During the last few years, a number of studies aimed at interfacing ontologies and lexical resources have been done. This chapter aims to clarify the current picture of this domain. It compares ontologies built following different methodologies and analyses their combination with lexical resources. A point defended in this chapter is that different methodologies lead to very different characteristics for the resulting systems. We classify these methodologies and show how current projects, among which many contributions to this book figure, fit into this classification. We also present the tools available for facilitating the interfacing between ontologies and lexical resources.

In Section 10.2, we will introduce our methodology classification for combining ontologies and lexical resources, and in the next section, we will detail some of the most popular top-level ontologies, namely DOLCE, which has been introduced in Chapter 3, OpenCyc[1] and SUMO (Niles and Pease, 2001), introduced in Chapter 2. These ontologies are all quite different from one another, although this might not be evident to the newcomer. Our purpose is to discuss the methodologies used to combine ontologies with lexical resources. In Section 10.4, based on the ground covered in the first two sections, we will show how actual initiatives fit into our classification. The lexical resources considered in the chapter are, for the most part, those of the WordNet family (Fellbaum, 1998) and are therefore good candidates for becoming linguistic ontologies. Section 10.5 presents two examples of populating and aligning ontologies with WordNet while Section 10.6 presents different tools that can be used to facilitate the combination of ontologies and lexical resources.

10.2   Classifying experiments in ontologies and lexical resources

The main aim of interfacing ontologies and lexical resources is the development of machine-understandable knowledge bases for future use within the

---

[1] See www.opencyc.org/releases/doc/

field of Human Language Technology. These knowledge bases are central to the next generation of tools envisaged by the Semantic Web, where knowledge sharing, information integration, interoperability, and semantic adequacy are the main requirements. Different methods may guide the linking of ontologies and lexical resources, depending on the final result one intends to achieve, which range from enhancing the coverage of an ontology to the building of a system that includes properties of an ontology and a lexical resource. A generalization of these tasks suggests the following methodological options:

1. *restructuring* a computational lexicon on the basis of ontological-driven principles;
2. *enriching* an ontology with lexical information;
   2.1 Populating an ontology with lexical entries
   2.2 Attaching lexical information to ontology concepts
3. *aligning* an ontology and a lexical resource.

Option (1) concentrates on the lexical resource and involves the ontology only at the *metalevel*: the ontological restructuring is carried out following formal constraints of ontological design, introducing, for instance, the ontological distinction between *role* or *type* for concepts. This dimension has been defended early in Guarino, 1998b, put into application in Gangemi *et al.*, 2003, and has been developed in Chapter 3 of this book.

Option (2) covers two different aspects of ontology enrichment with lexical information. The first one (2.1) attempts to improve the coverage of the ontology by populating it with lexical entries, thus significantly increasing the knowledge structure. The second one (2.2) consists of giving a lexical flavour to the ontological elements by enriching them with lexical information, such as part-of-speech, for example, but not with lexical entries.

In (2.1) lexical units are mapped to ontological entries focusing on the *object-level*: in this case, the formal constraints correspond to ontological categories and relations already implemented in an existing ontology. Roughly speaking, a computational lexicon and an ontology are taken as bare taxonomies of terms, the former containing only lexicalized concepts (e.g., SUBSTANCE) and linguistic relations (e.g., **hyponymy**), while the latter provides a formal structure of both lexicalized and non-lexicalized concepts (e.g., AMOUNT-OF-MATTER) and relations (e.g., **part-of**). It is clear that this method requires the inclusion of a comparative analysis of the ontology and the lexical resource, creating a bridge between the two, in order to find synonymous terms and possible homonyms.

(2.2) and (2.1) are different in several aspects. First, it is not the same nature of enrichment. In (2.1) the volume and coverage of the resource are aimed to be significantly increased; in (2.2) the knowledge structure remains the same but is decorated with precious linguistic and, in particular, lexical information.

This approach has been followed by LingInfo (see Chapter 12 of this volume) and LexOnto models (Cimiano *et al.*, 2007). This approach is deeply related to the development of metamodels for knowledge resources like SKOS (Simple Knowledge Organization System) (Miles *et al.*, 2005), which also deals with the representation of lexical knowledge.

Finally, (3), the most complete of the proposed approaches, combines both the *metalevel* and *object-level* character of the previous approaches, in order to produce a system that is ontologically sound and linguistically motivated. This track is followed by the OntoWordNet project described in Chapter 3 as well as by the SIMPLE lexicon (Lenci *et al.*, 2000).

The experiments described illustrate that ontologies and lexical resources generally keep their own peculiarities throughout the process of integration: in other words, neither (2) nor (3) bring about an actual *merging* of ontological properties and lexical information.[2]

Although it is possible for different ontologies to be coherently merged into a new one, associating semantically similar concepts by finding their points of intersection (Taboada *et al.*, 2005), the real benefit of integrating ontologies and computational lexicons consists of the advantage of being able to keep them as distinct layers of semantic information, albeit improved by their mutual linkings and other features. This is the main reason for singling out *alignment* (and not *merging*) as the most advanced interfacing method.

While both ontologies and lexical resources may be built around a taxonomic structure, they will generally include other types of information as well. An *axiomatic ontology* like DOLCE (Masolo *et al.*, 2003) provides an axiomatization of **part-of**, **constitution**, **dependence**, and **participation**, all of which are non-hierarchical relations. A lexical resource, such as the original WordNet (Fellbaum, 1998), is organized as a *semantic network* whose nodes (sets of synonym terms) are bound together by several lexical and conceptual relations (besides **hyponymy/hyperonymy**, there are, among others, **meronymy**, **antonymy**, **causation**, and **entailment**). This fact suggests the need for the introduction of another dimension to the characterization of resources presented in the introduction of this book, which we call *constraint density*.

Constraint density captures the density of the network of constraints that holds between the concepts, in contrast to the *concept density* that situates ontologies from top-level to domain-level (see Figure 10.1). *Constraint density* deals with non-hierarchical features of ontologies and lexical resources, such as the extension with axioms for dependence, participation and constitution, formalization of meronymy relation, and the translation of glosses into axioms and consistency checks (see, for instance, Gangemi *et al.*, 2003a).

---

[2] Method (1) is not considered since it provides only ontologically driven principles without any real ontological category or relation.

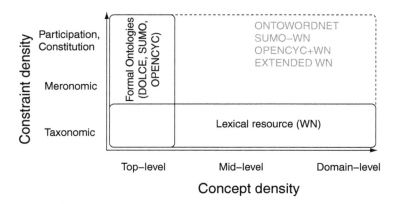

Figure 10.1 Concept and constraint density

To make an analogy containing the ontology development terminology, resources having very dense constraint networks correspond to *heavy-weight* ontologies, while loose constraint networks can be associated with *light-weight* ontologies (Guarino, 1998a; Gómez-Pérez *et al.*, 2004). Lexical resources are conceptually very dense; however, they do not have a dense network of constraints. On the other hand, foundational ontologies are not densely populated, but do offer a dense network of constraints for their concepts.

For a final remark on the nature of the lexical resources, we look at the following: although the experiments we consider in Sections 10.4 and 10.5 concern the interfacing of ontologies with WordNet, the methodologies we present here are general and apply to other resources, such as computational lexicons built on the basis of the original WordNet (e.g., EuroWordNet[3] (Vossen, 1998) modules).

The three methods isolated here have not been applied to other types of lexical resources other than WordNet until recently; in this respect, Chapter 4 about the FrameNet interface with SUMO, constitutes an exception. We believe that other initiatives related to WordNet will continue to emerge, especially in the context of the Global WordNet Association (see Chapter 2) in which the resource is developed for many languages.

10.3   Ontologies and their construction

Ontology, as a branch of knowledge representation, is a young research area with several weaknesses, two of which are the lack of established methodologies and the lack of reliable evaluation criteria. Thus, it should not come

---

[3] See www.illc.uva.nl/EuroWordNet/

as a surprise to discover that the ontologies available today have been built following disparate approaches resulting in quite different systems. This is particularly evident in the area of *top-level ontology* by which, in this chapter, we mean the research in *formal* and *foundational* ontologies. These ontologies, as we have seen in Chapter 1, are knowledge structures that (1) adopt a rich formal language (generally some kind of first-order logic) and (2) aim to classify basic notions of general interest, including process, event, object, quality, and so on.

The focus here is on three top-level ontologies, namely DOLCE, OpenCyc, and SUMO, the sum of which clearly indicates the variety of approaches possible. However, the main reason to focus on these ontologies is their attention to linguistic resources: these are the systems that have been used explicitly in relation to WordNet.

DOLCE (a Descriptive Ontology for Linguistic and Cognitive Engineering (Masolo *et al.*, 2003)) and SUMO (Suggested Upper Merged Ontology (Niles and Pease, 2001)) have been introduced respectively in Chapters 3 and 2. In this chapter, we consider the *lite* version of DOLCE (a.k.a. DOLCElite), namely an extension of the axiomatic ontology that does not consider modality, temporal indexing, and relation composition. This version contains more concepts and allows for the implementation of DOLCE-based resources (e.g., the alignment of DOLCE and WordNet called OntoWordNet presented in Chapter 1) in languages that are less expressive than FOL (First Order Logic), e.g. OWL-DL, OWL-Lite, and RDF.

OpenCyc is the ontology of Cyc, a project initiated in 1984 with the aim of building a knowledge base comprised of both scientific and commonsense knowledge. Cyc has grown to include hundreds of thousands of elements between atomic terms, concepts, and axioms. To overcome consistency issues, Cyc is now subdivided into hundreds of *microtheories*. Microtheories are, roughly speaking, bundles of assertions and rules within a specific domain of knowledge. They are supposed to be locally consistent, although no official claim has been made to this effect. OpenCyc is a byproduct of Cyc and is not part of the original Cyc project. Unfortunately, the OpenCyc ontology does not follow an ontologically tested methodology. Indeed, today the focus is still on coverage; on its website, one reads that OpenCyc includes 'an upper ontology whose domain is all of human consensus reality', which would explain the 47,000 concepts and more than 300,000 assertions it contains, a claim that nonetheless makes one wonder what indeed 'upper' means here! Initially, OpenCyc was obtained by isolating the taxonomy of the most general notions in Cyc (perhaps with minor adjustments), but it was never followed up with an ontological analysis, nor with a study of these notions. One can observe that OpenCyc adopts (at least in part) a cognitive viewpoint, since some categories capture naive conceptions of reality. For this reason, OpenCyc is compatible with the multiplicative approach (as seen in DOLCE), although this has not been followed in a systematic way. Since we lack a characterization of the ontological commitment as well as an analysis of the ontological choices embedded in the OpenCyc hierarchy, there is not much to say about its onto-logical relevance. A further problem is found in the scarcity of axiomatization in OpenCyc, which makes it impossible to analyse the adequacy of the system in a formal ontology.

10.4   How actual resources fit the classification

Generally speaking, projects interfacing ontologies and lexical resources are not easy to compare since often only generic statements are provided; the objectives are rarely addressed, and the results are not homogeneously eval-uated. Our classification of the methodologies outlined below is an attempt to create some measure of order as well as to properly situate these resources. This is not, however, meant to be a measure for ranking the resources.

10.4.1   OntoWordNet

The work underlying the OntoWordNet project, as described in Chapter 3 and 5, is rooted in early proposals about upper levels of lexical resources (Guarino, 1998b). We recall that the program of OntoWordNet includes:

1. re-engineering the WordNet lexicon as a formal ontology and, in particular:
    1.1 to distinguish synsets that can be formalized as classes from those that can be formalized as individuals;
    1.2 to interpret lexical relations from WordNet as ontological relations;
2. aligning WordNet's top level to the ontology by allowing re-interpretation of hypernymy, if needed;
3. consistency check of the overall result and consequent corrections;
4. learning and revising formal domain relations (from glosses or from corpora).

The point (1) corresponds to the restructuring task mentioned in Section 10.2, points (2) and (3) deal with populating an ontology and point (4) addresses the orthogonal issue of *constraint density* (axiomatizing the glosses).

The checking of constraints is a crucial aspect of the OntoWordNet project. It is at this step that the lexical resource benefits from ontological cleaning. OntoWordNet does not simply populate the top-level ontology by attaching WordNet terms under ontology concepts but rather determines which con-straints have to be satisfied for the integration of a WordNet synset into an ontology, in order to preserve its soundness. OntoWordNet also claims that WordNet itself benefits from this re-organization as well as from the application of the constraints. A full description of these constraints can be found in Chapter 3. Note that the restructuring has been systematically performed only up to the third (at some places fourth) upper level of WordNet nouns. The current OntoWordNet now comprises a restructured and cleaned upper level and a bare copy of WordNet at the lower levels which have not undergone any OntoClean check. For more details on OntoWordNet and OntoClean, see Chapter 3.

Finally, the axiomatization of WordNet glosses (in the spirit of eXtended-WordNet, as described in Section 10.4.4) is an active area of research for the OntoWordNet project as shown in Gangemi *et al.*, 2003a.

In conclusion, OntoWordNet is a costly methodology that, while not having yet been applied to the totality of WordNet, still offers general rules to clean the lexical resource and populate the ontology. This methodology falls into the third category: the *ontological alignment* between a lexical resource and an ontology.

10.4.2 OpenCyc and WordNet

The next proposal we present is the integration of OpenCyc with WordNet. This integration is obtained by adding into OpenCyc a synonym relationship between OpenCyc concepts and WordNet synsets (Reed and Lenat, 2002), the purpose of which is to enrich the ontology with WordNet information.

In our classification, this work falls under the *populating an ontology* option, since there is no interest in restructuring the lexical resource, nor is there any interest in merging the two systems.

Another initiative involving OpenCyc has been made by Kiryakov and Simov (2000), who propose a preliminary mapping between EuroWordNet top level and Upper OpenCyc, the very top level of OpenCyc. In this approach, only the top level of the resources is (partially) mapped. There is no attempt to restructure the resources, with the goal being to make EuroWordNet content available as an OpenCyc micro-theory. This experiment falls therefore under the *populating* methodology approach (although limited to a preliminary stage). The methodology for performing this approach is described in this chapter, but as the authors quite honestly admit, its quality may have to be improved upon for two main reasons: (1) the complexity of OpenCyc might result in some misunderstandings, and (2) the underspecification of some of EuroWordNet's top concepts.

10.4.3 SUMOwn

The result of the integration of SUMO and WordNet (hereafter SUMOwn) has been described in detail in Chapter 2. The result of this approach is a new resource whose entries are WordNet synsets tagged by SUMO categories. At first sight, this project seems to address the three methodologies we have identified: (1) restructuring a lexical resource (tagging WordNet entries with SUMO categories might constitute a first step towards re-structuring WordNet); (2) populating an ontology (tagging also allows the presentation of WordNet synsets as synonyms, hyponyms, and instances of SUMO concepts); and (3) aligning an ontology and a lexical resource because SUMOwn concerns both methodologies.

This brief description of SUMOwn integration makes it sound very complete; however, we need to take a closer look at the methodology, in order to understand exactly what has been accomplished with the integration of SUMO and WordNet into SUMOwn.

The interfacing between SUMO and WordNet results in a list of synsets annotated with SUMO concepts. The main task is, therefore, the annotation. In Niles and Pease, 2003, three unproblematic annotation cases are presented:

- the WordNet synset is a **synonym** of an existing SUMO concept
- the WordNet synset is a **hyponym** of an existing SUMO concept
- the WordNet synset is an **instance-of** of an existing SUMO concept

Unfortunately, the examples given in the original paper (Niles and Pease, 2003) are a bit confusing, as we will see in our discussion of some examples (Section 10.5). The ontology has been improved, but since our focus is on the methodology, we look at problems that arise from its application, disregarding subsequent ad hoc solutions.

Another problem with SUMOwn is the absence of verification during the integration process. The quality of the resulting resource relies totally on the quality of WordNet and SUMO. This is problematic, since the structural problems of WordNet are now well known. We believe that a more careful restructuring of WordNet is required before populating the ontology. SUMOwn mapping links are extremely useful, but they have no principled justification and, therefore, it is unlikely that such an approach could improve the accuracy of WordNet or SUMO. This point does not take away the interest and the usefulness of SUMOwn in applications, but the absence of an explicit methodology renders the evaluation or the repetition of the mapping by another impossible.

In conclusion, SUMOwn addresses only the second category of our classification (*populating*). Moreover, since there is no clear methodology for determining how to perform the tagging, the use of this tagging for modifying the resource would seem to be ill-advised.

10.4.4 Axiomatizing glosses

The EXTENDED WORDNET (eXtended-WordNet) project started with the objective of improving several weaknesses of WordNet. These weaknesses are described in Harabagiu and Moldovan, 1998 and include, in particular, the need for more conceptual relations, such as **causation** and **entailment**, which are not developed enough in WordNet as it stands currently.

The proposal (Harabagiu *et al.*, 1999) consists in *translating* WordNet glosses into logical formulas with the help of natural language analysis. WordNet glosses in the first step are parsed to produce logical forms. The second step consists in the transformation of the logical forms into semantic forms by taking into account finer semantic aspects, such as thematic relations. In this way, WordNet glosses will eventually become axioms that can be manipulated in a more precise and efficient way than current natural language glosses. Furthermore, the disambiguation of the terms in the glosses and their systematic linking to other WordNet entries or to terms in other glosses dramatically augment the connectivity between WordNet synsets.

This work is very promising. It nicely complements the approaches presented in Sections 10.4.1 and 10.4.3, which, at this point, provide mainly taxonomic axioms.

In our terminology, eXtended-WordNet wants to increase the constraint density, since the axioms derived from this method are potentially of all types. eXtended-WordNet does not, strictly speaking, propose to interface an ontology and a lexical resource because eXtended-WordNet does not explicitly involve an existing ontology. Since the ontological input is only implicit, eXtended-WordNet, therefore, does not enter into our classification. However, if this ontological input were to come from an existing ontology, eXtended-WordNet would belong to the *re-structuring* methodological option.

10.4.5 Summary

The results of our classification are summarized in Figure 10.2. Among the initiatives we have looked at here, OpenCyc is a clear example of a *populating*

	Level	Examples
Restructuring	Meta	OntoClean
Populating	Object	OpenCyc, SUMOwn
Aligning	Object&Meta	OntoWordNet

Figure 10.2 Methodology classification

methodology, and SUMOwn falls also into this category, while OntoWordNet includes both the *restructuring* methodology, through the application of OntoClean, and the *populating* methodology by linking WordNet synsets to DOLCElite categories. Finally, in terms of coverage, SUMOwn offers a complete interface with WordNet while OntoWordNet and OpenCyc are, for different reasons, incomplete.

10.5   Two practical examples

10.5.1   Christian_Science and Underground_Railroad examples

The first example, concerning the **hyponym** case, comes from the SUMOwn presentation (Niles and Pease, 2003). It is claimed that the SUMO concept RELIGIOUSORGANIZATION is a **hypernym** of WordNet synset { *Christian_Science* } *(gloss: 'religious system based on the teachings of Mary Baker Eddy emphasizing spiritual healing')*. Since RELIGIOUSORGANIZATION **are** ORGANIZATIONS, there is no clear reason for setting { *Christian_Science* } apart as an organization, because SUMO organizations are *'corporate or similar institutions (...)'*. The corresponding category for { *Christian_Science* } should be something like CHRISTIAN_SCIENCE_CHURCH. There is actually another WordNet synset for { *Christian_Science* } *(gloss: 'Protestant denomination founded by Mary Baker Eddy in 1866.')*. However, even if we accept this conceptual shortcut, it is still not clear why { *Christian_Science* } is a **hyponym** of RELIGIOUSORGANIZATION and not an **instance-of** it. For { *Christian_Science* } to be a sub-type of ORGANIZATION, there must exist at least two instances of { *Christian_Science* }. The WordNet gloss describes it more as a general doctrine and therefore as an instance of something like a RELIGIOUS_SYSTEM. The example provided better fits the second WordNet synset.

There is a lack of information regarding the notions of religious systems and organization to further pursue the investigation, but it is clear to us that the choices made in the 2003 paper on these topics were dubious. A later version corrected these problems, as illustrated in Figure 10.3. In this version, we can find both synsets. The first one is now an **instance-of** RELIGIOUSORGANIZATION, while the second one is a sub-type of SUMO's PROPOSITION. So, practically speaking, the resource is now correct; however, the mapping methodology seems to be a rather ad hoc one, appearing to rely essentially on the intuitions of the developers.

The example provided for illustrating the **instance-of** case is very similar to the previous one. In this case, { *Underground_Railroad* } *(gloss: abolitionist secret aid to escaping slaves)* is taken to be an **instance-of** and not a **hyponym** of SUMO ORGANIZATION.

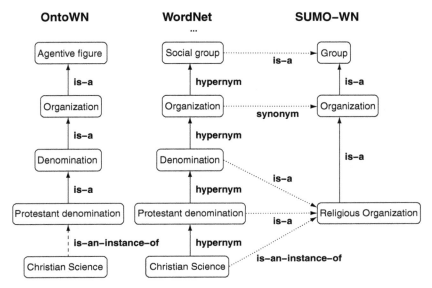

Figure 10.3 { *Christian_Science* } example

In OntoWordNet, { *Christian_Science* } and its hypernyms are integrated in the resource as shown in Figure 10.3. The hierarchy corresponds to that of WordNet up to the top level. Regarding the first sense, the last WordNet hypernym is { *Organization* }, and ORGANIZATION is also present in DOLCElite. The second sense is slightly trickier due to the presence of two hypernyms in the WordNet hierarchy.

Regarding the { *Underground_Railroad* }, the OntoWordNet version uses WordNet hierarchy { *Escape* }, a clear example revealing that the application of the methodology is incomplete in the current version of OntoWordNet. Due to its development cost, the checking and the restructuring of WordNet could not go deeper than the first four upper levels of the hierarchy. As a result, { *Underground_Railroad* } has not been checked and, therefore, has not been corrected yet, according to the cleaning principles advocated in OntoWordNet.

10.5.2   *{ Cement } example*

The second example concerns the need for WordNet restructuring (Figure 10.4). In WordNet, { *cement* } (*gloss: 'a building material that is a powder made of a mixture of calcined limestone and clay'*) is situated under { *building_material* } and further under { *artefact* } (see Figure 10.4). On the metaproperties level, { *artefact* } presents therefore both unitary concepts,

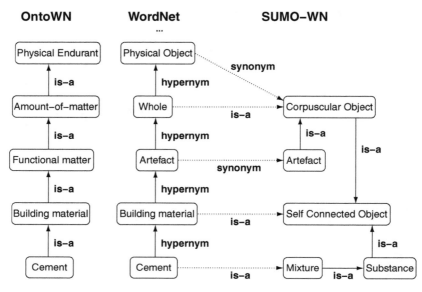

Figure 10.4 { *Cement* } example

such as regular artefacts ({ *chair, hammer,...* }) and non-unitary objects, such as { *cement* }. This constitutes a formal violation of OntoClean methodology.

In SUMOwn, this violation is repeated, since { *building_material* } **is-a** SELFCONNECTEDOBJECT, which is a unitary concept (+**U**) and SELFCON-NECTEDOBJECT, such as FOOD, which subsumes BEVERAGE and is clearly non-unitary (∼**U**).

On the other hand, OntoWordNet performs a restructuring at this level, which forces us to distinguish unitary and non-unitary concepts as explained in Chapter 3. { *building_material* } has therefore been removed from the { *arte-fact* } category and put under FUNCTIONAL-MATTER, which **is-subsumed** by AMOUNT_OF_MATTER (∼**U**). The { *artefact* } synset is put under ORDINARY_OBJECT. Finally, we do not discuss specific examples involving OpenCyc for the lack of public material.

10.6   Available tools for the ontology lexical resource interface

10.6.1   *A Protégé-based platform for interfacing ontologies and lexical resources*

So far, we have described the general methodologies that underlie the process of interfacing ontologies and computational lexicons, and we have shown concrete examples of populating and aligning distinct ontologies with WordNet. Here, we discuss a Protégé-based platform which can be exploited for such tasks.

Protégé[4] is the most successful tool for creating, editing, and visualizing ontologies. The recent implementation of an OWL plug-in makes Protégé a de facto standard for Semantic Web research and development. The platform described includes three modules: the first module concerns the creation (and possibly the import) of an ontology, and exploits the standard Protégé interface together with the above-mentioned OWL plug-in; the second one deals with the process of augmenting the ontology with a lexical resource using OntoLing[5] and finally, the third module adopts 'PAL Constraints'[6] to implement OntoClean metaproperties and to check for formal violations throughout the considered lexicon. In the following paragraphs, we focus on the last two issues only since the first is the standard practice in Protégé.

10.6.2 Enriching ontologies with OntoLing

OntoLing (see Figure 10.5) allows the user to populate the categories of a given ontology with any WordNet-like computational lexicon. Recall that the basic structure of a wordnet is the taxonomy that is then enriched with other semantic relations: synsets are mainly organized via hyponymy (equivalent to the **is-a** relationship for ontologies), potentially providing a huge number of lexical subclasses to the ontological nodes. For example, suppose one wanted to attach the children of the { *substance* } synset in WordNet to the concept { *amount of matter* } in DOLCE. By means of OntoLing, one simply 'moves' single synsets or even branches – that is, a node with its children – in a given ontology, a move which includes sense identifiers, glosses, and all other information available from the computational lexicon.[7] A user can also change the 'name' of a certain concept in the ontology according to a suitable term in the lexicon, which is done by selecting the appropriate lexical entry from a dedicated window. The OntoLing interface is user-friendly, and can also be employed for simple navigation in the lexical resource, easing the access with a minimal but effective combination of widgets. We think that this plug-in is a necessary tool for any developer desiring to create ontologies and lexicons in an intuitive way.

---

[4] Detailed information about Protégé can be found at http://protege.stanford.edu

[5] A tool for Protégé created by the University of Rome 'Tor Vergata'. For more information, see Pazienza and Stellato, 2005, 2006b, http://ai-nlp.info.uniroma2.it/software/OntoLing/

[6] PAL stands for Protégé Axiom Language.

[7] In this sense, lexical items actually become OWL classes.

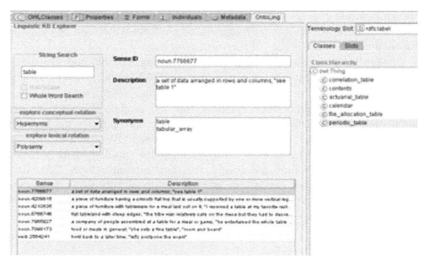

Figure 10.5 Protégé and OntoLing screenshot

10.6.3   OntoClean in PAL

An essential phase of interfacing ontologies and lexical resources consists
of the evaluation of the latter, according to suitable ontological principles
(which we termed *restructuring* in the previous sections). Our experience with
OntoWordNet showed that OntoClean provides such a principled methodology, helping the modeller to understand problems and guiding him or her
in finding suitable conceptual solutions. Nevertheless, one disadvantage of
restructuring a lexicon with OntoClean is its cost. Labelling lexical concepts with metaproperties and checking them for formal violations through
the **is-subsumed-by** arcs is incredibly time consuming, especially from a
practical perspective. For example, in building OntoWordNet, we could not
check all 100,000 synsets. Therefore, we needed to assume that the restructuring of higher levels of the WordNet taxonomy would have an effect on
the lower ones by proxy. A possible way to overcome this kind of problem
could be to automate OntoClean-labelling and/or OntoClean-checking. However, since performing OntoClean-labelling in an automatic way is extremely
difficult and breaks open the thorny issues of artificial intelligence,[8] our efforts
have been concentrated on the OntoClean-checking (see, however, current
investigations for automating OntoClean-labelling (Volker *et al.*, 2005)). By

---

[8] Such a goal would require a terribly huge amount of common-sense and natural language
knowledge to be inserted in a machine.

importing OntoClean formal rules into PAL[9] the knowledge engineer can exploit the Protégé internal language and reasoner in order to check for Onto-Clean violations. The 'PAL Constraints' widget looks like a split window: the left side shows OntoClean rules paraphrased in natural language (e.g., ~U cannot subsume +U); the right side elicits the formal violations, visualizing every father-son couple that exemplifies a violation-type. For example, in Figure 10.6, OntoClean detected a problem in the dependence relation between INTENTIONAL-AGENT and ANDROID.[10]

This concludes our brief sketch of the characteristics of two important tools that turn Protégé from an ontology-oriented application into an integrated platform for interfacing ontologies and lexical resources. By means of the OntoLing plug-in and OntoClean in PAL, we have shown the basic features of

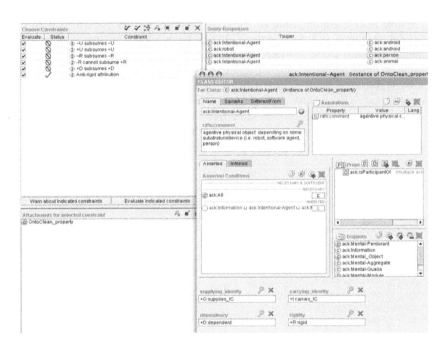

Figure 10.6 OntoClean in working with Protégé PAL: a problem of dependence

---

[9] See http://protege.stanford.edu/ontologies/ontoClean/ontoCleanOntology.html for further details about the translation performed by Nancy Ide.

[10] In the knowledge base considered – an extension of DOLCE – ANDROID was wrongly modelled as independent and INTENTIONAL-AGENT as dependent, causing an OntoClean violation.

an implementation of the methodological and experimental issues introduced in the previous sections of the chapter. Future work will concern the improvement of such tools, mainly with regard to new functionalities, in order to perform better and deeper interfacing. As of now, this seems to be the only platform available with a reasonable set of implemented features.

10.7   Conclusion

In this chapter, a way of classifying experiments and resources produced by interfacing ontologies and lexical resources has been proposed. This classification consists of a clear separation between restructuring a lexical resource on the grounds of an existing ontology hosting ontological principles and populating an ontology with lexical resources terms. A third option, called *alignment*, is a combination of these two aspects for the benefit of both the lexical resource and the ontology. It has been shown in this chapter how actual ongoing work fits into this classification through some examples. In light of these clarifications, we discussed the issue of *constraint density* for lexical resources and related it to the light-weight/heavy-weight distinction established in knowledge representation. It has also been shown that different construction methodologies lead to different features in the resulting resources. Finally, we have presented an overview of the tools and languages available for practical interfacing between ontologies and computational lexicons.

11 Sinica BOW (Bilingual Ontological WordNet): integration of bilingual WordNet and SUMO

Chu-Ren Huang, Ru-Yng Chang, and Hsiang-bin Lee

11.1 Background and motivation

The ontolex interface is anchored on two essential elements of human knowledge: conceptual structure and lexical access. A well-structured ontolex interface facilitates bilingual representation of both the conceptual structure and the lexical information which will be crucial in overcoming linguistic barriers. In this chapter we propose a robust and versatile approach for constructing the ontolex interface infrastructure: Bilingual Ontological WordNet (BOW). The Academia Sinica Bilingual Ontological WordNet (Sinica BOW) was constructed in 2003 using this approach. We argue that this novel combination of ontology and WordNet will (1) give each linguistic form a precise location in the taxonomy, (2) clarify the relation between the conceptual classification and its linguistic instantiation, and (3) facilitate a genuine crosslingual access of knowledge.

In terms of the ongoing research regarding ontologies and lexical resources, the issue of multilingual application remains an area of opportunity and challenge. On the one hand, an ontology provides a platform whereby knowledge can be represented uniformly across different languages. On the other hand, the complex mapping between linguistic forms and meanings needs to be explicitly represented in a lexical knowledge-base. The mappings are compounded when crosslingual correspondences are considered. For the successful application of ontology and lexical resources to multilingual language processing, it will be essential that these two components are integrated. In this chapter, we propose a framework for integrating bilingual WordNet with an upper ontology. This framework allows for the versatile manipulation of concepts and lexical items. In addition, the implications of this framework for crosslingual semantic relations are also explored in this chapter.

Our proposal to integrate multilingual resources with an upper ontology is an extension of the ongoing research on populating ontologies with lexical resources, as well as the development of multilingual WordNets. In particular, the work on mapping lexical resources to ontology was pioneered by the

SUMO team (Chapter 2), and the DOLCE team (Chapter 3). The work on multilingual WordNet is pioneered by the EuroWordNet team (Vossen, 1998). The work reported here, to the best of our knowledge, represents the first attempt to conduct a full-scale ontolex mapping for a new language without a previously constructed wordnet.

The BOW approach is also highly relevant to the Global WordNet Grid proposal,[1] see also Chapter 3, as well as the KYOTO project to build a global infrastructure for crosslingual knowledge synergy based on wordnets and ontologies (Vossen *et al.*, 2008). In essence, the architecture for a global and multilingual knowledge infrastructure requires both mappings between each language to an upper ontology as well as between each language pair. Each mapping should merge and yield new knowledge, as shown by the experiment of Bertagna *et al.* 2007 mapping Sinica BOW and ItalWordNet. The robustness of the BOW approach is supported by its interface role in our study to map domain texts to domain ontology (Huang *et al.*, 2004). In this study, the terms from two domains, animals and flowers, are extracted from the historical texts of 300 Tang poems and mapped to SUMO using Sinica BOW. Two small historical domain ontologies are constructed based on the mapping. The results are then integrated and accessed as domain ontology/lexicon under the Sinica BOW interface.

11.2   Resources and structure required in the BOW approach

The BOW approach, as exemplified by Sinica BOW, integrates three resources: WordNet, English–Chinese Translation Equivalents Database (ECTED), and SUMO (Suggested Upper Merged Ontology).

WordNet, introduced in Chapter 2, is a lexical knowledge base for the English language. Sinica BOW originally adopted WordNet 1.6, the version which has been used by most NLP applications to date. The WordNet 1.7 mapping was added later to attest to the versatility of this approach.

ECTED was constructed at Academia Sinica as a crucial step towards bootstrapping a Chinese wordnet with an English wordnet (Huang *et al.*, 2002; Huang *et al.*, 2003). The translation-equivalence database was handcrafted by the WordNet team at CKIP, Academia Sinica. First, all possible Chinese translations of an English synset word (from WordNet 1.6) were extracted from several available online bilingual (English–Chinese or Chinese–English) resources. These translation candidates were then checked by a team of translators with near-native bilingual ability. For each of the 99,642 English synsets, the translator selected the three most appropriate translation equivalents whenever possible. The default choice for translation equivalents

---

[1] See www.globalwordnet.org/

was lexicalized words, rather than descriptive phrases, whenever possible. The translation equivalences were then manually verified. Note that after the first round of translation, a Chinese translation for roughly 5% of the lemmas could neither be found in our bilingual resources nor be filled by the translators, which required another two person-years consulting various special dictionaries to fill in these gaps.

SUMO is an upper ontology constructed by the IEEE Standard Upper Ontology Working Group. It is a free resource owned by IEEE and edited by Adam Pease. SUMO contains roughly 1,000 conceptual nodes for knowledge representation. It can be applied to automated reasoning, information retrieval, and interoperability in E-commerce, education, and NLP tasks. Niles and Pease (2003) mapped synsets of WordNet and concepts of SUMO in three relations: synonymy, hypernymy, and instantiation (Chapters 2 and 3). Through the linking and the interface available at the SUMO[2] website, it is possible to map each English lemma to a SUMO ontology node.

The three above resources were originally linked in two pairs: WordNet 1.6 was mapped to SUMO (see Chapter 2, this volume), and ECTED mapped English synsets in WordNet to Chinese lexical equivalents, which encodes both equivalent pairs and their semantic relations (Huang *et al.*, 2003). Thus WordNet synsets became the natural mediation for our integration work, and with the successful integration of these three key resources, Sinica BOW can now function both as an English–Chinese bilingual WordNet and a bilingual lexical access point to SUMO. In other words, Sinica BOW allows a $2 \times 2 \times 2$ query design, whereby a query can be in either Chinese or English, in lexical lemmas of SUMO terms, and the query target can either be the WordNet content or the SUMO ontology.

The design of Sinica BOW also has an additional domain information layer, as shown in Figure 11.1. The domain information is represented by a set of Domain Lexico-Taxonomies (DLT) (Huang *et al.*, 2004). In this design, our main concern is domain interoperability. It can be safely assumed that if domain-exclusive words (i.e. lemma-sense pairs) are recorded only in a domain lexicon, there will be neither polysemy nor interoperability. Thus, we concentrate instead on the lexical items that intersect with the general lexicon. On the one hand, since these are the lemmas that may occur in more than one domain with one or more different meanings, domain specification would help resolve the ambiguity. On the other hand, these general lemmas with domain applicability can be effective lexical signatures for the applicable domains. The real challenge to domain interoperability involves the unknown domains, for which no comprehensive domain lexica/corpora are available. We argue that this

---

[2] See www.ontologyportal.org/

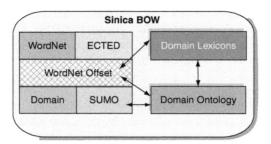

Figure 11.1 The resource and structure of Sinica BOW

problem can be greatly ameliorated by tagging the general lexicon with possible domain tags. When domain tags are assigned to lemmas whenever possible, the general lexicon will contain substantial partial domain lexica. Although we cannot expect to construct full-scale domain lexica within the general lexicon, these domain-tagged lexical items can be treated as seed domain lexica. These lexical items can also be used as signatures when guessing the domain of a new text.

11.3   Interfacing multiple resources: a lexicon-driven approach

The robustness and versatility of the BOW approach derive from the fact that it is lexicon-driven. As discussed in Chapter 1, the crucial foundation of the ontolex enterprise is that lexicalization is intimately related to linguistic conventionalization of concepts. Our approach takes advantage of this relation and anchors mappings to different language and knowledge resources with bilingual lexical pairs. What is crucial for the BOW approach is that, in addition to the interface between lexicon and ontology, lexical forms can be mapped to and interfaced with other linguistic resources. In addition to word-form mapping, morpho-lexical and lexical semantic structures can then be utilized to interface with other linguistic knowlege bases.

Sinica BOW illustrates how the BOW approach allows versatile access and facilitates a combination of lexical semantic and ontological information. The versatility is built-in, as Sinica BOW is fully bilingual, and is able to undertake the lemma-based merging of multiple language sources.

11.3.1   Lexicon-driven access

Since the main goal of Sinica BOW concerns knowledge representation, the lemma-based or conceptual-node-based query results are directly linked to the full knowledge base and are expandable. Sinica BOW access is lexicon-driven,

🔍 檢索條件值 Keyword：ant

- 詞類 POS：N
- 頻率 Frequency：參考詞彙 Reference word
  - WordNet1.6英中對譯
  - WordNet1.7.1英中對譯
  - HowNet
  - CIDE: Cambridge Internal Dictionary of English
  - The Brown Corpus
  - BNC: British National Corpus
  - ABC Chinese-English Dictionary

Figure 11.2 Initial return of lexical search

whereby each query returns a structured lexical entry, presented as a tree-structured menu. A keyword query returns with a menu arranged according to word senses, as shown in Figure 11.2. The top-level information returned includes POS, usage ranking, and cross-reference links. In addition to WordNet information, cross-references of up to five resources are precompiled for either language. For an English word, the main resource is of course the bilingual WordNet information constructed by our team, with direct hyperlinks to relevant major outside references. These resources include corpora and both English–Chinese and Chinese–English dictionaries. For Chinese, the main resource again is our bilingual WordNet. In addition, links are established to Sinica Corpus,[3] to WenLand (a learner's Lexical KnowledgeNet[4]), and to online monolingual and bilingual dictionaries. In addition to online access of multiple sources information, each lemma's distribution among these resources is also a good indicator of its usage level.

The access to the ontology and the domain taxonomy are also lexicon-driven, which is to say that in addition to using the predefined ontology or domain terms (in either English or Chinese), a query based on a lexical term is also possible. For SUMO, this query will return a node in which the word appears; a result which can also be achieved by looking up the ontological or domain node the word belongs to.

One last, but critical feature of the lexicon-driven access, is the possibility of restarting a query with any lexical node. When expansion reaches the leaf node and results in a new word, clicking on the word is equivalent to starting a new keyword search (see Figure 11.3).

[3] See Sinica corpus website www.sinica.edu.tw/SinicaCorpus
[4] See www.sinica.edu.tw/Wen

⊞ 詞義(Sense)2: 螞蟻

同義詞集和其他版本對應 Sense map with other version	WordNet1.7.1
該詞義中的ant和其他版本 對應 ant map with synset of other version	ant@WordNet1.7.1
領域 Domain	Entomology/insect(昆蟲學) 建議領域值
POS 詞類	Noun(名詞)
解釋 Explanation	social insect living in organized colonies; characteristically the males and fertile queen have wings during breeding season; wingless sterile females are the workers
翻譯 Translation	螞蟻, 蟻
同義詞集 Synset	pismire , emmet , ant
上位詞 Hypernym	hymenopteran⁅ⁿ⁆, hymenopteron⁅ⁿ⁆, hymenopterous_insect⁅ⁿ⁆, hymnenopter⁅ⁿ⁆
下位詞 Hyponym	Formica_rufa⁅ⁿ⁆, driver_ant⁅ⁿ⁆, little_black_ant⁅ⁿ⁆, slave-maker⁅ⁿ⁆, wood_ant⁅ⁿ⁆, slave_ant⁅ⁿ⁆, slave-making_ant⁅ⁿ⁆, bulldog_ant⁅ⁿ⁆, Monomorium_pharaonis⁅ⁿ⁆, Monomorium_minimum⁅ⁿ⁆, fire_ant⁅ⁿ⁆, legionary_ant⁅ⁿ⁆, pharaoh's_ant⁅ⁿ⁆, pharaoh_ant⁅ⁿ⁆, carpenter_ant⁅ⁿ⁆, army_ant⁅ⁿ⁆
（成員）群體詞 Member holonym	Formicidae⁅ⁿ⁆, family_Formicidae⁅ⁿ⁆
SUMO Concept ▣	▣ insect:Insect(昆蟲類)

Figure 11.3 WordNet search result: ant

11.3.2   Representing multiple knowledge sources

The BOW approach preserves the logical structure of both WordNet and the SUMO ontology, yet links them together to allow direct access to the merged resources. This is shown in Figure 11.3. In a WordNet search, the return includes an expandable list of the complete bilingual WordNet fields. The fields are listed under each sense and include: POS, synset, sense explanation, translation, and list of lexical semantic relations. In addition, we have included the domain information, translation equivalents, and a link to the corresponding SUMO node. Each field is expandable to present the database content. For instance, Figure 11.3 shows the query return for the lemma *ant*, with the full list of lexical semantic relations of sense 2 expanded. The field of domain and SUMO will lead directly to the corresponding node in the domain taxonomy of the ontology and allow further exploration. For instance, the menu item of the mapped SUMO node links to the SUMO representation and also permits browsing of the SUMO ontology and axioms.

Two more aspects of versatility can be achieved through the use of higher-level linguistic generalizations and the use of domain taxonomy to organize information. These aspects will be discussed in more details in the next section.

11.4 Integration of multiple knowledge sources

The architecture of Sinica BOW facilitates the integration of multiple knowledge sources. In this section, we discuss how knowledge from two different sources, linguistic generalization and domain knowledge, is integrated.

11.4.1 Integrating linguistic generalizations

Linguistic as well as inherent resource structures are utilized in Sinica BOW to facilitate the formation of generalizations as well as to assist in queries where the user is not sure of the precise lemma form. The non-lexical access methods include alphabetical (for English), prefix (for Chinese, including root compounds), suffix (for Chinese, including root compounds), POS, frequency, domain, SUMO concepts, as well as a combination of the above conditions. With this additional level of knowledge integration, generalizations such as the semantic correlation of senses and morphological heads can be easily explored.

Domain taxonomy can also be utilized to organize and access information. Our Domain Lexico-Taxonomy approach attempts to assign a domain tag to a word whenever applicable. We also encourage users of SUMO to offer feedback detailing their own domain use of lexical items because domain specifications cannot be covered by any single knowledge source, making Sinica BOW a rich source of domain information. We also allow structured access to the Sinica BOW knowledge content by specifying a node on the domain taxonomy, a feature which enables the quick extraction and checking of a domain lexicon.

11.4.2 Integrating domain knowledge

One of the most immediate and perhaps the most powerful applications of Sinica BOW is the construction of domain-specific ontologies, which is a crucial step towards providing a feasible infrastructure to facilitate the implementation of web-wide specific ontologies, as required by the vision of Semantic Web. The construction of domain-specific ontologies is also a critical test to see if the upper-ontology approach is really applicable to a wide range and diversity of knowledge domains. Lastly, for Sinica BOW, this provides a test ground for us to show that the combination of bilingual WordNet and ontology does in fact provide a better environment for knowledge processing.

Two preliminary attempts were carried out: Huang *et al.*, 2004 and Chang *et al.*, 2005. Both used a Shakespearean-garden approach to domain ontology, in which a domain lexicon was created from a target collection of texts. The first study entailed the collection of the 300 classical Tang poems, while the second study was based on the complete work of Su Shi, a major figure in Chinese literature. In each case, the domain lexicon was treated as the complete set of conceptual atoms from that domain. These conceptual atoms were then mapped to the SUMO ontology. This approach allowed us to examine the knowledge and/or experience of a specific domain, be it personal, historical, or regional, etc., as reflected in that collection of texts. This approach permitted us to make generalizations based on the full knowledge structure, not just on one lexical incident. Figures 11.5 and 11.4 illustrate our early

唐詩三百首知識本體 The Ontology of 300 Tang Poems

唐詩三百首中文詞彙（Keyword of 300 Tang Poems）：螻蟻	
SUMO 概念 SUMO Concept	昆蟲類（insect）
WordNet對應英文 English (Mapping with WordNet1.6)	ant
其它對應英文 English	black_and_white_ant
同義詞 Synset	螻蟻 图 国
相關詞 Related Word	蟻 国ant Ⓝ
出處 Source	螻蟻＞杜甫＞古柏行＞苦心豈免容螻蟻
相關網址 Related URL	溫柔在頌－唐詩三百首
其它資源查詢 Other Resource	全唐詩、國語辭典、唐詩典故、平衡語料庫

Figure 11.4 Tang animal ontology synset: ant

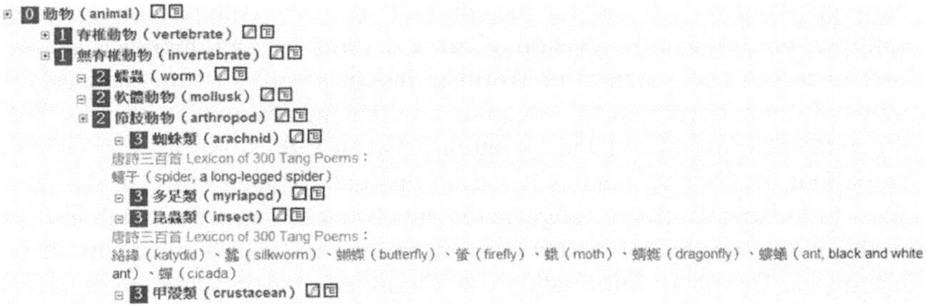

Figure 11.5 Tang animal ontology: ant

results with the animal ontology based on 300 poems from the Tang Dynasty
(AD 618–907). For instance, we were able to confirm the Tang civilization's
fascination with flying, by looking at the dominance of animal references in the
texts. The domain ontology is built upon a domain lexicon. Figure 11.4 shows
that a partial wordnet can be bootstrapped when we map historical domain
words to Sinica BOW and integrate both resources. Hence the lexical search
of 螻蟻 *black-and-white ant* returns its citation in Tang 300, as well as its
SUMO concept node and WordNet information. Alternatively, we can look
up the term in the Tang animal ontology (Figure 11.5). Our preliminary Tang
animal ontology is in essence an annotated version of SUMO. Our annotation shows whether a SUMO concept is attested in Tang 300 texts or not, and
if attested, the actual lexical forms attesting it. This presentation provides an
anchored overview of the conceptual structure of the (historical) domain and
will facilitate comparative studies as well as construction of a bona fide domain
ontology.

11.5   Updating and future improvements

As in any infrastructure work, one of the greatest challenges to the BOW
approach will be to keep the knowledge content updated. On the one hand, the
upper ontology may be presumed to be fairly stable, with infrequent updates or
additions easily performed. Lexical resources, on the other hand, are known to
change very fast. Take WordNet for example: there are no less than four major
versions that are being used currently: WordNet 1.6, WordNet 1.7, WordNet
2.0, and WordNet 3.2. Sinica BOW's approach to updating lexical resources
is anchored on the principle of representational versatility. The current version
of Sinica BOW has integrated both WordNet 1.6 and 1.7 information, with
each version fully mapped to Chinese. Based on complete mapping to both
versions, Sinica BOW allows a user to query either WordNet 1.6, WordNet
1.7, or a merged version of WordNet 1.6 and 1.7. Note that the differences

between WordNet 1.6 and 1.7 include both addition, deletion, merging, and splitting, not to mention revision of sense definitions. Our approach allows a user to access both versions of WordNet independently or simultaneously. In terms of future developments, we plan to utilize the design feature of ECTED: the annotated lexical semantic relation between English–Chinese translation pairs. Our preliminary studies based on this data (Huang *et al.*, 2005, 2006) show promising results and suggest that much can be learned through in-depth study of the conceptual mismatches between translation equivalents in two languages. This set of information was simplified to mere synonym in the current Sinica BOW. Spelling out the semantic relation between Chinese–English pairs, including implementation of relational inferences, will enrich the knowledge representation and allow a further exploration of the contrasts in linguistic ontologies.

11.6   Conclusion

Multilingual systems is one of the areas within NLP where the synergy between ontology and lexical resources can make an immediate and sizable contribution. An essential step to reaching this goal entails the construction of language resources which integrate a multilingual lexical knowledge base with an ontology. Building a linguistic resource that bridges crosslingual barriers as well as mapping intuitive lexical usage to a structured knowledge base is one of the major challenges currently facing computational linguists. The success of this resource can contribute to the resolution of the multilingual system challenges faced by both those on the Semantic Web and the computational linguistics community as a whole. Sinica BOW is one of earliest attempts in this direction, and in the future, an important development will be to construct and integrate a greater number of multilingual lexical resources with ontologies to build up a more complete knowledge map of all natural languages.

The BOW approach's contribution to the ontolex interface is twofold. First, it confirms the status of the lexicon as the interface between conceptualization and ontologies. Second, it provides a robust alternative for language without sophisticated lexical resources to interface effectively with ontologies. This approach should be crucial to attempts such as the Global Wordnet Grid or the KYOTO project for multilingual domain ontology and knowledge infrastructure. For both initiatives, the BOW approach not only allows quick bootstrapping of language WordNet, but also allows a simultaneous mapping to upper ontology. Availability of BOW's in different languages could be a crucial step towards a truly open knowledge infrastructure which is able to cross all language barriers. The validity of the BOW approach is attested both by the successful construction of Sinica BOW as well as its successful applications in future studies. In Chou and Huang's (Chapter 8) work on capturing the conventionalized ontological system of Chinese characters, Sinica BOW plays an essential role in providing mappings to SUMO ontology, and thus allows the conventionalized knowledge structure to be represented and studied in the framework of a formal ontology. In the Bertagna *et al.* 2007 experiment on bootstrapping WordNet information with two unrelated languages, Chinese and Italian, Sinica BOW also provided related WordNet information, as well as the semantic relations between the English and Chinese words. This experiment is important in the context of Global WordNet since it did not require any direct mapping or knowledge between the language pair, but succeeded in automatically augmenting semantic relation for both languages. It is not unreasonable to expect successful applications of the BOW approaches to allow quick construction of more language WordNets, in turn facilitating and mutually enriching both multilingual ontolex interfaces and WordNet-based knowledge bases.

12 Ontology-based semantic lexicons: mapping between terms and object descriptions

Paul Buitelaar

12.1 Introduction

An important requirement for the semantic analysis of textual documents, in areas such as document classification, information retrieval, and information extraction, is the annotation of terms with semantic classes. This allows for a normalization of semantically similar terms to the same semantic class. Such information is provided by a variety of semantic lexicons, ranging from synonym lists (Roget) and lexical semantic databases derived from machine-readable dictionaries (*Longman Dictionary of Contemporary English*, Webster) to wordnets (WordNet (Miller *et al.*, 1990), EuroWordNet (Vossen, 1998) and similar resources[1]).

However, the employment of such resources in real-world applications is hampered by a number of problems. On the one hand, in general, there are too many fine-grained senses represented, and second, many of those senses are of no relevance to the application, i.e., to the specific domain under consideration, whereas, on the other hand, domain-specific terms often carry interpretations (i.e., senses) that are not represented in the resource, for one of two reasons: either the interpretation is not associated with this term, or it is not available at all.

An application-oriented approach to semantic lexicons would instead focus on the semantics of the application, i.e., as represented by an ontology of the application domain. An ontology-based semantic lexicon would leave the semantics to the ontology, focusing instead on providing the mappings between domain-specific (and more general) terms and the class-based object descriptions in the ontology. It should be noted that this is fundamentally different from the traditional view on semantic lexicons as is current in linguistic and computational linguistic research; i.e., the semantics is not part of the linguistic description but is only referred to by it. Here, I propose exactly such an approach, based on the growing infrastructure of ontologies that are under development for Semantic Web applications. For an overview of

---

[1] www.globalwordnet.org/gwa/wordnet_table.htm

currently available (domain-specific) ontologies, consult SWOOGLE[2] (Ding *et al.*, 2004) or OntoSelect[3] (Buitelaar *et al.*, 2004).

The remainder of this chapter is structured as follows: in Section 2, I discuss why semantic lexicons are necessary, i.e., for semantic normalization; in Section 3, I discuss the problem of over-representation that is commonly found in traditional semantic lexicons, i.e., the representation of too many fine-grained, general purpose senses; and finally, in Section 4, I discuss the proposal for the development of ontology-based semantic lexicons.

12.2 Why we need semantic lexicons

Natural language is a redundant medium that allows the use of more than one possible sign to refer to the same object in the world. A term, which we take to be a simple or complex noun phrase, can refer to more than one concept and vice versa. That is, the ontology of concepts that represent the world on the one hand and the terms in the language on the other do not have a one-to-one relationship but, rather, are distributed many to many. Therefore, in many applications of natural language understanding, we need to undertake a semantic normalization that maps similar terms to the same concept. Normalization must be based both on class and structure, taking into consideration and using knowledge of the semantic class, as well as of the semantic context of the term under consideration.

12.2.1 Lexical semantic class

A set of semantically similar terms can be normalized to a certain semantic class. For instance, the nouns *church*, *mosque*, *cathedral*, and *synagogue* all refer to religious buildings and can therefore be mapped to a corresponding semantic class: RELIGIOUS_BUILDING. We can utilize this knowledge in natural language analysis by annotating (tagging) each occurrence of these nouns with the corresponding semantic class:

> *a Gothic* <sem class = RELIGIOUS_BUILDING > *church*</sem>
> *a Syrian* <sem class = RELIGIOUS_BUILDING > *mosque*</sem>

The kind of objects represented by the terms in the lexicon will be determined by the particular part of the world they collectively describe, commonly referred to as the 'ontology.' An ontology can be said to be an inventory of all possible sets of objects (formalized by class descriptions with their

---

[2] http://swoogle.umbc.edu/
[3] http://olp.dfki.de/OntoSelect

defining properties and relations) in a particular domain. See the introductory chapter (Section 1.1) for a broader 'ontology' definition, fitting with the one adopted here.

The level of detail of description of this particular part of the world may be more or less coarse-grained. An ontology with more detail naturally defines more concepts, and, as a consequence, more detailed ontologies increase the possibility of terms belonging to more than one semantic class. Therefore, the level of granularity of the ontology that underlies the semantic lexicon is closely connected to the level of ambiguity of each of the terms defined by it. See Section 1.1.3 of the introduction and Chapter 13 for more on this issue.

For instance, the well-known example of *bank* is commonly given to illustrate ambiguity between a FINANCIAL_INSTITUTE and a NATURAL_OBJECT. This ambiguity, however, depends entirely on the granularity level of the underlying ontology. If we assume a minimal ontology of only two kinds of objects – OBJECT and EVENT – then *bank* is not ambiguous at all. It could only be taken to introduce an object of the semantic class OBJECT. On the other hand, if we assume a much more detailed ontology specific to the financial domain, then *bank* could introduce objects of more specific semantic classes, such as INVESTMENT_BANK or BUILDING_SOCIETY.

12.2.2   Lexical semantic structure

A set of term variations can be normalized to a certain semantic structure. For instance, the following terms can be normalized to the same underlying semantic structure:

> the *x104 monitor for DELL computers*
> a *DELL computer monitor of type x104*

```
monitor [ type : x104,
          computer : DELL ]
```

In order to arrive at a given semantic structure, we need to analyse the dependency structure of a term to determine which structural components semantically depend on which others (Mel'cuk, 1987). The examples above allow for an analysis in which there are dependency relations between the noun *monitor* and two modifying constructions, one simple (*x104*), the other complex (*DELL computer*). In fact, in a recursive fashion, *DELL* is a modifier of *computer*:

> [*x104 monitor MOD] for [[DELL MOD] computers HEAD]*

The same dependency structure can be given for:

[[DELL MOD] [computer HEAD] [monitor of type x104 MOD]]

Terms may describe complex concepts: objects being modified in certain ways, undergoing actions and having relations with other objects. For instance, the term *computer monitor* expresses an object of class MONITOR that has a modifying relation with an object of class COMPUTER.

Similarly, the term *a monitor for a DELL computer with flat screen* expresses a complex concept as follows: the object of the class MONITOR has a modifying relation with an object of the class COMPUTER and with an object of the class SCREEN. In addition, the object of the class COMPUTER has a modifying relation with an object of the class COMPANY (*DELL*). Note that this same semantic structure can be expressed also by the sentential clause *DELL computer monitors come with a flat screen.*

12.3   More semantics than we need

Unfortunately, traditional semantic lexicons actually represent too much semantics, i.e., too many fine-grained senses that are of no direct relevance to real-world applications in specific domains. Here I discuss some methods that have been developed to address these problems.

12.3.1   Systematic polysemy and underspecification

Consider the following variation of the example given above, illustrating two different aspects of *church*, the religious building and the social group that gathers there. Each occurrence is annotated accordingly.

catholic<sem class = RELIGIOUS_BUILDING > *church*</sem>
catholic<sem class = SOCIAL_GROUP > *church*</sem>

It may not always be necessary to distinguish between these two aspects so clearly. In fact, a number of words share the same two aspects: *parliament*, *school*, *court*, etc, All of these are institutions, implying both a BUILDING and a SOCIAL_GROUP of people that work in this building. This phenomenon is referred to as regular or systematic polysemy.

Unlike homonyms, systematically polysemous words need not always be disambiguated, because such words have several related senses that are shared in a systematic way by a group of similar words. In many applications, it may be sufficient to know if a given word belongs to this group rather than to know which of its (related) senses exactly to pick (Buitelaar, 2000). In other words, it will suffice to assign a more coarse-grained sense, one that leaves several related senses underspecified, but which can be further specified on demand. Related senses are, however, only systematic (or regular) if more than one example in a language can be found as formulated by Apresjan (1973):

Polysemy of the word A with the meanings a_i and a_j is called regular if, in the given language, there exists at least one other word B with the meanings b_i b_j, which are semantically distinguished from each other in exactly the same way as a_i and a_j and if a_i and b_i, a_j and b_j are nonsynonymous.

Using this definition, we can construct classes of systematically polysemous words as shown in the CoreLex approach (Buitelaar, 1998). This method takes WordNet sense assignments and compares their distribution by reducing them to a set of basic types. For instance, WordNet assigns the following senses to the noun *book*: { *publication* }, { *product, production* }, { *fact* }, { *dramatic_composition, dramatic_work* }, { *record* }, { *section, subdivision* }, { *journal* }.

At the top of the WordNet hierarchy, these seven senses can be reduced to two basic types: the content that is being communicated and the medium of communication. We can arrive at systematically polysemous classes by investigating which other words share these same senses and are thus polysemous in the same way.

For instance, the seven different senses that WordNet assigns to the noun *book* can be reduced to two basic types: ARTEFACT and COMMUNICATION. We can do this for each noun in WordNet, and then group them into classes according to their combination of basic types. Among the resulting classes are a number that are to be expected, given the literature on systematic polysemy (Nunberg, 1979; Bierwisch, 1983; Pustejovsky, 1991; Lascarides and Copestake, 1995). For instance, the systematically polysemous classes ANIMAL/FOOD and PLANT/NATURAL_PRODUCT have been discussed widely. Other classes are less expected but, nonetheless, seem quite intuitive. The class ARTEFACT/ATTRIBUTE/SUBSTANCE, for instance, includes a number of nouns (*chalk, charcoal, daub, fiber, fibre, tincture*) that refer to an object that is at the same time an ARTIFACT made of some SUBSTANCE as well as an ATTRIBUTE.

Systematic polysemous classes that are obtained in this way can be used as filters on sense disambiguation in a variety of applications in which a coarse-grained sense assignment will suffice mostly but where an option of further specification exists. For instance, for information retrieval, it will not always be necessary to distinguish between the two interpretations of *baseball, basketball*, or *football*. Users looking for information on a baseball game may be interested also in baseball balls. On the other hand, a user may be interested specifically in buying a new baseball ball but does not wish to be flooded with irrelevant information on baseball games. In this case, the underspecified BALL/GAME sense needs to be further specified in the BALL sense only. Similarly, it will not always be necessary to distinguish exactly between the

VESSEL and MEASURE interpretation of, for instance, *bottle*, *bucket*, or *cask*, or between the COMMUNICATION and NOISE interpretation of *clamour, hiss,* or *roar*. In the case of verbs, a number of proposals for frame- or construction-based approaches exist to aggregate all of their polysemous senses into a common frame that covers different interpretations by variation in the combination and values of the different slots, i.e., verb arguments and adjuncts (Martin, 2001, and Chapter 4 in this volume).

12.3.2   Domain-specific tuning

An important aspect of semantic normalization entails the wider *semantic space* in which the word occurs. Semantic space may be instantiated by a specific domain (e.g., biomedicine), a subdomain (e.g., anatomy) or a specific task domain (e.g., heart transplantation). The influence of a particular domain on sense disambiguation can be clearly illustrated with some cross-lingual examples as they would appear in (machine) translation. Consider, for instance, the English word *housing*. In a more general sense, this translates into German *Wohnung (accommodation, dwelling)*. However, in engineering it translates into *Gehäuse (frame, casing)*. As senses are so strongly aligned with specific domains, it is actually possible to determine a 'most likely or dominant sense' given the specific application domain or, rather, a relevant corpus that represents this domain for training a model for sense selection.

One such method is described in Buitelaar and Sacaleanu, 2001, which determines the domain-specific relevance of WordNet synsets (i.e., senses) on the basis of the relevance of their constituent synonyms that co-occur within domain-specific corpora. For this purpose, the domain relevance of each of the synonyms (i.e., a simple or more complex term) in a synset is first computed, and then this information is used to compute the cumulative relevance of each synset.

The relevance measure for computing term relevance used is a slightly adapted version of standard TF.IDF (Term Frequency. Inverse Document Frequency) as used in vector-space models of information retrieval (Salton and Buckley, 1988). Given term relevance, the relevance of each synset can now be computed, which is simply the sum of the relevance of each term in the synset, defined as follows (see Buitelaar and Sacaleanu, 2001 for further details):

Definition 4 *Synset Relevance*

$$relevance(c|d) = \sum_{t \in c} relevance(t|d)$$

where t represents the term, d the domain-specific corpus, c is a synset.

In similar work McCarthy *et al.* (2004) report an approach in which they use untagged domain-specific corpora to determine predominant senses for corresponding domains. Their method produced a 64% precision on sense disambiguation of nouns with WordNet on the Senseval-2 English all-word task.

Some other work also deals with the idea of tuning a general sense inventory to an application domain (e.g. Basili *et al.*, 1997; Cucchiarelli and Velardi, 1998; Turcato *et al.*, 2000; Huang *et al.*, 2004). According to Cucchiarelli and Velardi (1998), a domain-specific sense inventory that is balanced (i.e., that has an even distribution of words to senses) and at the right level of abstraction (i.e., trading off ambiguity versus generalization) can be selected automatically given the following criteria: generality, discrimination power, domain coverage, and average ambiguity. Applying these criteria in a quantitative way to WordNet and a given domain-specific corpus automatically selects a set of relevant *categories* (i.e., groups of synsets). In more recent work in the context of SemEval 2007 a similar experiment by the same authors did not, however, provide conclusive evidence that automatically acquired domain-specific predominant senses improve performance on a WSD task (Koeling and McCarthy, 2007). One reason for this might be data sparseness due to a large collection of domains (forty-eight) as provided by the WN-DOMAINS resource (Magnini *et al.*, 2003), which has all WordNet synsets tagged with a domain label.

12.4   The semantics we need is in ontologies

As it is important to determine the appropriate set of semantic classes for a particular application, the methods discussed in the previous section have been developed to enable the use of a general lexical semantic resource. Alternatively, we could look at domain-specific semantic resources, such as ontologies, and enrich these ontologies with lexical information for their use in natural language processing applications. Here, I discuss such an ontology-based approach to semantic lexicon development, which involves a proposal for a lexicon model (LingInfo) for ontologies. Before proceeding, however, we must first look at the relation between ontologies and semantic lexicons, expanded somewhat from what has been presented in the introduction (Section 1.1.4)

12.4.1   Ontologies and semantic lexicons

Semantic lexicons represent different interpretations of words with senses. Consider, for instance, the following senses[4] of the English noun *article*:

---

[4] Dictionary definitions taken from http://dictionary.reference.com/

1. An individual thing or element of a class [...]
2. A particular section or item of a series in a written document [...]
3. A non-fictional literary composition that forms an independent part of a publication [...]
4. The part of speech used to indicate nouns and to specify their application
5. A particular part or subject; a specific matter or point

A sense represents the semantics of a word, very much like a class definition in an ontology. In fact, semantic lexicons such as WordNet are semi-formalized dictionaries that group words into classes (i.e., synsets, senses) for which we can give formal definitions (Moldovan and Rus, 2001). In this way, semantic lexicons are the reverse of ontologies in that they assign one or more classes (i.e., senses) to a given word, whereas ontologies assign labels (i.e., words or more complex terms) to a given class. To illustrate this fact, consider again the English noun *article*, which is used as a label for class definitions in a number of ontologies.

In the COMMA[5] ontology on document management, the definition of *article* corresponds to sense 2, with the class ARTICLE as **subclass** of the class DOCUMENT and of EXTRACTEDDOCUMENT[6]

```
<rdfs:Class rdf:ID='Article'>
 <rdfs:label xml:lang='en'>article</rdfs:label>
 <rdfs:subClassOf rdf:resource='#Document'/>
 <rdfs:subClassOf rdf:resource='#ExtractedDocument'/>
 <rdfs:comment xml:lang='en'>Document corresponding
  to a piece of writing on a particular\index{particular}
  subject and which purpose is to fully realize a
  particular objective in a relatively concise form e.g.:
  demonstrate something.</rdfs:comment>
</rdfs:Class>
```

In the GOLD[7] ontology on linguistics, the definition of *article* corresponds to sense 4, with *article* represented as a **subclass** of the class DETERMINER.

```
<owl:Class rdf:ID='Article'>
 <rdfs:label xml:lang='en'>article</rdfs:label>
 <rdfs:subClassOf rdf:resource='#Determiner'/>
 <rdfs:comment>An article is a member of a small
  class of determiners that identify a noun's
  definite or indefinite reference, and new or
  given status...</rdfs:comment>
</owl:Class>
```

---

[5] See http://pauillac.inria.fr/cdrom/ftp/ocomma/comma.rdfs
[6] http://visus.mit.edu/bibtex/0.1/bibtex.owl provides more detailed definitions of *article* in sense 2
[7] See www.linguistics-ontology.org/gold.html

Given these assumptions, we may thus view the collection of ontologies on the Semantic Web as a large, distributed semantic lexicon ('the Lexical Semantic Web') in which we can look up the meaning of words, just as in a regular dictionary. Consider, for instance, the meaning of *director* as provided by the following two ontologies.

According to the 'AgentCities ICSTM Shows'[8] ontology, a *director* is of class ROLE that somebody can assume:

```
<daml:Class rdf:ID='Director'>
 <rdfs:label>Director</rdfs:label>
 <rdfs:subClassOf>
  <daml:Class rdf:about='#Role'/>
 </rdfs:subClassOf>
</daml:Class>
```

Unfortunately, the ontology provides no additional information on what constitutes a ROLE but simply assigns it as a super-class to the DIRECTOR class as well as to the ACTOR and PLAYWRIGHT classes. From this information, we may infer something about the meaning of *director*, namely that it is something similar to being an *actor* and a *playwright* but not much more.

A more informative definition for a different sense of *director* is, for instance, provided by the 'University Benchmark'[9] ontology, which defines *director* as an object of the class DIRECTOR with super-class PERSON that has the property **headOf** with a value of the class PROGRAM:

```
<owl:Class rdf:ID='Director'>
<rdfs:label>director</rdfs:label>
<owl:intersectionOf rdf:parseType='Collection'>
 <owl:Class rdf:about='#Person'/>
 <owl:Restriction>
   <owl:onProperty rdf:resource='#headOf'/>
    <owl:someValuesFrom>
     <owl:Class rdf:about='#Program'/>
    </owl:someValuesFrom>
   </owl:Restriction>
 </owl:intersectionOf>
</owl:Class>
```

As the ontology further defines the class PROGRAM as a sub-class of ORGA-NIZATION, we may infer that *director*, in this sense of the word, refers to a person who is the head of a specific type of organization (i.e., a *program*).

---

[8] See www-agentcities.doc.ic.ac.uk/ontology/shows.daml
[9] See www.lehigh.edu/~zhp2/univ-bench.owl

12.4.2 A lexicon model for ontologies

However, to allow for the application of ontologies within natural-language processing applications, a richer linguistic representation is needed of domain terms, their synonyms, and multilingual variants for ontology classes and properties. Currently, such information is mostly missing, or represented only in an impoverished way (using RDFS Label), leaving the semantic information in an ontology without a linguistic grounding. Relevant linguistic information that should be represented includes: *language-ID* (ISO-based unique language identifier), *part-of-speech* (of the head of the term), *morphological and syntactic decomposition*, and *statistical/grammatical context models* (linguistic context represented by N-grams, grammar rules, etc.)

To allow for a direct connection of linguistic information with corresponding classes and properties in the domain ontology, Buitelaar *et al.*, 2006, developed a lexicon model (LingInfo) that enables the definition of LingInfo instances (each of which represents a term) for each class or property. The LingInfo model is represented by use of a metaclass (ClassWithLingInfo) and metaproperty (PropertyWithLingInfo), which allows for the representation of LingInfo instances for each class, where each LingInfo instance represents the linguistic features (feat:LingInfo) of a term for a particular class.

Figure 12.1 shows an overview of the model with example domain ontology classes and associated LingInfo instances. The domain ontology consists of the class o:FootballPlayer with subclasses o:Defender and o:Midfielder, each of which are instances of the metaclass feat:ClassWithLingInfo with the property feat:LingInfo.

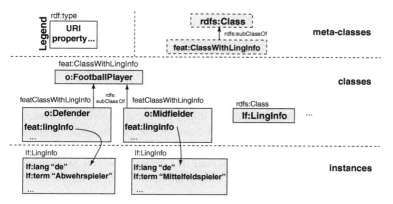

Figure 12.1 LingInfo model with example domain ontology classes and LingInfo instances (simplified)

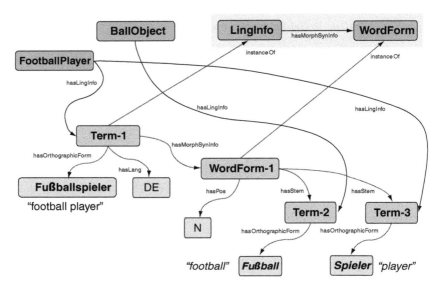

Figure 12.2 LingInfo instance (partial) for the morphosyntactic decomposition of *Fußballspieler* (football player)

Figure 12.2 shows a sample application of the model with a LingInfo instance that represents the decomposition of the German term *Fußball-spieler* (*football player*). The example shows the LingInfo object Term-1 that represents the word form *Fußballspieler* with language-ID German (DE) and part-of-speech (N), which can be decomposed into *Fußball* (Term-2, football) with semantics BALLOBJECT and *Spieler* (Term-3, player) with semantics FOOTBALLPLAYER.

The LingInfo approach in effect integrates a domain-specific multilingual wordnet into the ontology, although importantly, the original WordNet model does not distinguish clearly between linguistic and semantic information, whereas the LingInfo model is exactly based on this distinction.

Alternative lexicon models that are similar to the LingInfo approach include Bateman *et al.*, 1995 and Alexa *et al.*, 2002, but these models concentrate on the definition of a top ontology for lexicons instead of linguistic information for domain ontology classes and properties. This is also the main difference with the OntoWordNet model, presented in Chapter 3 which aims to merge the foundational ontology DOLCE with WordNet to provide the latter with a formal semantics.

The LingInfo[10] model is applied and/or developed further in the following domains:

- *Football Domain*: LingInfo has been applied in the context of the SmartWeb[11] project for defining multilingual terms of ontology classes in the SmartWeb Integrated Ontology (SWIntO, see Oberle *et al.*, 2007). This LingInfo instance is used currently also in the K-Space[12] project for text-mining support in semantic indexing of football video.
- *Biomedical Domain*: LingInfo is currently applied in the context of the MEDICO[13] project for inducing an ontology-based lexicon of biomedical terms (centred on lymphoma) from text corpora, using the Foundational Model of Anatomy ontology (or FMA[14]), RadLex[15] and the International Statistical Classification of Diseases and Related Health Problems (or ICD[16]) in combination with Wikipedia, WordNet and NLP annotation tools
- *Ontology Design*: In the context of the Theseus[17] project (Core Technology Cluster on Ontologies), LingInfo is considered as a model for including linguistic information in ontologies.

12.5   Conclusion

The traditional model of semantic lexicons assigns senses to lexical items, in which the set of senses is, for the most part, open-ended. Ontologies provide formal class definitions for sets of objects, which can be seen as a 'sense' for lexical items expressing such objects. In this chapter, I have presented the motivations leading up to and the subsequent ideas for organizing a semantic lexicon on the basis of an ontology, which brings these two disparate views together into a unified approach to lexical semantics and ontology-based knowledge representation.

---

[10] Current developments, download, and related publications for the LingInfo model can be obtained from http://olp.dfki.de/LingInfo
[11] http://www.smartweb-projekt.de/
[12] www.k-space.eu/
[13] http://theseus-programm.de/scenarios/en/medico
[14] http://sig.biostr.washington.edu/projects/fm/AboutFM.html
[15] www.rsna.org/radlex/
[16] www.who.int/classifications/icd/en/
[17] http://theseus-programm.de/about-theseus

13 Merging global and specialized linguistic ontologies

Manuela Speranza and Bernardo Magnini

13.1 Introduction

The increasing employment of ontologies to impart a greater level of meaning to the vast and continuously growing amount of data on the web (e.g. in electronic commerce and peer-to-peer systems) is converging, with multiple proposals coming from various communities both to build a Semantic Web that uses ontologies for the annotation of Web resources and to improve NLP applications such as information retrieval and question answering. Rather than contributing to the creation of a set of shared ontologies, however, this has the effect of raising both the degree of heterogeneity and other problems related to interoperability between ontologies. Ontology matching, which mainly consists of enabling two different ontologies to interoperate by finding correspondences between their concepts, has thus become an important topic in research communities across several disciplines.

The problem of ontology matching has been considered in three different dimensions, i.e. in relation to matching two ontologies, two linguistic ontologies (large lexical resources with an ontological structure which is generally semi-formal, such as WordNet), and two linguistic ontologies with different levels of specificity (a global one and one restricted to a particular domain). All three dimensions are relevant for this book, as mentioned in Chapters 1 and 5, especially in the perspective of the combination of ontologies with lexical resources (see Chapter 10 for a thorough discussion on this topic).

As for matching between ontologies, general surveys on recent approaches are provided in Euzenat and Shvaiko, 2007 and Doan and Halevy, 2005. In particular, the CtxMatch approach (Magnini *et al.*, 2004), which followed on from the plug-in approach described in this chapter, automatically finds mappings between concepts of different ontologies (or even less formal hierarchical classifications) by exploiting the implicit information derived from the context of the concepts, e.g. the relations with other concepts within the ontology. Specifically, it relies on both the semantic interpretation of the linguistic realization of the concepts and the hierarchical structure of the ontology itself. A related development to this approach is represented by the work on semi-automatic methods to revise automatically created mappings (Meilicke *et al.*, 2008), where non-standard reasoning methods are used to detect and propagate implications of expert decisions on the correctness of each mapping, which reduces the human effort required. The high number of proposed approaches strongly suggests a need to establish standards for evaluating ontology integration. In order to achieve this aim, a number of initiatives have been undertaken in the last few years (see, e.g., the OAEI evaluation campaigns that have been organized from 2004 to 2008).

As far as the mapping between linguistic ontologies is concerned, Daudé *et al.* (2000) exploit a constraint satisfaction algorithm (i.e. relaxation labelling) to discover relations between concepts. Among the various kinds of linguistic ontologies, it is important to underline the significance of those restricted to a particular domain, i.e. specialized resources as defined in Section 1.1.3. In particular, their role has been recognized as a major topic in a variety of content-based tasks, such as conceptual indexing and semantic-query expansion, where they can be used together with global linguistic ontologies for improving retrieval performance.

The third dimension, i.e. the problem of integrating specialized ontologies (as defined in Section 1.1.3) with global linguistic ontologies, is the focus of this chapter, where the solution proposed is a plug-in technique. We think that the possibility of merging information at different levels of specificity is a crucial requirement, at least for the case of large domains, where terminologies include both very specific terms and a significant amount of common terms which may be shared with global ontologies. The global-specialized scenario offers some simplifications with respect to the general problem of merging ontologies at a similar degree of specificity (Hovy, 1998); in the case of conflicting information, in particular, it is possible to define a strong precedence criterion according to which terminological information overshadows generic information. We take EuroWordNet as our assumed model and propose a methodology of 'plugging' specialized linguistic ontologies into global ontologies. The formal apparatus to realize this goal is based on plug relations that connect *basic concepts* of the specialized ontology to corresponding concepts in the global ontology. We provide experimental data to support our approach, which has been tested on a global and a specialized linguistic ontology for the Italian language.

The chapter is structured as follows. Section 13.2 presents the main features and uses of linguistic ontologies in contrast to formal ontologies. Section 13.3 introduces specialized linguistic ontologies, i.e. linguistic ontologies with domain-specific coverage, as opposed to global linguistic ontologies containing generic knowledge. Section 13.4 deals with the problem of the interoperability of linguistic ontologies and describes the relations and the procedure enabling integrated access to pairs of global and specialized linguistic ontologies. Section 13.5 provides quantitative data related to an implemented algorithm, which we have applied over a global and a specialized linguistic ontology for Italian. Finally, Section 13.6 discusses applications and extensions of the plug-in approach.

13.2   Linguistic ontologies versus formal ontologies

The increasing interest in ontologies for a variety of natural-language applications has led to the creation of ontologies designed for different purposes, which naturally possess different features; therefore, it would be worthwhile to elaborate on the distinction between ontologies, linguistic ontologies and lexica proposed in Section 1.1. In particular, linguistic ontologies such as WordNet, which has been presented and described in Chapters 2 and 3, can be seen both as a particular kind of lexical database and as a particular kind of ontology. In fact, they are large-scale lexical resources that cover most words found in a language, while at the same time also providing an ontological structure, for which the main emphasis is on the relations between concepts. As far as the degree of formalization is concerned, linguistic ontologies are typically semi-formal (see Section 1.1.2) in so far as they do not reflect all the inherent aspects of formal ontologies. For instance, as Guarino *et al.* (1999) have pointed out, WordNet's upper-level structure shows no distinction between types and roles, whereas most of the original Pangloss (Knight and Luk, 1994a) nodes in the SENSUS ontology are actually types; to give a further example, WordNet's hierarchical structure lacks information about mutual disjointness between concepts. Moreover, what distinguishes linguistic ontologies from most formal ontologies is their size: linguistic ontologies are very large (WordNet, for instance, has several dozen thousand synsets), while formal ontologies are generally much smaller.

The duality characterizing linguistic ontologies is reflected in their most prominent features. If considered at the linguistic level, they are strongly language-dependent, like classical lexica which focus on the words used in one specific language (in the case of monolingual resources) or in two or more specific languages (in the case of bilingual or multilingual resources). On the other hand, if we consider the semantic level (see Section 1.1.1), it can be observed that concepts denoted by different words in different languages can be shared, as sometimes happens with the concepts in formal ontologies.

One suggested approach is to keep these two levels separate as far as more application-oriented tasks are concerned. Buitelaar (Chapter 12), for example, proposes an ontology-based semantic lexicon, where an ontology of the application domain would represent the semantics of the domain, while the lexicon would provide the mappings between domain-specific terms and the classes of the ontology.

WordNet (Fellbaum, 1998), the best-known linguistic ontology, offers two distinct services: a lexicon, which describes the various word senses, and an ontology, which describes the semantic relations between concepts (see Section 1.2). Taking advantage of the semantic relations forged, WordNet could thus be adapted to a crosslanguage environment by employing the EuroWordNet multilingual database (Vossen, 1998), i.e. mapping synsets of different monolingual wordnets into the EuroWordNet InterLingual Index. In particular, the MEANING project (Rigau *et al.*, 2002), which adopted the EuroWordNet architecture, focused on automatic acquisition of semantic information and porting methodologies; for instance, as different languages often use different ways to realize the same meaning, it is possible to exploit semantic information available for one language so as to enrich wordnets of other languages (e.g. with domain labels).

One formal ontology based on linguistic motivation is the Generalized Upper Model (GUM) knowledge base (Bateman *et al.*, 1995), an ontology which has primarily been developed for NLP applications. An upper model is an abstract linguistically motivated ontology which simultaneously meets two requirements: (1) a sufficient level of abstraction in the semantic types employed, so as to escape the idiosyncrasies of surface realization and ease interfacing with domain knowledge, and (2) a sufficiently close relationship to surface regularities so as to permit interfacing with natural language surface components.

13.2.1   Uses of formal ontologies

Ontologies play a crucial role when viewed in the context of the Semantic Web as a means for establishing conceptually concise bases for knowledge communication. In fact, the most common approach to the creation of the Semantic Web relies on annotations of Web resources with respect to concepts and relations defined in ontologies (Antoniou and van Harmelen, 2004). The use of ontologies to associate meaning with data and thus with Web resources is meant to facilitate both humans' and artificial agents' access to documents. Regarding the retrieval of information from the Web, Luke *et al.* (1996) propose a set of simple HTML Ontology Extensions to manually annotate Web pages with ontology-based knowledge. This method performs with a high degree of precision, though it is very expensive in terms of time.

OntoSeek (Guarino *et al.*, 1999) is also based on content, but uses ontologies to find users' data in a large classical database of Web pages. Erdmann and Studer (1999) make use of an ontology to access sets of distributed XML documents on a conceptual level. Their approach defines the relationship between a given ontology and a document-type definition (DTD) for classes of

XML documents. Thus, they are able to supplement syntactic access to XML documents by employing conceptual-access methods.

However, as it has been previously noted by Guarino *et al.* (1999), the practical adoption of ontologies in information-retrieval systems is limited by their insufficient coverage as well as by their need to be constantly updated. On the one hand, linguistic ontologies encompass both ontological and lexical information, thus offering a way to partly overcome these limitations. On the other hand, automatic ontology learning and ontology population have recently emerged as new fields of application for knowledge-acquisition techniques (Buitelaar *et al.*, 2005); the automatic ontology population task consists of the extraction and subsequent classification of instances of concepts and relations defined in an ontology, whereas in ontology learning, new concepts and relations are supposed to be acquired, with the consequence of modifying the ontology itself.

13.2.2   Uses of linguistic ontologies

Linguistic ontologies (WordNet in particular) have been proposed for content-based indexing, where semantic information is added to the classic word-based indexing. As an example, *Conceptual Indexing* (Woods, 1997) automatically organizes words and phrases of a body of material into a conceptual taxonomy that explicitly links each concept to its most specific generalizations. This taxonomic structure is used to organize links between semantically related concepts, and to make connections between terms of a request and related concepts in the index.

Mihalcea and Moldovan (2000) designed an information retrieval (IR) system which performs a combined word-based and sense-based indexing system which makes use of WordNet. The input to IR systems consists of a question/query and a set of documents from which the information has to be retrieved, and adds lexical and semantic information to both the query and the documents, during a pre-processing phase in which the input question and the texts are disambiguated. The disambiguation process relies on contextual information, identifying the meaning of the words using WordNet.

The problem of sense disambiguation in the context of an IR task has been addressed by, among others, Gonzalo *et al.* (1998). In a preliminary experiment where the disambiguation had been accomplished manually, the vector-space model for text retrieval was found to give better results if WordNet synsets were chosen as the indexing space, instead of word forms.

Desmontils and Jacquin (2001) present an approach where linguistic ontologies are used as tools of information retrieval on the Internet. The indexing process is divided into four steps: (1) for each page a flat index of terms is built; (2) WordNet is used to generate all candidate concepts which can be labelled with a term of the previous index; (3) each candidate concept of a page is studied to determine its representativeness of this page content; (4) all candidate concepts are filtered via an ontology, selecting the most representative ones for the content of the page.

The role of linguistic ontologies has also emerged in the context of distributed agents technologies, where the problem of meaning negotiation is crucial (Bouquet and Serafini, 2001; Magnini *et al.*, 2004).

13.3   Specialized linguistic ontologies

A particular kind of linguistic ontology is represented by specialized linguistic ontologies, i.e. linguistic ontologies with domain-specific coverage, which stand in contrast to global linguistic ontologies, which contain only generic knowledge. Focusing on one single domain, specialized linguistic ontologies often provide many sub-hierarchies of highly specialized concepts, whose lexicalizations tend to assume the shape of complex terms (i.e. multiwords); high-level knowledge, on the other hand, tends to be simplified and domain oriented.

Many specialized linguistic ontologies have been developed, especially for practical applications, in domains such as art (see the *Art and Architecture Getty Thesaurus*), geography (see the *Getty Thesaurus of Geographical Names*), medicine (Gangemi *et al.*, 1999), etc., and the importance of these specialized linguistic ontologies has been widely recognized in a number of works. The role of terminological resources for NLP has been addressed, for instance, by Maynard and Ananiadou (2000), who point out the fact that high-quality specialized resources such as dictionaries and ontologies are necessary for the development of hybrid approaches to automatic term recognition combining linguistic and contextual information with statistical information.

Buitelaar and Sacaleanu (2002) address the problem of tuning a general linguistic ontology such as WordNet or GermaNet to a specific domain (the medical domain, in their specific case). This involves the selection of senses deemed to be most appropriate for the domain, along with the addition of novel specific terms. Similarly, the work of Turcato *et al.* (2000) describes a method for adapting a general-purpose synonym database, like WordNet, to a specific domain (in this case, the aviation domain), which is accomplished by adopting an eliminative approach based on the incremental pruning of the original database.

With the use of domain terminologies, the problem of the (automatic) acquisition of thematic lexica and their mapping to a generic resource (Buitelaar and Sacaleanu, 2001; Vossen, 2001; Lavelli *et al.*, 2002) arises. As far as automatic term extraction is concerned, Basili *et al.* (2001) investigate whether syntactic context (i.e. structural information on local term context) can be used for determining the 'termhood' of given term candidates, with the aim of defining a weakly supervised 'termhood' model which suitably combines endogenous and exogenous syntactic information.

13.4   The plug-in approach

One of the basic problems in the development of techniques for the Semantic Web is the integration of ontologies. Indeed, the Web consists of a variety of information sources, and in order to extract information from these sources, their semantic integration is required.

Merging linguistic ontologies introduces issues concerning the amount of data to be managed (in the case of WordNet we have several dozen thousand synsets), which are typically neglected when upper levels are to be merged (Simov *et al.*, 2001).

This work attempts to advance a step further in the direction of the interoperability of linguistic ontologies by addressing the problem of the integration of global and specialized linguistic ontologies. The possibility of merging information at different levels of specificity would appear to be a crucial requirement for success, at least in the case of certain domains, such as economics or law, which include both very specific terms and a significant number of common terms that may be shared by the two ontologies. We assume the EuroWordNet model and propose a methodology to 'plug' specialized ontologies into global ontologies, i.e. to enable them to be accessed in conjunction via the construction of an integrated ontology.

13.4.1   Correspondences between global and specialized
linguistic ontologies

Global and specialized linguistic ontologies naturally complement each other. The former contains generic knowledge without domain-specific coverage, while the latter focuses on a specific domain, providing sub-hierarchies of highly specialized concepts. This scenario allows for significant simplifications when compared to the general problem of merging two ontologies. On the one hand we have a specialized ontology, whose content should reflect a greater degree of accuracy and precision as far as specialized information is concerned; however, on the other hand, we can assume that the global ontology should guarantee a more uniform coverage as far as high-level concepts are concerned. Combined, these two assumptions provide us with a powerful precedence criterion for managing both information overlapping and inheritance in the integration procedure.

In spite of the differences that exist between the two ontologies, it is often possible to find a certain degree of correspondence between them. In particular, note the information *overlapping* which occurs when the same concept belongs to both the global and to the specialized ontology, and the information *over-differentiation* which happens when a terminological concept has two or more corresponding concepts in the global ontology or the other way round. Finally, some specific concepts referring to technical notions may have no corresponding concept in the global ontology, which indicates the presence of a *conceptual gap*; in such cases a correspondence to the global ontology can be found through a more generic concept.

The sections highlighted in the global and the specialized ontology represented in Figure 13.1 reflect the correspondences one typically finds between general and specialized ontologies.

As for the global ontology (the bigger triangle), area *B1* has been highlighted as it corresponds to the sub-hierarchies containing the concepts belonging to the same specific domain of the specialized ontology (the smaller triangle). The middle part of the specialized ontology, which we call area *B*, is also highlighted, and corresponds to concepts which are not only representative of the specific domain, but are also present in the global ontology.

When the two ontologies undergo the integration procedure, an integrated ontology is constructed (Figure 13.2). Intuitively, we can think of this process as though the specialized ontology had somehow shifted over to the global one. In the integrated ontology, the information of the latter is maintained, with the exclusion of the sub-hierarchies containing the concepts belonging to the domain of the specialized ontology, which are covered by the corresponding area of the specialized. The integrated ontology also contains the most specific concepts of the specialized ontology (area *C*), which are not provided in the global. What is excluded from the integrated ontology is the highest part of the hierarchy of the specialized ontology; it is represented by area *A*, which contains generic concepts not belonging to a specialized domain. These concepts are expected to be treated more precisely in the global ontology.

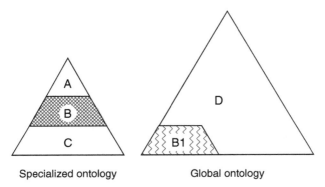

Specialized ontology   Global ontology

Figure 13.1 Separate specialized and global ontologies. Overlapping is represented in shaded areas

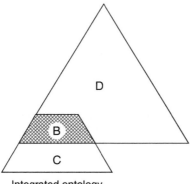

Integrated ontology

Figure 13.2 Integrated ontology. As to overlapping, precedence is given to the specialized ontology

13.4.2   Plug relations

The formal apparatus for realizing an integrated ontology is based on the use of three different kinds of relations (**plug-synonymy**, **plug-near-synonymy**, and **plug-hyponymy**) to connect basic concepts of the specialized ontology to the corresponding concepts in the global ontology, and on the use of eclipsing procedures that shadow certain concepts, either to avoid inconsistencies or as a secondary effect of a plug relation.

A plug relation directly connects pairs of corresponding concepts, one belonging to the global ontology and the other to the specialized ontology. The main effect of a plug relation is the creation of one or more 'plug concepts', which substitute the connected concepts, i.e. those directly involved in the relation. To describe the relations inherited by a plug concept, the following classification, adapted from Hirst and St-Onge, 1998, is employed: *up-links* of a concept are those whose target concept is more general (i.e. **hypernymy** and **instance-of** relations), *down-links* are those whose target is more specific (i.e. **hyponymy** and **has-instance** relations), and *horizontal-links* include all other relations (i.e. **part-of** relations, **cause** relations, derivation, etc.).

Plug-synonymy is used when overlapping concepts are found in the global ontology (hereafter *GLOB*) and in the specialized ontology (hereafter *SPEC*). The main effect of establishing a relation of plug-synonymy between concept C belonging to the global ontology (indicated as C^{GLOB}) and $C1^{SPEC}$ (i.e. concept $C1$ belonging to the specialized ontology) is the creation of a plug concept $C1^{PLUG}$. The plug concept gets its linguistic forms (i.e. synonyms)

Table 13.1 *Merging rules for plug-synonymy and plug-near-synonymy*

	CI^{PLUG}
Up links	*GLOB*
Down links	*SPEC*
Horizontal links	*GLOB + SPEC*

from *SPEC*, up-links from *GLOB*, down-links from *SPEC*, and horizontal-links both from *GLOB* and from *SPEC* (see Table 13.1). As a secondary effect, the up relations of CI^{SPEC} and the down relations of C^{GLOB} are eclipsed.

As an example, the creation of a **plug-synonymy** between { *fatturato* }^{GLOB} and { *fatturato* }^{SPEC} ('sales revenue') produces a new synset { *fatturato* }^{PLUG}, whose hypernym and hyponyms are, respectively, the hypernym of { *fatturato* }^{GLOB} and the hyponyms of { *fatturato* }^{SPEC}, and causes the eclipsing of the hypernym of { *fatturato* }^{SPEC}.

Plug-near-synonymy is used in two cases: (1) the over-differentiation of the *GLOB*, i.e. when a concept in the *SPEC* has two or more corresponding concepts in the *GLOB*; this happens, for instance, when regular polysemy is represented in the *GLOB* but not in the *SPEC*; (2) the over-differentiation of the *SPEC*, i.e. when a concept in the *GLOB* corresponds to two or more concepts in the *SPEC*; this situation may result as a consequence of subtle conceptual distinctions made by domain experts, which are not reported in the global ontology. Establishing a **plug-near-synonymy** relation has the same effect of creating a **plug-synonymy** (see Table 13.1).

Plug-hyponymy is used to connect concepts of the specialized ontology to more generic concepts in the case of conceptual gaps. The main effect of establishing a plug-hyponymy relation between C^{GLOB} (i.e. concept C of the global ontology) and CI^{SPEC} (i.e. concept C of the specialized ontology) is the creation of the two plug concepts C^{PLUG} and CI^{PLUG} (see Table 13.2). C^{PLUG} gets its linguistic forms from the *GLOB*, up-links from the *GLOB*, down-links are the hyponyms of C^{GLOB} plus the link to CI^{PLUG}, and horizontal-links from the *GLOB*. The other plug node, CI^{PLUG}, gets its linguistic form from the *SPEC*, C^{PLUG} as hypernym, down-links from the *SPEC* and horizontal-links from the *SPEC*. As a secondary effect, the hypernym of CI^{SPEC} is eclipsed.

To make an example, let us consider { *intermediazione_finanziaria* }^{SPEC} ('financial intermediation') and the more generic concept { *attività* }^{GLOB} ('activity').

Table 13.2 *Merging rules for plug-hyponymy*

	C^{PLUG}	C_1^{PLUG}
Up links	*GLOB*	C^{PLUG}
Down links	$GLOB + C_1^{PLUG}$	*SPEC*
Horizontal links	*GLOB*	*SPEC*

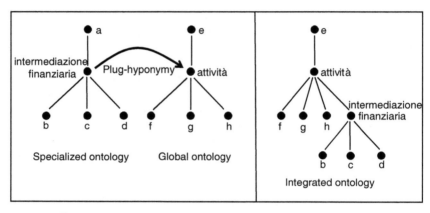

Figure 13.3 Example of **plug-hyponymy** between { *intermediazione_finanziaria* }^{SPEC} ('financial intermediation') and { *attività* }^{GLOB} ('activity')

As shown in Figure 13.3, the creation of a plug-hyponymy between them produces two new synsets in the integrated ontology, one the hyponym of the other:

- { *intermediazione_finanziaria* } ^{PLUG} (the hyponym), which gets its hyponyms from { *intermediazione_finanziaria* }^{SPEC} (i.e. *b*, *c*, and *d* in our example)
- { *attività* }^{PLUG} (the hypernym), which it gets its hypernym from { *attività* }^{GLOB} (i.e. *e*); among its hyponyms, we have not only { *intermediazione_finanziaria* } ^{PLUG}, but also all hyponyms of { *attività* }^{GLOB} (i.e. *f*, *g* and *h*);

In addition to this, it causes the eclipsing of the hypernym of { *intermediazione_finanziaria* }^{SPEC} (i.e. *a* in our example).

Eclipsing is a secondary effect of establishing a plug relation and is also an independent procedure used to avoid the case where pairs of overlapping concepts placed inconsistently in the taxonomies are included in the integrated ontology; this could happen, for instance, when 'whale' is placed under a 'fish' sub-hierarchy in a common-sense ontology, while also appearing in the mammal taxonomy of a scientific ontology.

13.4.3   Integration procedure

The plug-in approach described in the previous subsection has been realized by means of a semi-automatic procedure which consists of the following four main steps.

(1) **Basic concepts identification**. The domain expert identifies a preliminary set of 'basic concepts' in the specialized ontology. These concepts are highly representative of the domain and are also typically present in the global ontology. In addition, the basic concepts are required to be disjoint from each other, and they must also ensure complete coverage of the specialized ontology, i.e. it is required that all terminal nodes have at least one basic concept in their ancestor list. As examples of basic concepts, see { *fatturato* } ^{SPEC} ('sales revenue') and { *intermediazione_finanziaria* } ^{SPEC} ('financial inermediation') in Section 13.4.2.

(2) **Alignment**. This step consists of aligning each basic concept with the more similar concept of the global ontology, on the basis of the linguistic form of the concepts. Thus, for each pair a plug-in configuration is selected among those described in Section 13.4.2. For instance, { *fatturato* } ^{SPEC} is aligned to { *fatturato* } ^{GLOB} (the selected configuration is **plug-synonymy**); in the case of { *intermediazione_finanziaria* } ^{SPEC}, on the other hand, no similar concept is available, so it is necessary to select a more general concept (e.g. { *activity* } ^{GLOB}) and the **plug-hyponymy** configuration).

(3) **Merging**. For each plug-in configuration, an integration algorithm reconstructs the corresponding portion of the integrated ontology. For instance, in the case of { *intermediazione_finanziaria* } ^{SPEC}, the portion of integrated ontology to be created includes { *activity* } ^{PLUG} and { *intermediazione_finanziaria* } ^{PLUG} with their hypernyms and hyponyms (see Figure 13.3). If the integration algorithm detects no inconsistencies, the next plug-in configuration is considered, otherwise step 4 is called.

(4) **Resolution of inconsistencies**. Inconsistencies are detected automatically when the implementation of a plug-in configuration stands in contrast to a plug-in which has already been realized. In this case, the domain expert has to decide which configuration has priority and consequently modify the other configuration, which will be passed again to step 2 of the procedure.

Table 13.3 *IWN and ECOWN quantitative data*

	Specialized	Global
Synsets	4,687	49,108
Senses	5,313	64,251
Lemmas	5,130	45,006
Internal Relations	9,372	126,326
Variants/synsets	1.13	1.30
Senses/lemmas	1.03	1.42

13.5   Experiments

The integration procedure described in Section 13.4.3 has been tested within the SI-TAL project[1] to connect a global wordnet and a specialized wordnet that has been created independently. ItalWordNet (IWN) (Roventini *et al.*, 2000), which was created as part of the EuroWordNet project (Vossen, 1998) and further developed through the introduction of adjectives and adverbs, is the lexical database involved in the plug-in as a generic resource and consists of about 45,000 lemmas. Economic-WordNet (ECOWN) is a specialized wordnet for the economic domain and consists of about 5,000 lemmas distributed among approximately 4,700 synsets. Table 13.3 summarizes the quantitative data of the two resources considered.

As a first step, about 250 basic synsets (5.3% of the resource) of the specialized wordnet were manually identified by a domain expert, including, for instance { *azione* } ('share'), and excluding less informative synsets, such as { *azione* } ('action'). Alignment with respect to the global wordnet (step 2 of the procedure) was carried out with an algorithm that considers the match of the variants. Candidates were then checked by the domain expert, who also chose the proper plug relation. In the case of gaps, a synset with a more generic meaning was selected and a **plug-hyponymy** relation was chosen.

At this point we applied the merging algorithm to take each plug relation and reconstruct a portion of the integrated wordnet. In total, 4,662 ECOWN synsets were connected to IWN. Of these, 577 synsets (corresponding to area *B* in Figure 13.2) substituted the synsets provided in the global ontology to represent the corresponding concepts (area *B1* in Figure 13.1) and 4,085 synsets, corresponding to the most specific concepts of the domain (area *C* in Figure 13.2), were properly added to the database. Twenty-five high-level ECOWN synsets (area *A* in Figure 13.1) were eclipsed as the effect of plug relations. The

---

[1] Si-TAL (Integrated System for the Automatic Treatment of Language) is a National Project devoted to the creation of large linguistic resources and software for Italian written and spoken language processing.

number of plug relations established is 269 (92 plug-synonymy, 36 plug-near-synonymy and 141 plug-hyponymy relations), while 449 IWN synsets with an economic meaning were eclipsed, either as a consequence of plug relations (when the two taxonomic structures are consistent) or through the independent procedure of eclipsing (when the taxonomies are inconsistent). Each relation connects on average 17.3 synsets.

13.6   Applications and extensions

The plug-in approach we have proposed has been applied to a number of different resources, both for extensions of existing resources and for independently created resources. In this section, we discuss the main resources that have taken advantage of the plug-in approach, as reported in the literature.

Sagri *et al.* (2004) proposed applying the plug-in approach to Jur-WordNet, an extension of ItalWordNet for the legal domain aimed at providing multilingual access to sources of legal information.

Despite being developed to integrate independently developed resources, the plug-in approach has been used for the extension of linguistic ontologies. In the case of the extension of ItalWordNet with a database of maritime terminology (Marinelli *et al.*, 2006), the authors first identified the basic concepts which became the root nodes of the terminological database, and then populated the database with more specific concepts. The plug-in relations have been used to link each terminological sub-hierarchy (represented by its basic concept) to a node of ItalWordNet. The plug-hyponymy relation was used when the basic concept missing from ItalWordNet was considered a specific concept. On the other hand, if the basic concept was considered a generic concept, it was directly added to ItalWordNet.

The methodology developed to integrate MultiWordNet (Pianta *et al.*, 2002) and ArchiWordNet, a specialized resource for the architecture domain (Bentivogli *et al.*, 2004), is based on the plug-in approach, but elaborates it with the quite different aim of exploiting as much as possible the domain knowledge already provided in the global wordnet. The authors used the so-called substitutive plug-in (which is most similar to the plug-in we propose) for only three ArchiWordNet hierarchies, whereas in most cases they used integrative plug-ins. Another important difference between the two approaches is represented by the depth at which the plug-in takes place. This can be easily appreciated considering that, in our experiment, we individuated 250 basic synsets (i.e. 250 economy sub-hierarchies) whereas ArchiWordNet consists of 13 sub-hierarchies.

A recent extension of the plug-in approach has been suggested in Luengen *et al.*, 2008, where the plug-in approach is adapted and applied to resources represented in the Web Ontology language OWL, thus opening new perspectives for the ontologies of the Semantic Web. As the two resources (the domain-specific TermNet and the generic GermaNet) are both represented in OWL but with two different models, the authors defined OWL-properties that relate entities of the two resources. The authors primarily focus on modelling the relationships between general-language and domain-specific concepts, using the plug-in metaphor more for the relational model than for the integration process. Termnet concepts are modelled as classes and GermaNet synsets as individuals, so they realize the integration by restricting the range of a plug-in property to the individual that represents the corresponding GermaNet synset.

Finally, the significance of the plug-in approach is demonstrated by a series of subsequent attempts to fully automatize the process of finding candidate synsets for plug relations. Experiments have been performed in particular in the context of the CtxMatch approach (Magnini *et al.*, 2004), which exploits the implicit information derived from the context of a specific concept in an ontology (or other hierarchical structure), i.e. the relations of that concept with other concepts.

13.7   Conclusion

After discussing the main features and uses of linguistic ontologies as opposed to formal ontologies, we have addressed the problem of the interoperability between linguistic ontologies, and gone one step further by presenting a methodology for the integration of a global and a specialized linguistic ontology. The global-specialized scenario allows the definition of a strong precedence criterion to solve cases of conflicting information. The advantage of this approach is that a limited number of plug relations allows the connection of a large number of concepts (i.e. synsets) to take place between the two ontologies. Extensions of this methodology have been applied to other languages, e.g. German, and to other domains, e.g. the legal domain, the maritime domain and the architecture domain. Another potential domain for extension to be considered is the agricultural domain, with respect to the specialized ontology described in Chapter 17.

Part IV

Learning and using ontological knowledge

14   The life cycle of knowledge

Alessandro Lenci

14.1   Introduction

Due to its prima facie abstract character, we are often led to conceive of *knowledge* as a changeless entity inhabiting an extra-time realm, much like Plato's World of Ideas. Hence, we tend to forget or underestimate the crucial fact that knowledge has its own life cycle, similar to anything else in the universe. Newly created knowledge changes over time: it may reproduce itself, generating new knowledge; it may die out, as proven by the fact that our knowledge about artefacts, practices, people, or places can disappear forever. In technical domains (such as, for instance, biology, medicine, computer science, and agriculture), as claimed by Kawtrakul and Imsombut (Chapter 17 this volume), the rate of knowledge change can be very high, in which concepts become 'obsolete' because of new technological advances, which, in turn, may induce complex reorganizations or expansions of the knowledge system. These similar processes apply to ontologies as well, since ontologies are formal systems aimed at representing a certain body of knowledge.

The dynamics of knowledge and ontologies depend on their *contexts of use*. Knowledge is created or acquired for some purpose, e.g. to be used as a tool to achieve a certain goal or to perform a particular task. Its usage also changes our knowledge about entities and processes, and, consequently, leads us to revise our ontological systems. Moreover, employing some body of knowledge to perform a task may produce new knowledge that has to be added to our ontologies, possibly resulting in a major revision of their structure, if some breakthrough in the knowledge system has occurred. Actually, this is usually the main or ultimate purpose for us to carry out the task.

This book deals with ontological and lexical knowledge resources. The ontolex interface (see Chapter 10) is an attempt to address the increasing need of modelling the complex interrelationship between lexicons and ontologies. I will use the term *ontolexical resources* to stress the importance of investigating the substantial areas of overlapping between ontologies and lexicons. In this chapter, I will focus on the interaction between ontolexical resources and *natural language processing* (NLP). The interaction is bidirectional. First of all, NLP tools and applications are intensive *knowledge users*, because they have to access large amounts of different types of knowledge to carry out the tasks they are designed for. This raises the issue of how the particular goals of NLP systems act as constraints on ontological systems, so that the type and the organization of knowledge can optimally comply with the needs of NLP tasks. Second, NLP tools and applications are also powerful *knowledge creators*, because they can be used to create and modify ontolexical resources, for instance, by allowing the bits of knowledge to be represented in such resources to be carved out of the linguistic structures that encode them in natural language texts. Despite their prima facie differences, the two roles of NLP systems as knowledge users and knowledge creators are deeply interrelated. This integrated view is not an optional one, but rather, it represents the essential condition for NLP systems, on the one hand, to exploit at their best the incredible potential offered by large-scale ontolexical resources, and, on the other hand, to boost and enhance the process of knowledge creation.

14.2   Using ontolexical knowledge in NLP

From information extraction to question answering, the final goal of most NLP systems and applications is to access the information content of texts through the interpretation of their linguistic structures. To carry out their tasks, NLP systems need to know the relevant pieces of knowledge to be identified in texts, as well as how this knowledge is encoded in linguistic expressions. The role of ontolexical resources is to provide NLP systems with these two crucial types of information. In addition, there is a further important factor that assigns a key role to ontolexical knowledge in NLP, a factor that is not directly dependent on the specific system goals, but rather derives from the core principles of language. In fact, most of the constraints natural language grammars obey are *lexicalized*, and many aspects of complex linguistic structures depend on the properties of the lexical items that compose them. The *paradigmatic* properties of lexical items – the classes to which they belong in virtue of their morphosyntactic and semantic properties – constrain their possible *syntagmatic* distributional properties – the range of linguistic contexts in which they can appear. Thus, ontolexical knowledge plays a prominent role in most NLP architectures. Although there are approaches that dispense with this type of information altogether, the addition of ontolexical information usually proves to be a necessary step for enhancing the system performances in tackling the challenges set by natural language.

    In the sections below, I will focus on four major use contexts for ontolexical knowledge in NLP: *semantic typing, semantic similarity and relatedness, inference*, and *argument structure*. They represent some of the most important ways in which systems typically employ the information in ontolexical resources to achieve their specific applicative goals. While applications often change quite rapidly – following the waves of market needs or of technological developments – these use contexts provide us with general vantage points from which to observe the role of different aspects of semantic information in NLP, as well as the main problems and challenges that knowledge-intensive processing of natural language must face.

14.2.1 Semantic typing

The primary aim of ontolexical resources is to characterize the *semantic types* of linguistic expressions, i.e. the classes to which linguistic expressions belong in virtue of their meanings. Types can be regarded as formal, symbolic ways of identifying the concepts expressed by linguistic expressions. To the extent that meanings are related to entities in the world, semantic types also correspond to the categories of entities the linguistic items refer to. By assigning a lexical item to a semantic type, we characterize and focus on specific aspects of its semantic space. For instance, the type AEROPLANE can be used to explicitly represent one of the senses expressed by the word *plane*.

Ontologies and lexicons represent key resources for *semantic typing*, defined as the process of automatically identifying the semantic types of linguistic expressions in texts. As Pustejovsky *et al.* 2002 rightly claim, semantic typing is the backbone and prerequisite of most NLP applications to achieve content-based access to texts. For example, the goal of information extraction is to identify relevant facts from texts. Facts are typically defined by events involving a certain number of entities belonging to different categories (e.g. humans, locations, proteins, vehicles, etc.). The instances of the semantic categories relevant for the application domain must be identified in texts, and this amounts to assigning the proper semantic types to their linguistic descriptors. Take the following pair of sentences: *The new medicine is highly effective against pneumonia. This illness can still be quite dangerous.* An information-extraction system operating in the biomedical domain might need to understand that the word *pneumonia* belongs to the semantic type DISEASE and, therefore, the first sentence actually mentions a fact or event concerning this category of entities. Similarly, type identification is also critical for resolving the anaphorical link between the noun phrase *this illness* in the latter sentence and *pneumonia* in the former one.

Besides the semantic typing of entities, the problem of identifying the relations linking these entities is gaining increasing attention (Nastase and Szpakowicz, 2003; Girju *et al.*, 2005; Turney, 2006). Semantic relations can be explicitly encoded by lexical items, such as verbs or relational nouns, but they can also be implicitly expressed by linguistic constructions. For instance, the proper interpretation of noun compounds requires the understanding of the specific relation between their constituent words, such as **material** (*apple pie*), **location** (*lung cancer*), or **meronymy** (*door handle*). Conversely, the semantic relation of **causation**, besides being explicitly expressed by lexical items such as *cause* or *provoke*, is also implicitly encoded by compound nouns such as *food infection* or *flu virus*. Most of these relations are represented in *ontolexicons*, which are therefore often used as key knowledge resources for automatic semantic relation identification.

As is clear from these examples, semantic typing is actually a very complex task, which, in turn, presents a broad spectrum of possible variations, depending on the applicative and the domain-specific needs. In any case, it crucially relies on the identification of the semantic potential of lexical items, and more precisely on the possibility to characterize the way linguistic constructions express a certain system of semantic categories and the relations among these categories. This is the reason why semantic typing represents a crucial use context for *ontolexical resources*.

14.2.2   Semantic similarity and relatedness

Natural language expressions can share different aspects of their meanings and they can be *semantically similar* at various degrees. Semantic similarity is a very loosely defined notion, actually forming a wide spectrum of variation spanning from the full- or near-synonymy of pairs such as *king–monarch*, to much wider associative links. Budanitsky and Hirst 2006 (following Resnik, 1995) distinguish semantically similar pairs such as *horse–pony* from semantically related ones, such as *hot–cold* or *handle–door*. While similar pairs contain words referring to entities that share a certain number of salient 'features' (e.g. shape, position in a taxonomy, functionality, etc.), related pairs are formed by words that are connected by some type of semantic or associative relation – such as antonymy, meronymy, frequent co-occurrence – without being necessarily similar themselves (e.g. *handle–door*). Parallel distinctions are typically assumed in the psycholinguistic literature, where the notion of semantic similarity plays a crucial role in the explanation of phenomena such as priming effects (Moss *et al.*, 1995).

A huge literature exists in linguistics, philosophy, and cognitive science devoted to the many conundrums hidden behind such a prima facie natural aspect of semantic organization. The problem can be summarized as follows. It is more or less incontrovertible that *dog* is more semantically similar to *cat* than to *car*. However, turning such intuitions into effective and formal criteria to determine the degree of semantic similarity between two words is extremely hard. Yet, measuring the semantic similarity (or relatedness) between words has a key importance in any applicative context, such as word-sense disambiguation, information extraction and retrieval, machine translation. An illustration is provided on the use of similarity measures for question answering in Chapter 16 of this volume.

Ontolexical systems play an important role in computing semantic similarity (relatedness). Besides the fact that most of these resources explicitly contain lists of synonymous terms (like the synsets in WordNet), groups of similar words can be explicitly represented by assigning them to the same semantic type. For instance, *aeroplane*, *boat*, *car* and *bus* can all be assigned to the type VEHICLE, thereby making explicit the fact that they belong to the same paradigmatic class as determined by key features of the meaning they share (e.g. they can move, are designed for transportation, can be driven, etc.). If conversely *cat* and *dog* are assigned to the type ANIMAL, the 'dissimilarity' between *dog* and *car* immediately follows from their belonging to different semantic types. Even more crucially, it is the structure of the ontology that can be used to compute the degree of semantic similarity (relatedness) between words. In fact, semantic similarity (dissimilarity) between two words can be formally defined in terms of the closeness (distance) of their types in the semantic space defined by the ontology. Various types of metrics have been proposed in the literature that exploit the path (and types) of relations connecting two concepts to measure their semantic proximity. Budanitsky and Hirst (2006) provide an interesting survey and evaluation of different measures of semantic relatedness based on the topology of relations in WordNet.

14.2.3   Inference

The main function of the human conceptual system is to provide the basis for drawing inferences about the entities that belong to a certain category (Murphy, 2002). In a parallel fashion, this inferential ability is a characteristic property of our lexical competence: knowing the meaning of a word suggests that a speaker can draw some inferences from it (Marconi, 1997). For instance, if we understand the meaning of the sentence *Tweety is a bird*, we also infer that Tweety is an animal and that it is very likely to fly. Similarly, the meaning of the word *kill* in the sentence *The man killed the gorp* allows us to infer that the *gorp* – whatever this entity might be – was very likely to be a living being before the occurrence of this event, and became dead afterward. Inferences differ with respect to their type and strength, some of them being logical entailments (as in the case of a cat being an animal), others having instead just a probabilistic value. In fact, not all birds fly, but only the most prototypical ones. In either case, inferences depend on the properties and on the organization of our system of concepts and meanings.

Ontolexical resources represent the most direct way to explicitly capture the inferential relations between concepts and semantic types. Usually, they are not inferential system per se, but rather they are representational resources on which such systems can be defined. The definition of the classes of an ontology and the network of relations connecting them are the basis to define their inferential properties. Similar to the cognitive processes of categorization and concept formation, semantic types are designed at various levels of generality, abstracting away from specific features of meanings. Actually, semantic types usually form chains of conceptual classes ordered by subsumption relations: AEROPLANE, FLYING_VEHICLE, VEHICLE, INANIMATE_OBJECT, CONCRETE_OBJECT. Such chains allow systems to draw inferences that are crucial in many applicative contexts in NLP, such as information extraction, anaphora resolution, textual entailment recognition (Dagan *et al.*, 2006), etc. Consider, for instance, the following sequence of sentences: *The bus suddenly stopped along the road and the passengers went out of the vehicle. The engine was broken.* Capturing its information content requires NLP systems to resolve some cases of 'bridging' anaphora, defined as the referential phenomenon occurring when the referent of a linguistic expression can be determined only by recovering a meaningful implicit relation with an already mentioned entity or event. The co-reference between *vehicle* and *bus* can be resolved if the hyperonymic relation holding between these nouns is known to the system. Similarly, the availability in a computational lexicon of the information that engines are parts of buses can lead the system to infer the obvious fact that the broken engine belongs to the bus mentioned in the first sentence.

14.2.4   Argument structure

One of the most common use contexts for ontolexical resources in theoretical and computational linguistics is to specify the combinatorial constraints of lexical items. Some ontolexicons provide explicit representational devices of argument-structure properties, such as number and semantic types of arguments, semantic roles, argument alternations, and realizations (Levin and Hovav, 2005), etc. This is, for instance, the case of FrameNet (Baker *et al.*, 2003), Omega (cf. Chapter 15), VerbNet (Kipper-Schuler, 2005), SIMPLE (Lenci *et al.*, 2000), among others. It is also a common practice to start from a given ontology of types and then to try to use its conceptual atoms to specify the *selectional preferences* of predicative expressions. For instance, although WordNet itself does not encode argument-structure properties, it has been widely used as a source of semantic types for argument-semantic specification (Resnik, 1996). Light and Greiff 2002 and Brockmann and Lapata 2003 provide interesting surveys and evaluations of various WordNet-based approaches to selectional preferences. Generally, the structure of the ontology is exploited in order to identify the suitable level of semantic abstraction of the arguments that can typically occur in a certain predicate role (e.g. as direct objects of *eat*, or as subjects of *drive*). Given the notorious difficulties of defining the predicate-selectional preferences as sets of necessary and sufficient conditions, probabilistic models are typically used to establish the proper mapping, i.e. to determine the type or types that best capture the combinatorial constraints of predicates.

It goes without saying that the role of ontolexical resources in providing suitable representations for predicative structures is of paramount importance for a large number of tasks in NLP. Selectional preferences can act as key constraints for parsing, question answering, and relation extraction. Moreover, event identification in texts also requires access to information about the semantic roles expressed by predicates. Semantic-role labelling (Gildea and Jurafsky, 2002; Erk and Padó, 2006b) exploits resources such as FrameNet that provide the information about predicate argument structures, argument semantic roles, and the inferential relations between these roles (e.g. that a driver is a type of agent).

14.2.5 *The challenges of the ontolex interface*

As discussed, ontolexical resources appear to be undoubtedly important components in knowledge-intensive NLP applications involving tasks that crucially depend on knowledge about the structure and organization of a conceptual domain, and on the semantic content of the lexical and grammatical constructions describing this domain. Ontolexical systems can fulfil this role to the extent that they are able to provide suitable formal characterizations of the repertoire of semantic types and of the mapping between the language system and the conceptual system. But what are the challenges to achieving these goals?

The main problem is that the interface between language and concepts that ontolexicons purport to represent is notoriously highly complex. The principles governing this interface are still in many respects obscure and to a large extent defy precise formalizations. In general, no naive mapping between lexical and conceptual systems can pretend to capture the order of complexity shown by the semantic behaviour of natural language expressions. Polysemy, metaphor, metonymy, and vagueness are only some examples of the rich semantic phenomenology through which this complexity manifests ubiquitously in language. These phenomena are *systematic*, in the sense that they present specific regularities within a language and across languages (Pustejovsky, 1995). At the same time, they represent also *systemic* features of natural language, since they are inherent properties of its semantic organization and of the way the mapping between the conceptual and language systems have become established.

These pervasive semantic phenomena point towards a non-naive relation-ship between *concepts* – as representations of categories of entities – and *meanings* – as the semantic content of linguistic expressions. Most of the theo-retical and computational literature in semantics (this chapter included) usually tends to treat these two terms as essentially interchangeable, with meanings being regarded as concepts mapped on or linked to linguistic symbols that are conventionally used to communicate them. Actually, this equation is more or less explicitly assumed in many computational lexicons (e.g. WordNet), whose word-sense descriptions are often interpreted as concepts of an ontology.[1] Its widespread use notwithstanding, the meaning–concept equation is, however, not granted at all. Indeed, in recent psychological research on human seman-tic representation and categorization systems, there is rich evidence supporting the view that these two notions should be kept well distinguished (Murphy, 2002; Vigliocco and Vinson, 2007). This, obviously, does not mean to deny that concepts and meanings are related, but rather that this relation cannot be assumed to be one of straightforward 'ontological' identity. In fact, if this assumption is dropped, the notion itself of ontolexical interface gains much more relevance as the place at which the complex interplay between concep-tual systems and the semantics of natural language can be represented and investigated.

A second issue raised by semantic phenomenology is the relationship between the meanings of lexical expressions as captured by ontolexical resources and their interpretation in context. Ontolexical resources are gen-erally systems of semantic types which are defined and characterized more or less independently of the typical linguistic contexts in which these types are used. The crucial issue is to understand the extent to which context enters into the semantic constitution of linguistic expressions. In fact, lexical meaning is to a large extent a context-sensitive reality, and phenomena like polysemy or metonymy should be more properly modelled as the results of sense-generation processes in context (Pustejovsky, 1995). Lexical expressions have a seman-tic potential that gets realized as specific senses or interpretations when they combine with other linguistic expressions in syntagmatic contexts. It is worth emphasizing that the importance of these issues greatly exceeds their central-ity for theoretical semantic research. Given the aim of ontolexical systems at being effective knowledge resources for NLP systems, they cannot but face the challenges set by the different creative ways in which lexical items are used in texts. Tackling these phenomena raises the key question of whether they should be accounted at the representational level, within the lexicon or

---

[1] There are also exceptions. An example is provided by the *Omega Ontology* (Chapter 15), which includes an explicit distinction between the level of word-sense description and the level of conceptual representation.

the ontology, or rather at the processing level, by those systems that will use ontolexical knowledge within the larger perspective of text understanding. The answer to this notorious dilemma deeply affects the structure of ontolexical resources themselves, as well as the way they can be used in NLP tasks. For instance, wiring too many polysemous or metaphorical uses in the lexicon typically results in very granular sense distinctions. These will in turn negatively impact on systems that need to map such fine-grained sense distinctions on texts, e.g. for word sense disambiguation or machine translation. Therefore, enhancing the usability of lexical semantic resources for NLP tasks necessarily requires a better understanding of the theoretical principles governing the ontolex interface. Actually, its domain should not be limited to the characterization of binary relations between concepts and lexical items, but should instead cover the threefold interaction between the conceptual system, lexical expressions, and the linguistic contexts that shape and modulate their senses.

14.3   Creating ontolexical knowledge with NLP

Every time we introduce a new item in an ontology we perform 'an act of creation' (Hovy, 2005). Typically, this demiurgic experience is carried out by a domain expert, who builds the ontology either directly or indirectly, in the latter case by providing another 'ontologizer' with the necessary information about the domain structure. In either case, the human expert is supposed to be the most reliable knowledge source, from which the various components of an ontology can be made explicit and formalized. The key role of human expertise notwithstanding, another no less crucial knowledge source for ontology building is represented by natural language texts. Indeed, documents – from Wikipedia to scientific papers and technical reports – are the primary repository of the knowledge of a certain community. Therefore, they can be mined to identify the knowledge items most relevant to characterize a particular domain, and use them to feed the ontology creation process.

The challenge in using document sources for ontology development is obviously how to carve the formal structure of the conceptual system out of the implicit and informal ways in which knowledge is expressed and encoded in texts. The role of NLP methods and tools is exactly to help to bridge this gap, by extracting the relevant pieces of knowledge from texts, through various levels of processing and analysis of their linguistic structure. The use of NLP – in combination with machine learning, and AI-derived methods – to acquire knowledge from texts in support of ontology development is now commonly referred to (especially in the Semantic Web community) as *ontology learning*.[2] Indeed, ontology learning holds a high 'family resemblance' with the long-standing line of research in computational linguistics concerning (semi-)automatic acquisition of lexical information from texts (Manning and Schütze, 1999) in support of the development of computational lexical resources. Although there are some reasons to keep these two fields apart (Buitelaar *et al.*, 2005), the existence of a strong commonality of methods and intents is undeniable. Indeed, many popular techniques for ontology learning were originally born and developed in the context of lexical acquisition. The possible complementarity between ontology learning and lexical acquisition rather lies in a difference of emphasis with respect to their goals. While the purpose of ontology learning is to support the development of conceptual resources, lexical acquisition is generally more oriented towards the text-driven acquisition of specific linguistic properties of lexical items (e.g. subcategorization patterns, selectional preferences, synonymy relations, etc.).

In the context of ontolexical resources – with their strong interaction and interplay between ontological and lexical knowledge – clearly the overlap between ontology learning and lexical acquisition also increases. The boundaries between these two enterprises become so tenuous that the term *ontolexical learning* seems to be perfectly justified. What is worth emphasizing is that in both cases NLP directly enters into the life cycle of knowledge, by supporting the process of creation and growth of ontolexical resources. The latter is surely the phase in which the role of text-driven learning is most effective. In fact, although there are cases in which a whole ontology is bootstrapped from natural language sources, a much more common scenario is the one in which NLP techniques are used to extend and enrich an existing, human-made ontolexical resource. For instance, there are countless works focusing on the (semi)-automatic extension of WordNet through lexical information automatically harvested from corpora. Pustejovsky *et al.* (2002) apply NLP and statistical techniques to extend and adapt UMLS, the most important knowledge organization system in the medical domain. Similar techniques are also used by Kawtrakul and Imsombut (Chapter 17, this volume) for the maintenance of an ontology in the agricultural domain.

The spectrum of solutions offered to the problem of ontolexical learning is incredibly wide, and the number of publications devoted to it huge. Rather than attempting an impossible not to say useless survey of existing approaches to create knowledge with NLP methods, I will here focus on three general questions: *What pieces of knowledge can we extract with NLP? From which sources? How is NLP used to extract ontolexical knowledge?* There is a fourth

[2] Actually, ontology learning is a much broader field encompassing also knowledge acquisition from non-textual sources. Nevertheless, I will use this term only to refer to knowledge acquisition from texts.

issue that is also worth touching: *What for?* In other terms, *What are the advantages of using NLP and learning methods for ontolexical building?* Apparently, there is a very simple and direct answer, which usually appears at the beginning of every paper on this topic, i.e. because it is convenient, since it makes the process of ontolexical development easier and faster. However, we will see that this is not the only rationale, and there are actually more theoretical reasons that suggest that extracting ontolexical information from text data may actually enhance its quality and usability.

14.3.1 *Which ontolexical information can be extracted with NLP?*

Ontologies are complex entities that contain different types of components (cf. Chapter 10 this volume): classes representing categories of objects, properties and relations, link to the linguistic constructions that express these conceptual entities in a given language, cross-lingual links, etc. Actually, this whole spectrum of entities can be the target of NLP-based acquisition processes. Buitelaar *et al.* (2005) propose to arrange the possible targets of knowledge acquisition in what they refer to as the *ontology learning layer cake*: from the bottom to the top, this includes *terms, synonyms, concepts, concepts hierarchies, relations*, and *rules*. As is clear from this list, the layers differ with respect to the increasing degree of abstraction from the linguistic surface, and consequently with respect to the complexity of the learning task itself. Extracting the relevant domain terminology from a text collection is a crucial step within ontology learning and is now mature for real-scale applications (Frantzi and Ananiadou, 1999; Jacquemin, 2001). Synonymy detection methods have achieved impressive results, and their performance is now approaching human-like performance (Lin, 1998b; Rapp, 2003). Much effort is also devoted to the text-driven identification of taxonomical and other non-hierarchical relations (Hearst, 1992; Cimiano *et al.*, 2005; Pantel and Pennacchiotti, 2006), although further research is needed to improve the accuracy of relation learning.[3]

Besides the entities mentioned in the 'layer cake', other important pieces of knowledge that can be acquired automatically from texts are the instances of the ontology classes. This issue is usually considered to lie outside the specific field of ontology learning and receives the name of *ontology population*. Yet it is surely an important part of the general ontology development cycle: for instance, acquiring information about which entities in a domain are instances of a particular ontology class is an important condition to enhance the usability of the ontology for various tasks or applications (cf. Chapter 16 in this volume, for the case of question answering). Interestingly, Nédellec and Nazarenko

---

[3] For further references on these issues, cf. Buitelaar *et al.*, 2005.

(2005) point out the connections between information extraction – as the task of extracting factual information about events and entities – and ontology population. This is an important case of a virtuous circle in which an NLP core task such as information extraction at the same time can play the role of ontolexical knowledge user and developer.

Moving towards the linguistic side of ontolexical resources, the range of information types that are targeted by text-driven acquisition processes is equally extremely wide. Besides term extraction and synonymy detection that are shared with the ontology learning enterprise, we can mention the acquisition of subcategorization frames (Korhonen, 2002), predicate selectional preferences (McCarthy, 2001), lexicalized concept properties (Almuhareb and Poesio, 2004; Cimiano and Wenderoth, 2007), etc. Again the state-of-the-art performances are strictly correlated with the type of targeted lexical information. In general, however, it is safe to assume that automatically extracted information is constantly gaining centrality and importance for the development and extension of ontolexical resources.

14.3.2   Which text sources can be used?

Until now we have generally talked of text-driven knowledge extraction, but actually an important parameter in ontolexical learning methods concerns the type of natural language source. A major divide exists between knowledge extraction from *semi-structured texts* such as thesauri, glossaries, and machine readable dictionaries, and knowledge extraction from *text corpora*. In the former case, the input is represented by texts that are already designed to act as knowledge and lexical resources, although their structure is typically not a formal one and usually addressed to a human user. For instance, a long-standing line of research in computational linguistics has applied NLP techniques to convert dictionary definitions into structured semantic entities to populate computational lexicons (cf. for instance the ACQUILEX projects (Copestake, 1992)).

The advantage of using existing human-oriented knowledge resources is the possibility to exploit their partial structure (e.g. the conceptual categories of a thesaurus or the sense distinctions in a dictionary) to spell out the domain-conceptual organization. In fact, the thesauri or glossaries already available in many technical domains represent major repositories of the knowledge shared by a community, and therefore provide key input to determine the relevant domain concepts and structure. On the other hand, the use of these semi-structured text sources have shortcomings as well, the most important one being the fact that they are themselves limited and biased by the fact of being originally designed for human users. For instance, a dictionary entry for a word may give useful information for a human reader to understand bits of its meaning, but at the same time fail to provide key semantic properties necessary for an application to process that same word in a certain NLP task.

To overcome the limitations of semi-structured lexical resources, most approaches to ontolexical learning use *text corpora*.[4] The basic assumption is that the concepts relevant for organizing a particular domain of knowledge can be extracted from texts representative of that domain. Although the fact that the relevant pieces of knowledge are only implicitly encoded in texts provides a high challenge for NLP methods, corpus processing is surely the most promising source for ontology population, extension, and maintenance. Since ontology learning is mostly directed towards the vertical enrichment of domain ontologies, specialized corpora represent the preferred data source. For instance, the Medline collection of medical abstracts can be an endless knowledge mine to refine and extend medical ontologies (Pustejovsky *et al.*, 2002). On the other hand, large-scale, open-domain corpora are used as well. Large corpora are in fact useful to address or limit the negative effect of data sparseness, and many approaches now regard the Web itself as an important resource to extract semantic information. The applications of NLP methods to online encyclopedias such as Wikipedia could represent an interesting compromise between the use of semi-structured knowledge sources and corpus processing for ontology learning.

14.3.3   How to use NLP to extract ontolexical knowledge

Ontolexical learning is typically carried out through some mixture of text analysis with NLP tools – from lemmatization and POS tagging to different forms of shallow and deep parsing – together with machine learning or statistical methods to identify and weigh the extracted pieces of knowledge. The particular types of linguistic processing and statistical method provide the main parameters of variation among existing approaches to *ontolexical learning*. Within this large spectrum, one major family of algorithms is based on the a priori identification of *linguistic patterns* univocally associated with particular types of knowledge or semantic relations. This trend of research has been opened by the seminal work of Hearst (1992), who used automatically extracted patterns like *such NPh as NP1 or NP2* to identify pairs of concepts linked by hyperonymic or co-hyponymic relation. For instance, the identification in a corpus of the expression *such aircraft as jets or helicopters* as an instance of the above pattern, would be taken as evidence that *jet* and *helicopter* are **hyponyms** of *aircraft*. This method includes a sort of weak

---

[4] Hybrid approaches also exist, which use combinations of text corpora and structured knowledge resources for ontology learning. Cf. for instance Kawtrakul and Imsombut (Chapter 17 in this volume).

supervision, since the linguist must decide a priori which patterns are associated with which semantic relations. The patterns can be more or less abstract depending on the type of text processing that is performed (e.g. tokenization, shallow parsing, etc.). They are then searched on a large corpus and then statistically filtered to reduce noise. The increasing popularity of pattern-based methods (Berland and Charniak, 1999, Widdows and Dorow, 2002, Almuhareb and Poesio, 2004, Cimiano and Wenderoth, 2007, among many others) is due to the fact that they are very promising in allowing the explicit 'typing' of the extracted knowledge, thereby facilitating its possible mapping onto existing ontologies. Yet this strategy also has various shortcomings. First of all, it often runs into data-sparseness problem, since the relevant patterns are generally very rare. A common way to mitigate this problem is to use Web searches to have reliable statistics of linguistic patterns. Secondly, and most crucially, this approach works well only provided that we are able to identify easy-to-mine patterns, univocally associated with the target knowledge type. The problem is that this univocity is very rare in natural language, and most patterns are ambiguous or polysemous, since they encode very different types of semantic relations. For instance, the pattern X has Y can be used to express a meronymic relation (e.g. *a car has four wheels*), but also a possessive relation (e.g. *this man has a car*). This may result in high levels of noise, negatively impacting on the system precision.

Other methods for knowledge extraction instead adopt a fully unsupervised approach, and try to construct lexical semantic representations out of word-statistical distributions in corpora. Rather than searching for the words that instantiate a number of pre-selected and (supposedly) semantically meaningful patterns, *semantic space models* represent a target word as a point in an n-dimensional vector space, constructed from the observed distributional patterns of co-occurrence of its neighbouring words. Co-occurrence information is usually collected in a frequency matrix, where each row corresponds to a target word and each column represents its linguistic context. The assumption lying behind this type of semantic representation is the so-called 'distributional hypothesis', stating that two words are semantically similar to the extent that they occur in similar contexts (Harris, 1968; Miller and Charles, 1991). Vectorial representations are used to estimate the semantic relatedness between two words on the grounds of their distance in the n-dimensional vector space. A huge spectrum of variation exists among these models, mostly due to the particular statistical and mathematical technique used to process the co-occurrence vectors, and to the definition of linguistic context. In *Latent Semantic Analysis* (Landauer and Dumais, 1997) the context is represented by a whole document in a collection, and the word-semantic similarity is computed in a reduced dimensionality space, obtained through the Singular Value Decomposition of the original frequency matrix. Alternatively, the context can be provided by a window of *n* words surrounding the target word (cf. *Hyperspace Analogue to Language*, Burgess and Lund, 1997).[5] Other approaches instead adopt a syntactically enriched notion of context (Lin, 1998b; Padó and Lapata, 2007), and two words are said to co-occur if they are linked by a certain syntactic relation (e.g. subject, modifier, etc.). This latter method is often claimed to be able to produce much more accurate semantic spaces, although a much heavier corpus pre-processing is required.

Semantic-space models are very good in finding synonym pairs. For instance, Rapp (2003) reports 92.50% accuracy in the synonym-detection task carried out on the TOEFL dataset. Still, a major shortcoming of these methods is represented by the fact that their outcome is typically formed only by a quantitative assessment of the degree of semantic association between two words, with the type of relation remaining totally underspecified. Actually, the space of semantic neighbours of a target word can be highly heterogeneous, and besides synonyms it is typically populated by meronyms, co-hyponyms, or simply words belonging to the same semantic domain. Therefore, while the output of these methods can surely provide useful hints for evaluating the degree of semantic relatedness between two or more words, much work is still needed to carve actual semantic structure out of distributional spaces.

14.3.4   Why extract ontolexical knowledge using NLP?

It is well known that the process of developing ontologies and computational lexicons by hand is a very time-consuming and expensive enterprise. Thus, the possibility offered by ontology-learning methods to automatize parts of this process seems to be a promising way to overcome the 'knowledge acquisition bottleneck' of ontolexical resources, i.e. the fact that they are absolutely needed to perform new innovative steps in information technology, and yet they are very slow and complex to develop. The possibility of speeding up this process thus surely counterbalances the fact that the extraction methods are far from being perfect and noise free. Moreover, knowledge acquisition is commonly regarded not as a stand-alone method for ontology expansion or population, but rather as a support to the unavoidable human intervention by domain experts. Within the context of the so-called *Balanced Cooperative Modeling* (Morik, 1993), text-driven knowledge extraction is just a phase in the ontology-development cycle that must be complemented by manual pruning and refinements to integrate the acquired knowledge within existing knowledge resources.

---

[5] But see also *Random Indexing* (Karlgren and Sahlgren, 2001), *Infomap* (Widdows, 2003), and *Distributional Memory* (Baroni and Lenci, 2009).

Their importance notwithstanding, the practical needs of the ontolexical development process should not be the main rationale to pursue NLP-based approaches to knowledge acquisition. Actually, the use of text-driven learning methods appears as a necessary condition for ensuring the effective usability of ontolexical resources by NLP systems. Ontologies are nowadays used in many information-processing contexts, most of them not directly concerned with natural language understanding. In these cases, documents can be important sources of knowledge for ontology development, but nevertheless still just complementary ones. Conversely, when we talk about using ontologies by NLP systems for the purposes of understanding and extracting information content encoded in natural language documents, then the situation is totally different. In fact, NLP needs ontolexical resources that are well 'adapted' to the texts that they are going to process. Pustejovsky *et al.* (2002) present various cases in which even a very rich and fine-grained domain ontology such as UMLS cannot be effectively used for an NLP task such as anaphora resolution because of the very frequent type-mismatching. In fact, words that in texts are used co-referentially and as belonging to the same type may happen to be not assigned to the same type in the ontology. Notice that this mismatch is not due to accidental mistakes, but rather to the inherent multidimensional character of ontolexical systems, which may even require orthogonal principles of organization depending on the specific use contexts. These may actually impose different perspectives on the same conceptual system. Cognitive research has recently pointed out the fact that this context-dependency is an inherent feature of the human conceptual system (Barsalou, 2005). The phenomena of sense creation and semantic dynamics we saw above also point towards the same direction. Consistently, ontolexical resources cannot be regarded as fixed repositories of semantic descriptions, but at most as core sets of meanings that need to be customized and adapted to different domains, applications, texts, etc. NLP and learning methods can be used to achieve this sort of 'textual attunement' of ontolexical resources, as a key condition to make them better fitted for semantic-processing tasks.

14.4   Conclusion

There is a natural connection between NLP and ontolexical resources. One of the main goals of the former is to understand the information and knowledge content that is encoded in natural language structures. The latter purports to represent knowledge systems that also happen to be expressed through natural language expressions. The problem is that the naturalness of this link is often hindered by the way ontolexical knowledge is represented, organized, and acquired. In fact, the effective usability of ontolexical systems for practical NLP tasks is not granted per se, and in some cases these resources have intrinsic limits that negatively impact on the way they can be used in processing tasks. This is the main reason why the two apparently independent moments of knowledge creation and knowledge use are inevitably interconnected within the 'circle of life' of ontolexical systems. Indeed, NLP is both a part and a key protagonist of this circle. Better understanding of how knowledge can be automatically carved out of texts can lead to ontolexical resources that are more 'attuned' to the way knowledge is expressed with natural language. In turn, this promises to lead to a better way of creating knowledge resources that can boost performance in NLP technology.

15   The Omega ontology

Andrew Philpot, Eduard Hovy, and Patrick Pantel

15.1   Introduction

We present the Omega ontology, a 120,000-node terminological ontology constructed at USC ISI as the synthesis of WordNet 2.0 (Miller, 1990; Fellbaum, 1998), a lexically oriented network constructed on general cognitive principles, and Mikrokosmos (Mahesh, 1996; O'Hara *et al.*, 1998), a conceptual resource originally conceived to support translation, whose result is subordinated under a new feature-oriented upper model, created expressly in order to facilitate the merging of lower models into a functional whole.

Omega, like its close predecessor SENSUS (Knight and Luk, 1994b), can be characterized as a shallow, lexically oriented, term taxonomy – by far the majority of its concepts can be stated in English using a single word. At present, Omega contains no formal concept definitions and only relatively few interconnections (semantic relations) between concepts, in contrast to work such as DOLCE (Chapter 3) and SUMO (Chapter 2). Besides the core concept base, Omega has been extended to connect with a range of auxiliary knowledge sources (including instances, verb-frame annotations, and domain-specific sub-ontologies) incorporated into the basic conceptual structure and representation. By making few commitments to any specific theories of semantics or particular representations, Omega enjoys a malleability that has allowed it to be used in a variety of applications, including question answering and information integration.

We describe ongoing work on the manual reorganization of Omega terms and their connection to a large corpus of manually disambiguated word senses in three languages. This effort involves manually developing pre-formal sets of definitional features, derived from a variety of sources, from which partial formalized descriptions of concepts will be derived.

Omega is available for browsing at http://omega.isi.edu/.

15.2   Constituents of Omega

WordNet, the largest constituent of Omega by size, has a cognitive science orientation, modelling conceptual entities (synonym sets or *synsets* as explained in previous chapters) as the shared meaning of a set of lexical items, but having relatively few kinds of inter-concept relationships. Accordingly, it is richer in the lower part of the network, which houses more concrete concepts named by many lexical items, but unfortunately possesses less structure in the upper part, which contains more general concepts named by fewer or no specific lexical items (e.g., TANGIBLE OBJECT, DISPOSITIVE MATERIAL ACTION).

In contrast, Mikrokosmos is a much smaller network, possessing a wider range of conceptual links, but with a lesser focus on lexicalizations of the concepts. Its strength lies in its upper structure and representational expressiveness, not its breadth of coverage.

A major aim in constructing Omega was to leverage the strengths and minimize the weaknesses of the two major constituents: to have a large, lexically rich resource work with a clear comprehensive organization, supporting both inference and lexical access. To support this, we began with a newly designed upper model (Philpot *et al.*, 2003) of about 200 nodes, referred to here as the NUM (New Upper Model). Rooted in a single point, NUM is constructed by successive refinement over a set of mutually exclusive features. Figure 15.1 illustrates a subset of Omega's upper

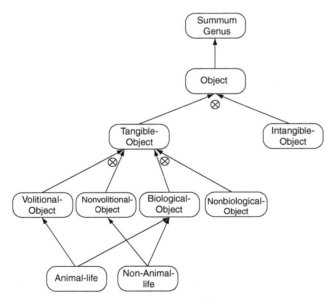

Figure 15.1 A subset of Omega's upper structure (NUM) with lattice points. Junctions marked with ⊗ indicate points where a superconcept is elaborated by choosing some value from an exhaustive and mutually exclusive feature set

ontology. Top-level children of the root concept SUMMUM GENUS are OBJECT, EVENT, and PROPERTY, which are mutually disjoint. Subtypes of OBJECT are two sets of mutually disjoint lattice points: TANGIBLE-OBJECT, INTANGIBLE-OBJECT and MENTAL-OBJECT, PHYSICAL-OBJECT, SOCIAL-OBJECT. Children of TANGIBLE-OBJECT are the two lattice point sets NONVOLITIONAL-OBJECT, VOLITIONAL-OBJECT and BIOLOGICAL-OBJECT, NONBIOLOGICAL-OBJECT. The leaves of this upper structure are high-level conceptual categories such as NONVOLITIONAL-OBJECT and INTANGIBLE-MULTI-PARTICIPANT-EVENT. As these are equivalent to conjunctions of (mutually exclusive) features, they provide an excellent place to root lower-level subtrees of concepts. For example, all plant life belongs under NONVOLITIONAL-OBJECT, while interpersonal actions without an intrinsic material effect (e.g., *to cooperate*) are subtypes of INTANGIBLE-MULTI-PARTICIPANT-EVENT.

15.3   Structure of Omega

Like most ontologies, the heart of Omega is a network of concepts linked by a set of instantiated relationships. Drawing its relationships from both Mikrokosmos and WordNet, and much like that of SENSUS, Omega's concept space is articulated in terms of hierarchical relations such as **is-a**, **part-of**, **substance-of**, and **element-of**, as well as lateral ones such as **theme**, **instrument**, and **pertains-to**. Concepts also possess nonsemantic attributes such as **gloss**.

As in SENSUS, paralleling the concept hierarchy, we collect all lexical items into what can be called language-specific *lexical spaces*. As with concepts, lexical items may have attributes and lateral links to other entities; in particular, each lexical item contains spelling, morphology, and other orthographic information, and is indirectly, via senses, attached to all concepts it names.

In Omega, rather than directly attaching a lexical item to an appropriate concept as is usually done, we created a sense object that sits between the two and is linked to both. This step permitted us to treat more accurately the information in WordNet, Mikrokosmos, PropBank (Kingsbury *et al.*, 2002), and other resources. We group together all senses for all languages into a single *sense space* (see Figure 15.2).

Sense space considerably simplifies resource alignment and the creation of concepts. Over time it has become apparent that builders of larger-scale lexico-semantic resources like dictionaries, WordNet, and PropBank find it most convenient to work with word senses rather than concepts. On the other hand, builders of ontologies and knowledge representation schemes prefer to work with concepts. Lexico-semanticists prefer word senses because it is easier to illustrate small shades of difference in word usage with examples than to

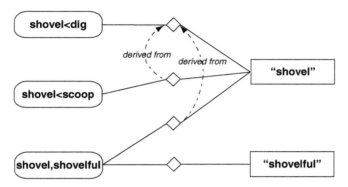

Figure 15.2 Concept/Sense/Lexical linkage, where senses are unlabelled diamonds, solid lines indicate concept–sense and sense–lexical links, and dashed arrows are sense–sense links

provide (formalizable) differentiae that adequately distinguish concepts from one another. For this reason, also, the granularity of word senses tends to be rather finer grained than that of concepts. One estimate based on several French and English dictionaries estimates that people will tend to define two to three times as many senses as concepts (Cooper, 2005). This implicit methodology employs as criterion for distinguishing sense vs concept the ability (or inability) of a new sense for a word to be metaphorically generated from the existing pool of senses.

In almost all existing large-scale ontology alignment studies using WordNet, Levin classes, and similar, word senses have been viewed as if they were concepts. The mismatches in term granularity and definition style lead to an awkward hybridization if one mixes WordNet-style and Mikrokosmos-style entities, but are resolvable following a process of controlled sense compression going from sense to concept space (see Hovy, 2005).

Sense space also facilitates linkage of words from different languages. In a project to manually annotate the nouns and verbs of texts (in Hindi, Arabic, Korean, French, Spanish, and Japanese, as well as their translations into English) with Omega concepts (Farwell *et al.*, 2004; Reeder *et al.*, 2004), we found it useful to gather the various languages' word senses into a single sense space, where overlaps and differences could be identified, before defining the actual Omega contents. Here the granularity of the concept in question had to be such as to represent the meaning distinctions common across the various translations, while their individual language-idiosyncratic facets of difference could remain in the sense hierarchy.

One can thus think of *ontology space* as the *interlingual* representation symbols (symbols capturing common, or common enough, meaning aspects), of *sense space* as the *multilingual* representation symbols (symbols for senses that may or may not co-occur across languages, but that are mapped to meanings no more specific than they denote themselves), and of *lexical space* as the *monolingual* representation symbols (namely, the words of each language).

In general, there is a complex many-to-many mapping across both gaps. Accordingly, we created a sense space as part of Omega to make explicit the nature of the attachments between concepts and lexical items. Besides providing a clean substrate for expressing sense–sense relationships, such as syntactic or morphological derivation links, sense objects are useful for lexical annotations of verb frames (e.g., as in Fleischman *et al.*, 2003), where one is focusing on making relationships between concepts as expressed in texts. See Figure 15.2, where three concept nodes (on the left), denoting different concepts which can be expressed using the lexical item *shovel* are linked to two different lexical items, via four unlabelled sense nodes. Two of these senses, SHOVEL < SCOOP (a garden implement) and SHOVEL, SHOVELFUL (the amount of material a shovel contains) are derived from a third sense corresponding to the act of shovelling; these sense–sense links are labelled with *derived-from*. Since such links are predicated on the uses of a particular word in context, they belong in the sense space rather than in the concept or lexical item spaces.

In Omega, concepts are interned, i.e., attached to identifying names which are referenced relative to name spaces; additionally, sets of related name spaces (e.g., lexical items expressed in different natural languages) are grouped together into vocabularies. These constructs allow modularity and flexibility in concept and lexical item name orthography.

Names for Omega concepts derived from WordNet synsets are constructed using a local constraint relaxation procedure, described more fully in Philpot *et al.*, 2003. While use of arbitrary identifiers such as WordNet synset offsets would be possible, having names based on distinguishing characteristics greatly assists users when browsing and reusing the ontology. Human-specified concept names are prohibitively expensive to generate for a network of this size.

First, for each synset, a set of candidate names is generated using attributes of the concept or its neighbours. Some of these generation methods include: word(s) from the associated synset (RATTLESNAKE, PORT, LEFT), reference to parent or children concepts (OLIVE<FRUIT, MOB>MAFIA), and suffixing with usage, region or subject domain tags (TONIC(MUSIC), CLASS(BIOLOGY)). Each name is assigned a score, based on local metrics such as simplicity and brevity as well as global metrics (primarily avoiding ambiguity). Local constraint cost minimization is used to choose names while approximating the maximum global utility of the assignment.

15.4   Construction of Omega via merging

Figure 15.3 shows our merging framework. We constructed Omega using WordNet (reorganized into concepts (named per the above), senses, and lexical items) and Mikrokosmos (slightly reformulated to satisfy minor orthographic and structural issues); together these are termed the source ontologies. The remainder of this section describes the procedure we used to merge WordNet and Mikrokosmos.

With the NUM in place, the upper models of the source ontologies were first removed and the remaining concepts were linked into the leaf nodes of the NUM. Identification and removal of the upper ontology of the WordNet portion was trivial because it had been previously linked to the Penman upper model (Bateman *et al.*, 1989) that we used in SENSUS and our previous version of Omega. For Mikrokosmos, we considered the top four levels to be the upper model in general. The remnants of the source ontologies then formed a set of isolated sub-lattices of related concepts. The root of each of these was either merged with or made a child of a node (typically a leaf node) of NUM, by manual inspection using the glosses, the local lexical item names, and the feature definition of the NUM concept (e.g., lattice points in Figure 15.1). The result of this process was one single top region (the NUM) below which hang strands of concepts once linked into the upper ontologies of Mikrokosmos and WordNet. These strands are linked together at the leaf nodes of the NUM and form two *curtains* that hang below, as yet unconnected. On one curtain typically there exists a strand of Mikrokosmos concepts and on the other side exists a strand of WordNet concepts. In the next two phases we sewed up the curtain by first merging the leaf of one side of the curtain into the other, forming a *concept bubble*. Then, the bubble was flattened out by merging the interior elements of one side of the curtain into the other. See Figure 15.4.

At this point, we merged leaves from one curtain (typically the Mikrokosmos curtain) into (possibly leaf) nodes from the other curtain. Then, the

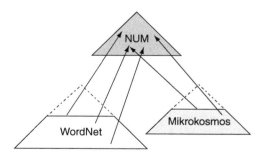

Figure 15.3 Schematic: merging WordNet and Mikrokosmos into NUM

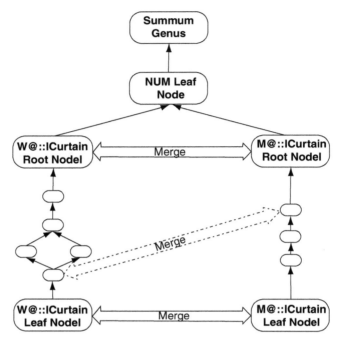

Figure 15.4 Merging ontology 'curtains'. M@ indicates concepts derived from Mikrokosmos whereas W@ indicates concepts derived from WordNet. Concept nodes interior to the curtains are unlabelled

resulting bubbles were sewn together. All combinations of pairs of concepts, one from each side of a given bubble, were compared using a learned classifier based on a few hand-aligned examples. The combination which provided the largest number of consistent high-quality matches was presented to a human to accept, reject, or edit. The relatively small number of rejected bubbles was retained not merged. For more details on the merging process, see Philpot *et al.*, 2003.

15.5   Omega's auxiliary knowledge sources

The Omega ontology, constructed as outlined above, contains about 120,000 concepts, 156,000 English-language lexical items, 28,000 Spanish-language lexical items, and 270,000 senses. As such, it has shown great utility for research and applications such as information integration and translation. Beyond these, in this section we provide summary descriptions of the various tools we have developed and other knowledge resources we have linked to the ontology core.

15.5.1 Tools

A web-based browser called Mammoth is available at http://omega.isi.edu/. Mammoth allows interactive visualization of both the current and research versions of Omega, as well as the older ontology SENSUS, also developed at ISI. A command-line interface to Omega, suitable for calling by client programs, is available. Omega is currently implemented using the persistent storage mechanism of the PowerLoom description logic (Chalupsky and Russ, 2003), which also exposes a relational database view of the concepts, senses, and lexical items.

15.5.2 Frames

As part of a semantic annotation experiment, we have used Omega as the substrate for merging various available data collections which define the semantic frame structures having the predicates used for annotation: FrameNet, PropBank, and LCS database. Each has a different view and a different coverage, so we integrate all information into the Omega ontology. We currently assign frame information only to verb senses and align frame roles among frames.

FrameNet (Baker *et al.*, 1998) defines semantic frames involving various participants, properties, and other conceptual roles, and for each frame, corresponding words are associated. FrameNet II (as of January 2004) defines 487 distinct frames and 6,743 predicate lexicons (2,300 verbs). In Omega, these frames are represented as a set of 73,000 links between sense objects and interned frame pseudo-concepts.

PropBank (Kingsbury *et al.*, 2002) defines predicate-argument structures on a per-predicate basis, and the core elements of each predicate are simply numbered. PropBank (as of February 2004) covers 3,323 predicate verbs and 4,659 framesets, for a total of 40,000 links in Omega.

LCS (Lexical Conceptual Structures) database (Dorr and Habash, 2001) contains hand-tagged structures organized based on Levin's English verb classes and alternations (Levin, 1993); it contains 4,452 verbs in 492 classes and corresponds to 73,000 links in Omega.

Additionally, we have reformulated the simple verb frame schemata that are provided within WordNet itself into a similar format (35 frames, 63,000 links).

The frame alignment, and, once that is accomplished, the alignment of individual roles within each pair of frames, was first produced automatically, by an algorithm that considered thirteen features of frames and the ontology organization, and was then manually checked by two humans. More details are provided in Kwon and Hovy, 2006.

15.5.3   Instances and mined knowledge

Omega's implementation contains infrastructure for representing and managing large numbers of concept instances (including a database-backed persistent storage mechanism). Instance sets which have been linked into Omega include named entities mined at ISI (470,000 from Fleischman *et al.*, 2003; 764,000 from Pantel *et al.*, 2004) and noun-noun compounds[1] (36,000 terms). Additionally, two geographic gazetteers (GNIS[2] from USGS: 1.9 million points of interest and GNS[3] from NGA: 5.4 million points of interest) have been fully linked into Omega, including part–whole relations, a feature typology, and lexical items for all known place names.

15.5.4   Concept annotations

Leveraging Omega's deep relationship to WordNet, we have incorporated other WordNet-based corpora, including the Semcor (Miller *et al.*, 1993) corpus[4], WordNet Topic Signatures (Agirre and López de Lacalle Lekuona, 2004) (197 million links), and WordNet Subject Domains (Magnini and Cavagliá, 2000) (200 concepts, 86,000 links) (see Chapter 13). We have also begun looking at incorporating eXtended WordNet (Moldovan and Rus, 2001).

15.5.5   Domain models and domain-specific extensions

In support of various applications, we have automatically linked the results of domain-specific ontologies (Klavans *et al.*, 2002; Hovy *et al.*, 2003) into Omega.

15.6   Applications

Omega has been used to support information integration across databases. In Hovy *et al.*, 2001, the conceptual hierarchy was extended with a domain-specific model describing aspects of energy time series. These aspects expressed the metadata conceptualizations of several information sources containing tens of thousands of different time series, which were thereby linked

---

[1] Available from www.isi.edu/~pantel/Content/demos.htm
[2] Available from http://geonames.usgs.gov/domestic/
[3] Available from http://earth-info.nga.mil/gns/html/
[4] Available from www.cs.unt.edu/~rada/downloads.html

to the appropriate Omega concepts. Users could browse the ontology to find the time series of interest, and computer systems accessing the time series data could use the feature descriptions of domain-model concepts to plan and execute multisource queries.

A related use of Omega was in supporting a related multilingual question-answering application called AskCal (Philpot *et al.*, 2002). The user's natural-language question was parsed using Omega's lexical items; the question type and other aspects of the parse were dynamically constrained using ontological relationships existing among already understood fragments of the sentence.

Omega has been used as a term repository in two projects that manually construct shallow 'literal' semantic representations for text. The IL-Annot project (Farwell *et al.*, 2004; Reeder *et al.*, 2004), containing six partners, had humans annotate text translated from six languages into English; the symbols for nouns, verbs, and adjectives were taken by specialized annotation interface directly from Omega. A similar, ongoing project, OntoBank, is collaborating with PropBank and other partners to perform the same type of annotation at a very large scale (Hovy *et al.*, 2003). Omega has also served more passively as the substrate for integrating hierarchical information harvested from online glossaries (Klavans *et al.*, 2002).

15.7 Omega 5 and the OntoNotes project

Omega is undergoing a major revision, which will be published eventually as Omega 5. In this version, the ontology serves as the repository of word senses for a large collection of text, in which each polysemous noun and verb has its meaning (its sense) manually assigned. Each meaning sense corresponds to a concept in Omega 5.

The multi-year multi-site OntoNotes collaboration (Hovy *et al.*, 2006) has the goal of annotating over 1 million words of English, Chinese, and Arabic text, of various genres (including newspaper articles and transcriptions of broadcasts), over the period 2005–2009. The annotations, which in addition to word senses include coreference links and propositional structure for verbs, are being made public year by year via the LDC. Each sense choice is made by two annotators, and their work is accepted (and corrected) only when they agree over more than 90% of their decisions. That is, the contents of the ontology are 'anchored' in a large multilingual body of text, based on the agreed decision of at least two people. This allows the user to observe in Omega 5 not only the traditional ontology content such as definition and example, but also to study the actual usage of each concept in naturally occurring text.

Naturally, creation of the senses is a major part of this work. Our sense-creation expert, a full-time lexicography professional, for each word draws on resources such as Omega, WordNet, various dictionaries, and natural text. In creating the list of senses for a word, she considers related words, some of whose senses may (partially) overlap in meaning. She defines each sense using an interface that supports not only the insertion of a definition and examples, but also the specification of one or more *differentiae*, namely atomic feature labels that help differentiate a sense from its conceptual neighbours. At present, the differentiae number over 3,100, where the majority of the most-frequent ones are typical Upper Model notions such as *animate* and *concrete*.

The 90% agreement rule serves as an important control measure on the granularity and quality of senses. Without it, the sense creator could build arbitrarily finely grained concepts, with arbitrarily specific definitions. However, if the sense annotators cannot achieve 90% agreement in their sense allocations for a word in the corpus (and each word appears in at least 100 sentences, and often in several thousand), then either the sense definitions are unclear or the senses are too finely split and hence indistinguishable. (Palmer, a member of the OntoNotes project, has determined, for example, that sense annotation using WordNet senses produces an agreement level of only 76%, meaning that one quarter of its senses are simply indistinguishable to a normal annotator.) In OntoNotes, when the 90% agreement level is not reached, the sense creator goes back and either refines and sharpens the definitions and examples, or adds helpful differentiae, or regroups the senses at a coarser granularity. This process is repeated until the annotators can reach agreement.

The 90% requirement brings into the picture a type of empirical quality and granularity control. Given our experience to date (having created senses for and annotated approximately 500 nouns and 350 verbs), we expect Omega 5 to contain about half the number of concepts of the current Omega. Each of these concepts will contain a definition, examples, differentiae, and links to hundreds of sentences that illustrate the concept in actual use.

15.8   Discussion and future work

Creating an ontology requires repeated decisions about concept creation and placement. Different decision criteria and methodologies give rise to legitimate but different ontologies (see Hovy, 2005 for a discussion of the five major methodologies in use). Omega's growth is grounded in our desire to avoid committing to any specific semantic theory or representation. That way, we avoid falling into theory-derived black holes and besides can support more users who can tease out the parts of Omega that suit their tasks. The future of Omega lies then in merging together more ontologies, including upper models such as DOLCE (see Chapter 3) and SUMO (Niles and Pease, 2001 and Chapter 2) as well as automatically harvesting and integrating instances, entailments, and other knowledge from the Web, domain documents, video, speech, and other media, and making sure this is all supported by agreements of decisions made by more than one individual.

The need for machine-assisted ontology construction is stronger than ever. It is increasingly clear that humans cannot manually structure the available knowledge at the pace it becomes available. In efforts to automatically update and grow ontologies, many researchers, including the authors, have proposed algorithms for harvesting shallow semantic resources such as term lists, conceptualizations, and semantic relations from text corpora and the Web. Though few have succeeded in automatically incorporating this knowledge into a formal ontology, there are encouraging signs of progress (Maedche and Staab, 2001; Rigau and Rodriguez, 2005; Caraballo, 1999; Farreres, 2005).

In testing some algorithms for automatically harvesting semantic knowledge, such as new term lists, concepts, similarity relations, subclass–superclass relations, and several fine-grained verb semantic relations, we have encountered several challenging issues when deploying these resources in natural-language applications, since the knowledge is not integrated into any formal knowledge representation.

In response, we have developed a general computational approach for representing a lexical ontology, such as Omega, that enables the automatic integration of certain kinds of shallow semantic resources into the ontology (Pantel, 2005). The approach assigns syntactic features to each node in an ontology and then attaches shallow semantic resources by matching on these features. We term *ontologizing* a lexical-semantic resource as the task of sense disambiguating the resource. This problem is different but not orthogonal to word-sense disambiguation. If we could disambiguate large collections of text with high accuracy, then current methods for building lexical-semantic resources could easily be applied to ontologize them by treating each word's senses as separate words. Our method does not require the disambiguation of text. Instead, it relies on the principle of distributional similarity, which links the semantics of words with their syntactic behaviour, and the observation that polysemous words that are similar in one sense tend to be dissimilar in their other senses.

Our collaboration in the OntoNotes project, described above, represents a different approach to try to provide some empirical and verifiable methodology to the enterprise of ontology creation.

15.9   Conclusion

In this chapter, we introduced Omega, ISI's 120,000-node terminological ontology. Omega was constructed by merging WordNet 2.0 and Mikrokosmos into a new upper model, created expressly in order to facilitate the merging of lower models into a functional whole. Several auxiliary knowledge sources (such as FrameNet, PropBank, automatically mined knowledge and concept annotations) have also been integrated.

At present, Omega contains no formal concept definitions and only relatively few interconnections between concepts. By making few commitments to any specific theories of semantics or particular representations, Omega enjoys a malleability that has allowed it to be used in a variety of applications, including question answering and information integration.

The future of Omega lies in harvesting and integrating more knowledge sources such as existing ontologies, like DOLCE and SUMO, and new concepts and relations mined from media such as textual documents and the Web.

16 Automatic acquisition of lexico-semantic knowledge for question answering

Lonneke van der Plas, Gosse Bouma, and Jori Mur

16.1 Introduction

Lexico-semantic knowledge is becoming increasingly important within the area of natural language processing, especially for applications such as word sense disambiguation (WSD), information extraction (IE), and question answering (QA). Although the coverage of handmade resources, such as WordNet (Fellbaum, 1998) (introduced in Chapters 1, 2 and 3), in general is impressive, coverage problems still exist for those applications involving specific domains or languages other than English.

We are interested in using lexico-semantic knowledge in an open-domain question-answering system for Dutch. Obtaining such knowledge from existing resources is possible, but only to a certain extent. The most important resource for our research is the Dutch portion of EuroWordNet (Vossen, 1998); however its size is only half that of the English WordNet. Therefore, many of the lexical items used in the QA task of the Cross Language Evaluation Forum (CLEF[1]) for Dutch cannot be found in EuroWordNet. In addition, information regarding the classes to which named entities belong, e.g. *Narvik* **is-a** HARBOUR, has been shown to be useful for QA, but such information is typically absent from hand-built resources. For these reasons, we are interested in investigating methods which acquire lexico-semantic knowledge automatically from text corpora. See also Chapters 5 and 14 for more support of such an approach.

The chapter is organized as follows: in the next section, we briefly describe the question types for which lexico-semantic knowledge will be used, and in Section 16.3 we describe related work. In Section 16.4, we outline our approach to finding words with a distributional similarity. Sections 16.5 and 16.6 detail how the acquired knowledge is employed to improve the performance of our QA system with regards to specific question types, i.e. questions asking for the names of persons who have a specific function in an organization, e.g. *Who is the secretary general of the UN?*, WHICH questions, and

---

[1] See http://clef-qa.itc.it/

definition questions. Finally, the results of an evaluation on three years of CLEF test sets are reported in Section 16.7, while Section 16.8 summarizes our conclusions and proposes suggestions for future research.

16.2   Lexico-semantic knowledge for QA

We will now briefly describe the four question types whose performance we hope to improve using automatically acquired lexical knowledge: WHICH questions, definition questions, questions that can be answered by off-line methods, and in particular, function questions.

A question type where the use of lexical knowledge is potentially useful are WHICH questions such as:

> Which volcano erupted in June 1991?

A QA system may find various named entities, such as *Philippines* and *Pinatubo*, as potential answers to the question, and knowing that *Pinatubo* **is-a** *volcano* can help to identify the correct answer. Information about named entities is typically absent in handmade lexical resources.[2] In Section 16.6, we describe a method for acquiring such categorized named entities automatically from a parsed corpus.

Definition questions are the second type of question where lexical knowledge proves to be useful:

> Who is Javier Solana?

For CLEF 2005, definition questions were restricted to persons and organizations, with the expectation that answers should provide 'some fundamental information' to users who know nothing about the named entity. Generally speaking, it is hard to determine which information should be used to provide an answer to such questions in general. We tried an approach whereby we used automatically acquired and categorized named entities (NEs) in order to find an appropriate category which is required to be included in the answer. In Section 16.6, we describe how this information can be used to determine answers to definition questions.

In addition, off-line methods (Fleischman *et al.*, 2003) can be used to improve the performance of QA systems. In off-line QA, plausible answers to highly likely questions are extracted before the actual question has been asked.

For example, if a user asks for the age of a person, the answer is extracted from the table, and it is not necessary to search the source text. Bouma *et al.*

---

[2] See, however, Chapters 2, 3, and 10 for a discussion about the treatment of instances within WordNet and related resources.

(2005) describe how syntactic patterns are used to extract answers for highly likely question types. A table is constructed for relations, such as the age of a person, the location and date of birth, and the death of a person. To expand the number of facts comprised in these tables, we have applied anaphora resolution.

For instance, consider the following question:

> How old is Ivanisevic?

In order to extract the answer to the above question from the text provided below, it is necessary to analyse it at the discourse level.

> Todd Martin was the opponent of the quiet Ivanisevic. The American, who defeated the local hero Boris Becker a day earlier, was beaten by the 26-year [3] old Croatian during the finals of the Grand Slam Cup ...

Among other things, one must correctly identify *Ivanisevic*, located in the first sentence, as the denotation of *the Croatian*, located in the second sentence, in order to extract the correct answer that is stated in the second sentence.

In Section 16.6, we explain how automatically acquired and categorized named entities are used to establish that *Ivanisevic* **is-a** *Croatian*. This information is referred to by the terms *categorized named entities* or *instances*.

Often, questions are asked about the function or role of a particular person:

> Who is the chair of Unilever?

These so-called function questions are also answered by the off-line module. The following syntactic pattern could serve as a method of extracting ⟨*Person,Role,Organization*⟩-tuples from the corpus:

$$name(PER) \xleftarrow{\text{app}} noun \xrightarrow{\text{mod}} name(ORG)$$

Here, the *name(PER)* constituent provides the *Person* argument of the relation, the *noun* provides the role, and the *name(ORG)*-constituent provides the name of the *Organization*. An important source of noise is revealed when this pattern is applied to the parsed corpus in cases where the *noun* is not indicating a role or a function:

> colleague Henk ten Cate of Go Ahead

Here, the noun *colleague* does not represent a role within the organization *Go Ahead*.

---

[3] We use the CLEF-corpus for our experiments. This corpus consists of newspaper text from 1994 and 1995.

To remedy this problem, we have collected a list of nouns denoting functions or roles from the Dutch version of the multilingual resource EuroWordNet (Vossen, 1998), and restricted the search pattern to nouns occurring in this list:

$$name(PER) \xleftarrow{\text{app}} function \xrightarrow{\text{mod}} name(ORG)$$

While the above modifications help to improve precision, they also hurt recall, as many valid function words present in the corpus are not present in EuroWordNet. In Section 16.5, we report an experiment in which we have expanded the list of function words extracted from EuroWordNet semi-automatically with words of distributional similarity found in the corpus.

16.3   Related work

Syntactic relations have been shown to provide information that can be used to acquire clusters of semantically similar words automatically (Lin, 1998a). With a fully parsed version of the Dutch CLEF QA corpus (4.1 million sentences containing a total of 78 million words) at our disposal, we were naturally interested in applying this method to Dutch. In particular, we have followed the strategy of Curran and Moens (2002), who evaluate various similarity measures and weight functions against various thesauri (Macquarie (Bernard, 1990), Moby (Ward, 1996) and Roget (Roget, 1911)). We implemented the majority of the best-performing similarity measures and weights according to the evaluation of Curran and Moens (2002) and evaluated their performance against Dutch EuroWordNet. The results of this experiment are given in Section 16.4.[4]

Automatically acquired clusters of semantically similar words can be used to extend and/or enrich existing ontological resources. Alfonseca and Manandhar (2002), for instance, describe a method for expanding WordNet automatically, whereby new concepts are placed in the WordNet hierarchy according to their distributional similarity to words already in the hierarchy. Their algorithm performs a top-down search and stops at the synset that is most similar to the new concept. In Section 16.5, we implement a similar technique to expand the class of function words obtained from EuroWordNet.

Paşca (2004) and the team of Pantel and Ravichandran (2004) both present methods for acquiring class labels for instances (categorized named entities) from unstructured text. Paşca (2004) applies lexico-syntactic extraction patterns based on Part-of-Speech tags: patterns were hand-built initially, and extended automatically by scanning the corpus for the pairs of named entities and classes found with the initial patterns. Patterns which occur frequently

---

[4] More background on semantic similarity studies is provided in Chapter 14, p. 244.

in matching sentences could then be added as additional extraction patterns. Pantel and Ravichandran (2004) have proposed an algorithm that takes a list of semantic classes in the form of clusters of words as input. Labels for these clusters are found by looking at four lexico-syntactic relationships: **apposition** (*ayatollah Khomeini*), **nominal subject** (*Khomeini is an ayatollah*), **such as** (*ayatollahs such as Khomeini*), and **like** (*ayatollahs like Khomeini*).

The above mentioned types of lexico-semantic information have been applied to several QA and QA-related tasks.

As described in Chapter 15, the Omega ontology, a large terminology ontology resulting from the merging of WordNet (Fellbaum, 1998), Mikrokosmos (Mahesh, 1996; O'Hara *et al.*, 1998), and various other sources, has been applied to the multilingual QA application called AskCal (Philpot *et al.*, 2002).

As for the use of categorized named entities, Pantel and Ravichandran (2004) conducted two QA experiments – one answering definition questions and the other performing QA information retrieval (IR). These experiments show that both tasks benefit from the use of automatically acquired class labels. Pasça (2004) then applies this information to Web searches in order to process list-type queries: *SAS*, *SPSS*, *Minitab*, and *BMDP* are returned in addition to the top documents for the query *statistical packages*. Other researchers have used lexico-semantic information for anaphora resolution (Poesio *et al.*, 2002; Markert *et al.*, 2003). In particular, Markert and Nissim (2005) have extended the corpus-based approach with the introduction of a method that extracts the required knowledge from the Web using shallow lexico-syntactic patterns.

16.4   Extracting semantically similar words

An increasingly popular method for acquiring semantically similar words is to extract words with a distributional similarity from large corpora, the underlying assumption of this approach being that semantically similar words are used in similar contexts. The context of a word W may be defined as the document in which W occurs or the n words surrounding W (n-grams, bag of words). Alternatively, the context may be defined syntactically whereby words are found in syntactic relations with other words: the syntactic relation of a target word plus its accompanying words form the context of a target word. Approaches which do not use syntax tend to find more associative relations between words, e.g., between *patient* and *hospital*, whereas approaches using syntactic context tend to find concepts belonging to the same class, such as *doctor* and *surgeon*. As we are ultimately interested in extending the coverage of a resource such as Dutch EuroWordNet, we have focused on the latter approach.

Most research has been undertaken using a limited number of syntactic relations (Lee, 1999; Weeds, 2003). However, Lin (1998a) shows that a system

Table 16.1 *Types of dependency relations extracted*

subject–verb	*cat_eat*
verb–object	*feed_cat*
adjective–noun	*black_cat*
coordination	*cat_dog*
apposition	*cat_Garfield*
prep. complement	*look + after_kitten*

which uses a wide range of grammatical relations outperforms Hindle's (1990) results that were based on using information from just the subject and object relation. Apart from the subject and object relation, we have used several other grammatical relations: adjective, coordination, apposition, and prepositional complement. Examples are given in Table 16.1.

16.4.1   Data collection

The Dutch CLEF QA corpus, which consists of 78 million words of Dutch newspaper text (Algemeen Dagblad and NRC Handelsblad 1994/1995) comprises the data used in this experiment. This corpus was parsed automatically using the Alpino parser (Van Noord, 2006), and the result of parsed sentences are dependency graphs that adhere to the guidelines of the Corpus of Spoken Dutch (Moortgat *et al.*, 2000).

From these dependency graphs, we have extracted tuples consisting of the (non-pronominal) head of an NP (either a common noun or a proper name), the dependency relation, and either (1) the head of the dependency relation (for the object, subject, and apposition relation), (2) the head plus a preposition (for NPs occurring inside PPs which are prepositional complements), (3) the head of the dependent (for the adjective and apposition relation), or (4) the head of the other elements of a coordination (for the coordination relation). Examples are given in Table 16.1. The number of tuples and the number of non-identical ⟨Noun, Relation, OtherWord⟩ triples (types) found are given in Table 16.2. Note that a single coordination can give rise to various dependency triples, as from a single coordination like *bier, wijn, en noten* (*beer, wine, and nuts*) the triples ⟨*bier, coord, wijn*⟩, ⟨*bier, coord, noten*⟩, ⟨*wijn, coord, bier*⟩, ⟨*wijn, coord, noten*⟩, ⟨*noten, coord, bier*⟩, and ⟨*noten, coord, wijn*⟩ can be extracted. Similarly, from the apposition *premier Kok* ⟨*premier, hd_app, Kok*⟩ and ⟨*Kok, app, premier*⟩ are extracted.

A vector was built for each noun that was seen at least ten times in any dependency relation. After applying this cut-off, vectors are present for 83,479 nouns.

Table 16.2 *Number of tuples and non-identical dependency triples (types) extracted per dependency relation*

Grammatical relation	Tuples	Types
subject	5,639,140	2,122,107
adjective	3,262,403	1,040,785
object	2,642,356	993,913
coordination	965,296	2,465,098
prep. complement	770,631	389,139
apposition	526,337	602,970

16.4.2 Similarity measures and weights

Various vector-based methods can be used to compute the distributional similarity between words. Curran and Moens (2002) report on a large-scale evaluation experiment, where they evaluated the performance of various commonly used methods. Van der Plas and Bouma (2005) present a similar experiment for Dutch, in which they tested most of the best-performing measures, as defined by Curran and Moens (2002), where Pointwise Mutual Information (I) and *Dice*† were awarded the best performance rating. We will now explain this weight and similarity measure in further detail.

The information value of a cell in a word vector, which lists how often a word occurs in a specific grammatical relation to a specific word, is not equal for all cells. For instance, a large number of nouns can occur as the subject of the verb *have* whereas only a few nouns may occur as the object of *squeeze*.

Intuitively, the fact that two nouns both occur as subject of *have* tells us less about their semantic similarity than the fact that two nouns both occur as object of *squeeze*. To account for this intuition, the frequency of occurrence in a vector can be replaced by a weighted score. The weighted score is an indication of the amount of information carried by the particular combination of a noun and its feature (the grammatical relation, and the word heading the grammatical relation). For this experiment we used Pointwise Mutual Information (I) (Church and Hanks, 1989).

$$I(W, f) = log\frac{P(W, f)}{P(W)P(f)}$$

where W is the target word,
P(W) is the probability of seeing the word,
P(f) is the probability of seeing the feature,
and P(W,f) denotes the probability of seeing the word and the feature together.

Dice is a well-known combinatorial measure that computes the ratio between the size of the intersection of two feature sets and the sum of the sizes of the individual feature sets. We used a variant of the Dice-measure, which Curran and Moens (2002) refer to as *Dice†*, which incorporates weighted frequency counts:

$$Dice† = \frac{2\sum_f min(I(W_1, f), I(W_2, f))}{\sum_f I(W_1, f) + I(W_2, f)}$$

where f is the feature,
W_1 and W_2 are the two words that are being compared,
and I is a weight assigned to the frequency counts, here the Pointwise Mutual Information.

16.4.3   Performance

The Dutch version of the multilingual resource EuroWordNet (Vossen, 1998) was used for evaluation. One thousand target words from Dutch EWN with a frequency of more than ten were randomly selected, according to the frequency information present in Dutch EuroWordNet. For each word we collected its 100 most similar words (nearest neighbours) in accordance with the system under evaluation, and for each pair of words (target word plus one of the most similar words) we calculated the semantic similarity according to Dutch EuroWordNet. A system scores well if the nearest neighbours found by the system also have a high semantic similarity according to EuroWordNet.

Lin (1998b) evaluates a number of measures for computing WordNet similarity. From the measures, which are defined in terms of **is-a** relations only, the Wu and Palmer (1994) measure correlated best to human judgment. The Wu/Palmer measure for computing the semantic similarity between two words W1 and W2 in a wordnet, whose most-specific common ancestor is W3, is defined as follows:

$$Sim = \frac{2(D3)}{D1 + D2 + 2(D3)}$$

where D1 (D2) is the distance from W1 (W2) to the lowest common ancestor of W1 and W2: W3, and D3 is the distance of that ancestor to the root node.

Table 16.3 reports average EuroWordNet similarity for the 1, 5, 10, 20, 50, and 100 most similar words for the 1,000 words in our test set. If a word is ambiguous according to EuroWordNet, i.e. it is a member of several synsets, the highest similarity score is used. The EuroWordNet similarity of a set of word pairs is defined as the average of the similarity between the pairs. The baseline for this task is 0.26, which is the score obtained by picking 100

Table 16.3 *Average EuroWordNet similarity at (k)*
candidates when combining dependency relations
based on Dice†+ I

	EuroWordNet Similarity at					
$k =$	1	5	10	20	50	100
system	0.60	0.54	0.52	0.49	0.46	0.44

random words to be the nearest neighbours of a given target word. The upper-bound ranges from 0.99 (if only the most similar word is selected) to 0.84 (if 100 similar words have to be selected). Van der Plas and Bouma (2005b) show that the system using data obtained from all syntactic relations outperforms systems using only a subset of the syntactic relations. Furthermore, their work reveals that Dice † + I outperforms various other combinations of weight functions and similarity measures.

16.5   Using automatically acquired role and function words

In Section 16.2, we explained that for QA we are interested in extracting, off-line, all instances of the following pattern in our corpus:

$$name(PER) \xleftarrow{\text{app}} function \xrightarrow{\text{mod}} name(ORG)$$

To obtain a list of words describing a role or function, all words under the node { *leider* } (*leader*), numbering 255 in total, were extracted from Dutch EuroWordNet. The majority of hyperonyms of this node appeared to indicate function words we were interested in, e.g. it contained (the Dutch equivalents of) *king, queen, president, director, chair*, etc., while other potential candidates, such as *beroep* (*profession*), seemed less suitable. However, the coverage of this list, when tested on a newspaper corpus, is far from complete. On the one hand, the list contains a fair number of archaic items, while on the other hand, many functions that occur frequently in newspaper text are missing, e.g. Dutch equivalents of *banker, boss, national team coach, captain, secretary-general*, etc.

To improve recall, we extended the list of function words obtained from EuroWordNet semi-automatically with words with a distributional similarity. In particular, for each of the 255 words in the EuroWordNet list, we retrieved the 100 words with the highest distributional similarity. We gave each retrieved word a score that corresponds to its reverse rank (first word: 100, second: 99, third: 98, etc.). The overall score for a word is comprised of the sum of the

Table 16.4 *Coverage of function*
table with (EWN+) and without
(EuroWordNet) expansion

EWN		EWN+	
tuples	unique	tuples	unique
34,191	16,530	77,028	46,589

scores it obtained for the individual target words. Thus, words that are semantically similar to several words in the original list will obtain a higher score
than words that were returned only once or twice. Words that were already
present in the EuroWordNet list were filtered out.

From an informal evaluation of the results obtained, we have learned that
many false positives in the expanded list were either named entities or nouns
referring to groups of people, e.g. *board*, *committee*, etc. The distinction
between groups and functions of individuals is difficult to make on the basis
of distributional data. For instance, both a *board* and a *director* can make
decisions, report results, be criticized, etc. We attempted to filter both proper
names and groups automatically, by discarding both noun stems that start with
a capital and noun stems which are listed under the node { *groep* } (*group*) in
EuroWordNet.

Finally, we selected the top 1,000 of the filtered list and validated it manually. This list contains 644 valid roles or function nouns, which are absent
in EuroWordNet. A substantial number of the errors that are found in the list
are, in fact, nouns which refer to a group, but which are not listed as such in
EuroWordNet.

The 644 valid nouns were merged with the original EuroWordNet list to
form a list of 899 function or role nouns. Next, the relation extraction process
was executed using both the original EuroWordNet list and the expanded list.
The effect its use has on recall is illustrated in Table 16.4. The number of
extracted tuples increases by 125%, while the number of types increases by
181%. The effect of this increase on the performance of our QA system is
described in Section 16.7.

16.6   Using automatically acquired categorized NEs

Both Paşca (2004) and Pantel and Ravichandran (2004) describe methods
for acquiring labels for named entities from large text corpora and evaluate
their results in the context of Web search and question answering. Pantel and
Ravichandran (2004) use the apposition relation to find potential labels for

named entities. As we already had extracted all appositions from the CLEF corpus as part of the vector-based method for finding semantically similar words, we decided to use this information for two other QA tasks as well.

Apart from applying the apposition relation to acquire categorized NEs for which results were given in Van der Plas and Bouma 2005a, we used the relation of nominal predicate compliment, e.g. *Monica Seles is a tennis player*, in which a NE is found with a predicate complement comprising a noun as well.

We extracted 342,180 categorized NE types from 550,198 tokens; 90.6% of the data was obtained using the apposition relation and 9.4% was found by scanning the corpus for predicate complements. For instance, this database contains 391 names of ISLANDS (*Bali, Bonaire, Aruba*, etc.) and 186 different QUEENS (*Elizabeth, Wilhelmina, Beatrix*, etc.). The class labels extracted for each named entity may contain a certain amount of noise. However, by focusing on the most frequent label for a named entity, most of the noise can be discarded. For instance, *Beatrix*, occurs 1,210 times in the extracted tuples: 1,150 times as QUEEN, and not more than 60 times with various other labels (PLAY, NAME, HAT, POSSIBILITY, etc.).

Regarding the ambiguity of the classified named entities, we can say that on average a named entity has 1.9 labels; however, the distribution is skewed: 80% have only one label, while, in an extreme example from the remaining 20%, the most ambiguous named entity, *the Netherlands*, has 704 labels in total. Off-line answer extraction is a technique that tries to extract answers to highly likely question types before the question is posed. We used the extracted class labels to improve the performance of our QA system on WHICH questions such as:

> Which ferry sank southeast of the island Utö?

Question analysis and classification tells us that this is a question of type which(ferry). Candidate answers that are selected by our system are: *Tallinn, Estonia, Raimo Tiilikainen*, etc. The QA system uses various strategies to rank potential answers, i.e. the score assigned to the passage by information retrieval (IR), the presence of named entities from the question in the sentence in which the answer is found, the syntactic similarity between question and answer sentence, the frequency of the answer in the set of potential answers, etc. Still, selecting the correct named entity for answers to WHICH questions poses considerable problems to our system.

To improve the performance of the system regarding these questions, we have incorporated an additional strategy for selecting the correct answer. Potential answers which have been assigned the class corresponding to the question stem (in this case, FERRY) are ranked higher than potential answers for which this class label cannot be found in the database of **is-a** relations. Since *Estonia* is the only potential answer which **is-a** ferry, according to our database, this answer is selected. Note that in answering WH-questions we do not just select the most frequent label assigned to a named entity, but rather check as to whether the named entity occurs at least once with the appropriate class label.

A second question type for which the acquired class labels are relevant is definition question. The CLEF 2005 QA test set contains no less than sixty questions of the form:

> What is Sabena?

The named entity *Sabena* occurs frequently in the corpus, but often with class labels assigned to it, which are not suitable for inclusion in a definition (POSSIBILITY, PARTNER, COMPANY, etc.). By focusing on the most frequent class label assigned to a named entity (AIRLINE COMPANY in this case), a more appropriate label for a definition can be found. While frequency is important, often the class label by itself is not sufficient for an adequate definition. For this reason, we have expanded the class label with modifiers which typically need to be included in a definition.

In particular, our strategy for answering definition questions consists of two phases:

- Phase 1: The most frequent class found for a named entity is taken.
- Phase 2: The sentences which mention the named entity and the class are selected, and then searched for additional information which might be relevant. Snippets of information that are found in an adjectival relation or a prepositional complement to the class label are selected accordingly.

In the example above, our system produces *Belgian airline company* as the answer.

However, it must be stressed that deciding beforehand what information is relevant is far from being a trivial step. As explained above, we decided to expand only the label with adjectival and PP modifiers that are adjacent to the class label in the corresponding sentence, and this is the reason for a number of answers being inexact. Given the constituent *the museum Hermitage in St Petersburg*, this strategy fails to include *in St Petersburg*, for instance. We did not include relative-clause modifiers, as these tend to contain information which is not appropriate for a definition. However, in the case of the question, *Who is Iqbal Masih?*, an answer that includes at least the first conjunct of the relative clause of the constituent *twelve year old boy, who fought against child labour and was shot Sunday in his home town Muritke* would have been preferable over just selecting *twelve year old boy*. Similarly, we did not include purpose clauses, which leads the system to respond *large scale American attempt*, in response to the question *What was the Manhattan project?*, instead of *large scale American attempt to develop the first (that is, before the Germans) atomic bomb.*

The extracted class labels were employed in order to be able to extract potential answers from a corpus not only when answers are clearly stated with the accompanying named entity in the same sentence, but also when an anaphoric expression is used to refer to an earlier mentioned named entity. More specifically, we have attempted to resolve the definite NPs, and to find the named entities they refer to. Our strategy is as follows: we scan the left context of the definite NP for named entities from right to left, i.e. the closest named entity is selected first. For each named entity we encounter, we check whether it is in an **is-a** relation with the definite NP. If so, the named entity is selected as the antecedent of the NP. As long as no suitable named entity is found we select the previous named entity and so on until we reach the beginning of the document. We have limited our search to the current document. If no suitable named entity is found, i.e., no named entity is found that is in an **is-a** relation with the definite NP, then a fallback is used. This fallback comes down so as to extract the NE in the previous sentence that is nearest to the anaphoric expression, if there is a NE present. If no NE is present in the previous sentence, the NP is not resolved.

If the NP is resolved, this fact is added to the facts table. In order to explain our strategy for resolving definite NPs, we will now apply it to the example from the introduction:

> Todd Martin was the opponent of the quiet Ivanisevic. The American who defeated the local hero Boris Becker a day earlier, was beaten by the 26-year old Croatian during the finals of the Grand Slam Cup . . .

In the example above, the left context of the NP *the 26-year old Croatian* is scanned from right to left. The named entity *Boris Becker* is selected before the correct antecedent *Ivanisevic*. The fact that *Boris Becker* is not found in an **is-a** relation with *Croatian* renders it an unsuitable candidate, and it is put aside. Then, *Ivanisevic* is selected and this candidate *is* found to be in an **is-a** relation with *Croatian*, so *Ivanisevic* is taken as the antecedent of *Croatian*, and the fact *Ivanisevic, 26-year old* is thus added to the Age table.

16.7   Evaluation

In this section, we evaluate the effect of using lexico-semantic knowledge for QA. We discuss the effect of using categorized NEs for anaphora resolution for relation extraction in terms of recall. Furthermore we run an evaluation on the Dutch questions from CLEF '03, '04, and '05 showing the effect of using categorized NEs for which and definition questions, and finally we state the results for using the expanded function list for function questions.

Table 16.5 *Number of facts found for the different tables for relation extraction*

	Original	Anaphora
age	20,229	24,917
born_date	2,297	2,395
born_loc	795	948
died_age	923	966
died_date	1,011	1,204
died_how	1,834	2,336
died_loc	720	744

Table 16.6 *Distribution of facts that differ between original tables and tables that use anaphora resolution for sample of 400 differences*

	Correct	Incorrect
new	168	128
increase freq.	95	9
total	263	137

Using categorized NEs for anaphora in relation extraction leads to improvements in terms of coverage, as can be seen in Table 16.5. The added facts fall into two categories: they are either facts that were already present in the original table or facts that are new. It should be noted that the facts that are not new do contribute to the overall reliability of the table, as facts that are found more frequently are more often correct than facts that are found only once.

We have extracted all differences between entries (types) in the original table and in the table that uses anaphora resolution. These differences are either new facts or increases in frequency. From these differences, we then randomly extracted 400 entries. Two of the authors determined the correctness of the found facts in both tables, the results of which are given in Table 16.6. A large number of facts (104 from 400) show a rise in frequency and, in fact, 95 of these 104 examples are correct facts. These are positive results, with regard to the reliability of the table. The precision of the facts, however, is not very encouraging. Overall 263 (66%) of the 400 facts are correct. For the new facts the percentage of correct items is even lower (57%). In Mur and Van der Plas (2007) we reported a very high precision for the facts added by using anaphora resolution. There was a difference in precision between the original

Table 16.7 *Overall performance of the baseline and improved QA system on the CLEF ('03, '04, '05) Dutch QA test set.*

q-type	baseline			improved		
	# q	MRR	CLEF	# q	MRR	CLEF
WH	137	0.39	0.33	114	0.52	0.48
definition	88	0.47	0.39	88	0.58	0.52
person	94	0.72	0.68	30	0.73	0.70
funct	0	0.00	0.00	87	0.78	0.75
funct_of	0	0.00	0.00	6	0.67	0.67
...	...	...	...	...	...	...
total	**773**	**0.48**	**0.45**	**773**	**0.54**	**0.50**

and the expanded tables of only 1%. The difference with the method used in the current experiment lies in the fact that we did not use a fallback in the previous study, but rather resolved the anaphora if and only if an **is-a** relation was found between the co-referring NP and the candidate antecedent. Although the precision of the added facts was high, the number of facts found proved to be disappointing, and for this reason, we have chosen to include a fallback in this experiment.

We evaluated the use of lexico-semantic information for QA on the Dutch questions from CLEF '03, '04, and '05. We then compared the performance of two versions of our QA system: the baseline is the version that does not make use of lexico-semantic information, while the improved system uses the different types of lexico-semantic knowledge discussed in this chapter.

This performance of the baseline and improved system is shown in Table 16.7. In the first column, the question type is given (question types not relevant to this chapter are left out). In the second and fifth columns the number of questions classified as being of the corresponding question type are shown. In columns 3 and 6, the corresponding mean reciprocal rank (MRR) score is given,[5] while in columns 4 and 7 the CLEF score is given. The CLEF score gives the precision of the first (highest ranked) answer only.

The baseline of our QA system was the Joost QA system, without a special question type for function questions, and without access to **is-a** relations. The baseline treats function questions as person questions, i.e. as questions which require a named entity of type PERSON as an answer. WHICH questions and definition questions are answered by selecting the most highly ranked answer from the list of relevant paragraphs returned by the IR component. Answers

---

[5] The MRR score is the average of 1/R where R is the rank of the first correct answer computed over the five highest ranked answers only

to definition questions are in essence selected by means of the same strategy as described for the improved system above, the only exception being that answers must now be selected from the documents returned by IR, rather than from sentences known to contain a relevant class label.

The improved system makes use of the question type *function* and *function_of* and the related tables in which information about functions is stored. This last type refers to questions, such as *Yeltsin is president of which country?* Furthermore, it uses **is-a** relations when answering WHICH questions and definition questions.

The overall effect of adding lexico-semantic information is an improvement in MRR score of 6%, and an improvement in CLEF score of 5%.

Adding a question class for functions and a table for this relation has the effect that 94 person questions and 23 WHICH question in the baseline system are now classified as function or function_of questions. The effect on accuracy of this change appears to be small, as person questions are already answered relatively well; however, on the other hand, for WHICH questions, answered with a much lower precision, the effect is more noticeable. The shift from person and WHICH questions to function and function_of questions is beneficial. Of the 93 questions that are classified as function or function_of questions in the improved system, 19 involve question stems, such as *weduwe (widow)*, *adviseur(advisor)*, *secretaris-generaal (secretary-general)*, and *vriendin (girl friend)*, which were present in our extended list of function nouns only.

Adding **is-a** relations as an additional knowledge source for answering WH-questions improves the MRR score of 114 WH-questions with 13% and improves the CLEF score with 15%. In addition, using the same information to provide answers to definition questions improves the MRR score of 88 definition questions by 11%, and improves the CLEF score by 13%.

We were not able to show that using lexico-semantic driven anaphora resolution for relation extraction improves the performance of the system on the CLEF test set. We believe that this is due to the fact that the test set contains only 19 questions with a question type for which anaphora resolution potentially could make a difference, i.e. questions that were of one of the question types (see Table 16.5) for which the relation extraction module using anaphora resolution provides answers.

16.8   Conclusion and future work

We have demonstrated that lexico-semantic knowledge can be acquired from syntactically parsed corpora, and that the inclusion of such knowledge in a QA system has a positive effect on the overall performance of the QA system, thus providing some answers to the evaluation issue of Ontolex resources raised in Chapter 5. First, it can be seen that the use of off-line techniques in general has a positive effect on the accuracy of QA. Here, we have demonstrated that the resources required for the off-line extraction of function relations can be acquired semi-automatically, by expanding a given list of relevant function words. Furthermore, coverage of a number of tables can be increased by including anaphora resolution. Second, the performance of the system on WHICH questions and definition questions was shown to improve considerably if it has access to automatically acquired class labels.

The research reported here can be extended and improved upon in several ways. For instance, alternative ways of exploiting the class labels in QA can be explored. Pantel and Ravichandran (2004), for example, use class labels to index the document collection, i.e. every paragraph which mentions a named entity known to be a FERRY is labelled with this class as well. This strategy allows the IR component to make use of class information. Pantel and Ravichandran (2004) show this modification to improve the precision of IR considerably. In future work, we would like to explore this possibility as well.

The lexico-semantically driven anaphora resolution can be improved in several ways. The fallback we have used introduced many false positives. We plan to investigate different methods of improving recall without hurting the precision. One possibility is the expansion of the list of categorized named entities by using more corpora and possibly also the Internet as a source. Another possible method is to expand the list by using semantically similar words in the same way as we employed it for expanding the function list.

Acknowledgments

This research was carried out in the project *Question Answering using Dependency Relations*, which is part of the research program for *Interactive Multimedia Information eXtraction*, IMIX, financed by NWO, the Dutch Organization for Scientific Research.

17 Agricultural ontology construction and maintenance in Thai

Asanee Kawtrakul and Aurawan Imsombut

17.1 Introduction

In this chapter, our ontology is meant to structure the knowledge we possess within the domain of agriculture.[1] We encode real-world, taxonomical and non-taxonomical, task-oriented aspects (see Figure 17.1). Typical taxonomical relations are the **hyponym-hypernym** relations; non-taxonomical relations; **synonyms, meronyms**, or roles (i.e., functional relations), of which **made-of, located-in, purpose-of, consist-of** are a few examples; and task-oriented relations, both specific non-taxonomical and specific-action relations.

While the manual building of an ontology by an expert is time-consuming and expensive, maintaining it throughout its life cycle is an endless task, since new terms are created, and others become obsolete. In the domain of agriculture, certain terms grow very quickly, for example, plant species, disease names, etc., while others tend to disappear. Those that disappear have lived out their time, or they have simply been made obsolete by the appearance of new technology, for example: in 2002 *pineapple* was an example of an economic plant, while in 2008, *oil palm* had become an economic plant instead (see Figure 17.2).

In order to reduce the costs and to support this open-ended task, research on (semi-) automatic ontology building has been conducted using a variety of resources, such as *raw text* (Hearst, 1992; Maedche and Staab, 2001; Kietz *et al.*, 2000; Yamaguchi, 1999; Navigli and Velardi, 2003; Li *et al.*, 2005; Pustejovsky *et al.*, 2002), *dictionaries* (Jannink, 1999; Kietz *et al.*, 2000; Aramaki *et al.*, 2005) and *thesauri* (Soergel *et al.*, 2004; Clark *et al.*, 2000; Wielinga *et al.*, 2001; Kawtrakul *et al.*, 2005). Each of these resources has different characteristics, and hence, each one is based on a different approach with regard to rules, natural language processing, statistics for term and relationship extraction, etc. Among the terminological resources considered, thesauri best lend themselves to ontology construction, because their explicit semantic structure eases natural language processing in the extraction of terms and

---

[1] See Chapter 1 for a presentation of the different scope of ontologies and lexical resources.

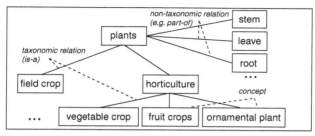

(a) Domain specific ontology for plants

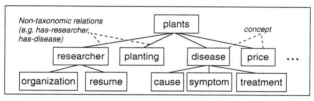

(b) Task-oriented ontology for plants

Figure 17.1 Examples of domain-specific and task-oriented ontologies

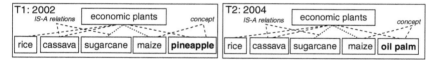

Figure 17.2 Examples of economic-plant ontologies at different points in time

relationships, whereas raw text contains huge amounts of frequently updated information.

This chapter presents a hybrid approach for building and maintaining (semi-) automatically an ontology of agriculture in Thai. To this end, we rely on the following three resources: a thesaurus, a domain-specific dictionary, and text corpora. We take AGROVOC,[2] a multilingual thesaurus that also includes Thai, as a seed. AGROVOC deals with two domains: food and agriculture. A domain-specific dictionary, such as the *Thai Plant Names Dictionary* (Smitinand, 2001) used here, is another good resource for extending the ontology. Of all these resources, text corpora present the biggest challenge, since they contain new, up-to-date terms, and thus a great deal more work is required in order to acquire the ontological terms and to mine their relationships. Hence,

---

[2] See www.fao.org/agrovoc

we do not only construct an ontology from the existing resources, but we also provide a means of maintaining it throughout its life cycle. Moreover, we also provide a tool for ontology aggregation into a tree structure with a verification system (Suktarachan *et al.*, 2008).

The outline of this chapter is as follows: the next section describes the framework of ontology building and maintenance. Section 17.3 shows how ontological terms are acquired from text corpora. In Section 17.4, we describe how terms and relationships are required from the dictionary and the thesaurus, while in Section 17.5, we present the method used to build the ontological tree. Finally, we summarize and conclude our present work and discuss our intended future work.

17.2   A framework of ontology construction and maintenance

Figure 17.3 shows the architecture of the Automatic Ontology Construction and Maintenance System of Thai. It is composed of the following modules: Ontology Acquisition, Ontology Tree Organization, and Verification.

17.2.1   Ontology acquisition

There are three sources for ontology acquisition: unstructured (raw) texts, a semi-structured dictionary, and a structured thesaurus. Unstructured texts

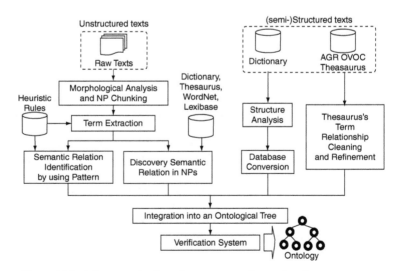

Figure 17.3 A framework of ontology construction and maintenance

should be dealt with by way of a hybrid approach, whereby natural language processing shall be dealt with by rule-based and statistical-based techniques being used in concert with the identification of the related ontological terms and their relationships. With the semi-structured dictionary, only a task-oriented parser is needed to extract the terms and relations. However, the parser will work well if, and only if, the dictionary has a certain structure. Since ontological terms can be transformed in a straightforward fashion, as in the case of a structured thesaurus, we must be sure to have clean relationships between terms and, if necessary, make certain refinements to ensure that this be the case. However, even if we have acquired the appropriate ontological relationships, we still need to perform natural language processing at the phrase level and, in addition, rely on various machine-learning techniques.

17.2.2   Integration into an ontological tree

During this step, we unite the related word/phrase pairs collected from our sources: texts on agriculture, the plant dictionary, and AGROVOC. The latter is used here as a core tree, since it is richly laden with concept hierarchies covering various subdomains of agriculture, of which animals, plants, plant/animal pathology, and chemicals are but a few. The ontological terms and their relationships taken from the dictionary and the texts will then be added to the core tree.

17.2.3   Verification tool

Verification is required in order to ensure a high-quality system, able to guide the expert in the maintenance of the existing ontology. For this reason, we have developed a user interface, thereby allowing the expert to verify the quality of the output and to add related word pairs to the ontological tree. Moreover, nodes can be moved or deleted from the ontology tree.

17.3   Ontology acquisition from texts

As mentioned above, AGROVOC is used as a seed to transform thesaurus terms into ontological terms. To this end, we start with the collection of necessary lexical patterns with clue words applied for ontology acquisition from texts at the sentence level by using AGROVOC's relations as a navigator.[3] Next, state-of-the-art NLP technologies are applied in order to identify

---

[3] See also Chapter 16 for an example of knowledge extraction from raw text exploiting richer syntactic information available on Dutch data.

Table 17.1 *Lexico-syntactic patterns extracted from the corpora*

Patterns	Cue-word translation	Occurrences	%
is-a			
NP_1 /pen/ $N P_0$	is/am/are	640	67
NP_0 /dai-kae/ $N P_1, \ldots N P_n$	such as/i.e.	85	9
NP_0 /chen/ $N P_1, \ldots N P_n$	for example	230	22
part-of			
NP_0 /prakop-douy/ $N P_1, \ldots N P_n$	consist of	80	100
SYNONYM			
NP_0 /chu-wittayasart/ $N P_1$	scientific name	25	31
NP_0 /chu-sanum/ $N P_1$	formal name	20	25
NP_0 /chu-tong-thin/ $N P_1$	local name	15	19
NP_0 /chao-ban-reak-wa/ $N P_1$	local name	10	12.5
Other patterns	-	10	12.5

potentially interesting terms, followed by heuristics and statistically based techniques, which identify the intended terms and relationships. In addition, machine-learning techniques are used to mine the semantic relationships embedded in the text's noun phrases by taking advantage of existing lexical resources, such as WordNet (Miller, 1995) and a general Thai–English Dictionary, LEXiTRON.[4]

17.3.1   Collecting lexical patterns and clue words

We select terms by considering relations like **is-a** (BT/NT), **part-of** (RT) and **synonym** (UF) from AGROVOC, taking into account lexico-syntactic patterns in Thai. The process is as follows:

- Selection of terms occurring in relations, such as: **is-a**, **part-of**, and **synonym** with 100, 50, and 50 term pairs, respectively.
- Extraction of all sentences from a corpus of 150 agricultural documents, containing these selected terms.
- Collection of lexico-syntactic patterns saved into a database.

The number of times lexico-syntactic patterns containing an **is-a, a-part-of**, or **synonym** relation in our experiment occured was 1,035, 80, and 80 times, respectively. The most frequently used patterns are shown in Table 17.1.

---

[4] See http://lexitron.nectec.or.th/

Given these results, we decided to focus on only the top eight patterns. Among the clue words, only */pen/* (*to be*)[5] is problematic when attempting to identify its **hypernym** relation, as it is highly polysemous, i.e. a word having several meanings. For example, it might signal any of the following relations, **hypernym**, **is-a-kind-of**, **have-symptom**, or **having-property**. It is therefore necessary to filter out inappropriate relationships.

17.3.2 Extraction of terms and relations

The acquisition of terms and ontological relations is accomplished in three steps, detailed below.

17.3.2.1 Morphological analysis and noun phrase chunking
As in many other Asian languages, there are no delimiters (blank spaces) in Thai to signal word boundaries. Hence, word segmentation and part-of-speech (POS) tagging (Sudprasert and Kawtrakul, 2003) techniques are necessary for the identification of a term unit and its syntactic category. Once this has been completed, words are clumped into phrases (Pengphon *et al.*, 2002) so that shallow noun-phrase (NP) boundaries within a sentence may be identified. In Thai, NPs are sometimes sentence-like patterns; this is why it is not always easy to identify the boundary of NPs composed of several words that include the presence of a verb. The candidate NP might then be signalled by another occurrence of the same sequence in the same document. The to-be-selected sentence-like NPs should be those that occur more than one time.

17.3.2.2 Identification of terms and relations at the sentence level
This process consists of sentence anchoring, generation of term candidates, ontological term selection, and identification of the semantic relation (Kawtrakul *et al.*, 2004; Imsombut and Kawtrakul, 2008).

Sentence anchoring: The sentence-anchoring process identifies plausible sentences whose content bears its ontological relation. A sentence σ is said to be anchored if σ contains at least one clue word (CW) that is a member of (CW). CW is a set of clue words: = [*/dai-kae/* (*i.e.*), */chen/* (*for example*), */pen/* (*to be*), */prakopduai/* (*consists of*), */chue-witthayasat/* (*scientific name*)...].

Term candidate generation: This process checks whether some NPs occurring at the left and right sides of the clue word qualify as term candidates in order to identify the corresponding terms. To do so, it will consider only

---

[5] The transcription system used in this chapter is not the standard system. It is semi-standard between IPA and Thai pronunciation rules. The use of such transcription system is only for computing purposes.

NPs respecting the grammatical ontological rules, such as [ncn+adj] and [ncn+prep+ncn].

Ontological term selection: In the texts analysed, we have often found that the ontological terms occurred in a variety of positions within the sentence, being more or less close to the clue word. In order to identify the intended ontological terms, two heuristic rules will be applied. The first technique is based on the assumption that ontological terms should have common head nouns. The second technique assumes that ontological terms should have strong mutual information. For example:

> (17.1) **samunphrai** lai chanit mi sabphakhun pen **ya-raksa-rok** lae mi kan nam ma phalit nai **radab utsahakam** laeo <u>chen</u> **krathiam, bai-pae-kuai**
>
> (*Many 'herbs' can be used as 'medicine' and some of them are manufactured at the 'industrial level', <u>such as</u> 'garlic, ginkgo biloba'*)

As shown in Example 17.1, the candidate terms in this example are *herbs*, *medicine*, and *industrial level*. If the word *herbs* co-occurs with *garlic* and *ginkgo biloba* more frequently than with *medicine* and *industry* in the document, the system will select *herbs* together with *garlic* and *ginkgo biloba* as ontological terms.

Identification of the semantic relation: The goal is to identify the correct relation (**hyponym**, **meronym**, or **synonym**) at the sentence level. Each relation has been extracted by using the clue word, such as: */dai-kae/* (*i.e.*) and */chen/* (*for example*) for extracting hyponym relations, */prakopduai/* (*composed of*) for extracting meronym relations, and */chue-witthayasat/* (*scientific name*), */chue-saman/* (*formal name*), and */chue-thongthin/* (*local name*) for extracting synonym relations.

As mentioned above, clue words, especially */pen/* (*be*), cause a lot of problems in the identification of the **hypernym** relation because of their polysemy, i.e., they possess multiple meanings. This is why it is necessary to filter out these inappropriate relationships at the next stage. Here are examples of a rule and a strategy that we used:

> *Rule: If one of two terms is a named entity, and if both of them belong to different classes, they cannot be ontological terms.*

Let us consider three cases, 17.2, 17.3, and 17.4.

> (17.2) /saphapwaetlom <u>pen</u> patchai-phainok/ (*Environment <u>is the</u> external factor.*)
>
> Here, /saphapwaetlom/ (*environment*) should not be extracted as the hyponym of /patchai-phainok/ (*external factor*), since it is a fairly generic term.

(17.3) /kalampli <u>pen</u> rok-naole/ (*Cabbage* <u>*is*</u> *rotten* or *Cabbage got disease as* Soft-Rot* (the literal translation))
Here, *Soft-Rot* is not a hypernym of *Cabbage*, but of a hyponym of PLANT DISEASE. We filter this pair of ontological terms by considering the difference between the two objects defined by the Named Entity (NE) extraction (Chanlekha and Kawtrakul, 2004).

(17.4) /kap-bai <u>pen</u> si-namtan/ (*The leaf* <u>*is*</u> *of brown-colour.*)
Brown-colour is not the hypernym of *leaf*, but a property of the object leaf. This being so, we have defined a set of properties in order to determine which terms are concepts and which are not. The domain of agriculture has within it three types of property lists: colours, shapes, and appearances.

In this step, precision is calculated for extracting ontological concepts and relations by using pattern matching. The fact that many sentences contain anaphorical terms constitutes an important cause of error, preventing the system from extracting the correct ontological terms. The results of the experiment show that filtering of inappropriate relations can increase the precision value by 14%, i.e., raise the level from 59% to 73%, because there are many general concepts and relations.

17.3.2.3 Terms and relations extraction at the phrasal level   Information concerning semantic relations can be extracted not only at the sentence level, but also at the noun phrase level. The problem in the case of the latter is how to identify the semantic relation between the nouns, since it is implicit. Moreover, in the case of compound nouns, we need to identify the correct ontological terms before being able to mine their relationships. For example:

(17.5) */pui/ (fertilizer)*:ncn + */in see/ (organic)*:ncn : *organic fertilizer*

(17.6) */pui/ (fertilizer)*:ncn + */nai-tro-chen/ (Nitrogen)*:ncn :*Nitrogen fertilizer*

(17.7) */kuad/ (bottle)* + */nam/ (water)* + */plad-sa-tik/ (plastic)*: *plastic water bottle*

(17.8) */kuad/ (bottle)* + */nam/ (water)*+ */phon-la-may/ (fruit)*: *fruit juice bottle*

The two nouns of noun phrases 17.5 and 17.6 both have the same patterns, yet they could express different semantic relationships, namely **made-of** and

Table 17.2 *A list of semantic relationships*

	Relation	Examples	Translation
1	**is-a**	/ka-fae/(coffee) /ro-bus-ta/(Robusta)	Robusta coffee
2	Location	/kai/(kitchen) /pun-muang/(local)	local kitchen
3	Purpose	/cream/(cream) /sa-lad/(salad)	salad cream
4	Possessor	/ran-kha/(shop) /khong/(to belong to) chum-chon/(commnunity)	community shop
5	Made-of	/sous/(sauce) /tua-luang/(soybean)	soy sauce
6	Source	/dok-mai/(flower) /tang-pra-ted/(foreign country)	foreign flower
7	Topic	/kor-mul/(data) /pra-mong/(fishery)	fishery data
8	Property	/ku-lab/(rose) /see-deang/(red)	red rose
9	Part-Whole	/perk/(husk) /kao/(rice)	rice husk
10	Produce	/puch/(plant) /nam-man/(oil)	oil crop

composed-of. In 17.7 and 17.8, they have different segmentations, one (17.8) is */plastic/-/water bottle/*, while the other is */fruit juice/- /bottle/*.

In Table 17.2, we list the semantic relations of NPs that our system is able to analyse by taking as input a Thai corpus in the domain of agriculture. The semantic relations in the list are the most frequent ones found in the data, and are based on the relations given in Vanderwende, 1994, Barker and Szpakowicz, 1998, and Soergel *et al.*, 2004. Even though our analysis is based on texts dealing with agriculture, the extracted semantic relations are still domain independent.

During this step, the system will extract semantic relations from NPs by learning the common ancestral concept of their head and modifier. The following features are taken into account by our learning component:

1. The semantic class of the head noun: the system will extract the head noun's sense and its hypernyms by using WordNet.
2. The semantic class of the modifier noun or head noun of a modifier phrase: like the head noun, the system will extract the sense of the modifier noun, or the head noun of a modifier phrase and its hypernyms with the help of WordNet.
3. The semantic class of the preposition: this is applied only to NPs composed of a prepositional phrase, and is meant to provide information about the semantic role of the prepositions used in the NPs. The value of this feature has been determined by Lexibase (Kawtrakul, 2004), a resource developed in our laboratory.

Since our learning features are based on the semantic information provided by WordNet, the examples to be learnt must be translated from Thai to English by using a Thai–English thesaurus, AGROVOC, a Thai–English dictionary, and LEXiTRON. Next, the WordNet sense of the nouns and the semantics of prepositions are identified. Here are some details concerning the algorithm.

Head noun and modifier segmentation: This step is similar to the approach taken by Lauer (1995) and Barker (1998). For a given sequence of X-Y-Z, segmentation is determined by comparing occurrences of X-Y, with Y-Z being occurrences in a corpus. If X-Z occurs in the corpus, the segmented phrase is [X-Y]-Z, otherwise it is X-[Y-Z]. For example, in case of the phrase in (17.7), if a corpus never contains a phrase like */nam/ /plad-sa-tik/ (water plastic)*, then it will be segmented as [[*/kuad/ (bottle) /nam/ (water)*] */plad-sa-tik/ (plastic)*].

In the case of the phrase in (17.8), if */nam/ /phon-la-may/ (fruit juice)* occurs in a corpus, then it will be segmented as [*/kuad/ (bottle)* [*/nam/ (water) /phon-la-may/(fruit)*]].

Translating each Thai NP constituent into English and disambiguation of the semantics: There are basically two techniques to accomplish this task in order to identify the sense of the head noun. The first technique conjointly employs the AGROVOC thesaurus and WordNet. The second strategy consists of drawing conjointly on a Thai–English dictionary and WordNet.

Technique 1: The system uses the Thai-English AGROVOC in order to translate the Thai source-word (tw) into its English correspondence (ew), all words having a one-to-one mapping, i.e. translation equivalent. However, ew might yield several word senses in WordNet, in which case it requires disambiguation. To this end, the system will compute the most likely similarity between each sense s and the hyponyms of ew in the thesaurus by determining the Number of Common Edges (CE).

$$s^* = argmax_{s \in S} \sum_{h \in H} NCE(s, h)$$

$h \in H$, H is the set of hyponyms of ew.

S is the set of all senses of ew in WordNet.

$NCE(s, h)$ is the function of the Number of Common Edges. It returns the number of edges having common paths from h to the root and s to the root.

Figure 17.4 shows an example of a thesaurus-based semantic disambiguation of */phon-la-may/ (fruit)*. Fruit has three senses in WordNet. If our decision is based on thesaurus information, we can conclude that sense number one is a fruit, part of the domain of agriculture. If the word does not exist in the thesaurus, it will be processed according to the second technique.

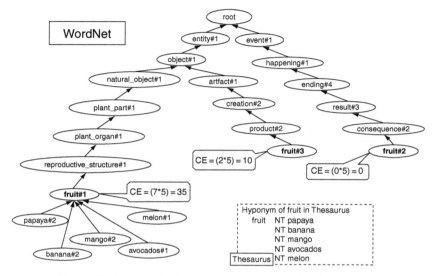

Figure 17.4 An example of thesaurus-based semantic disambiguation of /phon-la-may/ (*fruit*), with fruit #x having the sense #x

Technique 2: A Thai–English dictionary is used to translate a Thai word (*tw*) into English (*ew*). However, there are many words in Thai, each of which could be translated into several words in English (about 70%). In this case, we take the first English word or one of its synonyms, assuming that this word is the one most frequently used. This word is then compared to those in WordNet. If there are several senses in WordNet, the system will select the sense with the highest number of *synset* terms, similar to the set of translated words, by using the following equation:

$$s^* = argmax_{s \in S} sizeof(Synset(s) \cap T)$$

Synset(*s*) is a synset of *s* in WordNet.

T is the set of translated terms of *tw* in a dictionary.

Figure 17.5 shows an example of a dictionary-based semantic disambiguation of /krong/ (*cage*)

If the Thai word has several meanings, or if it has only one translation, the system will alert the expert, who will then manually select the sense of the word in WordNet. If the NP is a compound word and absent from WordNet, the system will select only the head noun for semantic disambiguation. For example, given the term /tang-pra-ted/ (*foreign_country*), the system will choose only *country* in *foreign_country* to disambiguate it semantically.

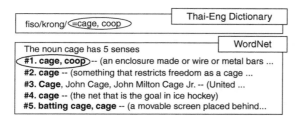

Figure 17.5 Examples of dictionary-based semantic disambiguation of /krong/ (*cage*).

Defining hypernym class and the semantics of the preposition: Having translated and disambiguated the semantics of the head and the modifier of the NP, we then proceed to extract from WordNet the complete hypernym path of each constituent of the NP for the learning system. For example, the hypernym path of NP /kuad/ (*bottle*) /nam phon-la-may/ (*fruit-juice*): *fruit-juice bottle* is as follows:

> { *bottle#1* } < { *vessel#3* } <{ *container#1* } < { *instrumentality#3* } < { *artefact#1* } < { *object#1* } < { *entity#1* }
> { *fruit_juice#1* } <{ *beverage#1* } < { *food#1* } <{ *substance#1* } < { *entity#1* }

Moreover, for NPs containing a preposition, such as /dok-mai/ (*flower*) /jak/ (*from*) /tang-pra-ted/ (*foreign_country*) : *flower from foreign country*, the system will define the semantic group to which it belongs by using Lexibase. In Thai, there are ten semantic groups for prepositions, such as location, purpose, time, etc. These groups are mapped into ten features. Their values are set to 1, if the preposition has the same semantic group as the feature. Some prepositions belong to several groups, such as /nai/ (*in*), which can express either a location or time. Hence, the system will set the value of these features to 1. For NPs without prepositions, the values are set to 0.

Learning of relationships: To obtain vectors of equal length, all hypernym list classes of the examples are united as a hypernym class, and then the features will be converted into binary representations. Next, the features' vector starts with the list of hypernym classes of the head, followed by the list of the hypernym classes of the modifier and the list of the semantics, i.e.

> *features_vector{{list of hypernym class of head},{list of hypernym class of modifier},{list of preposition semantic}}*

The learning algorithm will be used to learn the common ancestral concept of the head and the modifier, in order to generate then a model capable of

Table 17.3 *The experimental results of ontology acquisition from texts*

Technique	Relation	Precision
Lexical patterns and cue words	1,764	73%
Extraction at the Phrasal level	1,091	84%
Total	2,855	77%

extracting the NP's semantic relationship. Two machine-learning techniques, i.e. C4.5 of the decision-tree learning system and SVM using linear kernel, are applied by our system, using the software package Weka.[6]

For the purpose of this experiment, the decision-tree learning system has generated about ninety classification rules to discover ten semantic relations (see Table 17.2). For example:

> *Rule A: If the concept of a head-noun is body-path#1, then we are dealing with a **part-whole** relation.*

> (17.9) */kha/* (*leg*) */kai/* (*chicken*) : *chicken leg*

> *Rule B: If the modifier's concept is a country#5, then the relation is* **locatedAt** *or* **comeFrom**.

> (17.10) */pra-sal-mon/* (*salmom*) */aus-tra-lia/* (*Australia*) : *Australian salmon*

By applying Rule B, it can be seen that the semantic relationship between the nouns */pra-sal-mon/* (*salmon*) and */aus-tra-lia/* (*Australia*) is **comeFrom**.

In addition, the SVM learning system generated ten learning models according to the relationships. When comparing the performance of the two algorithms, the following results are obtained: the SVM and C4.5 scores respectively 84.10% and 78.82% in terms of precision. Both learning systems show that the 'Topic' relationship achieves the best results, because all NPs containing this relationship have the head word in the class of data or information. Moreover, the **is-a** relationship is the most problematic, as it is often embedded in NPs containing a number of modifiers, such as plant and animal species.

Table 17.3 shows the results of the experiment as generated by using the techniques outlined above. The average of the accuracy of ontology acquisition from agricultural texts is 77%.

---

[6] See www.cs.waikato.ac.nz/ml/weka/

17.4   Ontology acquisitions from a dictionary and a thesaurus

17.4.1   Acquisition based on a dictionary

A domain-specific dictionary is the best way to extract relational information, as this sort of dictionary has a specific structure in addition to clear and accurate information. In this chapter, we use as a case study the *Thai Plant Names Dictionary* (Smitinand, 2001), developed by Tem Smitinand and edited by the Forest Herbarium Royal Forest Department in 2001. The most frequent relationships of this specific dictionary are hyponymy and synonymy. Two steps are needed for extracting the ontological terms: structure analysis and database conversion.

Structure analysis: The analysis of the structure of the dictionary is an important step to undertake in order to be able to distinguish elements of word entries as sub-parts. The characteristics of term positions are analysed, and irrelevant parts, such as author name, are filtered out. The relevant portion is then transferred to a relational database by using a task-oriented parser.

Figure 17.6 illustrates the analysis of the dictionary's structure. The position of the terms in the text, such as top rightmost corner and top leftmost corner, is also considered. A relational database's fields are predefined as hierarchical relations such as **Family**, **Sub-Family**, **Genus**, **Specific Epithet**, **Formal Name** and **Local Name**, respectively.

Database conversion: After undergoing the parsing process, all of these terms are then defined and given an identifying number and converted into a relational database. The system is able to extract 24,966 terms, which express 5,519 concepts and entertain 33,956 relationships. The experiment of dictionary-based ontology extraction achieves an accuracy rating of 100%.

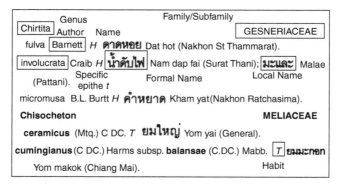

Figure 17.6 Dictionary structure

17.4.2   Ontology acquisition by using the AGROVOC thesaurus

AGROVOC is a multilingual agricultural thesaurus, which has been developed and is maintained by the Food and Agriculture Organization (FAO) of the United Nations. AGROVOC is a good resource to start with. Its relationships are of at least three types: **UF/USE, BT/NT** (*Broader/more Narrow Term*), and **RT** (*Related Term*). However, AGROVOC is not perfect, as some of its relations are incorrectly assigned and others are too broadly defined.

A cursory review of the data in AGROVOC reveals some **USE/UF** and **BT/NT** relationships to be incorrect or reflect inconsistent uses of the relationships. The **USE/UF** relationship links not only synonyms, but also quasi-synonyms, such as closely related and hierarchically related terms (Soergel *et al.*, 2004). Likewise, the **BT/NT** relationship is highly ambiguous. AGROVOC incorrectly[7] uses **NT**, approximately equivalent to **superclassOf** or **hypernymOf**, in *milk* **NT** *milk fat*, while a more specific and probably more correct relationship would be **containsSubstance**.

In particular, **RT** has been used to link any two, usually non-hierarchically related terms that seem to be associated with each other. This relationship needs to be defined in order to reflect the more meaningful and specific associative semantics between the terms in the thesaurus. For example, **RT** is under-specified, subsuming numerous relationships like **RT** in *mutton* **RT** *sheep*. This relationship should be refined to a more specific one, such as **madeFrom** (Soergel *et al.*, 2004) to distinguish it from other uses of **RT**.

We have divided the process of data cleaning and refinement of semantic relations, before being used for ontology construction, into three main steps: acquisition of refinement rules, detection and suggestion, and, finally, verification (Kawtrakul *et al.*, 2005).

17.4.2.1 The rule acquisition module: expert-defined rules and learning by examples   To mine the implicit relationship of some NPs, this module acquires a set of rules used to suggest the most likely relationships in case the relationship given by AGROVOC is under-specified (defined too broadly), especially RT. The rules will be provided by both experts and by machine learning.

Expert-defined rules: The experts can simply define a set of rules for allowing the correction of inappropriate relationships. These experts observe AGROVOC's data and subsequently define rules using data concerning

---

[7] Within a hierarchy based on partiality, the use of **NT** does not need to be incorrect, e.g., 'milk **NT** milk fat **NT** milk fat globule', etc. However, the refined AGROVOC will probably use **BT/NT** only to express hierarchical, super/subclass-type relationships. In addition, its conversion into an ontology requires that each relationship corresponds only to a unique sense.

concept types given in AGROVOC's database. For example, the rules are constrained by the data in 'concept type data', the category of terms such as GC (Geographic term: Country level), and TP (Taxonomic term: Plant).

Given these rules, a relationship satisfying them will be revised automatically. For example, consider the following rule:

If X and Y are marked as TP in the concept type field, and if X **BT** Y, then X **subclassOf** Y

According to AGROVOC, the concept types of *Rosaceae* and *Malus* are TP, related by **BT**. Hence, the original relationship **BT** of *Malus* **BT** *Rosaceae* will be replaced by **subclassOf**.

Learning rules-by-example: In this case, the rules are prepared to learn by example in order to refine a relationship, called **RT**.

To prepare the learning set, we provide an annotation tool allowing the domain expert to manually tag term senses (labelled by a sense ID number in WordNet). This annotation tool also allows the specification of the appropriate semantic relationship between terms, for example, ({ *sheep#1* } **usedToMake** { *mutton#1* }).

In the case of compound nouns, only the noun heads are used. For example, *rice* and *rice flour* will be annotated as follows: ({ *rice#1* }**usedToMake** { *flour#1* }).

Having prepared the examples, their complete hypernym path will be extracted from WordNet and used as the basis of the features' vectors, i.e.,

features_vector{{list of hypernym class of all term1},{ list of hypernym class of all term2}}

The learning system C4.5 will be applied to learn the common ancestral concept for term1, e.g. { *animal#1* }, and term2, e.g. { *meat#1* }, to then generate the rules. Figure 17.7 shows the example of the data set for training the **usedToMake** relationship. Table 17.4 displays the revision rules learned from the training set.

By applying Rule 1 in Figure 17.7, the original relationship RT of *chicken* **RT** *chicken meat* will be replaced by **usedToMake**.

17.4.2.2 The detection and suggestion module   In this module, the system detects incorrect and inconsistently applied relationships, suggests appropriate relationships, and then waits for the expert's confirmation of its analysis. We propose three techniques to achieve this goal: applying rules for semantic relationships, noun phrase analysis, and WordNet alignment. A full discussion of the relationship revision rules can be found in Kawtrakul *et al.*, 2005. In the following section, we briefly describe the procedures used for the analysis of noun phrases and the WordNet alignment.

Table 17.4 *Examples of training statistical-based rule*

	Rule
1	If class X is { *animal#1* } and class Y is { *meat#1* }, and X **RT** Y Then X **usedToMake** Y **Example** *sheep* **RT** *mutton, swine* **RT** *pork* *calf* **RT** *veal*
2	If class X is { *plant#2* } and class Y is { *food#1* }, and X **RT** Y Then X **usedToMake** Y **Example** *rice* **RT** *rice flour, oat* **RT** *oat meal* *sugar cane* **RT** *cane sugar*
3	If class X is { *fruit#1* } and class Y is { *oil#3* }, and X **RT** Y Then X **usedToMake** Y **Example** *castor bean* **RT** *castor oil* *cottonseed* **RT** *cottonseed oil*

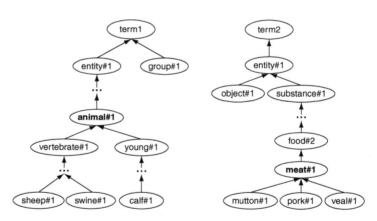

Figure 17.7 Examples of hierarchical data used for training the **usedToMake** relationship

Using noun phrase analysis: This technique is used to analyse the surface form of a compound term's head word. If the head word of a term has the same surface form as its broader term, the system will apply the **subclassOf/superclassOf** relationship. For example:

milk **BT** *cow milk*

From the analysis of the compound noun, it can be seen that the head word of *cow milk* is *milk*, which obviously has the same surface form as *milk*, the broader term of *cow milk*. Hence, the system will apply the **subclassOf** relationship to *cow milk* and *milk*.

> *milk* **BT** *milk fat*

The result of the analysis shows the head word of *milk fat* to be *fat*, which is not compatible with the broader term *milk*. This will be detected, and the system will be trained by examples, as mentioned before, in order to extract the rule for refining the relationship.

Using WordNet's relationships: During this step, we employ WordNet's **hyper-hyponymy** relationships to align the **BT/NT** relationship in AGROVOC. The synset of a term in WordNet is used to align the **UF/USE** relationship in AGROVOC. As the relationships in WordNet are checked by experts, and since it contains a great number of general, domain-specific terms, including agricultural terms, WordNet is a good resource for aligning certain relationships of AGROVOC, such as taxonomic and synonym relationships.

At this stage, the system commences with the retrieval of the synset offset number of the AGROVOC **UF/USE** term in WordNet. If it is able to find these terms, and if they have the same synset ID number, the system will consider them to be 'synonyms'. The system will also check AGROVOC's broader term and the narrower term in WordNet. If it discovers that the broader term is the ancestor of the narrower term in the WordNet hierarchy, it will conclude that we are dealing here with a **subclassOf/superclassOf** relationship. For example:

> *cabbage* **BT** *vegetable*

Query results for *cabbage* and *vegetable* in WordNet show that { *cabbage* } is a **hyponym** of { *cruciferous vegetable* }, and that { *cruciferous vegetable* } is a **hyponym** of { *vegetable* }.

Since { *vegetable* } is an ancestor of { *cabbage* }, the system will define VEGETABLE as a **superclassOf** CABBAGE. In the case of *milk* **NT** *milk fat*, the relationship is not refined by this technique, because { *milk* } and { *fat* } follow different hypernym paths in WordNet.

An experiment was performed, testing the training rules technique, in which 100 examples for five semantic relationships were gathered. The system produced roughly ten classification rules. The experimental results of the noun phrase analysis and the WordNet alignment based on these rules, including the ones given by the experts, are all shown in Table 17.5.

The precision of the training rules technique was estimated to achieve an accuracy of 72%. Sources of error include ambiguity concerning the concept classes used as arguments for a given rule, such as, 'If class X is { *food#1* }

Table 17.5 *The experimental results of thesaurus, classified according to the technique used*

Technique	Relation refinement	Precision
Expert rules	17,209	100%
NP Analysis	2,602	95%
WordNet Alignment	5,976	80%
Training rules	798*	72%*
Total	**26,045**	**94%**

Remark: * indicates that the experiment is run with some data

and class Y is { *food#1* }, and X **RT** Y, then X **usedToMake** Y', where the system cannot distinguish between X and Y, generating possibly erroneous relationships, e.g., *pork* **usedToMake** *hams*, and *hams* **usedToMake** *pork*, as both X and Y belong to the same concept class. These cases can only be revised manually by an expert.

17.5   Integration into an ontological tree

In this step, we united the related word/phrase pairs collected from our sources: texts, some dictionaries, and a thesaurus. In order to integrate them (Suktarachan *et al.*, 2008), two heuristics are applied:

> *If the separated ontological trees have the same label nodes, then merge them.*
> *If the terms' head words match partially, then merge them.*

There are three operations involved in this process of integration: addition, insertion, and deletion.[8] Examples of these operations are shown in Figure 17.8.

Addition: A child node will be added to the core tree if the parent node has the same label or head-word consistency as the existing node in the core tree.

Insertion: If the children nodes have the same label as the head word of the parent nodes, then the new, more specific term will be inserted between two existing ontological terms.

Deletion: If there are duplicate relations, the system will delete the tree with less nodes.

The remaining terms that could not be integrated will be kept for the expert, who will manually add them at a later date.

---

[8] See Chapters 10 and 13 for more discussions about the integration of new elements within an existing knowledge organization.

Table 17.6 *Experimental results*

	Terms	Concepts	Relations	Precision of relation
Thesaurus	42,145	24,345	26,045	94%
Dictionary	25,937	6,409	25,585	100%
Text	3,785	3,308	2,855	77%
Total	69,888	32,516	53,450	-%

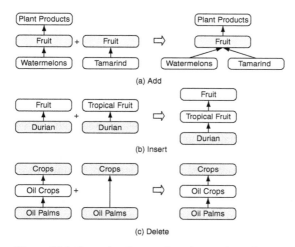

Figure 17.8 Operation for ontology integration of a core-tree (left tree) into a new ontological tree (right tree)

Table 17.6 shows the number of terms, concepts, and relationships extracted from each resource, as well as the total number of terms, concepts, and relationships in the ontology resulting from the process of organization. After a random check of 1,000 integrated terms, the organizing system's accuracy is deemed to be 87%. The errors are due to the particular characteristics of the corpus extraction terms.

17.6 Conclusion

The development of an ontology having precise semantics has important and far-reaching implications for the improvement of information systems by and large, as well as for automating reasoning and for the sharing and management of knowledge. In this work, we are interested in building an ontology that is both taxonomic and non-taxonomic; hence, we have included relations such as

synonyms, **meronyms**, and functional relations. One of our primary goals is to solve the ontology development bottleneck problem, which has been described in Chapters 5 and 14, by exploiting the enormous body of knowledge that has been gathered over the years in the form of various types of classification systems and thesauri. Next, AGROVOC and a plant dictionary have been used as seeds to transform these terms into ontological terms. As noted above, terms grow quite quickly in many domains. In the case of agriculture, this growth is illustrated by terms found in the categories of *plant species*, *disease name*, *chemical names*, and *pathogen names*. Likewise, certain terms tend to disappear because they have lived out their time, or because they have simply been rendered obsolete by the appearance of new technology. Hence, we should not only build an ontology, but also provide a means of maintaining it throughout its life cycle. This is where text corpora become extremely useful, since they contain a massive quantity of frequently updated information. However, texts also present the hardest challenge, as they require much more work concerning the acquisition of ontological terms and the mining of their relationships.

We have employed state-of-the-art NLP technologies in our experiments in order to identify potentially interesting terms, followed by heuristics and statistically based techniques used to identify the intended terms and their relationships. In addition, we used machine-learning techniques to mine the relationships embedded in the text's noun phrase, by taking advantage of existing lexical resources, such as WordNet. Our initial results look quite promising, and we look forward to continuing this avenue of research.

We have focused here only on noun phrases in order that the ontology be built monotonically. However, we plan to allow for non-monotonic growth, since the terms and relationships might very well change over time.

Acknowledgements

The authors would like to express their debt of gratitude towards Michael Zock, research director at the CNRS-LIF (Faculté de Luminy, Marseille, France), who put considerable time and effort into discussing and commenting on our work. We also would like to thank all of those people who have given their time in the preparation of the data found in this body of work, with a special thanks to Mukda Suktarachan and Chalatip Thumkanon, in particular. Of course, we hold ourselves solely responsible for any remaining mistakes or areas that lack clarity. The work described above has been supported by a grant from NECTEC (No. NT-B-22-14-12-46-06) and to some extent by a grant from FAO.

References

Agirre, E. and López de Lacalle Lekuona, O. (2004). Publicly Available Topic Signatures for All WordNet Nominal Senses. In *Proceedings of LREC*, Lisbon, Portugal.

Alexa, M., Kreissig, B., Liepert, M., Reichenberger, K., Rostek, L., Rautmann, K., Scholze-Stubenrecht, W., and Stoye, S. (2002). The Duden Ontology: An Integrated Representation of Lexical and Ontological Information. In *Proceedings of the OntoLex Workshop at LREC*, Germany. Fraunhofer Publica.

Alexander, C. (1979). *The Timeless Way of Building*. New York: Oxford University Press.

Alfonseca, E. and Manandhar, S. (2002). Improving an Ontology Refinement Method with Hyponymy Patterns. In *Proceedings of the International Conference on Language Resources and Evaluation*.

Almuhareb, A. and Poesio, M. (2004). Attribute-Based and Value-Based Clustering: An Evaluation. In *Proceedings of EMNLP 2004*, pages 158–65, Barcelona, Spain.

Antoniou, G. and van Harmelen, F. (2004). *A Semantic Web Primer*. Cambridge, MA: The MIT Press.

Apresjan, J. (1973). Regular Polysemy. *Linguistics* 142, 5–32.

Apresjan, J. (2000). *Systematic Lexicography*. Oxford: Oxford University Press. Translated by Kevin Windle.

Aramaki, E., Imai, T., Kashiwagi, M., Kajino, M., Miyo, K., and Ohe, K. (2005). Toward Medical Ontology via Natural Language Processing. In *Proceedings of the OntoLex workshop at the International Joint Conference on Natural Language Processing*, pages 53–8, Jeju Island, Korea.

Asher, N. and Denis, P. (2004). Dynamic Typing for Lexical Semantics. In *Proceedings of FOIS 2004*.

Assem, M. v., Gangemi, A., and Schreiber, G. (2006). Conversion of WordNet to a Standard RDF/OWL Representation. In *Proceedings of the International Conference on Language Resources and Evaluation (LREC), Genoa, Italy*. ACL.

Baader, F., Calvanese, D., McGuinness, D. L., Nardi, D., and Patel-Schneider, P. F. (eds.) (2003). *The Description Logic Handbook: Theory, Implementation, and Applications*. New York: Cambridge University Press.

Bach, E. (1986a). The Algebra of Events. *Linguistics and Philosophy* 9, 5–16.

Bach, E. (1986b). Natural Language Metaphysics. In Marcus, R. B., Dorn, G., and Weingartner, P. (eds.), *Logic, Methodology, and Philosophy of Science*, volume VII, pages 573–95. Amsterdam: North Holland.

Baker, C., Fillmore, C., and Cronin, B. (2003). The Structure of the Framenet Database. *International Journal of Lexicography*, 16(3), 281–96.

Baker, C. F., Fillmore, C., and Lowe, J. B. (1998). The Berkeley FrameNet Project. In *Proceedings of the COLING-ACL*.

Barker, K. (1998). A Trainable Bracketer for Noun Modifiers. In *Proceeding of the Twelfth Canadian Conference on AI*, Vancouver.

Barker, K. and Szpakowicz, S. (1998). Semi-Automatic Recognition of Noun Modifier Relationships. In *Proceeding of COLING-ACL*, Montréal.

Baroni, M. and Lenci, A. (2009). One Distributional Memory, Many Semantic Spaces. In *Proceedings of the EACL Workshop on Geometrical Models of Natural Language Semantics*, Athens, 31 March.

Barsalou, L. (1999). Perceptual Symbol Systems. *Behavioral and Brain Sciences*, 22, 577–609.

Barsalou, L. (2005). Situated Conceptualization. In Cohen, H. and Lefebvre, C. (eds.), *Handbook of Categorization in Cognitive Sciences*, pages 619–50. St. Louis: Elsevier.

Bartlett, F. (1932). *Remembering: An Experimental and Social Study*. Cambridge: Cambridge University Press.

Basili, R., Pazienza, M., and Zanzotto, F. (2001). Modelling Syntactic Context in Automatic Term Extraction. In *Proceedings of Recent Advances in Natural Language Processing*, Tzigov Chark, Bulgaria.

Basili, R., Rocca, M. D., and Pazienza, M.-T. (1997). Contextual Word Sense Tuning and Disambiguation. *Applied Artificial Intelligence*, 11, 235–62.

Bateman, J. (1997). The Theoretical Status of Ontologies in Natural Language Processing. In *Text Representation and Domain Modelling – Ideas from Linguistics and AI.*, pages 50–99. Technische Universität Berlin. Also available from the Computation and Language E-print archive: cmp-lg/9704010.

Bateman, J., Henschel, R., and Rinaldi, F. (1995). *Generalized Upper Model 2.0: Documentation*. Technical report, GMD/Institut für Integrierte Publikations- und Informationssysteme.

Bateman, J., Magnini, B., and Fabris, G. (1995). The Generalized Upper Model Knowledge Base: Organization and Use. In *Proceedings of International Conference on Building and Sharing of Very Large-Scale Knowledge Bases*, Twente, The Netherlands.

Bateman, J. A., Kapser, R. T., Moore, J. D., and Whitney, R. A. (1989). *A General Organization of Knowledge for Natural Language Processing: The Penman Upper Model*. Technical report, Information Sciences Institute, Marina del Rey, CA, USA.

Beale, S., Nirenburg, S., and McShane, M. (2003). Just-in-Time Grammar. In *2003 International Multiconference in Computer Science and Computer Engineering*, Las Vegas, Nevada.

Bechhofer S., Harmelen F., Hendler J., Horrocks D., McGuinnes I., Patel-Schneider P., and Stein L.A. (2004). *OWL Web Ontology Language Reference*. Technical report, W3C.

Beneventano, D., Bergamaschi, S., Guerra, F., and Vincini, M. (2003). Synthesizing an Integrated Ontology. *IEEE Internet Computing*, 07(5), 42–51.

Bentivogli, L., Bocco, A., and Pianta, E. (2004). ArchiWordNet: Integrating Wordnet with Domain-Specific Knowledge. In *Proceedings of the Second Global Wordnet Conference*, Brno, Czech Republic.

Berland, M. and Charniak, E. (1999). Finding Parts in Very Large Corpora. In *Proceedings of the 37th Meeting of the Association for Computational Linguistics*, pages 57–64.

Bernard, J. (1990). *The Macquarie Encyclopedic Thesaurus*. Sydney: The Macquarie Library.

Berners-Lee, T., Hall, W., Hendler, J. A., Shadbolt, N., and Weitzner, D. J. (2006). Creating a Science of the Web. *Science*, 313(5788), 769–71.

Berners-Lee, T., Hendler, J., and Lassila, O. (2001). The Semantic Web. *Scientific American*, May, 35–43.

Bertagna, F., Monachini, M., Soria, C., Calzolari, N., Huang, C.-R., Hsieh, S.-K., Marchetti, A., and Tesconi, M. (2007). Fostering Intercultural Collaboration: A Web Service Architecture for Cross-fertilization of Distributed Wordnets. In Ishida, T., Fussell, S., and Vossen, P. (eds.), *Intercultural Collaboration I*. Lecture Notes in Computer Science State-of-the-Art Survey, pages 146–58. Heidelberg: Springer Verlag.

Bierwisch, M. (1983). Semantische und konzeptuelle Repräsentationen lexikalischer Einheiten. In Ruzicka, R. and Motsch, W. (eds.), *Untersuchungen zur Semantik*, pages 61–99. Berlin: Akademische Verlag.

Bisiach, E. (1988). Language without Thought. In Weiskrantz, L. (ed.), *Thought without Language*, pages 464–84. Oxford: Clarendon Press.

Bouma, G., Mur, J., and van Noord, G. (2005). Reasoning over Dependency Relations for QA. In *Knowledge and Reasoning for Answering Questions, Workshop associated with IJCAI*, pages 15–21.

Bouquet, P. and Serafini, L. (2001). Two Formalizations of a Context: A Comparison. In *Proceedings of Third International Conference on Modeling and Using Context*, Dundee, Scotland.

Bouquet, P., Serafini, L., and Zanobini, S. (2003). Semantic Coordination: A New Approach and an Application. In *Proceedings of 2nd International Semantic Web Conference*, volume LNCS 2870, pages 130–45.

Brachman, R. J. (1977). A Structural Paradigm for Representing Knowledge. PhD thesis, Harvard University, USA.

Brockmann, C. and Lapata, M. (2003). Evaluating and Combining Approaches to Selectional Preference Acquisition. In *Proceedings of the 11th Conference of the European Chapter of the ACL*, pages 27–34, Budapest, Hungary.

Budanitsky, A. and Hirst, G. (2006). Evaluating WordNet-Based Measures of Semantic Distance. *Computational Linguistics*, 32(1), 13–47.

Buitelaar, P. (1998). CoreLex: An Ontology of Systematic Polysemous Classes. In *Proceedings of Formal Ontology in Information Systems*.

Buitelaar, P. (2000). Reducing Lexical Semantic Complexity with Systematic Poly-semous Classes and Underspecification. In *Proceedings of the ANLP2000 Workshop on Syntactic and Semantic Complexity in Natural Language Processing Systems*.

Buitelaar, P., Choi, K., Gangemi, A., Huang, C., and Oltramari, A. (2007). *Proceedings of ISWC 2007 Workshop OntoLex2007*, Busan, Korea. http://olp.dfki.de/OntoLex07/.

Buitelaar, P., Cimiano, P., and Magnini, B. (2005). *Ontology Learning from Texts*. Amsterdam: IOS Press.

Buitelaar, P., Declerck, T., Frank, A., Racioppa, S., Kiesel, M., Sintek, M., Engel, R., Romanelli, M., Sonntag, D., Loos, B., Micelli, V., Porzel, R., and Cimiano,

P. (2006). LingInfo: Design and Applications of a Model for the Integration of Linguistic Information in Ontologies. In *Proceedings of the OntoLex06 Workshop at LREC*.

Buitelaar, P., Eigner, T., and Declerck, T. (2004). OntoSelect: A Dynamic Ontology Library with Support for Ontology Selection. In *Proceedings of the Demo Session at the International Semantic Web Conference*.

Buitelaar, P. and Sacaleanu, B. (2001). Ranking and Selecting Synsets by Domain Relevance. In *Proceedings of the NAACL 2001 Workshop on WordNet and Other Lexical Resources: Applications, Extensions and Customizations*.

Buitelaar, P. and Sacaleanu, B. (2002). Extending Synsets with Medical Terms. In *Proceedings of the First Global WordNet Conference*, Mysore, India.

Buitelaar, P., Sintek, M., and Kiesel, M. (2006). A Lexicon Model for Multilingual/Multimedia Ontologies. In *Proceedings of the 3rd European Semantic Web Conference*.

Burchardt, A., Erk, K., and Frank, A. (2005). A WordNet Detour to FrameNet. In Fisseni, B., Schmitz, H.-C., Schröder, B., and Wagner, P. (eds.), *Computer Studies in Language and Speech*. VIII. *Sprachtechnologie, mobile Kommunikation and linguistische Resources*, pages 408–21. Frankfurt: Peter Lang.

Burgess, C. and Lund, K. (1997). Modelling Parsing Constraints with High-Dimensional Context Space. *Language and Cognitive Processes*, 12, 1–34.

Burns, K. and Davis, A. (1999). Building and Maintaining a Semantically Adequate Lexicon Using Cyc. In Viegas, E. (ed.), *Breadth and Depth of Semantic Lexicons*. Dordrecht: Kluwer.

Busa, F., Calzolari, N., Lenci, A., and Pustejovsky, J. (1999). Building a Semantic Lexicon: Structuring and Generating Concepts. In *Proceedings of The Third International Workshop on Computational Semantics*, Tilburg, The Netherlands.

Calzolari, N., Lenci, A., Bertagna, F., and Zampolli, A. (2002). Broadening the Scope of the EAGLES/ISLE Lexical Standardization Initiative. In *COLING '02: Proceedings of the 3rd Workshop on Asian Language Resources and International Standardization*, pages 1–8, Morristown, NJ: ACL.

Campbell, K. (1990). *Abstract Particulars*. Cambridge, MA: Blackwell.

Caraballo, S. A. (1999). Automatic Construction of a Hypernym-Labelled Noun Hierarchy from Text. In *Proceedings of the 37th Annual Meeting of the Association for Computational Linguistics*.

Carlson, G. N. (1980). *Reference to Kinds in English*. New York: Garland Publishing.

Casati, R. and Varzi, A. (eds.) (1996). *Events*. Aldershot: Dartmouth Publishing Company.

Chalupsky, H. and Russ, T. A. (2003). *The PowerLoom Knowledge Representation and Reasoning System*. Marina del Rey, CA: USC Information Sciences Institute.

Chang, N., Feldman, J., Porzel, R., and Sanders, K. (2002). Scaling Cognitive Linguistics: Formalisms for Language Understanding. In *Proceedings of the First International Workshop on Scalable Natural Language Understanding (ScaNaLU2002)*.

Chang, R.-Y., Huang, C.-R., Lo, F.-J., and Chang, S. (2005). General Ontology to Specialized Ontology: A Study Based on a Single Author Historical Corpus. In *Fourth OntoLex Workshop*.

Chanlekha, H. and Kawtrakul, A. (2004). Thai Named Entity Extraction by Incorporating Maximum Entropy Model with Simple Heuristic Information. In *Proceeding of IJCNLP 2004*, Hainan Island, China.

Chao, Y.-R. (1968). *A Grammar of Spoken Chinese*. Berkeley: University of California Press.

Chi, M., Glaser, R., and Farr, M. (1988). *The Nature of Expertise*. Hillsdale, NJ: Erlbaum.

Choi, N., Song, I., and Han, H. (2006). A Survey on Ontology Mapping. *SIGMOD REcord*, 35(3): 34–41.

Chou, Y. (2005). Hantology – The Knowledge Structure of Chinese Writing System and its Applications. PhD thesis, National Taiwan University.

Chou, Y.-M. and Huang, C.-R. (2006). Hantology – A Linguistic Resource for Chinese Language Processing and Studying. Paper Presented at the 5th International Conference on Language Resources and Evaluation, Genoa, Italy.

Chou, Y.-M., Hsieh, S.-K., and Huang, C.-R. (2007). HanziGrid: Toward a Knowledge Infrastructure for Chinese Characters-Based Cultures. In Ishida, T., Fussell, S. R. and Vossen, P. (eds.), *Intercultural Collaboration*, pages 133–45. Lecture Notes in Computer Science, State-of-the-Art Survey. Heidelberg: Springer-Verlag.

Chou, Y. and Huang, C. (2005). Construction of a Knowledge Structure Based Chinese Radicals. In *Proceedings of the Sixth Chinese Lexical Semantics Workshop*, Xiamen.

Church, K. W. and Hanks, P. (1989). Word Association Norms, Mutual Information and Lexicography. In *Proceedings of the 27th Annual Conference of the Association of Computational Linguistics*, pages 76–82.

Churchland, P. S., Ramachandran, V. S., and Sejnowski, T. J. (1994). A Critique of Pure Vision. In Koch, C. and Davis, J. (eds.), *Large Scale Neuronal Theories of the Brain*. Cambridge, MA: MIT Press.

Cimiano, P., Hotho, A., Stumme, G., and Tane, J. (2004). Conceptual Knowledge Processing with Formal Concept Analysis and Ontologies. In Eklund, P. (ed.), *Concept Lattices*, pages 189–207. Heidelberg: Springer Verlag.

Cimiano, P., Haase, P., Herold, M., Mantel, M., and Buitelaar, P. (2007). LexOnto: A Model for Ontology Lexicons for Ontology-based NLP. In *Proceedings of the OntoLex07 Workshop held in conjunction with ISWC'07*.

Cimiano, P., Hotho, A., and Staab, S. (2005). Learning Concept Hierarchies from Text Corpora using Formal Concept Analysis. *Journal of Artificial Intelligence Research*, 24, 305–39.

Cimiano, P., Staab, S., and Tane, J. (2003). Automatic Acquisition of Taxonomies from Text: FCA Meets NLP. In *Proceedings of the International Workshop on Adaptive Text Extraction and Mining*.

Cimiano, P. and Wenderoth, J. (2007). Automatic Acquisition of Ranked Qualia Structures from the Web. In *Proceedings of the 45th Annual Meeting of the Association of Computational Linguistics*, pages 888–95, Prague, Czech Republic.

Clark, A. (1993). *Associative Engines: Connectionism, Concepts, and Representational Change*. Cambridge, MA: MIT Press.

Clark, P., Thompson, J., Holmback, H., and Duncan, L. (2000). Exploiting a Thesaurus-Based Semantic Net for Knowledge-Based Search. In *Proceedings of 12th Conference on Innovative Applications of AI AAAI/IAAI'00*, pages 988–95.

Clark, P., Thompson, J., and Porter, B. (2000). Knowledge Patterns. In Cohn, A. G., Giunchiglia, F., and Selman, B. (eds.), *KR2000: Principles of Knowledge Representation and Reasoning*, pages 591–600, San Francisco: Morgan Kaufmann.

Cole, R., Mariani, J., Uszkoreit, H., Zaenen, A., and Zue, V. (eds.) (1997). *Survey of the State of the Art in Human Language Technology*. Cambridge: Cambridge University Press.

Collins, A. M. and Quillian, R. (1969). Retrieval Time from Semantic Memory. *Journal of Verbal Learning and Verbal Behavior*, 8, 240–7.

Condoravdi, C., Crouch, D., de Paiva, V., Stolle, R., and Bobrow, D. (2003). Entailment, Intensionality and Text Understanding. In *HLT-03 Workshop on Text Meaning*, Edmonton.

Cooper, M. C. (2005). A Mathematical Model of Historical Semantics and the Grouping of Word Meanings into Concepts. *Computational Linguistics*, 31(2), 227–48.

Copestake, A. (1992). The ACQUILEX LKB: Representation Issues in Semi-automatic Acquisition of Large Lexicons. In *Proceedings of the 3rd Conference on Applied Natural Language Processing (ANLP-92)*, pages 88–96.

Copestake, A. and Briscoe, E. J. (1995). Semi-productive Polysemy and Sense Extension. *Journal of Semantics*, 12, 15–67.

Croft, W. (2001). *Radical Construction Grammar: Syntactic Theory in Typological Perspective*. Oxford: Oxford University Press.

Croft, W. and Cruse, D. A. (2004). *Cognitive Linguistics*. Cambridge: Cambridge University Press.

Cruse, A. (1986). *Lexical Semantics*. Cambridge: Cambridge University Press.

Cucchiarelli, A. and Velardi, P. (1998). Finding a Domain-Appropriate Sense Inventory for Semantically Tagging a Corpus. *Natural Language Engineering*, (4), 325–44.

Curran, J. and Moens, M. (2002). Improvements in Automatic Thesaurus Extraction. In *Proceedings of the Workshop on Unsupervised Lexical Acquisition*, pages 59–67.

Dagan, I., Glickman, O., and Magnini, B. (2006). The PASCAL Recognising Textual Entailment Challenge. In Quiñonero, C. *et al.* (eds.), *MLCW 2005*, number 3944 in *Lecture Notes in Artificial Intelligence*, pages 177–90. Heidelberg: Springer-Verlag.

Damasio, A. R. (1994). *Descartes' Error: Emotion, Reason, and the Human Brain*. New York: A Grosset/Putnam Book.

Daudé, J., Padró, L., and Rigau, G. (2000). Mapping Wordnets Using Structural Information. In *Proceedings of the 38th Annual Meeting of the Association for Computational Linguistics(ACL00)*, Hong Kong.

Davidson, D. (1967a). The Logical Form of Action Sentences. In Rescher, N. (ed.), *The Logic of Decision and Action*. Pittsburgh: University of Pittsburgh Press.

Davidson, D. (1967b). The Logical Form of Action Sentences. In *The Logic of Decision and Action* (2nd edn). Pittsburgh: University of Pittsburgh Press.

De Giacomo, G., Lenzerini, M., and Rosati, R. (2008). Towards Higher-Order DL-Lite. In *Proceedings of the 21st International Workshop on Description Logics (DL2008)*, Dresden, Germany.

De Luca, E., Eul, M., and Nürnberger, A. (2007). Multilingual Query-Reformulation using an RDF-OWL EuroWordNet Representation. In *Improving Web Retrieval for Non-English Queries Workshop (iNEWSOT)* in conjunction with the 30th Annual International ACM SIGIR Conference 2007, Amsterdam.

Desmontils, E. and Jacquin, C. (2001). Indexing a Web Site with a Terminology Oriented Ontology. In *Proceedings of SWWS International Semantic Web Working Symposium*, Stanford University, USA.

Ding, L., Finin, T., Joshi, A., Pan, R., Cost, R. S., Peng, Y., Reddivari, P., Doshi, V. C., and Sachs, J. (2004). Swoogle: A Search and Metadata Engine for the Semantic Web. In *Proceedings of the 13th ACM Conference on Information and Knowledge Management*.

Doan, A., Domingos, P., and Halevy, A. (2003). Learning to match the Schemas of Data Sources: A Multistrategy approach. *Machine Learning*, 50(3), 279–301.

Doan, A. and Halevy, A. (2005). Semantic Integration Research in the Database Community: A Brief Survey. *AI Magazine*, 26(1), Special Issue on Semantic Integration, 83–95.

Doan, A., Madhavan, J., Domingos, P., and Halevy, A. (2002). Learning to Map between Ontologies on the Semantic Web. In *WWW '02: Proceedings of the 11th International Conference on World Wide Web*, pages 662–73, New York: ACM.

Dolbey, A., Ellsworth, M., and Scheffczyk, J. (2006). BioFrameNet: A Domain-specific FrameNet Extension with Links to Biomedical Ontologies. In *Proceedings of KR-MED 06: Biomedical Ontology in Action*.

Dölling, J. (1993). Commonsense Ontology and Semantics of Natural Language. *Zeitschrift für Sprachtypologie und Universalienforschung*, 46(2), 133–41.

Dong, Z. and Dong, Q. (1999). *HowNet*. Technical report, KEENAGE.com. (available online at www.keenage.com).

Dorr, B. L. and Habash, N. (2001). Lexical Conceptual Structure Lexicons. In Calzolari, N., Grishman, R., Palmer, M., Atkins, S., Bel, N., and Bertagna, F. (eds.), *Survey of Major Approaches towards Bilingual/Multilingual Lexicons*, volume D2.1–D3.1. Pisa: ISLE CLWG Deliverable.

Dowty, D. (1990). Thematic Proto-Roles and Argument Selection. *Language*, 67(3), 547–619.

Dowty, D. R. (1977). Toward a Semantic Analysis of Verb Aspect and the English imperfective progressive. *Linguistics and Philosophy*, 1(1), 45–77.

Eco, U. (1975). *Trattato di semiotica generale*. Milan: Bompiani.

Edelman, G. M. (1989). *The Remembered Present: A Biological Theory of Consciousness*. New York: Basic Books.

Elkateb, S., Black, W., Rodríguez, H., Alkhalifa, M., Vossen, P., Pease, A., and Fellbaum, C. (2006). Building a WordNet for Arabic. In *Proceedings of The Fifth International Conference on Language Resources and Evaluation*.

Erdmann, M. and Studer, R. (1999). Ontologies as Conceptual Models for XML Documents. In *Proceedings of the Twelfth Workshop on Knowledge Acquisition, Modeling and Management (KAW '99)*, Voyager Inn, Banff, Alberta, Canada.

Erk, K. and Padó, S. (2005). Analysing Models for Semantic Role Assignment Using Confusability. In *Proceedings of HLT/EMNLP-05*.

Erk, K. and Padó, S. (2006a). Shalmaneser – a Toolchain for Shallow Semantic Parsing. In *Proceedings of LREC-06*.

Erk, K. and Padó, S. (2006b). Shalmaneser – a Flexible Toolbox for Semantic Role Assignment. In *Proceedings of the LREC 2006*, Genoa, Italy.

Euzenat, J. and Shvaiko, P. (2007). *Ontology Matching*. Berlin: Springer-Verlag.

Evens, M. (ed.) (1988). *Relational Models of the Lexicon*. Cambridge: Cambridge University Press.

Farrar, S. and Langendoen, T. (2003). A Linguistic Ontology for Semantic Web. *GLOT International*, 7(3), 200–3.

Farreres, J. (2005). Automatic Construction of Wide-Coverage Domain-Independent Lexico-Conceptual Ontologies. PhD thesis, Universitat Politècnica de Catalunya, Spain.

Farwell, D., Helmreich, S., Reed, F., Dorr, B. L., Habash, N., Hovy, E. H., Levin, L., Miller, K., Mitamura, T., Rambow, O., and Siddharthan, A. (2004). Interlingual Annotation of Multilingual Text Corpora. In Meyers, A. (ed.), *HLT-NAACL 2004 Workshop: Frontiers in Corpus Annotation*, Boston, MA: ACL.

Fauconnier, G. (1994). *Mental Spaces*. New York: Cambridge University Press.

Feldman, J. (2006). *From Molecule to Metaphor: A Neural Theory of Language*. Cambridge, MA: MIT Press.

Fellbaum, C. (1998). *WordNet: An Electronic Lexical Database and Some of its Applications*. Cambridge, MA: MIT Press.

Fikes, R., Jenkins, J., and Frank, G. (2003). JTP: A System Architecture and Component Library for Hybrid Reasoning. In *Seventh World Multiconference on Systemics, Cybernetics, and Informatics*, Orlando, Florida.

Fillmore, C. (1976). Frame Semantics and the Nature of Language. In *Annals of the New York Academy of Sciences: Conference on the Origin and Development of Language and Speech*.

Fillmore, C. (1982). Frame Semantics. In Linguistic Society of Korea (ed.), *Linguistics in the Morning Calm*, pages 111–37. Seoul: Hanshin.

Fillmore, C., Johnson, C., and Petruck, M. (2003). Background to Framenet. *International Journal of Lexicography*, 16, 235–50.

Fillmore, C., Kay, P., and O'Connor, C. (1988). Regularity and Idiomaticity in Grammatical Constructions: The Case of Let Alone. *Language*, 64, 501–38.

Fillmore, C. J. (1968). The Case for Case. In Bach, E. and Harms, R.T. (eds.), *Universals in Linguistic Theory*, pages 1–88. New York: Holt, Rinehart, and Winston.

Fleischman, M., Hovy, E. H., and Echihabi, A. (2003). Offline Strategies for Online Question Answering: Answering Questions before they Are Asked. In Hinrichs, E. and Roth, D. (eds.), *Proceedings of the 41st Annual Meeting of the Association for Computational Linguistics (ACL-2003)*, pages 1–7, Sapporo, Japan.

Fleischman, M., Kwon, N., and Hovy, E. H. (2003). Maximum Entropy Models for FrameNet Classification. In Collins, M. and Steedman, M. (eds.), *Proceedings of the 2003 Conference on Empirical Methods in Natural Language Processing*, pages 49–56.

Foerster, H. v. (1974). Notes pour une épistémologie des objets vivants. In Morin, E. and Piattelli-Palmarini, M. (eds.), *L'unité de l'homme: invariants biologiques et universaux culturels*. Paris: Seuil.

Francopoulo, G., Bel, N., George, M., Calzolari, N., Monachini, M., Pet, M., and Soria, C. (2006). Lexical Markup Framework for NLP Multilingual Resources. In *Proceedings of COLING-ACL Workshop on Multilingual Lexical Resources and Interoperability*.

Francopoulo, G., George, M., Calzolari, N., Monachini, M., Bel, N., Pet, M., and Soria, C. (2006). Lexical Markup Framework (LMF). In *Proceedings of the International Conference on Language Resources and Evaluation (LREC)*, Genoa, Italy. ACL.

Frantzi, K. and Ananiadou, S. (1999). The C-Value / NC-Value Domain Independent Method for Multi-word Term Extraction. *Journal of Natural Language Processing*, 6(3), 145–79.

Frege, G. (1884). *Die Grundlagen der Arithmetik/The Foundations of Arithmetic*. Evanston, IL: Northwestern University Press. Translated by J. L. Austin.

Gallese, V. and Lakoff, G. (2005). The Brain's Concepts: The Role of the Sensorymotor System in Conceptual Knowledge. *Cognitive Neuropsychology*, 22, 455–79.

Gallese, V. and Metzinger, T. (2003). Motor Ontology: The Representational Reality of Goals, Actions and Selves. *Philosophical Psychology*, 16, 365–88.

Galton, A. (1995). Time and Change for AI. In *Handbook of Logic in Artificial Intelligence and Logic Programming*, Vol. 4, pages 175–240. Oxford: Clarendon Press.

Gangemi, A. (2005). Ontology Design Patterns for Semantic Web Content. In M. Musen *et al.* (eds.), *Proceedings of the Fourth International Semantic Web Conference, Galway, Ireland*. Berlin: Springer.

Gangemi, A. (2008). Norms and Plans as Unification Criteria for Social Collectives. *Journal of Autonomous Agents and Multi-Agent Systems*, 17(1), 70–112.

Gangemi, A., Catenacci, C., Ciaramita, M., and Lehman, J. (2006). Modelling Ontology Evaluation and Validation. In *Proceedings of the Third European Semantic Web Conference*. Heidelberg: Springer.

Gangemi, A., Guarino, N., Masolo, C., and Oltramari, A. (2001). Understanding Top-Level Ontological Distinctions. In *Proceedings of IJCAI-01 Workshop on Ontologies and Information Sharing*, pages 26–33. Seattle: AAAI Press.

Gangemi, A., Guarino, N., Masolo, C., and Oltramari, A. (2003). Sweetening WordNet with DOLCE. *AI Magazine*, 3(24), 13–24.

Gangemi, A., Guarino, N., and Oltramari, A. (2001). Conceptual Analysis of Lexical Taxonomies: The Case of WordNet Top-Level. In Welty, C. and Smith, B. (eds.), *2nd International Conference on Formal Ontology in Information Systems*, pages 285–96. Seattle: AAAI Press.

Gangemi, A., Navigli, R., and Velardi, P. (2003a). The OntoWordNet Project: Extension and Axiomatization of Conceptual Relations in WordNet. In *Proceedings of ODBASE03*.

Gangemi, A., Navigli, R., and Velardi, P. (2003b). The OntoWordNet Project: Extension and Axiomatization of Conceptual Relations in WordNet. In *CoopIS/DOA/ODBASE*.

Gangemi, A., Pisanelli, D., and Steve, G. (1999). Overview of the ONIONS Project: Applying Ontologies to the Integration of Medical Terminologies. *Data and Knowledge Engineering*, 31(2), 183–220.

Ganter, B. and Wille, R. (1997). *Formal Concept Analysis: Mathematical Foundations*. New York: Springer-Verlag.

Gärdenfors, P. (2000). *Conceptual Spaces: The Geometry of Thought*. Cambridge, MA: MIT Press.

Genesereth, M. (1991). Knowledge Interchange Format. In Allen, J., Fikes, R., and Sandewall, E. (eds.), *Proceedings of the Second International Conference on the Principles of Knowledge Representation and Reasoning*, pages 238–49. San Mateo, CA: Morgan Kaufman Publishers.

Gero, J. and Smith, G. (2007). Context, Situations and Design Agents. *Lecture Notes in Computer Science* 4635, 220–33.

Gibson, J. J. (1979). *The Ecological Approach to Visual Perception*. Hillsdale, NJ: Laurence Erlbaum.

Gildea, D. and Jurafsky, D. (2002). Automatic Labeling of Semantic Roles. *Computational Linguistics*, 28(3), 245–88.

Girju, R., Moldovan, D., Tatu, M., and Antohe, D. (2005). On the Semantics of Noun Compounds. *Computer Speech and Language*, 19, 479–96.

Gómez-Pérez, A., Fernández-López, M., and Corcho, O. (2004). *Ontological Engineering*. London: Springer.

Gonzalo, J., Verdejio, F., Chugur, L. and Cigarran, J. (1998). Indexing with WordNet Synsets Can Improve Text Retrieval. In *Proceeding of the Workshop 'Usage of WordNet in Natural Language Processing Systems'*, Montreal, Quebec, Canada.

Goodman, N. (1951). *The Structure of Appearance*. Cambridge, MA: Harvard University Press.

Grimshaw, J. (1990). *Argument Structure*. Cambridge, MA: MIT Press.

Gruber, T. (2007). Ontology of Folksonomy: A Mash-up of Apples and Oranges. *International Journal on Semantic Web and Information Systems*, 3(2), 1–11.

Gruber, T. R. (1995). Toward Principles for the Design of Ontologies Used for Knowledge Sharing. *International Journal of Human and Computer Studies*, 43(5–6), 625–40.

Guarino, N. (1998a). Formal Ontology in Information Systems. In Press, I. (ed.), *Proceedings of FOIS'98*, pages 3–15, Amsterdam: IOS Press.

Guarino, N. (1998b). Some Ontological Principles for Designing Upper Level Lexical Resources. In Rubio, A., Gallardo, N., Castro, R., and Tejada, A. (eds.), *Proceedings of First International Conference on Language Resources and Evaluation*, pages 527–34. Granada: ELRA.

Guarino, N., Masolo, C., and Vetere, G. (1999). OntoSeek: Content-Based Access to the Web. *IEEE Intelligent Systems and their Application*, 14(3), 70–80.

Guarino, N. and Welty, C. (2000a). A Formal Ontology of Properties. In Dieng, R. and Corby, O. (eds.), *12th International Conference on Knowledge Engineering and Knowledge Management: Methods, Models and Tools*, pages 97–112. Berlin: Springer Verlag.

Guarino, N. and Welty, C. (2000b). Ontological Analysis of Taxonomic Relationships. In Laender, A. and Storey, V. (eds.), *Proceedings of ER-2000: The International Conference on Conceptual Modeling*, pages 273–90. Salt Lake City: Springer-Verlag LNCS.

Guarino, N. and Welty, C. (2002a). Evaluating Ontological Decisions with OntoClean. *Communications of the ACM*, 45(2), 61–5.

Guarino, N. and Welty, C. (2002b). Identity and Subsumption. In Green, R., Bean, C., and Myaeng, S. (eds.), *The Semantics of Relationships: An Interdisciplinary Perspective*, pages 111–26. Amsterdam: Kluwer.

Guarino, N. and Welty, C. (2004). An Overview of OntoClean. In Staab, S. and Studer, R. (eds.), *Handbook of Ontologies*, pages 151–9. Berlin: Springer Verlag.

Gumperz, J. J. and Levinson, S. C. (1996). *Rethinking Linguistic Relativity*. Studies in the Social and Cultural Foundations of Language. Cambridge: Cambridge University Press.

Haav, H.-M. (2003). An Application of Inductive Concept Analysis to Construction of Domain-Specific Ontologies. In Thalheim, B. and Fiedler, G. (eds.), *Emerging Database Research in East Europe, Proceedings of the Pre-conference Workshop of VLDB 2003*, number 14 in Computer Science Reports, pages 63–7. Cottbus: Brandenburg University of Technology.

Harabagiu, S. M., Miller, G. A., and Moldovan, D. I. (1999). WordNet 2 – A Morphologically and Semantically Enhanced Resource. In *SIGLEX 1999*.

Harabagiu, S. M. and Moldovan, D. I. (1998). Knowledge Processing on an Extended WordNet. In Fellbaum, C. (ed.), *WordNet, An Electronic Lexical Database*, pages 379–406. Cambridge, MA: The MIT Press.

Harris, Z. S. (1968). *Mathematical Structures of Language*. New York: Wiley.

Hawley, K. (2001). *How Things Persist*. Oxford: Clarendon Press.

Hearst, M. (1992). Automatic Acquisition of Hyponyms from Large Text Corpora. In *Proceedings of the 14th International Conference on Computational Linguistics*, pages 539–45.

Hillel, Y. B. (1970). *Argumentation in Natural Language Aspects of Language*. Jerusalem: Magnes Press.

Hindle, D. (1990). Noun Classification from Predicate-Argument Structures. In *Proceedings of ACL-90*, pages 268–75.

Hirst, G. (1995). Near-Synonymy and the Structure of Lexical Knowledge. In *AAAI Symposium on Representation and Acquisition of Lexical Knowledge*.

Hirst, G. (2004). Ontology and the Lexicon. In Staab, S. and Studer, R. (eds.), *Handbook on Ontologies*, Series on Handbooks in Information Systems pages 209–30. Karlsrane: Springer.

Hirst, G. and St-Onge, D. (1998). Lexical Chains Representations of Context for the Detection and Correction of Malapropisms. In C. Fellbaum (ed.), *WordNet: An Electronic Lexical Database*. Cambridge, MA: The MIT Press.

Hobbs, J., Appelt, D., Bear, J., Israel, D., Kameyama, M., Stickel, M., and Ty-son, M. (1997). FASTUS: A Cascaded Finite-State Transducer for Extracting Information from Natural-Language Text. In Roche, E. and Schabes, Y. (eds.), *Finite-State Language Processing*, pages 383–406. Cambridge, MA: MIT Press.

Hobbs, J., Stickel, M., Appelt, D., and Martin, P. (1990). *Interpretation as Abduction*. Technical report, Artificial Intelligence Centre, SRI International.

Hobbs, J. R., Croft, W., Davies, T. R., Edwards, D., and Laws, K. I. (1987). Common-sense Metaphysics and Lexical Semantics. *Computational Linguistics*, 13(3–4), 241–50.

Horrocks, I. (1998). The FaCT System. In de Swart, H. (ed.), *Automated Reasoning with Analytic Tableaux and Related Methods: International Conference Tableaux'98*, volume 1397 of *Lecture Notes in Artificial Intelligence*, pages 307–12. Berlin: Springer-Verlag.

Hovy, E. (1998). Combining and Standardizing Large-Scale, Practical Ontologies for Machine Translation and Other Uses. In *Proceedings of the First International Conference on Language Resources and Evaluation*, Granada, Spain.

Hovy, E., Marcus, M., Palmer, M., Pradhan, S., Ramshaw, L., and Weischedel, R. (2006). OntoNotes: The 90% Solution. In *Proceedings of the Human Language Technology Conference at the Annual Meeting of the North American Association for Computational Linguistics (HLT-NAACL 2006)*, New York.

Hovy, E. H. (2005). Methodologies for the Reliable Construction of Ontological Knowledge. In Dau, F., Mugnier, M.-L., and Stumme, G. (eds.), *Conceptual Structures: Common Semantics for Sharing Knowledge. Proceedings of the 13th International Conference on Conceptual Structures (ICCS'2005)*, volume 3596 of *Lecture Notes in Artificial Intelligence*, pages 91–106, Kassel: Springer.

Hovy, E. H., Marcus, M., and Weischedel, R. (2003). OntoBank. Presentation at DARPA PI Meeting.

Hovy, E. H. and Nirenburg, S. (1992). Approximating an Interlingua in a Principled Way. In *Proceedings of the DARPA Speech and Natural Language Workshop*.

Hovy, E. H., Philpot, A. G., Ambite, J. L., Arens, Y., Klavans, J. L., Bourne, W., and Saroz, D. (2001). Data Acquisition and Integration in the DGRC's Energy Data Collection Project. In Hovy, E. and Arens, Y. (eds.), *Proceedings of the NSF's 2001 National Conference on Digital Government Research*, Los Angeles: Digital Government Research Center.

Hovy, E. H., Philpot, A. G., Klavans, J. L., Germann, U., Davis, P. T., and Popper, S. (2003). Extending Metadata Definitions by Automatically Extracting and Organizing Glossary Definitions. In Agouris, P. (ed.), *Proceedings of the NSF's 2003 National Conference on Digital Government Research*, Boston, MA: Digital Government Research Center.

Hsieh, C.-C. and Lin, S. (1997). A Survey of Full-Text Data Bases and Related Techniques for Chinese Ancient Documents in Academia Sinica. *International Journal of Computational Linguistics and Chinese Language Processing*, 2(1), 105–30. (in Chinese).

Huang, C., Chang, R., and Lee, S. (2004). Sinica BOW (Bilingual Ontological Wordnet): Integration of Bilingual WordNet and SUMO. In *Proceedings of the 4th International Conference on Language Resources and Evaluation*, Lisbon Portugal.

Huang, C.-R., Ahrens, K., and Jiann Chen, K. (1998). A Data-Driven Approach to the Mental Lexicon: Two Studies on Chinese Corpus Linguistics. *Bulletin of the Institute of History and Philology*, 69, 151–79.

Huang, C.-R., Chen, S.-Y., Hsieh, S.-K., Chou, Y.-M., and Kuo, T.-Y. (2008). Linguistically Conventionalized Ontology of Four Artifact Domains: A Study Based on Chinese Radicals. Presented at the Workshop on Linguistic Studies of Ontology. In *Proceedings of the 18th International Congress of Linguists*, Seoul.

Huang, C.-R., Li, X.-B., and Hong, J.-F. (2004). Domain Lexico-Taxonomy: An Approach towards Multi-Domain Language Processing. In *Proceedings of the Asian Symposium on Natural Language Processing to Overcome Language Barriers*, pages 25–6.

Huang, C.-R., Lin, W.-Y., Hong, J.-F., and Su, I.-L. (2006). The Nature of Cross-lingual Lexical Semantic Relations: A Preliminary Study Based on English–Chinese Translation Equivalents. In *Proceedings of the Third International WordNet Conference*.

Huang, C.-R., Su, I.-L., Hong, J.-F., and Bin Li, X. (2005). Cross-lingual Conversion of Lexical Semantic Relations: Building Parallel Wordnets. In *Fifth Asian Language Resources Workshop*.

Huang, C.-R., Su, I.-L., Hsiao, P.-Y., and Ke, X.-L. (2007). Paranyms, Co-hyponyms and Antonyms: Representing Semantic Fields with Lexical Semantic Relations. In *Proceedings of Chinese Lexical Semantics Workshop*. Hong Kong Polytechnic University.

Huang, C.-R., Tseng, E. I., and Tsai, D. B. (2002). Translating Lexical Semantic Relations: The First Step Towards Multilingual Wordnets. In *Proceedings of the COLING2002 Workshop: SemaNet: Building and Using Semantic Networks*.

Huang, C.-R., Tseng, E. I., Tsai, D. B., and Murphy, B. (2003). Cross-lingual Portability of Semantic Relations: Bootstrapping Chinese WordNet with English WordNet Relations. *Language and Linguistics*, 4(3), 509–32.

Imsombut, A. and Kawtrakul, A. (2008). Automatic Building of an Ontology on the Basis of Text Corpora in Thai. *Language Resources and Evaluation*, 42(2), 137–49. Special issue on Asian Language technology.

Jackendoff, R. (1983). *Semantics and Cognition*. Cambridge, MA: MIT Press.

Jacquemin, C. (2001). *Spotting and Discovering Terms through Natural Language Processing*. Cambridge MA: MIT Press.

Jakobson, R. (1990). Closing Statements: Linguistics and Poetics. In Sebeok, T. A. (ed.), *Style In Language*, pages 350–77. Cambridge, MA: MIT Press.

Jannink, J. (1999). Thesaurus Entry Extraction from an On-line Dictionary. In *Proceedings of Fusion '99*, Sunnyvale, CA.

Java, A., Finin, T., and Nirenburg, S. (2006). Text Understanding Agents and the Semantic Web. In *39th Hawaii International Conference on System Sciences*, Hawaii.

Jiang, G. and Ogasawara, K. (2003). Context-Based Ontology Building Support for Clinical Domains Using Formal Concept Analysis. *International Journal Med Inform*, 71(1), 71–81.

Johnson, M. (1987). *The Body in the Mind: The Bodily Basis of Meaning, Imagination, and Reason*. Chicago: University of Chicago Press.

Juang, D., Wang, J.-H., Lai, C.-Y., Hsieh, C.-C., Chien, L.-F., and Ho, J.-M. (2005). Resolving the Unencoded Character Problem for Chinese Digital Libraries. In *Proceedings of 2005 ACM/IEEE Joint Conference on Digital Libraries*, Denver, USA.

Karlgren, J. and Sahlgren, M. (2001). From Words to Understanding. In Uesaka, Y., Kanerva, P., and Asoh, H. (eds.), *Foundations of Real-World Intelligence*, pages 294–308. Stanford, CA, CSLI.

Karmiloff-Smith, A. (1994). Précis of 'Beyond Modularity: A Developmental Perspective on Cognitive Science'. *Behavioral and Brain Science*, 17(4) 693–745.

Katz, J. J. and Fodor, J. A. (1963). The Structure of Semantic Theory. *Language*, 39, 170–210.

Kawtrakul, A. (2004). *The Development of Resources on Network for NLP*. Technical report.

Kawtrakul, A., Imsombut, A., Thunyakijjanukit, A., Soergel, D., Liang, A., Sini, M., Johannsen, G., and Keizer, J. (2005). Automatic Term Relationship Cleaning and Refinement for AGROVOC. In *EFITA/WCCA2005, The Sixth Agricultural Ontology Service Workshop*, Vila Real, Portugal.

Kawtrakul, A., Suktarachan, M., and Imsombut, A. (2004). Automatic Thai Ontology Construction and Maintenance System. In *Workshop on OntoLex LREC conference*, Lisbon, Portugal.

Kietz, J.-U., Maedche, A., and Volz, R. (2000). A Method for Semi-Automatic Ontology Acquisition from a Corporate Intranet. In *Proceedings of Conference on Knowledge Engineering and Knowledge Management (EKAW 2000) Workshop Ontologies and Text*, France.

Kilgariff, A. (1997). I Do not Believe in Word Senses. *Computers and the Humanities*, 31, 91–113.

Kingsbury, P., Palmer, M., and Marcus, M. (2002). Adding Semantic Annotation to the Penn TreeBank. In *Proceedings of the Human Language Technology Conference (HLT'02)*, San Diego, CA.

Kipper, K., Dang, H. T., and Palmer, M. (2000). Class-Based Construction of a Verb Lexicon. In *Proceedings of the Seventh National Conference on Artificial Intelligence (AAAI-2000)*.

Kipper-Schuler, K. (2005). VerbNet: A Broad-Coverage,Comprehensive VerbLexicon. PhD thesis, University of Pennsylvania.

Kiryakov, A. and Simov, K. I. (2000). Mapping of EuroWordnet Top Ontology to Upper Cyc Ontology. In *Proceedings of Ontologies and Text workshop, EKAW 2000*.

Klavans, J. L., Davis, P. T., and Popper, S. (2002). Building Large Ontologies Using Web-Crawling and Glossary Analysis Techniques. In Hovy, E. (ed.), *Proceedings of the NSF's 2002 National Conference on Digital Government Research*. Los Angeles, CA: Digital Government Research Center.

Knight, K. and Luk, S. (1994a). Building a Large Knowledge Base for Machine Translation. In *Proceedings of the American Association of Artificial Intelligence Conference AAAI-94*, Seattle, WA.

Knight, K. and Luk, S. K. (1994b). Building a Large-Scale Knowledge Base for Machine Translation. In *Proceedings of the 12th National Conference on Artificial Intelligence*, volume 1, pages 773–8, Menlo Park, CA: AAAI Press.

Koeling, R. and McCarthy, D. (2007). Sussx: WSD Using Automatically Acquired Predominant Senses. In *Proceedings of the Fourth International Workshop on Semantic Evaluations*, SemEval-2007, pages 314–17.

Köhler, W. (1947). *Gestalt Psychology*. New York: Liveright.

Korhonen, A. (2002). Subcategorization Acquisition. PhD thesis, Cambridge University.

Kroeber, A. (1917). *California Kinship Systems*. Berkeley: University of California Press.

Kwon, N. and Hovy, E. H. (2006). Integrating Semantic Frames from Multiple Sources. In Dau, F., Mugnier, M.-L., and Stumme, G. (eds.), *Proceedings of the Seventh International Conference on Intelligent Text Processing and Computational Linguistics (CICLing)*, Lecture Notes in Computer Science, Mexico City: Springer Verlag.

Lakoff, G. (1987). *Women, Fire, and Dangerous Things: What Categories Reveal about the Mind*. Chicago: University of Chicago Press.

Lakoff, G. (1990). The Invariance Hypothesis: Is Abstract Reason Based on Image-Schemas? *Cognitive Linguistics*, 1(1), 39–74.

Lakoff, G. (1994). The Master Metaphor List. http://cogsci.berkeley.edu/, University of California, Berkeley.

Lakoff, G. and Johnson, M. (1980). *Metaphors we Live By*. Chicago: University of Chicago Press.

Landauer, T. and Dumais, S. (1997). A Solution to Plato's Problem: The Latent Semantic Analysis Theory of Acquisition, Induction and Representation of Knowledge. *Psychological Review*, 104, 211–40.

Langacker, R. (1990). *Concept, Image, and Symbol: The Cognitive Basis of Grammar*. Berlin and New York: Mouton de Gruyter.

Lascarides, A. and Copestake, A. (1995). The Pragmatics of Word Meaning. In *Proceedings of Semantics and Linguistic Theory V*.

Lauer, M. (1995). Corpus Statistics Meet the Noun Compound: Some Empirical Results. In *Proceeding of the 33rd Annual Meeting of the ACL*, Cambridge.

Lavelli, A., Magnini, B., and Sebastiani, F. (2002). Building Thematic Lexical Resources by Bootstrapping and Machine Learning. In *Proceedings of the Workshop 'Linguistic Knowledge Acquisition and Representation: Bootstrapping Annotated Language Data', Workshop at LREC-2002.*

Lee, L. (1999). Measures of Distributional Similarity. In *Proceedings of the 37th Annual Meeting of the ACL*, pages 25–32.

Lenat, D. (1995). CYC: A Large-Scale Investment in Knowledge Infrastructure. *Communications ACM*, 11(38), 33–8.

Lenat, D. (1998). *The Dimensions of Context-Space.* Technical report, Cycorp. (available online at www.cyc.com).

Lenci, A., Bel, N., Busa, F., Calzolari, N., Gola, E., Monachini, M., Ogonowski, A., Peters, I., Peters, W., Ruimy, N., Villegas, M., and Zampolli, A. (2000). SIMPLE: A General Framework for the Development of Multilingual Lexicons. *International Journal of Lexicography*, 13(4), 249–63.

Levin, B. (1993). *English Verb Classes and Alternations.* Chicago: The University of Chicago Press.

Levin, B. and Hovav, M. R. (2005). *Argument Realization.* Cambridge: Cambridge University Press.

Levinson, S. (1997). From Outer to Inner Space: Linguistic Categories and Non-linguistic Thinking. In Nayts J. and Pedesson E. (eds.), *Language and Conceptualization*, pages 13–45, Cambridge: Cambridge University Press.

Levinson, S. (2003). *Space in Language and Cognition: Explorations in Cognitive Diversity.* Cambridge: Cambridge University Press.

Li, S., Lu, Q., and Li, W. (2005). *Experiments of Ontology Construction with Formal Concept Analysis. OntoLex Workshop IJCNLP*, pages 67–75, Korea.

Light, M. and Greiff, W. (2002). Statistical Models for the Induction and Use of Selectional Preferences. *Cognitive Science*, 87, 1–13.

Light, P. and Butterworth, G. (eds.) (1992). *Context and Cognition: Ways of Learning and Knowing.* Hillsdale, NJ: Lawrence Erlbaum Associates.

Lin, D. (1998a). Automatic Retrieval and Clustering of Similar Words. In *Proceedings of COLING-ACL*, pages 768–74.

Lin, D. (1998b). An Information-Theoretic Definition of Similarity. In Kaufmann, M. (ed.), *Proceedings of 15th International Conference on Machine Learning*, pages 296–304. San Francisco: Morgan Kaufmann.

Link, G. (1983). The Logical Analysis of Plurals and Mass Terms: A Lattice-Theoretical Approach. In Bauerle, R., Schwartze, C., and von Stechow, A. (eds.), *Meaning, Use and Interpretation of Language*, pages 302–23. Berlin: de Gruyter.

Litowski, K. (2004). Senseval-3 Task: Automatic Labeling of Semantic Roles. In *Senseval-3: Third International Workshop on the Evaluation of Systems for the Semantic Analysis of Text*, pages 9–12.

Loux, M. J. (2002). *Metaphysics: A Contemporary Introduction* (2nd edn). Routledge Contemporary Introductions to Philosophy. London: Routledge.

Lowe, E. J. (1998). *The Possibility of Metaphysics.* Oxford: Clarendon Press.

Luengen, H., Kunze, C., Lemnitzer, L., and Storrer, A. (2008). Towards an Integrated OWL Model for Domain-Specific and General Language WordNets. In *Proceedings of the Fourth Global WordNet Conference*, Szeged, Hungary.

Luke, S., Spector, L., and Rager, D. (1996). Ontology-Based Knowledge Discovery on the World-Wide-Web. In *Proceedings of the AAAI1996 Workshop on Internet-Based Information Systems*, Portland, Oregon.

Maedche, A., Motik, B., Stojanovic, L., Studer, R., and Volz, R. (2003). Ontologies for Enterprise Knowledge Management. *IEEE Intelligent Systems*, 18(2), 26–33.

Maedche, A. and Staab, S. (2000). Discovering Conceptual Relations from Text. In *Proceedings of the 14th European Conference on Artificial Intelligence (ECAI 2000)*. Amsterdam: IOS Press.

Maedche, A. and Staab, S. (2001). Ontology Learning for the Semantic Web. *IEEE Intelligent Systems*, 16(2), 72–9.

Magnini, B. and Cavagliá, G. (2000). Integrating Subject Field Codes into WordNet. In Gavrilidou, M., Crayannis, G., Markantonatu, S., Piperidis, S., and Stainhaouer, G. (eds.), *Proceedings of Second International Conference on Language Resources and Evaluation (LREC-2000)*, Athens, Greece.

Magnini, B., Speranza, M., and Girardi, C. (2004). A Semantic-Based Approach to Interoperability of Classification Hierarchies: Evaluation of Linguistic Techniques. In *Proceedings of COLING-2004*, Geneva, Switzerland.

Magnini, B., Strapparava, C., Pezzulo, G., and Gliozzo, A. (2003). The Role of Domain Information in Word Sense Disambiguation. *Natural Language Engineering*, 8(04), 359–73.

Mahesh, K. (1996). *Ontology Development for Machine Translation: Ideology and Methodology*. CRL report MCCS-96-292, New Mexico State University, Las Cruces, NM, USA.

Mandler, J. M. (2004). *The Foundations of Mind: Origins of Conceptual Thought*. Oxford: Oxford University Press.

Manning, C. and Schütze, H. (1999). *Foundations of Statistical Natural Language Processing*. Cambridge MA: MIT Press.

Marconi, D. (1997). *Lexical Competence*. Cambridge MA: MIT Press.

Marek, O., Vaclav, S., and Jan, S. (2004). Ontology Design with Formal Concept Analysis. In Snasel, V. and Belohlavek, R. (eds.), *Proceedings of the CLA 2004 International Workshop on Concept Lattices and their Applications*, pages 111–19, Ostrava, Czech Republic.

Marinelli, R., Roventini, A., and Spadoni, G. (2006). Using Core Ontology for Domain Lexicon Structuring. In *Proceedings of LREC 2006*, Genova, Italy.

Markert, K. and Nissim, M. (2005). Comparing Knowledge Sources for Nominal Anaphora Resolution. *Computational Linguistics*, 31(3), 367–401.

Markert, K., Nissim, M., and Modjeska, N. (2003). Using the Web for Nominal Anaphora Resolution. In *Proceedings of the EACL Workshop on the Computational Treatment of Anaphora*.

Martin, W. (2001). A Frame-Based Approach to Polysemy. In Cuyckens, H. and Zawada, B. E. (eds.), *Polysemy in Cognitive Linguistics: Selected Papers from the International Cognitive Linguistics Conference, Amsterdam, 1997*. Amsterdam: John Benjamins Publishing Company.

Masolo, C., Borgo, S., Gangemi, A., Guarino, N., and Oltramari, A. (2003). *WonderWeb DeliverableD18, Ontology Library (final)*. Technical report, LOA-ISTC, CNR.

Masolo, C., Vieu, L., Bottazzi, E., Catenacci, C., Ferrario, R., Gangemi, A., and Guarino, N. (2004). Social Roles and their Descriptions. In Dubois, D., Welty, C. A., and Williams, M.-A. (eds.), *Proceedings of the 9th International Conference on*

Principles of Knowledge Representation and Reasoning, pages 267–77. Seattle: AAAI Press.

Maynard, D. and Ananiadou, S. (2000). Creating and Using Domain-Specific Ontologies for Terminological Applications. In *Proceedings of Second International Conference on Language Resources and Evaluation (LREC-2000)*, Athens, Greece.

McCarthy, D. (2001). Lexical Acquisition at the Syntax-Semantics Interface: Diathesis Alternations, Subcategorization Frames and Selectional Preferences. PhD thesis, University of Sussex.

McCarthy, D., Koeling, R., Weeds, J., and Carroll, J. (2004). Finding Pre-dominant Senses in Untagged Text. In *Proceedings of the 42nd Annual Meeting of the Association for Computational Linguistics*.

McCormick, S., Lieske, C., and Culum, A. (2004). OLIF v.2: A Flexible Language Data Standard. http://www.olif.net/.

McGuinness, D., Fikes, R., Rice, J., and Wilder, S. (2000). The Chimaera Ontology Environment. In *Proceedings of the 17th National Conference on Artificial Intelligence – AAAI*.

McShane, M. (2005). *A Theory of Ellipsis*. New York: Oxford University Press.

McShane, M., Beale, S., and Nirenburg, S. (2004). Some Meaning Procedures of Ontological Semantics. In *LREC 2004*, Lisbon, Portugal.

McShane, M., Nirenburg, S., and Beale, S. (2005). An NLP Lexicon as a Largely Language Independent Resource. *Machine Translation*, 19(2), 139–73.

McShane, M., Zabludowski, M., Nirenburg, S., and Beale, S. (2004). OntoSem and SIMPLE: Two Multi-lingual World Views. In *ACL 2004 Workshop on Text Meaning and Interpretation*, Barcelona, Spain.

Meilicke, C., Stuckenschmidt, H., and Tamilin, A. (2008). Supporting Manual Mapping Revision using Logical Reasoning. In *Proceedings of the Twenty-Third AAAI Conference on Artificial Intelligence (AAAI-08)*, Chicago, USA.

Mel'cuk, I. A. (1987). *Dependency Syntax: Theory and Practice*. Albany: State University Press of New York.

Meyer, J. and Dale, R. (2002). Using the WordNet Hierarchy for Associative Anaphora Resolution. In *Proceedings of SemaNet'02: Building and Using Semantic Networks*, Taipei, Taiwan.

Mihalcea, R. and Moldovan, D. (2000). Semantic Indexing Using WordNet Senses. In *Proceedings of the ACL Workshop on Recent Advances in Natural Language Processing and Information Retrieval*, Hong Kong.

Miles, A., Matthews, B., Wilson, M., and Brickley, D. (2005). SKOS Core: Simple Knowledge Organisation for the Web. In *Proceedings of the International Conference on Dublin Core and Metadata Applications (DC-2005)*, Madrid, 5–13.

Miller, G., Beckwith, R., Fellbaum, C., Gross, D., and Miller, K. J. (1990). Introduction to WordNet: An On-line Lexical Database. *International Journal of Lexicography*, 3, 235–312.

Miller, G. and Charles, W. (1991). Contextual Correlates of Semantic Similarity. *Language and Cognitive Processes*, 6, 1–28.

Miller, G., Leacock, C., Randee, T., and Bunker, R. (1993). A Semantic Concordance. In *Proceedings of the DARPA Workshop on Human Language Technology*, Plainsboro, New Jersey.

Miller, G. A. (ed.) (1990). *WordNet: An On-Line Lexical Database. Special Issue, International Journal of Lexicography*.

Miller, G. A. (1995). WordNet: A Lexical Database for English. *Communications of the ACM*, 38, 39–41.

Miller, G. A. (1998). Nouns in WordNet. In Fellbaum, C. (ed.), *WordNet: An Electronic Lexical Database*, pages 23–46, Cambridge, MA: MIT Press.

Miller, G. A. and Hristea, F. (2006). WordNet Nouns: Classes and Instances. *Computational Linguistics*, 32(1), 1–3.

Minsky, M. (1975). A Framework for Representing Knowledge. In Winston, P. (ed.), *The Psychology of Computer Vision*, pages 211–77, New York: McGraw-Hill.

Mitra, P., Noy, N., and Jaiswlas, A. (2005). OMEN: A Probabilistic Ontology Mapping Tool. In *Proceedings of 4th International Semantic Web Conference*.

Moldovan, D. and Rus, V. (2001). Explaining Answers with Extended WordNet. In *Proceedings of the 39th Annual Meeting of the Association for Computational Linguistics*.

Moortgat, M., Schuurman, I., and van der Wouden, T. (2000). CGN Syntactische Annotatie. Internal Project Report Corpus Gesproken Nederlands, see http://lands.let.kun.nl/cgn.

Morik, K. (1993). Balanced Cooperative Modeling. *Machine Learning*, 11(1), 217–35.

Moss, H. E., Ostrin, R., Tyler, L., and Marslen-Wilson, W. (1995). Accessing Different Types of Lexical Semantic Information: Evidence from Priming. *Journal of Experimental Psychology: Learning, Memory, and Cognition*, 21(4), 863–83.

Mur, J. and van der Plas, L. (2007). Anaphora Resolution for Off-line Answer Extraction using Instances. In *Proceedings from the First Bergen Workshop on Anaphora Resolution (WAR I)*.

Murphy, G. L. (2002). *The Big Book of Concepts*. Cambridge, MA: MIT Press.

Murphy, M. L. (2003). *Semantic Relations and the Lexicon*. Cambridge: Cambridge University Press.

Narayanan, S. (1999). Moving Right Along: A Computational Model of Metaphoric Reasoning about Events. In *Proceedings of the National Conference on Artificial Intelligence (AAAI'99)*, pages 121–28. Seattle: AAAI Press.

Narayanan, S., Baker, C., Fillmore, C., and Petruck, M. (2003). FrameNet Meets the Semantic Web: Lexical Semantics for the Web. In Fensel, D., Sycara, K., and Mylopoulos, J. (eds.), *The Semantic Web – ISWC 2003*, pages 771–87. Berlin: Springer-Verlag.

Narayanan, S. and McIlraith, S. (2003). Analysis and Simulation of Web Services. *Computer Networks*, 5(42), 675–93.

Nastase, V. and Szpakowicz, S. (2003). Exploring Noun-Modifier Semantic Relations. In *Fifth International Workshop on Computational Semantics (IWCS-5)*.

Navigli, R., Velardi, P., and Gangemi, A. (2003). Ontology Learning and its Application to Automated Terminology Translation. *IEEE Intelligent Systems*, 18, 22–31.

Nédellec, C. and Nazarenko, A. (2005). Ontology and Information Extraction: A Necessary Symbiosis. In Buitelaar, P., Cimiano, P., and Magnini, B. (eds.), *Ontology Learning from Texts*, pages 155–70. Amsterdam: IOS Press.

Niles, I. and Pease, A. (2001). Towards a Standard Upper Ontology. In Welty, C. and Smith, B. (eds.), *Proceedings of the 2nd International Conference on Formal Ontology in Information Systems (FOIS-2001)*, Ogunquit, Maine.

Niles, I. and Pease, A. (2003). Linking Lexicons and Ontologies: Mapping WordNet to the Suggested Upper Merged Ontology. In *Proceedings of the 2003 International Conference on Information and Knowledge Engineering (IKE 03)*, Las Vegas, Nevada.

Nirenburg, S., McShane, M., and Beale, S. (2004). The Rationale for Building Resources Expressly for NLP. In *LREC 2004*, Lisbon, Portugal.

Nirenburg, S., McShane, M., Zabludowski, M., Beale, S., and Pfeifer, C. (2005). *Ontological Semantic Text Processing in the Biomedical Domain*. Technical report, Institute for Language and Information Technologies, University of Maryland Baltimore County.

Nirenburg, S. and Raskin, V. (2001). Ontological Semantics, Formal Ontology and Ambiguity. In *Proceedings of FOIS 2001*.

Nirenburg, S. and Raskin, V. (2004). *Ontological Semantics*. Cambridge, MA: MIT Press.

Noy, N. and Musen, M. (2000). PROMPT: Algorithm and Tool for Automated Ontology Merging and Alignment. In *Proceedings of the National Conference on Artificial Intelligence – AAAI*.

Nozick, R. (2001). *Invariances*. Cambridge, MA: The Belknap Press at Harvard University Press.

Nunberg, G. (1979). The Non-uniqueness of Semantic Solutions: Polysemy. *Linguistics and Philosophy*, 3, 143–84.

Nunberg, G. and Zaenen, A. (1992). Systematic Polysemy in Lexicology and Lexicography. In *Proceedings of Euralex*.

Oberle, D., Ankolekar, A., Hitzler, P., Cimiano, P., Sintek, M., Kiesel, M., Mougouie, B., Vembu, S., Baumann, S., Romanelli, M., Buitelaar, P., Engel, R., Sonntag, D., Reithinger, N., Loos, B., Porzel, R., Zorn, H.-P., Micelli, V., Schmidt, C., Weiten, M., Burkhardt, F., and Zhou, J. (2007). DOLCE ergo SUMO: On Foundational and Domain Models in SmartWeb Integrated Ontology (SWInto). *Web Semantics: Sci. Services Agents World Wide Web*, doi:10.1016/j.websem.2007.06.002.

O'Hara, T., Mahesh, K., and Nirenburg, S. (1998). Lexical Acquisition with WordNet and the Mikrokosmos Ontology. In Harabagiu, S. (ed.), *Proceedings of the COLING/ACL Worskshop on Usage or WordNet in Natural Language Processing Systems*, pages 94–101. Montreal: ACL.

Padó, S. and Lapata, M. (2007). Dependency-Based Construction of Semantic Space Models. *Computational Linguistics*, 33(2), 161–99.

Pantel, P. (2005). Inducing Ontological Co-occurrence Vectors. In *Proceedings of the 43rd Annual Meeting of the Association for Computational Linguistics (ACL-2005)*, Ann Arbor, MI.

Pantel, P. and Pennacchiotti, M. (2006). Generic Patterns for Automatically Harvesting Semantic Relations. In *Proceedings of the Conference on Computational Linguistics / Association for Computational Linguistics*.

Pantel, P. and Ravichandran, D. (2004). Automatically Labeling Semantic Classes. In Susan Dumais, D. M. and Roukos, S. (eds.), *HLT-NAACL 2004: Main Proceedings*, pages 321–8, Boston, MA, USA.

Pantel, P., Ravichandran, D., and Hovy, E. H. (2004). Towards Terascale Knowledge Acquisition. In *Proceedings of the 20th International Conference on Computational Linguistics (COLING-2004)*, Geneva, Switzerland.

Parsons, T. (1990). *Events in the Semantics of English: A Study in Subatomic Semantics*. Cambridge, MA: MIT Press.

Paşca, M. (2004). Acquisition of Categorized Named Entities for Web Search. In *Proceedings of the Thirteenth ACM Conference on Information and Knowledge Management*, pages 137–45.

Pazienza, M. T. and Stellato, A. (2005). The Protégé Ontoling Plugin – Linguistic Enrichment of Ontologies. In *Semantic Web 4th International Semantic Web Conference (ISWC-2005)*.

Pazienza, M. and Stellato, A. (2006a). Linguistic Enrichment of Ontologies: A Methodological Framework. Second Workshop on Interfacing Ontologies and Lexical Resources for Semantic Web Technologies (OntoLex 2006), held jointly with LREC2006, Genoa, Italy.

Pazienza, M. and Stellato, A. (2006b). An Open and Scalable Framework for Enriching Ontologies with Natural Language Content. In Huang, C.-R., Oltramari, A., Buitelaar, P., Fellbaum, C., and Lenci, A. (eds.), *OntoLex (Ontologies and Lexical Resources) – LREC 2006 (Linguistic Resources and Evaluation)*, pages 20–7, Genoa: ELDA.

Pease, A. (2003). The Sigma Ontology Development Environment. In *Working Notes of the IJCAI-2003 Workshop on Ontology and Distributed Systems*, volume 71. CEUR Workshop Proceeding Series.

Pease, A. and Fellbaum, C. (2004). Language to Logic Translation with PhraseBank. In *Proceedings of the Second International WordNet Conference (GWC 2004)*. Masaryk University Brno, Czech Republic.

Pease, A. and Murray, W. (2003). An English to Logic Translator for Ontology-Based Knowledge Representation Languages. In *Proceedings of the IEEE International Conference on Natural Language Processing and Knowledge Engineering*. Beijing, China.

Peirce, C. S. (1958). On Signs and the Categories. In Hartshorne, C., Weiss, P., and Burks, A. (eds.), *Collected Papers of C. S. Peirce*, pages 327–41, Cambridge, MA: Harvard University Press.

Pelletier, F. J. (1979). Non-Singular References: Some Preliminaries. In Pelletier, F. J. (ed.), *Mass Terms: Some Philosophical Problems*, pages 1–14. Dordrecht: Reidel.

Pengphon, N., Kawtrakul, A., and Suktarachan, M. (2002). Word Formation Approach to Noun Phrase Analysis for Thai. In *Proceedings of Symposium on Natural Language Processing 2002*, pages 277–82., Thailand.

Peters, W., Montiel-Ponsoda, E., Aguado de Cea, G., and Gómez-Pérez, A. (2007). Localizing Ontologies in OWL. http://olp.dfki.de/OntoLex07/.

Petitot-Cocorda, J. (1995). Morphodynamics and Attractor Syntax: Constituency in Visual Perception and Cognitive Grammar. In Port, R. and van Gelder, T. (eds.), *Mind as Motion: Explorations in the Dynamics of Cognition*, pages 227–81. Cambridge, MA: MIT Press.

Philpot, A. G., Ambite, J. L., and Hovy, E. H. (2002). DGRC AskCal: Natural Language Question Answering for Energy Time Series. In *Proceedings of the NSF 2002 National Conference on Digital Government Research*, Los Angeles, CA: Digital Government Research Center.

Philpot, A. G., Hovy, E. H., and Fleischman, M. (2003). Semi-Automatic Construction of a General-Purpose Ontology. In *Proceedings of the International Lisp Conference (ILC-2003)*, New York.

Piaget, J. (1968). *Six Psychological Studies*. New York: Vintage.

Pianta, E., Bentivogli, L., and Girardi, C. (2002). Multiwordnet: Developing an Aligned Multilingual Database. In *Proceedings of the First International Conference on Global Wordnet*, Mysore, India.

Picca, D., Gangemi, A., and Gliozzo, A. (2008). LMM: An OWL Metamodel to Represent Heterogeneous Lexical Knowledge. In *Proceedings of the International Conference on Language Resources and Evaluation (LREC)*, Marrakech, Morocco: ACL.

Poesio, M., Ishikawa, T., Schulte im Walde, S., and Vieira, R. (2002). Acquiring Lexical Knowledge for Anaphora Resolution. In *Proceedings of the Third International Conference on Language Resources and Evaluation*.

Poesio, M., Vieira, R., and Teufel, S. (1997). Resolving Bridging Descriptions in Unrestricted Text. In *Proceedings of the ACL-97 Workshop on Operational Factors in Practical, Robust, Anaphora Resolution For Unrestricted Texts*, pages 1–6, Madrid, Spain.

Porzel, R., Micelli, V., Aras, H., , and Zorn, H.-P. (2006). Tying the Knot: Ground Entities, Descriptions and Information Objects for Construction-Based Information Extraction. In *Proceedings of OntoLex 2006*, Genoa, Italy.

Presutti, V. and Gangemi, A. (2008). Content Ontology Design Patterns as Practical Building Blocks for Web Ontologies. In *Proceedings of the 27th International Conference on Conceptual Modeling (ER 2008)*. Berlin: Springer.

Presutti, V., Gangemi, A., David, S., Aguado de Cea, G., Suarez-Figueroa, M., Montiel-Ponsoda, E., and Poveda, M. (2008). *Library of Design Patterns for Collaborative Development of Networked Ontologies*. Deliverable D2.5.1, NeOn project.

Priss, U. (1998). The Formalization of WordNet by Methods of Relational Concept Analysis. In Christiane, C. (ed.), *WordNet: An Electronic Lexical Database and Some of its Applications*, pages 179–96. Cambridge, MA: MIT press.

Priss, U. (2005). Linguistic Applications of Formal Concept Analysis. In Ganter, B., Stumme, G., and Wille, R. (eds.), *Formal Concept Analysis, Foundations and Applications*, number 3626 in *Lecture Notes in Artificial Intelligence*, pages 149–60. Berlin: Springer Verlag.

Pustejovsky, J. (1991). The Generative Lexicon. *Computational Linguistics*, 4, 409–41.

Pustejovsky, J. (1995). *The Generative Lexicon*. Cambridge, MA: MIT Press.

Pustejovsky, J. and Boguraev, B. (1993). Lexical Knowledge Representation and Natural Language Processing. *Artificial Intelligence*, 63, 193–223.

Pustejovsky, J., Castaño, J., Zhang, J., Cochran, B., and Kotecki, M. (2002). Robust Relational Parsing over Biomedical Literature: Extracting Inhibit Relations. In *Proceedings of the Pacific Symposium on Biocomputing*.

Pustejovsky, J., Rumshisky, A., and Castaño, J. (2002). Rendering Semantic Ontologies. In *Proceedings of the LREC 2002 Workshop on Ontologies and Lexical Knowledge Bases*.

Quan, T., Hui, S., and Cao, T. (2004). FOGA: A Fuzzy Ontology Generation Framework for Scholarly Semantic Web. In *Knowledge Discovery and Ontologies (KDO-2004), Workshop at ECML/PKDD 2004*.

Quine, W. (1951). Two Dogmas of Empiricism. *The Philosophical Review*, 60, 20–43.

Quine, W. O. (1960). *Word and Object*. Cambridge, MA: MIT Press.

Rapp, R. (2003). Word Sense Discovery Based on Sense Descriptor Similarity. In *Proceedings of the 9th Machine Translation Summit*, pages 315–22.

Reed, S. and Lenat, D. (2002). Mapping Ontologies into Cyc. In *AAAI 2002 Conference Workshop on Ontologies for the Semantic Web*, Edmonton, Canada.

Reeder, F., Dorr, B. L., Farwell, D., Habash, N., Helmreich, S., Hovy, E., Levin, L., Mitamura, T., Miller, K., Rambow, O., and Siddharthan, A. (2004). Interlingua Development and Testing through Semantic Annotation of Multilingual Text Corpora: Interlingual Annotation for MT Development. In Frederking, R. E. and Taylor, K. B. (eds.), *Proceedings of the 6th Conference of the Association for Machine Translation in the Americas (AMTA-2004)*, pages 87–95, Georgetown University, Washington DC, USA. Association for Machine Translation in the Americas. Berlin: Springer-Verlag.

Reinach, A. (1983). The Apriori Foundations of the Civil Law. *Aletheia*, 3, 1–142.

Resnik, P. (1995). Using Information Content to Evaluate Semantic Similarity. In *Proceedings of the 14th International Joint Conference on Artificial Intelligence*.

Resnik, P. (1996). Selectional Constraints: An Information-Theoretic Model and its Computational Realization. *Cognition*, 61, 127–59.

Rigau, G., Magnini, B., Agirre, E., Vossen, P., and Carrol, J. (2002). MEANING: A Roadmap to Knowledge Technologies. In *Proceedings of the Workshop 'A Roadmap for Computational Linguistics' at COLING-2002*, Taipei, Taiwan.

Rigau, G. and Rodriguez, H. (2005). Combining Resources and Methods for a Semi-automatic Construction of Large Scale Ontologies. In Lenci, A., Montemagni, S., and Pirrelli, V. (eds.), *Acquisition and Representation of Word Meaning: Theoretical and Computational Perspectives*, pages 366–76. Linguistica Computazionale – Fascicoli Monografici 22–3, Pisa: Istituto Editoriale e Poligrafici internazionale.

Roget, P. (1911). *Thesaurus of English Words and Phrases*. London: Bloomsbury.

Rohrer, T. (2005). Image Schemata in the Brain. In Hampe, B. (ed.), *From Perception to Meaning: Image Schemas in Cognitive Linguistics*, pages 165–96. Berlin: Mouton de Gruyter.

Rosch, E. (1973). Natural Categories. *Cognitive Psychology*, 4, 328–50.

Rosch, E. (1978). Principles of Categorizations. In Rosch, E. and Lloyd, B. (eds.), *Cognition and Categorization*, pages 15–35. Mahwah, NJ: Lawrence Erlbaum Associates.

Roventini, A., Alonge, A., Bertagna, F., Magnini, B., and Calzolari, N. (2000). Ital-WordNet: A Large Semantic Database for Italian. In *Proceedings of the Second International Conference on Language Resources and Evaluation (LREC-2000)*, Athens, Greece.

Rumelhart, D. (1980). Schemata: The Building Blocks of Cognition. In Spiro, R., Bruce, B., and Brewer, W. (eds.), *Theoretical Issues in Reading Comprehension*, pages 33–58. Mahwah, NJ: Lawrence Erlbaum.

Ruppenhofer, J., Ellsworth, M., Petruck, M., Johnson, C., and Scheffczyk, J. (2006a). *FrameNet II: Extended Theory and Practice*. Technical report, ICSI Berkeley, www.icsi.berkeley.edu/framenet/book/book.html.

Ruppenhofer, J., Ellsworth, M., Petruck, M. R. L., Johnson, C. R., and Scheffczyk, J. (2006b). FrameNet II: Extended Theory and Practice. http://framenet.icsi.berkeley.edu/book/book.html.

Ryle, G. (1971). Categories. In *Collected Papers: Collected Essays*, volume II. New York: Barnes and Noble.

Sagri, M., Tiscornia, D., and Bertsgna, F. (2004). Jur-WordNet. In *Proceedings of the Second Global Wordnet Conference*, Brno, Czech Republic.

Salton, G. and Buckley, C. (1988). Term-Weighting Approaches in Automatic Text Retrieval. *Information Processing and Management*, 24(5), 513–23.

Saussure, F. de (1906). *Cours de linguistique générale*. Lausanne: Payot.

Schalley, A. and Zaefferer, D. (2006). *Ontolinguistics: How Ontological Status Shapes the Linguistic Coding of Concepts*. Trends in Linguistics. Studies and Monographs. Berlin: Mouton de Gruyter.

Scheffczyk, J. and Ellsworth, M. (2006). Improving the Quality of FrameNet. In *Proceedings of the Workshop on Quality Assurance and Quality Measurement for Language and Speech Resources*, pages 8–13.

Scheffczyk, J., Pease, A., and Ellsworth, M. (2006). Linking FrameNet to the Suggested Upper Merged Ontology. In *Proceedings of the 2006 International Conference on Formal Ontology in Information Systems (FOIS 2006)*.

Searle, J. R. (1969). *Speech Acts: An Essay on the Philosophy of Language*. Cambridge: Cambridge University Press.

Searle, J. R. (1995). *The Construction of Social Reality*. New York: Free Press.

Serhiy, A. Y. (2000). System of Data Analysis 'Concept Explorer'. In *Proceedings of the 7th National Conference on Artificial Intelligence KII-2000*, pages 127–34 (In Russian).

Shcherba, L. V. (1995). Towards a General Theory of Lexicography. *International Journal of Lexicography*, 8(4), 314–50. Translated from Russian and Introduced by D. M. T. Cr. Farina, Re-edited in Lexicography, Critical Concepts, Vol. III (2003). R.R.K. Hartmann (ed.).

Simons, P. (1987). *Parts: A Study in Ontology*. Oxford: Oxford University Press.

Simons, P. (2000). How to Exist at a Time when you Have No Temporal Parts. *The Monist*, 83(3), 419–36.

Simov, K. I., Kiryakov, K., and Dimitrov, M. (2001). OntoMap – the Guide to the Upper-Level. In *Proceedings of SWWS International Semantic Web Working Symposium*, Stanford University, USA.

Singh, U. N. (ed.) (2002). *Proceedings of the First Global WordNet Conference*. Mysore: Central Institute for Indian Languages.

Smith, B. (1990). Towards a History of Speech Act Theory. In *Speech Acts, Meanings and Intentions: Critical Approaches to the Philosophy of John R. Searle*, pages 29–61. Berlin: de Gruyter.

Smitinand, T. (2001). *Thai Plant Names Dictionary*. Bangkok: The Forest Herbarium Royal, Forest Department.

Soergel, D., Lauser, B., Liang, A., Fisseha, F., Keizer, J., and Katz, S. (2004). Reengineering Thesauri for New Applications: The AGROVOC Example. *Journal of Digital Information*, 4(4). Article No. 257, 2004-03-17.

Sojka, P., Choi, K.-S., Fellbaum, C., and Vossen, P. (eds.) (2006). *Proceedings of the Third Global WordNet Conference*. Brno: Masaryk University.

Sojka, P., Pala, K., Smrz, P., Fellbaum, C., and P. Vossen, P. (eds.) (2004). *Proceedings of the Second International WordNet Conference*. Brno. Masaryk University.

Sowa, J. F. (2000). *Knowledge Representation, Logical, Philosophical, and Computational Foundations*. Pacific Grove, CA: Brooks/Cole Thomson Learning.

Strawson, P. F. (1959). *Individuals: An Essay in Descriptive Metaphysics*. London: Routledge.

Stumme, G. (2002). Formal Concept Analysis on its Way from Mathematics to Computer Science. In Priss, U., Corbett, D., and Angelova, G. (eds.), *Conceptual Structures: Integration and Interfaces, Proc. ICCS 2002*, number 2393 in *Lecture Notes in Artificial Intelligence*, pages 2–19. Heidelberg: Springer.

Sudprasert, S. and Kawtrakul, A. (2003). Thai Word Segmentation Based on Global and Local Unsupervised Learning. In *Proceedings of National Computer Science and Engineering Conference 2003 (NCSEC'03)*, Chonburi, Thailand.

Suktarachan, M., Thamvijit, D., Rajbhandari, S., Noikongka, D., Mahasarakram, P. P. N., Panita Yongyuth, A. K., and Sini, M. (2008). Workbench with Authoring Tools for Collaborative Multi-lingual Ontological Knowledge Construction and Maintenance. In *Proceedings of the Sixth International Conference on Language Resources and Evaluation, LREC 2008*, pages 2501–8, Marrakech, Morocco.

Taboada, M., Martinez, D., and Mira, J. (2005). Experiences in Reusing Knowledge Resources Using Protégé and PROMPT. *International Journal of Human-Computer Studies*, 62, 597–618.

Takenobu, T., Sornlertlamvanich, V., Charoenporn, T., Calzolari, N., Monachini, M., Soria, C., Huang, C.-R., YingJu, X., Hao, Y., Prévot, L., and Kiyoaki, S. (2006). Infrastructure for Standardization of Asian Language Resources. In *Proceedings of ACL-COLING*.

Talmy, L. (2003). *Toward a Cognitive Semantics*. Cambridge, MA: MIT Press.

Thomasson, A. L. (1999). *Fiction and Metaphysics*. Cambridge: Cambridge University Press.

Thomasson, A. L. (2004). Methods of Categorization. In Varzi, A. C. and Vieu, L. (eds.), *Proceedings of the Third International Conference Formal Ontology in Information Systems (FOIS)*. Amsterdam: IOS Press.

Tomasello, M. (2003). *Constructing a Language: A Usage-Based Theory of Language Acquisition*. Cambridge, MA: Harvard University Press.

Turcato, D., Popowich, F., Toole, J., Fass, D., Nicholson, D., and Tisher, G. (2000). Adapting a Synonym Database to Specific Domains. In *Proceedings of Workshop on Information Retrieval and Natural Language Processing*, Hong-Kong, held in conjunction with ACL2000.

Turner, M. (2007). Conceptual Integration. In Geeraerts, D. and Cuyckens, H. (eds.), *The Oxford Handbook of Cognitive Linguistics*. Oxford: Oxford University Press.

Turney, P. (2006). Similarity of Semantic Relations. *Computational Linguistics*, 32(3), 379–416.

van der Plas, L. and Bouma, G. (2005a). Automatic Acquisition of Lexico-semantic Knowledge for QA. *Proceedings of the Workshop on Ontologies and Lexical Resources* (Ontolex).

van der Plas, L. and Bouma, G. (2005b). Syntactic Contexts for finding Semantically Similar Words. *Proceedings of the Meeting of Computational Linguistics in the Netherlands* (CLIN).

van Noord, G. (2006). At Last Parsing Is Now Operational. In *Actes de la 13e conférence sur le traitement automatique des langues naturelles*.

Vanderwende, L. (1994). Algorithm for Automatic Interpretation of Noun Sequences. In *Proceedings of International Conference on Computational Linguistics (COLING-94)*.

Varzi, A. C. (2000). Foreword to the Special Issue on Temporal Parts. *The Monist*, 83(3).

Vertan, C., von Hahn, W., and Gavrila, M. (2005). MANAGELEX – A Tool for the Management of Complex Lexical Structures. In *GLDV Workshop 'Exchange of Lexical and Terminological Resources in Machine Translation (MT), Computer-Aided Translation (CAT) and Terminology Management Systems (TMS)'*.

Viezzer, M. and Nieuwenhuis, C. (2005). Learning Affordance Concepts: Some Seminal Ideas. Submitted to IJCAI05 Workshop on Modeling Natural Action Selection.

Vigliocco, G. and Vinson, D. (2007). Semantic Representation. In Gaskell, M. (ed.), *The Oxford Handbook of Psycholinguistics*, pages 195–215. Oxford: Oxford University Press.

Vigotsky, L. S. (1962). *Thought and Language: A Usage-Based Theory of Language Acquisition*. Cambridge, MA: MIT Press.

Volker, J., Vrandecic, D., and Sure, Y. (2005). Automatic Evaluation of Ontologies. In *Proceedings of ISWC 2005*.

Vossen, P. (1998). *EuroWordNet: A Multilingual Database with Lexical Semantic Networks*. Dordrecht: Kluwer Academic Publishers.

Vossen, P. (2001). Extending, Trimming and Fusing WordNet for Technical Documents. In *Proceedings of NAACL Workshop WordNet and Other Lexical Resources: Applications, Extensions and Customizations*, Pittsburgh, held in conjunction with NAACL2001.

Vossen, P., Agirre, E., Calzolari, N., Fellbaum, C., Hsieh, S., Huang, C., Isahara, H., Kanzaki, K., Marchetti, A., Monachini, M., Neri, F., Raffaelli, R., Rigau, G., Tescon, M., and van Gent, J. (2008). KYOTO: A System for Mining, Structuring, and Distributing Knowledge across Languages and Cultures. In *Proceedings of the Fourth International Global Word Net Conference*, Szeged, Hungary.

W3C (2004). OWL Web Ontology Language Family of Specifications. http://www.w3.org/2004/OWL.

Ward, G. (1996). *Moby Thesaurus*. Moby Project. Sheffield: The Institute for Language Speech and Hearing, University of Sheffield.

Weeds, J. (2003). Measures and Applications of Lexical Distributional Similarity. PhD thesis, University of Sussex.

Welty, C. (1999). Formal Ontology for Subject. *Journal of Knowledge and Data Engineering*, 31, 155–82.

Welty, C., Mahindru, R., and Chu-Carroll, J. (2003). Evaluating Ontological Analysis. In *Proceedings of the ISWC-03 Workshop on Semantic Integration*.

Wessel, M. and Möller, R. (2005). A High Performance Semantic Web Query Answering Engine. In *Proceedings of the International Workshop on Description Logics*.

West, M., Sullivan, J., and Teijgeler, H. (2008). Industrial Automation Systems and Integration of Life-Cycle Data for Process Plants Including Oil and Gas Production Facilities, ISO 15926.

Widdows, D. (2003). *Geometry and Meaning*. Stanford CA: CSLI.

Widdows, D. and Dorow, B. (2002). A Graph Model for Unsupervised Lexical Acquisition. In *Proceedings of the 19th International Conference on Computational Linguistics*, pages 1093–9, Taipei, Taiwan.

Wielinga, B., Schreiber, A. T., Wielemaker, S., and Sandberg, J. A. C. (2001). From Thesaurus to Ontology. In *Proceedings of International Conference on Knowledge Capture*, Victoria, Canada.

Wierzbicka, A. (1990). Prototypes Save: On the Uses and Abuses of the Notion of 'Prototype' in Linguistics and Related Fields. In Tsohatzidis, S. L. (ed.), *Meaning and Protoypes: Studies in Linguistic Categorization*, pages 347–67, London: Routledge.

Wierzbicka, A. (1996). *Semantics: Primes and Universals*. Oxford: Oxford University Press.

Wildgen, W. (2004). *The Evolution of Human Language*. Amsterdam: Benjamins.

Woods, W. (1997). *Conceptual Indexing: A Better Way to Organize Knowledge*. Technical report, SUN Technical Report TR-97-61.

Wu, Z. and Palmer, M. (1994). Verb Semantics and Lexical Selection. In *Proceedings of the 23rd Annual Meeting of the ACL*, pages 133–8.

Xyu, S. (121/2004). *ShuoWenJieZi*. Beijing: ZhongHua.

Yamaguchi, T. (1999). Constructing Domain Ontologies Based on Concept Drift Analysis. In *Proceedings of International Joint Conference on Artificial Intelligence 1999 (IJCAI-99) Workshop on Ontologies and Problem-Solving Methods*, Sweden.

Yu, S., Duan, H., Zhu, X., and Yasuhito, T. (2001). Some Experiences in the Development of the Large Scale Tagged Chinese Corpus. *Journal of Chinese Language and Computing*, 11(2), 101–10.

Zaefferer, D. and Schalley, A. (2003). Report of the Workshop 'Ontological Knowledge and Linguistic Coding'. In *Bulletin of the DGfS* 57, 42–4. German Linguistic Society.

Index

abduction, 118
abstract, 43, 50
adjective, 43, 50, 276
adjunct, 110
affordance, 162
agentivity, 38, 46
AGROVOC, 289, 291, 292, 297, 302, 303, 305, 308
alignment, ontological, 186, 191
amount of matter, 45
anaphora, 24, 75, 246, 273, 275, 283–7, 295
    bridging, 246
    resolution, 273, 275, 283, 284, 286, 287
annotation ontology, 58
anti-rigid, property, 51
antonymy, 12
application, 201, 212, 217, 218, 221, 222, 226, 267, 275
argument structure, 16, 246
artificial intelligence, 14, 117, 152
AskCal, 267, 275
associative anaphora, *see* anaphora bridging
attribute set, 83, 86, 88–91, 94
axiomatization, 22, 41, 47, 71, 152, 154, 156, 171, 187, 190, 191
    glosses, 52, 191

backbone taxonomy, 48
basic concept, *see* concept

categorization, 15, 16, 57, 82, 246, 248
categorized, 272, 273, 275, 280, 281, 283, 284, 287
Chinese character, 122–8, 130, 133–5, 137, 139, 141–3, 211
circumstantial context, 149, 150, 152
CLEF, 271, 272, 274, 276, 281–3, 285, 286
clue word, 291, 293, 294
coercion, 16, 21, 130
cognitive bias, 42, 43
commitment, ontological, 190
common sense, 39

componential semantics, 15
compound, noun-noun, 114
computational lexicon
    restructuring, 186
concept, 37
    basic, 74, 82, 125, 129, 130, 133, 139, 143, 235, 237
    lexicalised, 186
concept bubble, 263
concept density, 187
conceptual context, 149, 150
conceptual gap, 231
conceptual indexing, 225, 228
conceptual space, 43, 148
conceptualization, 4–7, 19, 23, 36, 72, 82, 126, 128, 145, 150, 151, 155, 161, 210
constraint density, 51, 187, 190, 193
constructivism, 147, 149, 166
continuant, 41
contrast, principle of relation by, 13
conventionalization, 5, 204
core, 258, 265
CoreLex, 216
corpus, 32, 81, 86, 87, 90, 92, 95, 96, 98, 110, 119, 120, 172, 181, 205, 217, 218, 223, 250, 252–5, 258, 266, 268, 269, 271–6, 279–83, 286, 287, 289, 290, 292, 296, 297, 307, 308
countable, 69, 112
crosslinguistic, 27, 34
cumulativity, 47
curtain, 263

deduction, 73, 118
dependence, ontological, 45
dependency, 51, 214, 215, 276, 277, 279
descriptive approach, 129
dictionary
    encyclopedic, 19
    ideological, 19
disambiguation *see* Word Sense Disambiguation

For EU product safety concerns, contact us at Calle de José Abascal, 56–1°, 28003 Madrid, Spain or eugpsr@cambridge.org.